UNHOLY WARS

Mercenaries and auxiliaries are useless and dangerous ... For mercenaries are disunited, thirsty for power, undisciplined, and disloyal; they are brave among their friends and cowards before the enemy; they have no fear of God, they do not keep faith with their fellow men; they avoid defeat just so long as they avoid battle; in peacetime you are despoiled by them, and in wartime by the enemy ... Mercenary commanders are either skilled in warfare or they are not: if they are, you cannot trust them, because they are anxious to advance their own greatness, either by coercing you, their employer, or by coercing others against your own wishes. If, however, the commander is lacking in prowess, in the normal way he brings about your ruin ... Experience has shown that only princes and armed republics achieve solid success, and that mercenaries bring nothing but loss.

Niccolo Machiavelli, *The Prince*

Unholy Wars

Afghanistan, America and International Terrorism

THIRD EDITION

John K. Cooley

Pluto Press

LONDON • STERLING, VIRGINIA

First published 1999 by Pluto Press
345 Archway Road, London N6 5AA
and 22883 Quicksilver Drive, Sterling,
VA 20166–2012, USA

Third edition published 2002

British Library Cataloguing in Publication Data
A catalogue record for this book is available from the British Library

ISBN 0 7453 1918 1 hbk
ISBN 0 7453 1917 3 pbk

Library of Congress Cataloging in Publication Data
Cooley, John K., 1927–
    Unholy wars : Afghanistan, America, and international terrorism /
John K. Cooley.
        p.   cm.
    Includes bibliographical references and index.
    ISBN 0–7453–1918–1 (hbk)
    1. United States—Foreign relations—Afghanistan. 2. Afghanistan–
–Foreign relations—United States. 3. Espionage, American—Islamic
countries. 4. Terrorism. 5. United States. Central Intelligence
Agency. I. Title.
JZ1480.A57A3   1999
958.104'5—dc21   98–50370

10   9   8   7   6   5   4   3   2   1

Designed and produced for Pluto Press by
Chase Publishing Services, Fortescue, Sidmouth EX10 9QG
Typeset from disk by Stanford DTP Services, Towcester
Printed in the United States of America

Contents

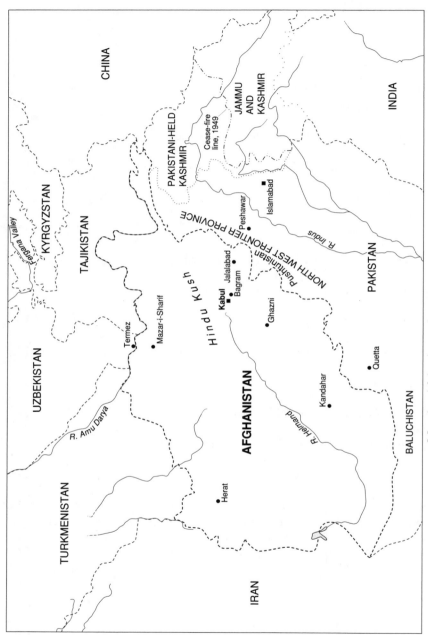

Map 1   Afghanistan after the 1989 cease-fire.

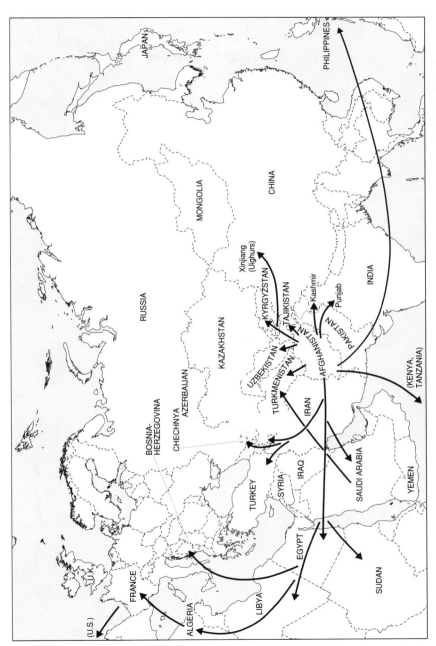

Map 2 Movements of CIA-trained guerrillas and drugs outwards from Afghanistan after the 1979–89 Afghanistan war.

to Vania Katelani Cooley

Acknowledgements

I am indebted to publications of friends, colleagues and many other persons I have never met. They are journalists, travelers, scholars, diplomats and members or former members of government and the military. They are mentioned in the endnotes.

Among those so mentioned and others who are not, deserving special thanks are Helga Graham, author of excellent books on the Mideast; my old friend and neighbor during my years as a news correspondent in Beirut, David Hirst of the *Guardian* and his colleague on that newspaper, Martin Woolacott. In Cairo I was helped generously by the distinguished Egyptian author and publicist, Muhammad Hasseinine Haykal and many others, including journalist and former ABC News producer Miss Hinzada al-Fikry, now teaching journalism and mass communications at the American University in Cairo.

Flora Lewis, both in her syndicated column in the *International Herald Tribune (IHT)* and in private conversations offered great encouragement when it was needed most, as she knows. Robert Donahue, editor of the *IHT*'s editorial page, has allowed me to publish my ideas on the theme of this book in the premium space he commands. In Germany, Wilhelm Dietl, investigative reporter and author, expert and frequent traveler in South Asia, generously opened to me his unique files and archives. At ABC News, my old friend anchorman Peter Jennings, investigative team chief Chris Isham and a few other colleagues have always been supportive. Dr. William R. Polk, former professor of Arab history at Harvard University and Mideast advisor to Presidents John F. Kennedy and Lyndon B. Johnson, has been a constant friend and scholarly guide.

In Washington DC, Georgetown University professors Michael Hudson and Hisham Sharabi are foremost among many helpers. Charles Cogan, a retired senior CIA official in the Afghanistan war program, now a visiting scholar at Harvard University and elsewhere, was informative, courteous and helpful. William Charles Maynes, now president of the Asia Foundation, has always been supportive. So have Tom Hughes, former president and Selig Harrison, former senior associate of the Carnegie Endowment for International Peace. Eric Rouleau, ex-Mideast editor of *Le Monde,* and former French ambassador to Tunisia and Turkey, is another old friend who has always helped.

Robin Raphel, widow of former US Ambassador to Pakistan Arnold Raphel, an American victim of the 1979–89 Afghan war, former assistant secretary of state for South Asian Affairs and now US Ambassador in Tunisia, graciously received me in Tunis in the spring of 1998, giving generously of her time and her insights. At Brown University, Professor Jim Blight and his associate, graduate student Michael Corkery, shared with me transcripts and thoughts about the Oslo meetings of Russian and US diplomats in the early 1990s, dealing with the origins of the 1979–89 Afghanistan war. Declassified Soviet documents on this subject were obtained and passed to me by the ABC News Moscow bureau. Senior Russian diplomat Alexander Zotov steered me to Soviet historians who helped. During research and production work for ABC News documentaries on terrorism and the Mideast, I benefitted from US government expertise not ordinarily available to journalists. Highly placed individuals evidently opposed publication of my earlier work on this subject. Their opposition, real or suspected, spurred my enthusiasm for my task.

I would have been lost without the technical help with the manuscript of Samir Srouji and Alexander Halliday, both students in Nicosia. Natalie Kovalenko provided fine translations from the Russian.

Others who cannot be named provided extremely valuable information and judgements. They know who they are, and I hope to repeat my gratitude to them in person.

Finally, Roger van Zwanenberg, the director of Pluto Press, my publisher, deserves my thanks for his patience with my delays and for his constant support. My son, Dr Alexander Cooley, an assistant professor of political science at Barnard College, Columbia University and my daughter, Katherine Anne Cooley, a news anchorwoman on French television in Paris, both gave me substantial and well-informed advice and help. Opinions and any errors of fact or judgement are, of course, entirely my own responsibility.

John K. Cooley
Athens, Greece,
April 2002

Preface to the Third Edition

In September 2001, following the worst terrorist attack against it in its history, the United States for the second time in a generation became embroiled in an air and ground war in Afghanistan. This time, the war was not a proxy war against Russian invaders. It was a direct one, fought with allies who had varying degrees of commitment, against the presumed terrorist attackers. By the winter of 2001–02, the new Afghan war had caused innumerable civilian casualties in Afghanistan. It had thrown many of the world's one billion or more Muslims into a state of new political ferment. The war, and the terrorist assault against America which caused it, had bred a state of global insecurity and instability, fed by fears of biological warfare after the autumn anthrax outbreaks in the US and had accelerated a global economic downturn which had begun long before the war, into a global economic recession.

This book aims to explain some of the reasons why all this came about.

Histories of World War II record that an American soldier, arriving in a devastated Normandy village evacuated by the Germans in June 1944, exclaimed, "We sure liberated the hell out of this place!" Many of the American or British commandos, searching a ruined Afghan village for Osama bin Laden and his men, or for his Taliban protectors, might have said the same, during the bitter new Afghan war which raged onward from the autumn of 2001.

The unprecedented and devilishly well-planned assaults by suicide terrorists crashing three hijacked American airliners against New York's World Trade Center towers and the Pentagon in Washington on September 11, 2001, had killed close to 3,000 people in those cities, hearts of a United States which had previously felt itself immune from such unthinkable violence. They triggered a retaliatory and punitive war, aimed at rooting out the presumed terrorist chiefs and their hosts. Once again, as during the 1980s war and afterward, Afghanistan's villages, towns, cities and countryside were laid waste. Millions of its unhappy people again fled in refugee tides, seeking food, shelter and safe havens amid Afghanistan's hills and mountains – or across the borders in Pakistan and Iran; or in Tajikistan, Uzbekistan, Turkmenistan. These last three lands had once been bases for the futile and fateful Soviet invasion and occupation of Afghanistan in 1979–89. Now, some of their territory, along with that of America's once enthusiastic, but now highly reluctant ally, Pakistan, had become bases for the third invading army, that of the United States, with its junior political and military partner, Britain.

Britain had already lived through its own bitter experiences of Afghan history. In the mid-nineteenth century, the fierce Afghan royal and tribal warriors inflicted stinging defeats on a British colonial army which thought it was protecting the flanks of the imperial British raj in India, and forced the British to take to their heels.

That Anglo-Afghan war of 1839–42 was precipitated by the fears of Lord Auckland, one of British India's colonial warlords. Auckland felt that the Russians were gaining ground in Afghanistan on the English, and so were winning "The Great Game," as the Anglo-Russian rivalry for empire in Asia came to be called. In a similar vein was President Jimmy Carter's fateful decision, urged by his Polish-born, Cold Warrior national security advisor Zbigniew Brzezinski, to fight the Russian invaders of Afghanistan by proxy. It was prompted in large measure by fear of a serious Russian threat to communication lines on the Indian Ocean and the nearby oilfields of Arabia and the Persian Gulf.

Although 16,000 British and Indian sepoy troops had succeeded in occupying Kabul in 1839–41, a popular revolt of most of the major Afghan ethnic groups forced their evacuation on January 6, 1842 and the headlong flight of most of them through the snowdrifts and bitter cold to the Khyber Pass. Of that British force of well over 12,000, most were massacred on the way home to India. Only 121 survived.

Looking back on that and several other ignominious defeats, in 1889 British statesman Lord Curzon wrote that

> For fifty years, Afghanistan has inspired the British people with a feeling of almost superstitious apprehension ... It is only with the greatest reluctance that Englishmen can be persuaded to have anything to do with so fateful a region ... In the history of most conquering races is found some spot that has invariably exposed their weakness like the joints in armour of steel. Afghanistan has long been the Achilles' heel of Great Britain in the East.

Winston Churchill, wearing one of his hats as military historian, took matters somewhat less seriously, but recognized an important fact of Afghan life which yesterday's Russian generals learned and today's American and allied planners are learning again, to their grief. "Except at harvest time, when self-preservation enjoins a temporary truce," Churchill wrote in 1898, "the Pathan [Pushtun] tribes," the majority of today's Taliban and indeed, more than half of the entire Afghan population, "are always engaged in private or public war. The life of the Pathan is thus full of interest."

On the bright, sunlit morning skies of September 11, 2001 in New York's downtown Manhattan financial district, and on the banks of the Potomac river dividing Washington, DC from northern Virginia, three suicidal pilots changed American and world history forever. With their fellow Muslim conspirators and supporters, they had quietly trained and prepared for this moment for years. They had betrayed few, if any, signs of religious hatred or fanaticism during their lives as quiet students in Hamburg and Bochum, Germany, and in flying schools in Vero Beach and Venice, Florida, and other American towns. The thunderous, fiery end of their lives, those of their passengers, and of thousands already at breakfast or at work in the fallen twin New York towers and in a wing of the Pentagon in Washington, brought to some thoughtful Americans apocalyptic flashbacks of the war they had commissioned others to fight in the 1980s, but had largely ignored themselves, except to think of it as a distant, but righteous campaign. Unlike the wars in Vietnam and Korea, which had cost the lives of upwards of 100,000 Americans, most ordinary Americans, apart from a few thousand Central Intelligence Agency and Army, Navy and Air Force special warriors who had served as trainers or instructors in guerrilla and terrorist techniques in the Afghan war of 1979–89, knew or cared much about it.

Nevertheless, there is a direct chain of related events linking that seemingly distant war with the events in the United States and South Asia in the fall of 2001. That war ended in 1989 with a defeated Soviet army retreating across Afghanistan's northern borders, just as the Afghans had sent the British across the Khyber pass back to British India in 1842. The chain is composed of political links, as well as military ones.

In describing these links, this book narrates the course and the consequences of a strange love affair which went disastrously wrong: the alliance, during the second half of the twentieth century, between the United States of America and some of the most conservative and fanatical followers of Islam.

World War II ended with the allies who had defeated the German–Italian–Japanese Axis seriously divided into two camps. In 1946 US President Harry Truman perceived the Soviet Union as the main threat to American interests. For the next half-century, US administrations regarded "world communism," embodied in dictator Joseph Stalin's system of Soviet hegemony, as their arch-enemy. Western Europe's leaders, under the American-forged shield of the NATO alliance since 1949, in general thought the same way. The new Central Intelligence Agency (CIA), seeking counter-measures, recognized that religion was one, if not the most important, of atheistic communism's foes. In France, Greece and Italy in particular, it gave massive financial aid to Rightist, often Christian-oriented parties, like Italy's Christian Democrats, to enable them to defeat the Communists.

Soon it became apparent to the Western planners that the fast-growing, dynamic religion of Islam was as resolutely anti-Communist, if not more so, than even the Roman Catholic Church. The tendency of the post-war US governments to support the colonial status quo in overseas possessions of Britain, France, Spain, Portugal and Italy was paralleled, and often contradicted, by a flirtation with Muslim groups which had politicized their religion. In Egypt, for example, the Muslim Brotherhood, formed in the 1920s, opposed President Gamal Abdel Nasser and his "Arab socialism," which the West perceived as a handmaiden of communism because Nasser accepted Soviet economic and aid and Russian armaments.

The Islamist politicians and groups like the Muslim Brothers began in the 1950s to receive covert, usually modest, American aid when they were engaged against local or Soviet Communists. By the mid-1960s, the Saudi Arabian kingdom had become a fountainhead of support for Islam and political Islamists everywhere. It was, of course, America's main oil supplier and political ally in the Arab Middle East (as opposed to the State of Israel, by 1967 the principal US ally in the entire region). There was talk of an anti-Nasser and anti-Soviet "Islamic Pact," led by the ultra-conservative and hyper-religious Saudi monarchy. Such talk, echoed by the military rulers in Islamic Pakistan, alarmed the Hindu-Muslim, but secularly-ruled giant state of India, which fought repeated battles and three wars with Pakistan over Kashmir, as well as the less conservative and secular-run Arab states like Egypt, Syria and Iraq.

The American flirtation with Islamism now became a more serious affair. Britain and France, in particular, helped the US to conduct this affair. Their governments and information media often sought to represent their colonial or post-colonial wars in Asia and Africa – Britain in Kenya or France in Algeria, for example – as part of the struggle against communism, and therefore worthy of US support. In a somewhat similar way, the US today seeks the support of its friends and allies for the "war against terror," as President George W. Bush named it following the murderous attacks of September 11, 2001 in New York and Washington, by reminding those friends and allies that terrorism threatens them too.

The US and its allies, including Britain, France and Portugal, with the aid until his overthrow in 1979 of Shah Muhammad Reza Pahlavi of Iran, waged proxy wars in Africa and Asia against adversaries considered as real or token allies of Moscow. Such proxy wars required no commitment of ground troops. They entailed few of the risks of casualties of the magnitude suffered by the United States and France in Southeast Asia from the 1950s through the 1970s, or by France during the Algerian revolution in 1954–62.

The fateful Soviet invasion of Afghanistan in 1979 was the event which was the fateful first link in the chain of dark destiny which has led the United States to its present serious crisis. The invasion was decided by a tiny coterie in the Brezhnev politburo. It jolted President Jimmy Carter and his administration (1977–81) out of their relative indifference to events in South Asia, then considered secondary to the main drama, the Arab–Israel conflict, which Carter and his advisors had applied mighty efforts to resolve, and had succeeded in inducing Israel and Egypt to sign peace in that same year of 1979.

When Soviets troops seized Kabul at Christmas 1979, murdering the incumbent Afghan president, Hafizullah Amin, some of Carter's advisors resolved on counter-measures. They would use the strategy and tactics of proxy warfare, already tested and applied in places like Angola, Somalia and Ethiopia, to say nothing of Central America. Carter's team, spearheaded by the viscerally anti-Communist and activist, Polish-born National Security Advisor, Zbigniew Brzezinski, perceived the foolhardy Soviet invasion not only as an international threat. They also saw it as an opportunity to undermine the already tottering Soviet empire lying north of Afghanistan, where huge Muslim populations stirred restlessly under Communist rule.

So the American love affair with Islamism was now raised another notch in intensity. It became a marriage of convenience. It was consummated in an alliance with General Zia al-Haq, the Islamist military dictator of Pakistan. He was desirous for his own reasons to cleanse Afghanistan of the Soviets and their Afghan satellite regime in Kabul and, if possible, advance Pakistan's strategic and commercial influence northward into South Asia. The Pakistani theorists reasoned that American support would strengthen Pakistan's position in Kashmir, and in general with India, the bigger adversary which had already defeated Pakistan on the battlefield in 1947, 1965 and 1971.

In cooperation with Zia al-Haq's military and intelligence services, the CIA, with Saudi finance as well as Pakistani logistical support, managed the raising, training, equipping, paying and sending into battle against the Red Army in Pakistan of a mercenary army of Islamist volunteers. Eventually, this army would be drawn not only from Arab and Muslim states everywhere, but also from minority Muslim communities in Western countries, including the United States. Many of those from the African or Asian continents were religious, political or criminal fugitives from their own governments. Others were simply soldiers of fortune.

It came to pass that the last quarter-century of conflict in South Asia had, as a centerpiece, this jihad or holy war against the Russian invaders of 1979. In 2002, there is an ironic reversal of history: the United States and Russia, formerly Cold War enemies, have become de facto allies. Their common foe is what both perceive as a terrorist threat of near-cosmic dimensions from the same radical Islamists, and their successors and those trained by them, who fought and ruined Afghanistan in the 1979–89 war.

In 1989, the Soviet invaders of Afghanistan were defeated and sent home. There they faced a collapsing Soviet society and empire. The war had in no small measure brought about the collapse which Mikhail Gorbachev, during his presidency (1985–91), fought desperately to manage and to impart a semblance of order and even a timid beginning of democratization.

In 1989, under the presidency of George Herbert Bush (1989–93), the CIA celebrated its victory with champagne. Nevertheless, the "holy" alliance of the Americans and Islamist forces against the Russians in South and Central Asia had ended in a series of distinctly unholy clan and tribal wars, affecting much more than the ex-Soviet Union. Afghanistan itself lay in ruins, wasted by the jihad. Its society and people were ravaged by drugs, poverty, and horrific war injuries from fighting and land mines.

This wasting process has continued almost incessantly, ever since the CIA "victory" of 1989. Two-thirds to one-half of the Afghan population, over four million people, became refugees in Pakistan, Iran, Central Asia, or beyond. As the new war began in October 2001, after the terrorist attacks in the United States, new tides of refugees from the American bombardments surged through the Afghan countryside and across the frontiers into its neighboring territories. Much of Kabul, the capital, and other main cities had already been rubble since the 1980s. The surviving population was further tried by a disastrous drought in the late 1990s. The new war created new rubble, new homeless, and new human tragedies of all descriptions. By the end of 2001, there was little work, food or proper homes for most Afghans. Many depended on begging and whichever international charities could brave the war to help keep them clinging to life.

Worse, the two Islamic powers who had become the uneasy allies of the United States in the new war of 2001–02, Saudi Arabia and Pakistan, had by 1994 hatched a monster of Islamist extremism, the Taliban movement, which the George W. Bush administration in 2001 asked these allies to combat. The first Taliban were religious students, armed by Pakistan's intelligence services, and former moujahidin or holy warriors of the anti-Soviet war. For a time they brought some order and stability to regions ravaged by warlords and bandits. The price paid by the remnants of Afghan society, however, was horrendous. It included the virtual enslavement and sequestration of women, and the crushing of all opposition to the Talibans' super-rigorous, pretended Sunni Muslim, laws and protocols of conduct. Transgressors suffered the harshest punishments systematically inflicted since Europe of the Middle Ages and the Inquisition. There were: beatings or floggings for violations of dress codes for men or women, or of prescribed beard lengths or shapes for men; amputation of hands and feet for theft; stoning to death for adultery; burial alive for sodomy – punishments carried out in public.

The cruelest punishment of all, for women and for the society as a whole, as the Taliban conquered most of Afghanistan from their ethnic foes by the fall of 1998, was total exclusion of women from the work place, including teaching and medicine.

Like the Taliban themselves, the anti-Soviet jihad which gave rise to them was essentially the creation of Pakistan's powerful Interservices Intelligence Directorate (ISI). From the mid-1980s on, the ISI steered the jihad into a new and trenchant, sectarian turn. By then, pro-Iranian Shi'ite militants beholden to the revolutionary and clerical regime which had overthrown the Shah in 1979 were bombing US Marines and diplomats, and kidnapping Americans and other Westerners in Lebanon.

In their sabotage and bomb attacks, they were already using methods which men like Saudi construction tycoon Osama bin Laden, allies of the CIA in the jihad of the 1980s, would perfect and apply later on. Fight fire with fire, was the US reasoning: combat the militant Shi'ism of the Iranians with the even greater militancy and violence of some of the groups who considered themselves orthodox, mainstream Sunni Muslims.

This served well the Saudi Arabian rulers, troubled by Iran's power, even though that power had been reduced in Iran's virtual defeat by Saddam Hussein's Iraq. In 1988 Baghdad had been aided vigorously by the United States, Britain, France and Germany, mainly in the form of financial credits and surreptitious arms and scientific aid which benefited his missile, chemical, biological and nuclear warfare projects. All of these were very much on the minds of US planners, as they wondered what new targets to attack in the 2001–02 American "war against terror."

So from the mid-1980s onward, the marriage of convenience between the United States and militant Sunni Islam became a more complicated, three-way working alliance – though a very uneasy one – of Washington with Islamabad and Riyadh. By the late 1990s, Russia, harassed by Islamist guerrillas with links to Osama bin Laden in its breakaway Muslim state of Chechenya, became another partner. Neither the Americans, stung and exhausted after the wars of the CIA and the US armed forces in Vietnam, Laos and Cambodia, nor the Saudis, who hate to get involved in fighting anywhere, wanted to commit their own forces. So they let Pakistan's ISI do the donkey work. As government funds for the anti-Soviet jihad ran out, the financing of the war and, most crucially, the new ISI program of training its militant veterans and the new recruits they attracted, mostly from Algeria, Egypt and other Arab states, became "privatized" – financed by the private fortunes of men like Osama bin Laden, Islamic banks and charities, and the huge proceeds of the drug trade, which the CIA had helped to promote and which flourished during and after the war.

Although this book is mainly about the disastrous consequences of US policies in South Asia, those consequences are inextricably linked to the Palestine–Israel crisis. Osama bin Laden and his followers – despite the disavowals of bin Laden's group by Palestine Authority president Yassir Arafat's mainstream Palestinian movement in the Israeli-occupied territories – have shrewdly perceived that the Palestinian struggle for an end to Israeli occupation and for full Palestinian statehood is by far the most popular cause among the world's more than one billion Muslims.

Especially since the September 2001 attacks in the United States, bin Laden's followers have endeavored in their fatwas, communiqués and interviews loudly to proclaim the Palestinian cause as their own. Strong in the collective memory of the Palestinians are generations of contradictory, often broken, American promises, both to the Arabs and Muslims, and to the Jewish and other supporters of the State of Israel. However, the US administration of George W. Bush, in order to hold together the shaky "coalition against terrorism" it tried to build in late 2001, to the dismay of Israel's supporters in the US, has repeated old assurances by the Clinton and some earlier US administrations that they would, after all, support an independent Palestinian state. The proof of the pudding, said skeptical Arab intellectuals and other sympathizers with the Palestinian cause, will be in the eating. Has any US administration, they asked, since the bold stand of President Dwight Eisenhower who in 1957 after the Anglo–French–Israeli Suez war against Egypt forced the Israelis to evacuate Egypt's Sinai and the Gaza Strip, ever stood up to Israel, or supported any just Arab cause?

The intentions of some hawks in the Bush administration, especially in the Pentagon, in late 2001 to move militarily to destroy President Saddam Hussein's despotic regime in Iraq in the "war against terror" could easily trigger a vicious new Arab–Israel war. Saddam has repeatedly proclaimed his intention to lead the Arabs in "the liberation of Palestine." Israeli strategists have always yearned for a final, military solution to the problem of Iraq, which is the only Arab belligerent in the various Arab–Israel wars since 1948 never to sign peace, an armistice, or even a cease-fire with the Jewish state. Some of them would be only too delighted to see the United States help Israel do the job, even at the expense of a bloody and ruinous new war, with the likely use of weapons of mass destruction. Such a war might make the previous Middle East conflicts look, by comparison, like minor regional skirmishes.

As I tried to warn in the first edition of this book in 1999, the societies and governments of both the Western and Islamic worlds have suffered mightily from their inattention and their lack of care about choosing and nurturing allies. These allies have been inclined to stab them in the back. Washington now finds itself battling them back in the same old arenas of South Asia, where millions of lives were lost and untold billions of dollars of damage was done in the savage unholy wars of the 1970s and 1980s. This book may succeed in some measure, if it reminds us all once again of the old historical truth that those who forget the mistakes of history are condemned to repeat them.

Foreword

Edward W. Said

The work of a veteran American journalist who has lived in and covered the Middle East for several decades, this book is a masterpiece of reportorial thoroughness, painstaking research, and serious reflection. Written originally in 1998, well before the world's focus had turned to Osama bin Laden and Afghanistan, it was first published in 1999, then revised and republished in English in 2000, then again in 2002. Its essential findings remain the same, profoundly relevant to the events that unfolded after the awful terrorist atrocities that befell New York, Washington and Pennsylvania on September 11, 2001. Cooley shows that during the last half of the Cold War, the United States searched for and found willing allies amongst the various Middle Eastern powers who were in its camp – Egypt, Pakistan, Morocco, Saudi Arabia, Jordan and a few others – and who were willing in the name of anti-communism and regional stability to finance, organize, train and deploy increasingly large and widespread brigades of anti-Communist moujahidin, warriors who could be sent as proxies to fight Communist forces when and where they threatened disruption and instability in strategic areas (like the oil-rich regions of the Middle East).

The apex of this effort was a response to the Soviet invasion of Afghanistan in 1979. In effect, and acting through secret groupings such as "the Safari Club" and the CIA as well as Egyptian, French, British, Iranian, and Israeli secret services, these newer warriors for Islam were trained and encouraged to do what they were to do so successfully, that they achieved their objectives, drove out the Soviet Union, but then stayed on as fervent defenders of the Islamic cause. After the Gulf War and the end of the Cold War, these same men, whose Afghan experience was central to their lives, sought new ways of vindicating their brand of Islam – by no means that of the majority of Muslims – whether in attacks on American encroachment in the Gulf or attempts to bring down local governments whose corruption and oppressiveness had made them extremely isolated and unpopular. New alliances between states and Islamic groups (for example between Pakistan and the emerging Taliban) were forming beyond public scrutiny. This testifies as much to the cynicism of the original sponsors of militant Islamic groups as it does to the laziness and indeed the absence of investigative journalism, with a few exceptions. The result is that we now have a worldwide quasi-hysteria about terrorism, which is as seriously unexamined and unanalyzed now as it was then, despite the enormous media hype that has built up around the US Afghanistan campaign against the Taliban.

There is no better single work in this regard than Cooley's dispassionate and meticulous book. Lucid, detailed, well-organized and superbly researched. *Unholy*

Wars is the only book to place Islamic militancy in the context created not just by desperately poor, hopelessly mismanaged, corrupt and oppressive societies, but also by great powers like the United States, which has tried to have and eat its cake in all ways, manipulating the militants one day, abandoning them the next, inadvertently keeping them in business, then attacked by and finally going to war against them. Cooley's tone is Olympian and does not dole out blame or indulge in name-calling of any kind. But, shining through the calm of his remorselessly plotted tale of drugs, violence, power, war, and religious madness, there is a rational, analyzable narrative being disclosed, which it behooves readers to pay close attention to. The great thing about *Unholy Wars,* though, is that it is an extremely well-written, and even gripping, work, not a collection of sound bites, or a confection made up of cliches and stereotypes. There is no work like it and we are fortunate to have it.

Edward W. Said
New York
December 19, 2001

1 Carter and Brezhnev in the Valley of Decision

Early in December 1971, I flew from my base in Beirut to cover the Western half of the war between India and Pakistan. The only way to reach Islamabad at the time, with West Pakistan's airports closed and under occasional Indian air attack, was overland through Afghanistan. As the Afghan airliner nosed past the snowy horizon of the Hindu Kush mountains and into a brown winter valley flanked by hills, Kabul's low buildings and higher minarets came into view. Soon my taxi threaded its way through moderate traffic, past mud huts, sternly styled administrative buildings and mosques not too unlike those I had grown used to in cities like Cairo, Damascus or Amman. There was the usual color and contrast of an Eastern city: turbaned folk on slowly trotting donkeys; women swathed in their coverall *burqahs* beside younger women and girls in 1950s-style Western dresses and stockings. Now and then a laden camel, decorated with red and gold tassels, growled wickedly at a passing Mercedes, BMW, or ancient Ford.

What I needed to find was the central bus station, to catch transport toward the Khyber pass and the Pakistani frontier. My quest led me down well-paved central avenues and then upward into narrow alleys and lanes, snaking around the hilly part of the city. Before long, I was able to board a bus which connected me with the truck route up the winding Khyber road. That afternoon and evening, I hitchhiked my way to Peshawar, Pakistan and a hostelry for the night before heading into Islamabad, capital of Pakistan. I was light years distant from the real war in the East – the battle for Dacca, detached East Pakistan's capital and soon, with India's help, to become the "liberated" capital of the new nation of Bangladesh.

In some cramming to overcome my ignorance at the time about South Asia, I had been re-reading James Michener's early Afghanistan novel, *Caravans*. Somehow this had led me into premonitions about this land, though I had crossed a mere corner of it in only a few hours. Here, Soviet and American meddling with an archaic, but slowly modernizing Muslim society, on terrain where Czarist Russia and Victorian Britain had played out their recent century of imperial rivalry called "The Great Game," would spawn mischief and evil. Both would spread into both the East and the West: a final act of the Soviet–American Cold War, ending the existence of the Soviet Union and attacking Western societies and governments and their allies.

Somewhere in my library, I had read the words of that wily British prophet and advocate of imperial power, Lord Curzon, published in 1889. For 50 years, he wrote, Afghanistan had "inspired the British people with a feeling of almost superstitious apprehension ... It is only with the greatest reluctance that Englishmen can be persuaded to have anything to do with so fateful a region ... Afghanistan

1

has long been the Achilles' heel of Great Britain in the East. Impregnable elsewhere, she has shown herself uniformly vulnerable here."[1]

After being checked into Pakistan's Northwest Frontier Province after a jolting and dizzy ride over the mountains, I found myself, after paying outrageous passage money, in the cab of a Pakistani truck, smeared with the largely symbolic camouflage (presumably against marauding Indian jets) of mud and a few leafy branches. "CRUSH INDIA" was the brave slogan spray-painted on the truck's sideboards. After some more grueling travel, I was trying to relax and then write a story for my newspaper in a grim but adequate Peshawar hotel. It was far beyond the reach of my imagination then to suppose that in less than a decade, this austere winter town near the Himalayan foothills would be the main base for the last major armed conflict of the US–Soviet Cold War. Or that within less than two decades, it would be a rear base for a movement to spread militant Islam around the world, as a consequence of that conflict.

What occurred to bring about both these developments could be briefly encapsuled between the Indo-Pakistan war of 1971, which had ended within three weeks of my journey over the Khyber Pass, and the fateful Soviet and American interventions in Afghanistan. These two armed interventions – the Russian one direct, the American one using an army of Muslim mercenaries – would seal the fate of the Soviet empire. They also uncorked the bottle containing the genies which would, in the 1980s and 1990s, unleash terrorist violence and help to spread the culture of drugs around the world, from New York to the Philippines.

Afghanistan had largely escaped the impact of World War II. What it did not escape were the after-effects of the partition and independence of British India in 1947. Once the British had withdrawn, the claim was revived of Afghan governments in Kabul to the lands peopled by the Pushtun (called by Rudyard Kipling and many other writers Pathan) and Baluchi ethno-tribal groups, across the border in what now became Pakistan. "Pushtunistan," as it came to be called, became an inflammatory issue between Kabul and Islamabad. Pakistan's rejection of the Afghan monarchy's revanchist claims meant that landlocked Afghanistan was prevented from gaining a port on the Indian Ocean; also a traditional goal of Russian foreign policy through long generations of Czarist rule before 1917.

King Zahir Shah, who had reigned since 1933, had chosen as prime minister a member of his own family, Prince Muhammad Daoud Khan, whose devotion to the cause of Pushtunistan was one of the factors which drew him somewhat closer to the Soviet Union, after a long post-World War II balance between Soviet and American influence. Each pursued aid projects and sought in this way and others to purchase more influence. From 1956 and 1961 onward, Moscow agreed to equip and train the Afghan army and air force respectively, after the US refused to sell arms to Kabul or provide it with loans on favorable terms. Soon, the Soviet Union began to build huge infrastructure projects of strategic importance, effectively seeking to incorporate the ancient monarchy into the power system of the Soviet borderlands: a highway from the border of Soviet Tajikistan to Kabul; port facilities along the Amu Darya river (where during the Afghan war of the 1980s, CIA-backed incursions of Afghan guerrillas and saboteurs into Soviet territory nearly provoked a major Soviet–Pakistani, if not Soviet–American war).

A giant new military air base was built at Bagram. In Afghanistan's north, development projects flourished, stimulated partly by discovery of huge reserves of natural gas in Jowzjan Province, close to the Soviet frontier. By 1968 Soviet engineers had completed a gas pipeline to pump low-priced Afghan gas to Soviet Central Asian industrial centers; a flow rarely interrupted even during the 1979–89 war, despite sabotage training given to prospective Afghan saboteurs by the CIA and Pakistan's Inter-Services Intelligence Directorate (ISI). The gas line was one of the few enduring Russian successes of the period. By 1985, Moscow was claiming annual gas production of 2400 million cubic meters (m m^3). Only three percent was used for Afghan needs; all the rest went to the Soviet economy.

Despite competition from US aid and that from West Germany, France, Russia, China and India, the USSR had loaned Afghanistan so much money, much of it at heavy interest charges, that by 1972 the Soviets were Afghanistan's biggest creditor. They had committed close to a billion dollars between 1957 and 1973. This was about 60 percent of all the civilian foreign aid reaching the country. A liberal constitution which King Zahir Shah initiated in 1964 brought in parliamentary democracy. Political parties, mainly small ones, flourished for a time: the Leftist one increasingly under Communist influence; the others growingly under the sway of Islamist ideology. Both the Communists and the Islamists militated most effectively in the high schools and Kabul's university, and among junior officers of the armed forces. The Leftists and Communists founded the People's Democratic Party of Afghanistan (PDPA). Its two wings were called Parcham (Banner) and Khalq (The People). Parcham recruited adherents chiefly from Persian-speaking, young urban elites; Khalq from mainly Pushtuns (Pathans) from a more humble rural background. On the fringe were a few small extremist groups, such as the "Maoist" and definitely non-religious group called *Sholah-e-Javed* (Eternal Flame), attracting non-Pushtuns, Shi'a Muslims (as opposed to the Sunni majority of about two-thirds of the population), and others discontented with the functioning of the Left-leaning constitutional monarchy of Zahir Shah.

Progressively, the King's indecisiveness and, some said, weakness, failed to prevent erosion of the democratic principles he had helped to launch with the new constitution of 1964. He was, his critics remarked, too spineless to support the more honest and capable prime ministers, five of whom tried successively to rule until 1973. Much of the blame for the mishandling of affairs, including foreign relief help at the time of the drought and famine which in 1972 killed up to 100,000 Afghans, fell on the King's son-in-law, General Abdul Wali. Then, in 1973, while the King was abroad, a junta of armed forces officers staged a sudden military coup, proclaiming a Republic and the monarchy's end. Their figurehead and in some senses their real leader, was one of Zahir Shah's cousins, Muhammad Daoud, who had functioned as an effective foreign minister from 1953 to 1963, but who was banned from power during the period of Zahir's democratic experience. Daoud tried to rule with an iron fist. He largely neglected social and economic problems. Western commentators – few of whom really understood Afghan politics or society then, nor understood their complexities later on, when the West became embroiled in its proxy war with the Russians – wrongly called Daoud "the Red Prince." They believed, though the Soviets themselves did not, that the support of Leftist PDPA elements in his successful bid for power made him automatically a tool or a satellite of Moscow.

The events which would provoke the fateful Soviet military intervention of December 1979 could be said to begin with the reunion of the two rival PDPA factions, Parcham and Khalq, in 1977. It was fragile and temporary, but it helped to make possible another military coup, this time fatal to Daoud who with most of his family was killed resisting it. Their murders happened on April 27, 1978. They brought the PDPA, now identified by the US Central Intelligence Agency (CIA) and other Western agencies as Communist and pro-Soviet, to power at last. The winning faction in his "Saur" or April Revolution, as it was called, was the Khalq, numerically superior to the less radical and more cautious Parcham. From April 1978, the new president, Nur Muhammad Taraki, was a sort of hack Marxist writer, and a front man for the much more able politician, Hafizullah Amin.[2]

From the beginning of Taraki's rule, the Kremlin of President Leonid Brezhnev carefully watched every development in Afghanistan. It suspected that Amin was pro-American, and possibly an agent of the CIA. In March 1979, there was a major revolt in Herat province against Taraki's government. Soviet intelligence noted that it was supported from abroad, mostly by the Iran of Ayatollah Khomeiny, the fiery cleric who had returned to Tehran from exile to become Iran's supreme religious and political chief following the Shah's departure in February 1979. Several Soviet advisory personnel were killed in suppressing the Herat uprising. To keep an eye on Amin, now prime minister, and other members of Taraki's clique who might have pro-Western leanings or worse, the Kremlin sent Vassily Safronchuk, a competent senior diplomat fluent in English, the foreign language in which Amin was most at home, to keep an eye on things in Kabul, as counselor to the Soviet Ambassador in Kabul, A.M. Puzanov.

Safronchuk found Amin to be "of middle height and solid build, with well-pronounced Pushtu features, a vigorous and polite man [who] if he wanted to, could charm any visitor from the very first." After hearing Amin's initial protestations of loyalty and friendship to Soviet Communist principles and people, Safronchuk found him actually to be "a commonplace petty bourgeois and an extreme Pushtu nationalist," both traits which Moscow considered dangerous. Amin, Safronchuk reported, was a political schemer with "boundless political ambitions and a craving for power" which he would "stoop to anything and commit any crimes" to fulfill.

Because of Amin's "suspicious" contacts with the Americans and persistent signs that the CIA, Iran and Pakistan had all begun to encourage agitation and ferment among the Islamist-minded tribal leaders (especially after the Herat uprising in March 1979), Taraki and Amin both began urging Moscow of the need for a "limited contingent" – soon to become the favorite phrase of Kremlin bureaucrats seeking to justify their military intervention – of Soviet troops. In June 1979, says Safronchuk, Amin at one of their first meetings asked him to inform the Soviet leadership of his and Taraki's request for sending "two or three battalions" of Red Army troops "to protect certain military communication lines and the Baghram airfield." Safronchuk says he told Amin he doubted there would be a positive response. Moscow, he said, feared the arrival of Soviet troops on Afghanistan's territory could be used by the West, Pakistan, Iran and China, all viewed as adversaries, to "discredit the Afghan revolution," and would be viewed in the Kremlin as an admission that the Taraki–Amin regime was weak.[3]

During the summer of 1979, during which the principal anti-Soviet "hawk" in President Jimmy Carter's administration, National Security Advisor Zbigniew Brzezinski, got Carter to sign a secret directive for covert aid to the nascent moujahidin, or anti-Russian resistance fighters, more trouble developed for Taraki, Amin and the Soviets. On June 23, an army mutiny erupted in the heart of Kabul, close to the central Chandaval bazaar. On August 6, carefully monitored by the CIA and Pakistani observers, if not directly encouraged by them, an Afghan army unit mutinied and tried to seize the ancient fortress of Balahisar, on the southeastern slope of the hill called Shir-Darviz, inside Kabul. From this fortress, guns could be trained on all the capital's main streets and neighborhoods. The Soviet diplomats and military advisors in Kabul, as well as the KGB station, suspected that Amin had provoked these rebellions, or had known about them in advance. In any case, these events consolidated Amin's power over the Afghan armed services The Soviets judged that Amin, long on friendly terms with the US Embassy in Kabul, was aiming for a personal dictatorship, possibly in collusion with the Americans.[4]

Selig Harrison, former *Washington Post* correspondent whose writings on South Asian events are authoritative, describes the setting for "Moscow's monumental blunder" in invading Afghanistan. He depicts a "Byzantine sequence of murderous Afghan intrigue complicated by turf wars between rival Soviet intelligence agencies and the undercover manipulations of agents for ... contending foreign powers" (presumably the US, the USSR, Iran, Pakistan, India and Britain). The Kremlin's fatal blunder, taken by a small coterie of President Leonid Brezhnev's advisors, and imposed when Brezhnev himself, "ailing and alcoholic," imposed the secret decision without calling a full Politburo meeting, "disregarding the opposition of three key generals in his Army General Staff."[5]

Many of the riddles and mysteries of the decision-making process in both Moscow and Washington concerning Afghanistan were elucidated in Oslo, Norway, in September 1995. Grandly entitled "Afghanistan and the Collapse of Détente," this was the fourth and final meeting of senior Russian and American policymakers, diplomats, soldiers and intelligence operatives; many, though not all, retired. Most if not all the participants took part in the crucial decisions in both capitals concerning intervention in Afghanistan's internal turmoil; the last great political chess game and military contest of the Cold War. Some important truths emerged from the meetings.

At the Oslo conference on Afghanistan, participants included key senior aides of President Carter: Zbigniew Brzezinski, his national security advisor; Admiral Stansfield Turner, CIA director; General William Odom, director of Soviet affairs in the National Security Council; Dr. Marshall Shulman, a special assistant to Secretary of State Cyrus Vance (who was not present at Oslo), Mark Garrison, a senior counselor at the US Embassy in Moscow and Dr. Gary Sick, former US Navy Captain and Iran expert on the National Security Council.

On the Russian side, there was Anatoly Dobrynin, in 1979 USSR Ambassador in Washington; Karen Brutents, deputy head of the Soviet Communist Party's Central Committee, international department; General Valentin Varennikov, deputy defense minister; General Mikhail Greev, first deputy chief of the Army General Staff and Sergei Tarasenko, a senior US and Middle East expert in the USSR Foreign Ministry.

Besides these heavyweights, a select group of 23 other American, Russian and Norwegian experts took part. Main questions on the agenda included: what was the exact sequence of behind-the-scenes events in the Soviet intervention? What were Soviet motives? Who were the main architects of the invasion? Finally, what kind of parallel thinking was going on in Washington? How might it have figured in Soviet calculations? These calculations were to result in tragedy for the USSR; for Afghanistan itself and its neighbors; and finally, in a Pyrrhic victory for Western and Muslim states which had taken part in the Crusade against communism and the Russian invaders.

Backed by all of the documentary and human resources of the Norwegian Nobel Institute (the conference host), the conferees got down to work, after the opening dinner had mellowed them, by watching a video and in this way, "enter a kind of time machine," as Russian participant Alexander Bessmertnykh called it. It was a real-time US media coverage of a prologue to the Afghanistan drama composed of three events: the June 1979 Vienna summit of Carter and Brezhnev; the mini-crisis over a largely phantasmagoric "Soviet brigade" in Cuba a few weeks later; and the news coverage in the West of the Soviet invasion of Afghanistan in the last week of December 1979.

There was some polite good humor and also some guffaws at what one participant called the "awkward and inadvertently hilarious kiss" between Carter and Brezhnev, after they signed the SALT II arms-reduction treaty at Vienna. Anatoly Dobrynin remarked, "Just imagine, such a kiss, and on their first date." On a less hilarious note was the observation of General Valentin Varennikov, former commander of Soviet ground forces in Afghanistan: "that kiss was like a dream when you are sick, kind of unreal, a product mainly of wishful thinking. With the events in Afghanistan later that year, we all woke up to reality again." In fact, mused Professor James G. Blight of the Watson Institute, one way to state the purpose of the conference was: how was it possible for relations between the US and the Soviet Union to self-destruct so quickly and so completely, following the triumphal signing of the SALT II arms-reduction treaty at Vienna?

What, indeed, wondered the pundits of early 1980, like the delegates at the Oslo gathering in 1993, had triggered the foolish Soviet decision to move into Afghanistan at Christmas 1979? There was, first of all, awareness among the senior chiefs of the Kremlin that the CIA, whether or not actively stirring the tribal and military revolts of 1978–79 against the Communist PDPA regime in Kabul, had been involved in intelligence and reconnaissance missions in and around the Hindu Kush mountains and beyond. There was apprehension about Western attempts to destabilize the Muslim republics of the Soviet Union. This, as we will see later, was something a famous Cold Warrior of France would seriously suggest to newly elected President Ronald Reagan before and during the start of Reagan's term in January 1981.

Anatoly Gromyko is the son of Andrei Gromyko, who after long years of service as Soviet Foreign Minister, earning himself the nickname in the West of Mr. *Nyet* (Mr. No) because of his dour demeanor and stiff intransigence, became state president of the USSR, a largely honorific post, once Mikhail Gorbachev took over as Communist Party general secretary in 1985. Andrei Gromyko died in 1989. He wrote, but never sent, a revealing letter to the Politburo. His son Anatoly, to whom he dictated the letter, published it in 1997. The letter tries to justify Andrei Gromyko's positive vote for intervention at the fateful December 12, 1979 decision-making meeting of the Politburo's inner circle through "subjective circumstances and objective ones."

Among the "objective" reasons Gromyko mentioned in 1989, as dictated to his son, were "the efforts of the US government ... to destabilize the southern borders of the Soviet Union and to create a threat to our security." This American mind-set, according to Gromyko, stemmed from the overthrow of America's faithful ally, the Shah of Iran, in February 1979; the resulting moves by the revolutionary clerical regime of the Ayatollah Ruhollah Khomeiny in Iran to close down the American bases there and the resulting "intentions of the Americans to replace Iran with Pakistan, and if possible, even Afghanistan, as anti-Soviet bases." Added to this, said Gromyko, was presumed American involvement in the political and social upheavals in Afghanistan in 1978–79. Gromyko denied that the decision to intervene was "taken behind closed doors." Then he contradicts himself. He admits that Central Committee decisions were not submitted even to the larger Congress of Peoples' Deputies, and that he participated and concurred in the crucial decision to invade Afghanistan. This was taken at a secret conclave of the Politburo's innermost circle in December 1979. Brezhnev presided. "Unfortunately," Gromyko observed, "Brezhnev, [Yuri] Andropov, [KGB chief 1967–82]; [Defense Minister Dmitri] Ustinov, [Premier Alexei] Kosygin; [Mikhail] Suslov are no longer alive. Only a few of us, including me, discussed this problem behind 'closed doors' ... Today I won't deny that after discussion, we unanimously agreed that temporarily

it was necessary to send a small Soviet military contingent to Afghanistan."
Gromyko added, "Brezhnev believed that [Hafizullah] Amin was capable of
reaching an agreement with the United States," something, Gromyko implied, to
be prevented at all costs.[6]

A top secret memo of a December 31, 1979 meeting of the Central Committee,
bearing in superscript Brezhnev's handwritten approval, summarizes the reasons
for the decision to intervene and formally confirms it. (The document, declassified
and released by Russian President Boris Yeltsin's aides in 1993, is reproduced in
the original and in translation, as an appendix of this book.) The memo mentions
how the pro-Soviet Taraki, before his replacement and then murder on September
17, 1979, probably in factional fighting, had been undermined by Amin's "personal
dictatorship." It complained of Amin's secret contacts with the American Embassy
in Kabul, and with "leaders of the Right-Wing Muslim opposition" whose "counterrevolutionary forces ... [had] practically established their control in many provinces
... using foreign support." All this, and such events as the splitting and
disintegration of the ruling PDPA "were threatening the achievements of the April
[Afghan] revolution and the security interests" of the USSR. So "in accordance with
the provisions of the Soviet–Afghan treaty of 1978, the decision was made to send
the necessary contingent of the Soviet Army to Afghanistan."[7]

Amin was first said by the Soviet media to have been accidentally killed when
Soviet troops entered Kabul on December 27. Later it was announced that he had
been found guilty of "crimes against the state and executed."

The Oslo conference of Russian and American leaders and scholars in September
1995 aired the reasons behind President Jimmy Carter's angry reaction. Marshall
Shulman deprecated talk at the Pentagon and among senior presidential advisors
such as Brzezinski about a Soviet threat to Persian Gulf oil fields. What was much
worse to most Americans, including Carter, he said, was the sudden, brutal and
cynical nature of the Soviet operation itself. Gary Sick, Malcolm Toon, former US
Ambassador in Moscow and several other US participants agreed.

General William Odom did not. He concurred with his former chief, Zbigniew
Brzezinski, that the Soviet move into Afghanistan was a strategic threat to the
United States; one of a long series. Odom, with Gary Sick's agreement, rebuked
his Russian colleagues:

> Your people take over in Angola. Then in Ethiopia. Then in South Yemen. Then
> comes the Iranian Revolution. I know, I know – you weren't behind the fall of
> the Shah ... But those events could still, in our view, have been used to your
> advantage in the region. And then you send massive numbers of troops into
> Afghanistan, giving you a capacity to strike deeply into our vital interests in the
> Persian Gulf. Are you gonna tell 'em that these events were *completely* unrelated
> in your own minds?

Anatoly Dobrynin, General Leonid Shebarshin, the 1979 KGB station chief in
Kabul and General Valentin Varennikov, who had been one of the decision-makers

at the decisive Kremlin meeting in December 1979, disagreed vehemently with the Odom–Brzezinski thesis which, said Varennikov, was "Cold War paranoia." What was more, Varennikov added, the Soviets felt they were being "kicked around" throughout the region:

> The US had long dominated Iran under [Shah Muhammad Reza] Pahlavi. The US Navy controlled the Indian Ocean. Pakistan – we, we can be honest here, I think – Pakistan took its orders from Washington. That was clear, and was [already] training and supplying the Islamic guerrillas that opposed the regime of Amin and Taraki, whom we supported. So the threat to the Soviet Union was not "from" Afghanistan. It was from the US, via its overwhelming influence in this region.

Varennikov then described a scenario in the minds of the Soviet leaders in 1979. Suppose, he said, that Afghanistan "fell" to US and Pakistani aggression. The US could then deploy short-range missiles there, threatening Soviet strategic missile fields including ICBMs, in Kazakhstan. If Washington then decided, as the Soviets believed it would, to counter the threat from revolutionary Iran by invading Iran "to replace Khomeiny with the Shah [then in exile but still alive] or someone else you liked," a Western "invasion" of Afghanistan would follow. The Kremlin's inner circle also believed by then that Amin was probably an American agent. This, Varennikov reminded the Americans, "was *our* sphere of influence" and "*our* borders, not yours." Therefore there was no choice but to get involved in Afghanistan. "It does not explain," Varennikov admitted, "why we did something as stupid as sending in the Soviet Army. But I think it explains why we did not want the regime in Kabul to fall."

Varennikov, along with Marshal Nikolai Ogarkov and Marshal Sergei Akhromyev, was one of Defense Minister Dmitri Ustinov's senior advisors in 1979. Until the final "go" order was given, all three marshals, like the entire Soviet general staff, strongly opposed sending troops. Varennikov revealed that he was in Turkmenistan in the fall of 1979, preparing for such contingencies as the possible entry of US troops into Khomeiny's Iran. In meetings on December 4 and 10 in Brezhnev's office, proposals by Andropov, Gromyko and Ustinov to send up to 75,000 troops were discussed. Operations were discussed but deferred. The final decision on December 12 set the operation to start from 1500 hours on December 25, and to be complete by December 27. General Alexander Lyakhovsky, an aide to Varennikov, confirmed that assassinating Hafizullah Amin was part of the plan, and was carried out as scheduled.

Brezhnev was ailing by this time. Andropov, it appears from the Oslo conference notes, convinced Brezhnev of the need for intervention in a private aide-memoire given to him in early December 1979. Dobrynin said that when he visited Brezhnev on January 20, 1980 (after Carter had announced the first public measures against the Soviet Union, and approved a shipment of rifles to the moujahidin), on his way to Washington, Dobrynin warned Brezhnev, "watch out for Carter. He's behaving like a bull in a china shop." Brezhnev told Dobrynin, "Don't worry. It will be over in three to four weeks." Dobrynin told the Oslo conferees that this was a sign of the confused state of Brezhnev's mind at the time.

The state of mind of Zbigniew Brzezinski, who had been stage-managing US covert aid to the moujahidin for months, was quite different. Until January 1998, Brzezinski had insisted to all questioners and researchers, including this author, that the official US histories of the Afghanistan war were correct: CIA aid to the Islamic fighters had begun only when President Carter, in December 1979, issued a presidential finding on covert action to supply them with "lethal" weapons, through the Pakistani authorities, in order to harass Soviet occupation troops in Afghanistan. "The first arms," reports Charles Cogan, until 1984 one of the senior CIA officials running the aid program, " – mainly .303 Enfield rifles [antiquated but still effective infantry weapons] – arrived in Pakistan on January 10, 1980, fourteen days after the Soviet invasion."

At the same time, Cogan agrees with Brzezinski – who claimed in an interview with a French news magazine in January 1998 that he was revealing a secret – that the first covert CIA aid to the Afghan resistance fighters was actually authorized *fully six months before the Soviet invasion – in July 1979, as the Communist government in Kabul was beginning to lose control of the country.*

Cogan says that in July 1979, President Carter "signed a presidential finding on covert action that began a modest program of propaganda and medical aid to the insurgents." This Cogan calls a "very modest beginning to US involvement."[8]

In his seeming desire to take credit as a major architect of the Soviet Union's defeat in the Cold War, Brzezinski told his French interviewer that the "secret reality is that on July 3, 1979, President Carter signed the first directive for clandestine aid to the enemies of the pro-Soviet regime in Kabul. On that day," he added, "I wrote a note to the President in which I explained to him that in my opinion, this aid would result in military intervention by the Soviets."

No, Brzezinski told his obviously shocked interviewer, it wasn't exactly that he wanted to provoke the Soviets to start a war. "We didn't push the Russians to intervene, but we consciously increased the probability that they would do so." He regretted the decision not at all: "This secret operation was an excellent idea. Its effect was to draw the Russians into the Afghan trap. You want me to regret that?" He added that as soon as the Soviets "officially" crossed the frontier, on December 23, 1979, he had written to President Carter that "now we can give the USSR its own Vietnam war." This compelled Moscow to wage a war over ten years which was "insupportable" for the Soviet regime; a conflict which, Brzezinski insisted, had brought about the "demoralization and finally the collapse of the Soviet empire."

Brzezinski, like President Carter's CIA director Admiral Stansfield Turner and lower-ranking but key players like Charles Cogan, freely acknowledges that the possible adverse consequences of the anti-Communist alliance with the Afghan Islamists (and shortly afterward, with their radical Muslim allies around the world)

– the growth of a new international terrorist movement and the global outreach of South Asian drug trafficking – did not weigh heavily, if at all, in their calculations at the time.

In post-mortems of the CIA's holy war in Iran, operating officials like Cogan have been more objective and cautious in their analysis of American motives, and their possible consequences, in concluding the alliance with the Islamists than senior figures like Brzezinski. As we will see later on, some very senior CIA and other administration officials had serious reservations and apprehensions. Cogan acknowledges that the Americans, as well as the Soviets, had already in 1979 become victims of the tide of Islamic revivalism sweeping the Muslim world. Main antagonists of the Americans were the Shi'ite Muslims, followers of the Ayatollah Khomeiny, in Iran; whereas the main adversaries of the Soviets were the Sunni Muslims – doctrinally and in many other ways quite different from the Shi'ites – of South and Central Asia. Cogan quotes an unnamed CIA colleague, still active in the Agency's clandestine operations in 1993, describing the CIA–Islamist partnership: "We took the means to wage war, put them in the hands of people who could do so, for purposes for which we agreed."[9]

Brzezinski's proclaimed goals were, and remain, far more grandiose and truly strategic. Asked whether he regretted favoring extremist Islamism or arming and training future terrorists, his reply was, "Which was more important in world history? The Taliban or the fall of the Soviet empire? A few over-excited Islamists or the liberation of Central Europe [Brzezinski's original Polish homeland was of course in Eastern Europe; perhaps this is what he meant] and the end of the Cold War?"[10]

In other revealing pronouncements in early 1998, when US and multi-national oil companies were eyeing possible pipeline routes to evacuate the oil and natural gas of Central Asia and the Caspian Basin to the West, Brzezinski expressed hope that the United States would, in Eurasia, build bridges to states having a "strong Muslim identity" and a manifest will to "become part of the world economy." This was a reference primarily to Turkey, America's favorite Muslim power in the late 1990s, and to his hope, for obvious commercial and political reasons, for an American rapprochement with the Iran of the ayatollahs.[11]

The US, having at first sympathetically watched (if not helped) the rise of the Pakistani-created Taliban, was observing with a mixture of sympathy and trepidation, the US oil company, UNOCAL, as it sought to negotiate with the Taliban authorization for energy pipelines from the ex-Soviet, now independent, republic of Turkmenistan, through Afghanistan and Pakistan. If successful, such agreements would probably be viewed by Brzezinski, the multi-national energy firms, and like-minded economic and political strategists as one of the *positive* long-range outcomes of the Afghanistan conflicts.

In addition to oil, trade routes, and Cold War geo-strategy, there were other American motives in concluding the alliance with the thousands of Islamist volunteers who would, during the decade of the 1980s, rally to the Stars and Stripes and the green-and-white star and crescent banner of Pakistan to fight the Soviet infidels. There was a spirit of romantic adventurism, inspiring some of the older Cold Warriors on the Western side. In a rather pale version of Orientalism of such European Arabophiles or Islamophiles as Lawrence of Arabia, some of them tended to idolize, or at least idealize, the sword of Islam, and the need to free it from Communist rule.

One such Cold Warrior was Archibald Bulloch Roosevelt, Jr., a Bostonian born in 1918, a Harvard man and grandson of the adventuresome President Theodore (Teddy) Roosevelt. Archie Roosevelt was a journalist turned army intelligence officer. Like his cousin, Kermit Roosevelt, who managed the counter-coup which returned the Shah of Iran to power in 1953, when nationalist supporters of Prime Minister Muhammad Mossadeq had driven the Shah out of the country, Archie became a Middle East specialist for the CIA. After a long career in the geographical space between Morocco and the Indian sub-continent, he retired in 1974 to work for the Chase Manhattan Bank.

Myself and fellow Mideast hands who attended a private publication party at a posh London club for Archie Roosevelt's book, *For Lust of Knowing, Memoirs of an Intelligence Officer,* a few months before his death in 1988, sensed his innate romanticism.

Where Afghanistan was concerned, Archibald Roosevelt considered himself a hard-headed realist. That evening in London he quoted for us a passage from his book, emphasizing his credo that the West had never properly responded to Soviet attacks. These had been taking place since Lenin's time. But there had been no counter-blows at "Russian imperialism in Asia." Although the US had sided with the Soviets in forcing World War II allies like France and the Netherlands to give up their colonies after that war, Roosevelt reminded us that "the subject races of Russia's Asian empire have continued to languish without any encouragement from us."[12]

The British, French, and to some extent the Italians, Spaniards and Portuguese (the latter three in various other parts of Africa) had other goals. One, as Archie Roosevelt saw it, was "to stem the course of [anti-colonial] nationalism ... fueled by the pan-Arab passions aroused by President Gamal Abdel Nasser" who ruled Egypt from the overthrow of King Farouk in 1952 until Nasser's death in 1970. US policy-makers, sympathetic to allied purposes, often confused the secular nationalist fervor of Nasser with that of the religion Islam. (This was even though Abdel Nasser, himself a pious Muslim, believed in separating church and state, and was a target of Muslim Brotherhood hitmen who tried unsuccessfully to murder him in 1954.) Also, the distinction between Communists and nationalists like Nasser was not always well understood in Washington, nor in the United States at large (where Israel's supporters made no effort to clear up the confusion). This was one reason why the anti-Communist religious conviction, occasionally zealotry, of conservative Muslim societies like those in Saudi Arabia and the Persian Gulf states, as well as the power (though not the Islamic religious conviction) of the Shah's Iran, were seen in Washington as strong allies against Moscow, as well as against Nasserism.

This was the kind of mind-set which would give rise to the belief, held in the Carter administration, and which hardened into articles of faith after President Ronald Reagan took office in 1981, that in Afghanistan especially, Islamists would make good allies for America in an anti-Communist crusade.

Added to this, the CIA "old boys' club," as some members of Archie Roosevelt's generation called it, felt strongly that the Soviet invasion of Afghanistan gave them a unique opportunity to challenge an enemy which had sought the West's downfall ever since the Russian revolution in 1917; a visceral as well as intellectual sense of historical revenge. It meant, in Archie Roosevelt's words, confronting "that [Russian] bear" which "has not changed since [Rudyard] Kipling's time – indeed we now see him in Afghanistan on the northern rim of the Khyber Pass." Roosevelt, like Zbigniew Brzezinski and other Carter advisors, felt the historic Khyber crossing between Afghanistan and Pakistan was the "true front line" where they felt "the chill winds of the Cold War blowing over those forbidding mountains."[13] Beyond those mountains, to the north, lay the vast reaches of Soviet Central Asia. There, along the roads to the ancient Muslim cities of Bokhara, Samarkand and Tashkent, lay the lands of Muslim Central Asia, restless under Russian and Communist rule; perhaps ripe for a "liberation" process which would end in independence.

It does seem clear from Brzezinski's 1998 musings that he, at least, among President Carter's top policy-makers shared this ambitious view in 1979, even if the vast energy resources which Central Asia might offer the West were still not known as well then as they were a decade later. What is certain is that Carter's men, especially those in the intelligence community who had survived the major CIA scandals of the 1960s and 1970s, were certain that helping the Afghan resistance against the Soviets might bring as yet unsuspected rewards – but this had to be a covert operation with a difference.

The CIA's Directorate of Operations was the only arm of the US government able to carry out what Archie Roosevelt called "truly covert functions like secret support to foreign leaders, political parties, or guerrilla forces in 'denied areas' such as Afghanistan." Definitely to be avoided was any repetition of the ill-conceived, unsupported and ill-fated Bay of Pigs invasion of Cuba in 1960, run by the CIA with a large body of poorly-trained Cuban exiles, mercenaries and adventurers as troops. Laos was a relative success; Cuba was disaster. The lessons of both were the same: use as few actual CIA personnel as possible, and be sure that the fighters used were motivated and trained as well as was feasible.

The Agency, it was decided, would co-opt specialized American military personnel, with the support of the Pakistani military once this had been obtained, to train an army of Muslim zealots. They could be well paid, and train and deploy with the help of anti-Communist and Muslim governments, like geographically proximate Pakistan and wealthy Saudi Arabia. Archie Roosevelt and his like-minded juniors conceived that the American responsibility should lie with the

[American] military, utilizing such units as the US Army's Special Forces. This was the core idea: using the Army's "Green Berets" and the Navy SEALS (Sea/Air/Land Commando teams). Both were veterans of major paramilitary operations which the CIA had managed in Indo-China. Other special military units would, in time, join them. They would train a huge foreign mercenary army; one of the largest ever seen in American military history. Virtually all would be Muslims. They would fervently believe that God had commanded them to fight His enemies, the Godless Communists and foreign Russian invaders. Their earthly rewards would be glory and generous pay. For those who died as martyrs, rewards would be in heaven.

It had fallen to the administration of President Gerald Ford, between 1974 and Carter's accession in 1977, to clean house after the CIA's notable scandals. These concerned Angola, use of drugs in covert wars in Indo-China and elsewhere and domestic spying on American citizens. These and other matters became known, after their exposure by the *New York Times* and acknowledgment by the CIA director William Colby in 1974–75, as "The Family Jewels" – dark secrets which the Agency had wanted to keep locked in its most top-secret safes forever.

After his inauguration in January 1977, President Jimmy Carter resolved to run as clean and tight an intelligence ship as possible. He felt it important to wipe out the stigma of a rogue CIA which had, as he put it in his memoirs, "a role in plotting murder and other crimes."[14] Soon Carter came to believe he could avoid the stigma of past covert operations gone wrong; yet accomplish certain tasks needed to win the Cold War against the Soviets. First, you found and appointed a "clean," highly moral Director of Central Intelligence; a super-spy who might also be an intellectual – Carter had a high respect for intellectuals – and who had a human face that bespoke a humane nature. Second, he gradually discovered, there was a way to accomplish Cold War missions, especially in the Third World, without direct avowable or accountable American involvement.

Jimmy Carter's first choice for his "clean" CIA chief was his friend Theodore Sorenson. Congress refused. Some congressmen pointed out that Ted Sorenson had been a conscientious objector in the Vietnam conflict. Others said he simply was not qualified for the job of heading the largest and most expensive spy agency in the world. Carter then chose Admiral Stansfield Turner, a Christian Scientist and former Rhodes scholar at Oxford who had made a brilliant career in the US Navy. When appointed in 1977, Turner was serving as commander-in-chief of NATO forces in southern Europe, headquartered in Naples, Italy.

During his three years between his appointment and his having to work with President Carter's National Security Advisor and enthusiastic Cold Warrior, Zbigniew Brzezinski, to launch the anti-Soviet war in Afghanistan, Turner worked to clean up the Agency further and to streamline it. After firing hundreds of human spies, analysts and assorted personnel from both the front lines and back rooms of intelligence gathering, and of encouraging new programs of electronic surveillance from satellites, aircraft and remote sensors to take their places, Turner found himself studying the whole subject of covert action. "The majority of the espionage professionals," he asserted, "from what I could see [after the exposed abuses of the 'Family Jewels'], believed that covert action had brought more harm and criticism to the CIA than useful return, and that it had seriously detracted from the Agency's primary role of collecting and evaluating intelligence."[15]

Nevertheless, Turner and his aides saw a lot of covert action in those last few years before Afghanistan. Much of it educated them for the working alliance with Muslim zealots, the first of its kind in American history, which was to come. None of it, apparently, prepared them to contemplate, or even to imagine, what the terrible consequences of that alliance were to be.

In 1977, as Turner's watch began, and on into 1978, Cuban mercenaries fought for the Leftist government in Angola, where the CIA had already meddled and supported anti-Communist warlords like Jonas Savimbi. Others, Turner noted, fought alongside forces of the Marxist government, which had replaced Emperor Haile Selassie in Ethiopia, against Somalia. In 1979, Marxist South Yemen, with active Soviet backing – and active opposition from British and CIA-backed groups – threatened the republican government of North Yemen, supported by Egypt and other outside Arab states. Finally, just before the main act began in the Afghanistan drama in 1979, the Shi'a Muslim zealots of the Ayatollah Khomeiny in Iran took command of a mass popular revolution, ousted the Shah and took the US Embassy in Tehran and over 50 of its incumbent American diplomats hostage.

The Carter team adopted a method of avoiding the stigma of direct CIA involvement in covert operations which could go wrong and backfire on the United States. It was a method which Henry Kissinger, first as President Richard Nixon's national security advisor, then as Secretary of State, had refined and applied with skill: get others to do what you want done, while avoiding the onus or blame if the operation fails. The "others," in Kissinger's era of the early 1970s, a time of rehearsal for the approaching adventure in Afghanistan, were a set of unlikely colleagues and allies of circumstance. These allies, in rough order of their actual value rendered to the US, were: France's late Count Alexandre de Marenches, chief of external French intelligence from 1972 to 1982; President Anwar al-Sadat of Egypt from 1970 until his murder in 1981; the Shah of Iran, until his dethronement in 1979 by Khomeiny's revolutionaries and King Hassan II of Morocco, a discreet but valuable friend of the United States since his enthronement in 1960. Finally, there was Kamal Adham, the doughty and super-rich chief of intelligence for Saudi Arabian King Faisal. Together, these gentlemen created an informal but for a time highly effective covert operation, christened by the Egyptian author and publicist who discovered it, Muhammad Hasseinine Haykal, advisor to the late President Nasser, "the Safari Club."

The Safari Club set a precedent and some guidelines for the subsequent CIA operation in Afghanistan. As its name implied, the Safari Club's main task was to carry out missions – always anti-Communist ones, for America, on the "good guys'" side of the Cold War – in Africa and other parts of the Third World. Some of its members – the intelligence establishments of France, Egypt, the Shah's Iran,

Morocco and Saudi Arabia – would eventually help out in the Afghanistan operation too.

Haykal discovered the Club's existence when, poking into Tehran archives of Iran's imperial era with the permission of the Ayatollah Khomeiny's post-1979 revolutionaries, he came up with a formal written agreement, signed by the heads of intelligence concerned. Africa was the first focus of the Club's founders. All had plenty to lose if what they viewed as communism should triumph there. The Shah and his family had big investments linked with South Africa's white supremacy regime, such as the Transvaal Development Company. Also, the Shah shared with President Sadat and Morocco's King Hassan (always ready to support the interests of the ex-colonial power, France, and its ally, the United States), a deep concern about Soviet and Cuban military intervention in Ethiopia and Angola, and about Marxist liberation movements elsewhere in Africa, Asia and Latin America. The Saudis, too, viewed such goings-on, especially those in the Horn of Africa, so geographically close to them, with an equally jaundiced eye. They were as enthusiastic about President Sadat's expulsion of the Soviet advisors whom his predecessor Nasser had invited into Egypt as the Americans were.[16]

The Shah, who dying in exile in 1980, found a safe haven only in Sadat's Egypt, had often sympathized and concurred with Sadat. His Imperial Majesty told the author in Tehran in 1972 that the US administration's "slowness and sluggishness," in failing to react swiftly and imaginatively to Sadat's shock expulsion of the Russians, had disappointed him. Ardeshir Zahedi, his son-in-law, then Iranian Foreign Minister, was constant in his efforts to impress American listeners with the urgency of the Soviet threat to South Asia; especially Afghanistan. Once in 1978 Zahedi spoke of Soviet efforts to "buy" certain tribes and warlords in Afghanistan (something the CIA and Pakistan's ISI would be doing more efficiently than the Soviets by 1980). He showed me a map of Baluchistan, a huge tribal area shared by Iran, Pakistan and Afghanistan which purported to show that Moscow planned to realize the old dream of Peter the Great and subsequent czars to push through to the warm-water ports of the Indian Ocean. Under such pretexts of a largely non-existent Soviet agitation among Baluchi tribal separatists, the Pakistani and Iranian armed forces waged a rude war, using jet planes and helicopter gunships, against the Baluchis in the late 1970s, providing a discordant overture to the main symphony of the Soviet and American interventions soon to follow in Afghanistan.

The Safari Club player who probably helped most to draw the US into the Afghan adventure was Count Alexandre de Marenches, who served under French President Valery Giscard d'Estaing as chief of the French external intelligence service, then called the *Service du Documentation et de Contre-Espionage* (SDECE). He had cooperated actively with the United States in warfare and covert operations since World War II. He believed it to be of advantage to France, as well as to his American friends and allies, to form a group like the Safari Club to protect and advance Western interests in the Third World. The SDECE was watching developments in South Asia closely. De Marenches sensed that a Western–Soviet confrontation was probably inevitable there.

From his Paris office in what French journalists nicknamed *la Piscine,* because SDECE headquarters was located near a large swimming pool, de Marenches, a big, bluff man who his close American friend, General Vernon A. Walters, a Cold Warrior and CIA official called a "real French Kissinger," sent out a series of suggestions to Egypt, Saudi Arabia, Iran and Morocco that they formalize their Safari Club collaboration in a written pact. Algeria was invited to join too, but the military regime of Houari Boumedienne, a self-avowed "Islamic socialist" (whatever that meant), veteran leader of the 1954–62 Algerian war for independence from France, said thank you, but no.

The agreement found by Haykal in Tehran was signed on September 1, 1976. De Marenches signed for France, with his approximate counterparts in the other participating intelligence services the other signatories. To face what they saw as the Russian and Communist danger in Africa and South Asia, they agreed to set up their main center in Cairo, divided into a secretariat, a planning section and an operations branch. President Sadat ordered his government to provide office space and living accommodations for personnel. France would supply technical equipment for security and communications. There would be a rotating chairmanship, with each member taking one-year turns in chair.

Safari Club conferences were held in secret during the 1970s in Saudi Arabia, France and Egypt. Millions of dollars were spent on acquiring real estate and equipment, including secure telephone hotlines (almost certainly accessible to the big electronic ears of the US electronic intelligence-gathering organization, the huge National Security Agency (NSA) at Fort Meade, Maryland, and its junior but ubiquitous ally, Britain's General Communications Headquarters (GCHQ) at Cheltenham, England). The Club's first success was in the Congo (later Zaire) when a dissident general threatened to seize the mineral-rich province of Katanga. The Belgian and French mining interests closely allied to Congo President Mobutu Sosi Seke, a corrupt favorite of the CIA, took fright and appealed to the Club for help. Moroccan and Egyptian troops, with French air transport and logistical support, flew to the rescue. The Club, with varying success, met bigger challenges, this time from the Soviets and regimes, Marxist or otherwise, they were helping, in Ethiopia and Somalia. In one of these operations, the Club provided Egypt's Sadat with experience and a precedent for the Afghanistan operation. Club members sold Somali president and strongman Siad Barre, suddenly deprived of Soviet support in his war with Ethiopia over disputed Ogaden territory, needed arms to finish trouncing the Ethiopians.

Just before the Afghanistan war began, and because the Safari Club was keeping both Israeli and US intelligence informed of its actions, the Club was able to help bring about President Sadat's historic peacemaking visit of November 1977 to Jerusalem, leading eventually to the US–Egyptian–Israeli peace treaty of 1979. The first letter suggesting an Israeli–Egyptian summit meeting came not from Sadat. It came from the late Prime Minister Yitzhak Rabin of Israel. Morocco's representative in the Safari Club hand-carried Rabin's letter to Sadat. King Hassan then sponsored the first secret meeting in Morocco between Israeli General Moshe

Dayan and Hassan Tuhamy, an Egyptian deputy prime minister with responsibilities for intelligence.[17]

In February 1979, the Shah, exiled and dethroned, could do no more. Count de Marenches, the Safari Club's initiator and most active member, was convinced that the Soviets would march into Afghanistan. He believed the credos of men like Zbigniew Brzezinski that geography, and the historic Russian aspiration to reach the warm waters of the Indian Ocean and perhaps lay hands on the oil of the Persian Gulf, made a Soviet push southward inevitable. The chief French spy, as he told his French biographer, Christine Ockrent, began to follow Afghan events closely when the last Afghan king, Zahir Shah, was ousted and went into exile in Italy in July 1973. For de Marenches, the subsequent murder of his successor, Prince Daoud and the subsequent assassinations of other senior Afghan figures including President Taraki were proof that Afghanistan was headed for Soviet conquest. SDECE reports observed that Afghanistan's highways had been built with both Russian and American aid; the Russian ones were clearly planned to facilitate strategic movement across the mountain barriers between Afghanistan and the USSR.

De Marenches recalled that a colleague in British intelligence informed him that Cheltenham's GCHQ electronic spooks had detected frequent comings and goings of the same large Soviet VIP plane at Kabul airport. The Soviets had been careless about taking routine precautions: the number and national emblem on the fuselage had not been hidden; nor had the aircraft's radio frequencies been changed, and so were easily detectable. De Marenches decided to send some French human spies to watch Kabul airport and see who got out each time the big Soviet bird arrived. One day, in the early summer of 1979, as tribal tumult and disorders boiled in Afghanistan, the French agents identified an arriving VIP as no less a personage than Marshal Ivan Pavlovsky, commander-in-chief of the Soviet ground forces since 1967.

Pavlovsky was a frequent visitor all that summer. De Marenches observed that Afghanistan, a rustic and rough country, "not St. Tropez or Hawaii," was hardly a place which a senior Soviet marshal accustomed to great luxury would choose for summer rest and recreation.

The CIA's analysts were more or less aware of all this, it appears; yet many of their analysts seem to have been taken by surprise with the sudden and fateful Soviet intervention in December. At least one distinguished American journalist fared better. About three weeks before Christmas, Arnaud de Borchgrave of *Newsweek* who is related to one of de Marenche's Belgian cousins, visited the French intelligence chief. He asked for advice on where to find, in the very near future, the best story. "If I were you," de Marenches told him, "I would go to Kabul."[18]

De Borchgrave took his advice, and sacrificed his Christmas holidays to covering what proved to be the start of one of the biggest stories of the next decade. He was one of the very few Western newsmen on the spot when the Soviets descended on Kabul, their guns blazing, at Christmas 1979.

2 Anwar al-Sadat

As I covered Pentagon briefings for *The Christian Science Monitor*, I recalled earlier briefings in Tehran and Washington by Ardeshir Zahedi, the Shah's son-in-law, foreign minister and last ambassador in the United States. The next big Soviet move, he had insisted, would be into Afghanistan. Brezhnev wanted access to the Indian Ocean. Once in Kabul he would be a lot closer to the sea and the oilfields.

Brzezinski's staffers and senior State Department aides had begun discussions with the allies Washington would need. Egyptian diplomats, under orders from President Anwar al-Sadat, and others commanded by Saudi Foreign Minister Prince Saud al-Faisal, relayed urgent messages to their capitals. Even more important than Egypt or Saudi Arabia to the coming enterprise was Pakistan, as President Carter pointed out to a formal National Security Council (NSC) meeting on December 28. There was serious disagreement, growing and well-publicized, with the Islamabad government over its developing, clandestine nuclear weapons capacity: US military aid had been cut by Act of Congress, the so-called Pressler Amendment, because the US President was unable to certify to Congress that Pakistan was not making a nuclear bomb.

Despite this major obstacle to good relations, Pakistan would be the indispensable geographic and political base for waging the coming proxy war in Afghanistan. So assistant secretary of state Warren Christopher – his superior, cautious and seasoned diplomatist Cyrus Vance, had serious reservations about the entire project – was sent on what CIA and diplomatic old-timers used to call a "hand-holding mission." The purpose was to placate and reassure Pakistan's military president (some called him a military dictator), General Zia al-Haq, whose cooperation and collaboration were indispensable.[1]

That New Year's Eve was raw and frosty on our quiet street in Arlington, Virginia, close to the Potomac River and Washington. My Greek wife Vania and myself welcomed old Middle East friends. Just before midnight, a new friend arrived. He was Alexander Zotov, then Middle East specialist at the Soviet Embassy in Washington. Zotov commanded several major Mideast languages. He looked, dressed and talked like an American academic, a courteous extrovert with a ready smile. He had (he told me) a great-grandfather who had fought against the Bolsheviks in the White Army in his native Caucasus in the 1919–20 civil war. He handed us a party gift, a little carved wooden Orthodox church, the kind you put under the Christmas tree, with its Russian steeple and onion top.

Why, I asked him, had the Russians moved into Afghanistan? He paused about five seconds, then replied: "I don't understand why. They didn't have to. They could have gotten on fine with Hafizullah Amin. There has been a great mistake."

Zotov went on to become chief of Mideast affairs in the presidium of the Soviet Communist Party and, during the Soviet Union's twilight years, ambassador to

Syria. In his wisdom and prescience he survived the rise and fall of Mikhail Gorbachev. It isn't too much to say, I think, that on that New Year's Eve, a premonition of disaster touched both Zotov and myself.

Even as the first old Lee-Enfield rifles from the CIA were reaching the moujahidin on the ground in Afghanistan, President Carter sent Zbigniew Brzezinski first to Egypt, then to Pakistan. Defense Secretary Harold Brown's destination was another potential ally, China.

Brzezinski's task in Cairo was to win President Anwar al-Sadat for the Afghanistan operation, or "get him on the team," in the parlance of Washington. Some of the American capital's Mideast experts realized that enlisting Sadat's Islamist critics and opponents as ideological leaders or recruiters was a key to raising a volunteer army of Egyptian mercenaries. A tiny handful of real Afghanistan experts in the West, such as the late Louis Dupree of the American Universities Field Service or the French student of political Islam, Olivier Roy, knew that Afghan Islamist leaders, who would be required for the fight to eject the Russians, had been in part educated in Egypt. They were heavily influenced by the traditions of the Muslim Brotherhood movement which had arisen in the then British-occupied Egyptian monarchy in the 1920s.

One link between Egypt's Islamists and the Afghans was Dr. Gholam Muhammad Niyazi, who became dean of the faculty of theology at the Afghan University in Kabul when he returned from studies in Egypt. Dr. Niyazi and other Afghan scholars were graduates of Cairo's al-Azhar.[2] This was considered by many the illustrious mother of all the world's Islamic universities. Its elders had an uneasy love–hate relationship with President Sadat, especially after his embrace of the United States after the 1973 war and in the peace agreements with Israel which President Carter catalyzed. At al-Azhar, secular nationalists and Islamists from all over the Muslim world, from Morocco to the Philippines, found a forum and platform for their dreams, plans and ideas. Here they also met leaders of the Muslim Brothers.

Founded in Egypt by a schoolteacher, Hassan al-Banna, in 1928, the Brotherhood propagated its theories of strict Islamic theocracy in an ideal Muslim state, to be guided only by the laws and precepts of the Holy Koran. The Brotherhood formed its cells throughout much of the Arab and Muslim worlds.

The Brothers had a record of militancy. This included fighting the Jewish armies in Palestine in 1948–49 and opposing the British in Egypt with terrorism and occasional guerrilla warfare during the 1950s and earlier. Egypt's long record of both a vigorous nationalist movement, led by intellectuals, and occasional tough armed opposition to foreign invaders, had already nourished other resistance movements in the Arab and Muslim worlds. Azharis, as the al-Azhar graduates came to be called, especially when they became chiefs of state like Houari Boumedienne of Algeria, a leader of the 1954–62 anti-colonial revolution against the French, lent a strongly Islamist flavor, even to the secular Arab nationalist movements like Algeria's FLN.

Since coming to power after President Nasser's death in 1970, Sadat had released from jail many of the Muslim Brotherhood and other Islamist leaders and militants whom Nasser had imprisoned, following conspiracies and attempts on his life by the Brothers in the 1950s. Sadat's flirtation with the Islamists made it easier for him to do what Brzezinski and his successors in the administration of President Ronald Reagan asked him to do. Sadat and his governments became, for a time, virtual recruiting sergeants and quartermasters to the secret army of zealots being mustered to fight the Soviets in South and Central Asia.

Besides flirtation with the Islamists, whom he relied upon to fight Communist influence in Egypt and counter Leftist plots against him, especially in the period just before his wholesale expulsion of Soviet military personnel from Egypt in 1972, Sadat had another card in his hand when he agreed with the Americans to help train, equip and supply volunteers for the Afghan jihad. From the American viewpoint, it looked like a strong card. Actually, it would help to doom Sadat, and would lead to the most serious Islamist insurgency Egypt has known in modern times.

After signing his March 1979 peace treaty with Israel with President Jimmy Carter and Prime Minister Menahem Begin in Washington, there was a loud chorus of denunciation from the Palestinians, Syria, Iraq, Saudi Arabia and much of the rest of the Muslim world. They accused Sadat of betraying the Palestinian cause, by not linking an Israeli evacuation of the West Bank, Gaza and Arab East Jerusalem to the Israeli commitment to evacuate Sinai. Sadat reacted by drawing even closer to the US administration and, indeed, to all things American. In public speeches, he termed the Arab leaders "dwarves and ignoramuses" with "putrid and corrupt" minds. However, as Cairo's establishment newspaper, Al-Ahram, quoted him on April 1, 1981, Egypt would "fly to help" its fellow Arabs and Muslims, "if ever help were sought – and even if it were not."

Within weeks of Brzezinski's visit in January 1980, Sadat had symbolically carried out this promise by authorizing US cargo planes, sometimes accompanied by Egyptian personnel, to fly from such bases in Egypt as Qena and Aswan to deliver arms and supplies to the moujahidin in Pakistan. Soon, Egypt's military inventories were being scoured for Soviet-supplied arms, many of them out of date, to send to the jihad. An old arms factory near Helwan, Egypt, was eventually converted to produce the same kind of weapons. Journalists were later told, when they had to be told anything about the weapons, that the bogus Russian weapons came from old surplus stocks in Egypt. Later, Israel would feed real Russian weapons, captured from Egypt, Syria and the PLO, into the supply pipeline for the Afghan jihad.[3]

By the end of 1980, Sadat was engaged in these efforts and in welcoming selected groups of US military trainers to Egypt to impart skills of the US Special Forces to those Egyptians who would, in turn, pass on the training to the Egyptian volunteers flying to the aid of the moujahidin in Afghanistan.

Sadat may have considered that his burgeoning alliance with the Americans in Afghanistan would ease the rancor of the Muslim Brothers and the various other

Islamist groups which had begun to spring up over his 1981 peace treaty with Israel and his growing friendship on other fronts, besides Afghanistan, with the Americans. The US political role in Egypt was fast becoming primordial. Sadat repeated several times in interviews and in public that "America holds 99 percent of the cards in the [Middle East] game." When, during one exchange with President Carter, the US President challenged this, Sadat is reported to have replied, "My dear Jimmy; you are right; it is not 99 percent but 99.9 percent." Both men, according to an Egyptian journalist's account, laughed.[4]

Only six months after signing the peace accord with President Carter and Israeli Prime Minister Menahem Begin in March 1979, Sadat further antagonized the Islamists by staging a huge public celebration. Originally, he had intended to hold a "World Peace Festival" with Muslim, Jewish and Christian religious ceremonies, on Mount Sinai, where Moses is supposed to have received the Ten Commandments from God. This proved impossible to organize. Instead, Sadat substituted a huge party which the *New York Times* described as an occasion where "a bunch of beautiful people have created their own island of conspicuous opulence in a sea of Egyptian poverty." This was a gathering of jet-setters, not far from the teeming huts and hovels of some of the Cairo suburbs' poorest of the poor. The party was to make Sadat, for a fleeting moment, into a kind of King of Glitz, a patron of international café society. This gala event took place in September 1979, on the ninth anniversary of President Nasser's death. In what some Egyptians, Islamists included, saw as a kind of symbol of the metaphysical distance he had already traveled from Nasser, his former chief, and from the Egyptian values of dignity and modesty which Nasser and Sadat had both extolled, Sadat for the first time stayed away from the commemoration of Nasser's death. The guest of honor at the Pyramids party was Frank Sinatra, who crooned for Sadat and his hundreds of guests. Sponsoring the party and paying the bills for it, according to the late historian Desmond Stewart, was Michel C. Bergerac, chairman of Revlon Inc., the giant cosmetics firm, to raise money for Mrs. Jihan Sadat, the First Lady, to use for her favorite charity. A normal ticket cost a mere $2,500, the equivalent of nine years' wages for an ordinary Egyptian. However, a $30,000 ticket would secure a table with an Egyptian cabinet minister. Those exclusive tables for six were all taken. Senior executives of Philip Morris, Pan-Am, TWA and Mobil Oil were able to get advice during the entertainment on their prospective investments in Egypt. For the really important guests, the evening ended in a dinner at a cinema club in Giza, the district of the Pyramids. The host was US Ambassador Alfred Atherton.[5] He would soon find himself helping to clinch the details of the US–Egyptian alliance for the jihad in Afghanistan.

During these preparations, Sadat and the US diplomats soon found that there was a senior and jealous rival for US affections: the State of Israel. Israeli leaders and commentators feared that the honeymoon with Sadat might obscure Israel's value as an ally, or, at least, as a "strategic asset" to the United States. So Jerusalem stepped up its self-promotion. In one typical statement, retired General Chaim

Herzog, former Israeli ambassador to the United Nations and later Israeli President, said that the best thing the United States could do would be to encourage the incorporation of Israel within the NATO treaty agreement, to defend Europe and the Western Levant against the expansion of the Soviet Union.

Although Israel has not to this time of writing made it into NATO, it did make a substantial contribution to the secret anti-Soviet Muslim army in Afghanistan. For this, Israel paid a heavy price: the holy warriors included Palestinians who, as we will see in more detail later on, became founders and movers of the Islamist HAMAS resistance movement in Gaza and the West Bank, which shot and bombed its way into world consciousness in the 1990s.

Sadat, while not going so far as to back Israel's candidacy for NATO, wholeheartedly agreed with the Carter administration about the Soviet threat. Although in the 1950s, as an aide of President Nasser, he had described the USSR as "an imaginary foe" made in America, he now described it as "more dangerous, much more dangerous" to the world than Adolf Hitler had ever been. Sadat's friend, the late Shah, who in his exile in 1979 came to briefly enjoy Sadat's hospitality in Egypt and then die there, had left the world stage. Sadat scornfully pointed out once to a Western TV interviewer that the Soviets had then "captured Afghanistan in broad daylight." What Sadat neglected to mention was that in January 1979, when the Shah first arrived in Egypt as a refugee from the Islamic revolution in Iran, Islamist activist groups in Assiut, Middle Egypt, later the stronghold of armed Islamist insurgents, conducted violent protests against the welcome Sadat had given the Shah. They looted Christian shops in a pattern often repeated later, and caused casualties. As Sadat's entente with Israel and the United States developed during 1979, friction arose between Islamists and Egypt's large Coptic Christian minority. The Copts in Egypt enjoy much support from the Coptic Christian community in the United States, which quickly took the side of their brothers in Egypt in the growing sectarian friction there. In his interviews and other public pronouncements for Western consumption, Sadat turned more and more to the theme of the Communist danger abroad. Increasingly he signalled his fatal turning to the West in statements, like one made to Brzezinski, that Egypt was the "gateway" to the Middle East for America. Soon, he said, "you will no longer need a gendarme at all."[6]

Sadat's engagement in the Afghan jihad came as early as December 1979, before Brzezinski's post-New Year's visit, and even as Soviet troops were descending upon Kabul. Sadat told his favorite Cairo magazine, *October,* that he was ready to do what neither Abdel Nasser nor most other Arab leaders had been prepared to do, and which Sadat had previously avoided doing himself: the US could now have military "facilities" – the word "bases" was taboo – in Egypt "to defend all the Arab countries."[7]

To reward Sadat and Egypt for making peace with Israel, the US Congress had already provided $1.5 billion on the same easy credit terms enjoyed by Israel. By the end of 1980, as Sadat proved his loyalty in the Afghan jihad, this had expanded into $3.5 billion more, spread over four years. This was the beginning of what proved to be a generation of Egyptian purchases of advanced US weaponry, including the F-16 fighter, earlier withheld due to Israeli objections. It was also the beginning of a huge boom for the US armaments industry, giving them government-subsidized sales which in some years since have almost rivalled those to Israel.

As regards the US military "facilities" needed for the Afghanistan jihad, when Sadat made his initial offer in December 1979, US Air Force AWACS reconnaissance planes had already been flying missions from Qena air base for months. This was well-known to most of the local inhabitants, among whom the Islamists had long been proselytizing. Qena lay 280 miles south of Cairo. In April 1980, during the first weeks of Sadat's hyperactive program to support the jihad in South Asia, Qena would serve as a staging-post for the failed US attempt to rescue the American diplomatic hostages in Tehran. By the summer of 1980, the Cairo West military air base, near Cairo International Airport, had also been opened to the US Air Force. It sent an initial squadron of F-4 Phantom fighter-bombers with about 300 personnel to prepare for high-profile joint maneuvers with the Egyptian air force. In November of the same year, 1,400 US ground troops with tactical air support would join the Egyptian armed forces in joint desert maneuvers, often repeated in the years to come. Later came small teams of US Special Forces, notably US Navy SEALS (Sea–Air–Land commandos) to train Egyptian military men who would be associated with the Afghanistan mission.

The supply operation for Afghanistan, however, dated from Brzezinski's meeting with Sadat in Cairo in January 1980. Sadat's own recollection of that meeting was that the White House advisor asked him to provide stocks of Soviet-made weapons (which Sadat probably hoped would soon be obsolete anyway, as the trickle of hi-tech American armaments gradually increased to a torrent). Soviet-made small-arms, ammunition, mortar and artillery shells, and even hand-held Strela and other anti-aircraft missiles, offered the US the plausible alibi that they had been captured from the Russians, if they fell into Soviet hands in Afghanistan. According to Sadat, Brzezinski proposed: "Please open your stores for us so that we can give the Afghanis the armaments they need to fight, and I gave them the armaments." USAF C-5 Galaxy and C-130 transports shortly began flying the Egyptian arms supplies to Pakistan. There, the CIA turned them over to the Pakistani military which, with a good deal of waste, corruption and loss, passed them on to the seven main groups of Muslim zealots training in the arts of guerrilla war and urban terrorism.

Sadat's relations with the Islamists worsened, as the mainstream Muslim Brotherhood (MB) movement distanced itself from the more extreme Islamists. During the first months of the Afghan jihad in 1980, the extremists began to urge their followers to attack the recently established Israeli Embassy in Cairo and to harm Israeli diplomats and foreign tourists, as well as the Egyptians who worked with them or facilitated their presence. In April 1980, the unofficial Muslim Brotherhood magazine, *Al-Dawa*, warned: "Now that disaster has fallen and Israel has an embassy in our country, what must we do? Do we blow up the Embassy? Do we seize the Jewish diplomats and kill them? No, a thousand times no! Blowing up the Israeli Embassy will never lead to any result but the reconstruction of another embassy at Egypt's expense." Instead, *Al-Dawa* urged a boycott of everything to do with Israel.

From 1980 on, the Muslim Brotherhood tried to gather the rapidly growing Islamist groups in the universities, one of the original foundations of its own power, under its wing. Some of the groups advocated extremism and violence; others followed the more moderate line of the mainstream MB. The emirs or princes heading each group elected a general emir over all of them. Then a coalition of other Islamist groups outside the universities formed a loose organization called the Permanent Islamic Congress for the Propagation of Islam. It elected the Muslim Brotherhood's Umar al-Telmisani as its president. It began organizing opposition against Sadat's foreign policy, including the Camp David accords with Israel (but not against the US-sponsored war against the Soviets in Afghanistan). Public meetings and rallies, attended by tens of thousands of people, called for the recovery of Jerusalem by the Muslims, punitive measures against Israel for bombing the Iraqi nuclear plant outside Baghdad in June 1981 and the opening of mosques to independent Muslim preachers, rather than just the government-appointed ones. As sectarian passions rose, serious rioting broke out in Zawiya al-Hamra, a poor Cairo neighborhood, on June 17, 1981. Muslims clashed with Coptic Christians; dozens died, hundreds were wounded and many shops and homes were burned.

Sadat in his public statements began more and more to blame even the "moderate" leadership of the Muslim Brotherhood for the rising tide of violence. He failed to understand that the Islamic Congress was an attempt by the Brotherhood to absorb the extremist danger to the regime. He also appears to have believed that the rising Islamist tide would endanger the negotiations with Israel and the United States for the peaceful recovery of the Sinai Peninsula from Israel. By concentrating attention on the Brotherhood and at the same time pursuing the Afghan adventure with the United States, Sadat chose to ignore the real source of danger which would cost him his life in October 1981: the small but determined and ruthless extremist groups.[8]

The final nine months of Sadat's career and life were devoted mainly to vindictive political crackdowns and the jailing of real and imagined adversaries. In the latter category was even Muhammad Hasseinine Haykal. These final nine months for Sadat happened to be the first nine months of President Ronald Reagan's new administration in the United States. Reagan's new CIA director – the lawyer, businessman and World War II Office of Strategic Surveys (OSS, the CIA's precedessor) chief William Casey – visited Cairo. He was even more excited than Brzezinski had been over Sadat's enthusiasm for the pursuit of the Afghan jihad.

By the time they killed Sadat, the Islamists seem to have taken this support for granted. Anyway, the support was not enough to forgive Sadat for signing peace with Israel under an American umbrella; nor for the toleration of rather massive financial corruption in his entourage (displayed, for the Islamists, in manifestations like Revlon Night at the Pyramids). This corruption, as they saw it, arose from the influx of Western private capital and the cynical attitude of "enrich yourself while you can" which was current in the United States during the Reagan years, and which flourished in Sadat's entourage.

The failure of Sadat's vision, when it came to evaluating his own countrymen's motives (as opposed to his grand and successful concept of concluding peace with Israel, by getting the United States involved in the process) emerged in an interview with NBC television's *Today* show in September 1981, after jailing thousands of real or imagined opponents. In this interview, Sadat bragged to the American public about the Afghan operation, still being treated as covert by the new Reagan administration and the US Congress. Today, he told NBC's Tom Brokaw, he was able to reveal a big secret. Aircraft (he didn't say US aircraft, nor did he mention the Egyptian "facilities" they were using) were ferrying planeload after planeload of arms from Egypt to the anti-Communist guerrillas in Afghanistan. Why was he doing it? "Because they are our Muslim brothers and are in trouble."

But hadn't some of the Egyptian and other Arab volunteers been involved in terrorism? (Muhammad Shawki Islambuli, brother of the young Islamist army lieutenant whose bullets would soon kill Sadat, was already in trouble with Egyptian law enforcement agencies for his militant Islamist activities. Soon, he would join the other volunteers heading for Afghanistan.) No, said Sadat. They weren't terrorists. They just held meetings (he added dismissively), but they didn't use weapons.[9]

To understand the impact of the Afghan adventure on the Egyptian society and state, and why it helped to produce such disasters for Egypt as the massacre of 58 foreign tourists by Islamists at the winter resort of Luxor in November 1997, all but destroying Egypt's vital tourist business, it is important to know who, exactly, Sadat's assassins were. Those behind them and seeking to profit from his murder, which they felt had been a righteous action in the name of Islam, would soon become the adversaries of Sadat's successor, President Husni Mubarak.

Khaled al-Islambuli was born at Mallawi, Upper Egypt, in November 1957. His father, Ahmed Shawki, was a lawyer who headed the legal department of the sugar company in Nag Hammadi, also in Upper Egypt where Egypt's sugar-cane fields abound. These fields offered shelter and sometimes cover for the terrorist bands arising in the 1980s, many led by Afghan war veterans. Khaled's elder brother Muhammad Islambuli, in 1998 aged 43, was in 1981, the year of Sadat's murder, in the commercial faculty of the University of Assiut, the main university of southern and central Egypt, and a traditional center of both Muslim and Coptic Christian zealotry. Sectarian tensions were common, if not usual; the Copts are a proud folk, comprising about 12 percent of Egypt's people. They stoutly defend their status and claim to be the oldest Mideastern Christian sect.

Khaled al-Islambuli's artillery unit was based at Huckstep. This kept him within easy range of his family and his Islamist friends and teachers in nearby Cairo. He belonged to a small group of these Islamists, calling themselves the *al-Gama'a al-Islamiya* or Islamic Group. It operated mainly underground. Originally, it was inspired by the Muslim Brotherhood and by the same intellectual forefathers – Jamal al-Din al-Afghani, Rashid Reda, Hassan al-Banna – who were firing the imagination and zeal of Afghans, like Dr. Gholam Muhammad Niyazi, who had lived and studied among Cairo intellectuals, before returning to Afghanistan and getting in trouble with the Left-leaning Afghan regimes of the period for their Islamic activist activities.

The Islamic Group's different geographical branches were divided into cells, called '*anquds,* Arabic for a bunch of grapes. Like other conspiratorial cells, each '*anqud* was self-contained. If it were plucked, as from a grapevine, its disappearance would not affect the others. The chief of each '*anqud* was often called the amir or prince, as in the student groupings already mentioned. He would make contact with followers and friends in places like mosques. Muhammad Hasseinine Haykal notes that the heads of the cells, meeting together, formed a kind of *majlis al-shura,* or consultative assembly. Curiously, many of the fighting groups which appeared in Afghanistan, financed or trained by the CIA, the Pakistanis and the Saudis, kept this same basically loose organizational structure when they fought the Russians. After they returned home or went looking for other regimes to attack and destabilize, in order, they thought, to establish Islamic states, they tended to keep the same pattern.

One strong influence on Islambuli was the blind sheikh, or religious reacher, Dr. Omar Abdel Rahman, who since 1997 has been serving a life sentence for terrorism in New York at a US Federal prison hospital facility in Missouri. Sheikh Omar worked in Fayoum, the great, green complex of oases and villages built around the town and lake of Fayoum, two hours' drive southwest of Cairo. Almost as though consulting an oracle, his students would pose theoretical or hypothetical questions to him.

Sheikh Omar's replies would often be honored among his younger devotees as *fatwas*, or religious opinions carrying the strength of religious law. During the 1970s, the blind teacher's fame spread among devout activists beyond the borders of his region of Fayoum. He became known to some of his students and followers as the "mufti" or religious suzerain, of *Al-Jihad (Al-Gihad* in Egyptian Arabic), a militant offshoot, later to become a rival of the Islamic Group. Unlike the godfather of both, the Muslim Brotherhood, which had foresworn political violence of all sorts including downright terrorism, and was consequently offered limited rehabilitation, *Al-Gihad* members could and did commit murders and, for purposes of gathering funds for the organization, made armed raids and robberies on jewelers or goldsmiths, many of whom happened to be Coptic Christians.

Between 1977 and 1980, private Muslim foundations in Saudi Arabia financed a tour of teaching for Sheikh Omar Abdel Rahman in that kingdom. Upon his return, he became notorious for his militant sermons and occasional *fatwas*, often recorded on audiotape cassettes. These were peddled openly on sidewalks in front of major mosques. During periods when the government forbade this, they were clandestinely passed from hand to hand, and from one mosque congregation to another.

It was known to intelligence specialists, though not the general public beyond a few academics, that by the beginning of 1981, and during the recruiting for Afghanistan which preceded Sadat's murder, *Al-Gihad* had managed to infiltrate its armed and teaching cells into many levels of Egyptian society, as the Muslim Brotherhood had already done decades earlier. It was at first strongest in the Cairo metropolitan areas, and in the four provinces of Upper Egypt, especially Assiut. Unlike its terrorist predecessor, an extremist group calling itself *Al–Takfir wa'l Hijra* (Withdrawal and Flight), its cell leaders preached not hermit-like isolation from society, but rather active measures to penetrate it. The particular targets of the disciples of Sheikh Omar Abdel Rahman in *Al-Gihad* were men and women (but mostly men) in the armed forces, the police and security services, professional associations such as those of lawyers and doctors (long strongholds of the Muslim Brotherhood) and education, especially at the university level.

Word had circulated among the *'anquds* since the beginning of 1981 that there was a de facto death contract on Sadat. The document contained a theoretical question to Sheikh Omar Abdel Rahman: "Is it lawful to shed the blood of a ruler who does not obey the laws of God?" The Sheikh's answer, like the question, contained neither the actual name of Sadat nor of any other ruler. The evidence presented at one of the trials following Sadat's assassination, and at which Sheikh Omar was acquitted, showed that the blind teacher had responded simply that it was lawful. Later, when asked to give a specific ruling about Sadat, without being told of the plot to kill him on October 8, 1981, Sheikh Omar is said to have waffled: "I cannot say that he has definitely crossed the line into infidelity." At this point, the conspirators dropped him from their discussions. This helped to make possible his future acquittal, and to empower him as helpmate to the CIA in recruiting young zealots, especially among Arab-Americans in the United States, for the jihad in Afghanistan.

The career of this blind cleric, described to me in 1993 by Dr. Usama al-Baz, President Mubarak's senior foreign affairs advisor, as "one prayer leader among men, and certainly not a leader of men," contained few hints of his future. Eventually, he would be indicted, convicted and imprisoned in the United States as a moving force in conspiracies to bomb such targets in New York as the World Trade Center, and to attempt to bomb others such as United Nations Headquarters and the Lincoln and Holland tunnels.

Because of his central role in inspiring and encouraging the militants of what was to become the Afghan terrorist International, his life deserves the close scrutiny which only a few careful writers, such as Mary Anne Weaver in the *New Yorker* magazine have given it.[10]

Sheikh Omar Abdel-Rahman Ali Abdel-Rahman (his full name) was born to poor parents in Egypt's Daqahliya Province, in the Nile Delta. He was blinded by diabetes while still a baby of ten months. His family launched him into Islamic religious studies, based on memorizing the entire Koran. At the age of 11, he had mastered a Braille copy of the Koran.

The future sheikh went through his secondary and university education during the Nasser regime, which imprisoned and executed Muslim Brotherhood leaders after their apparent attempt on Nasser's life in Alexandria in 1954. He received a Master's degree, with distinction, at Cairo University's School of Theology. By the outbreak of the June 1967 Arab–Israel war, he had begun writing rather bland political pamphlets and lecturing on the Koran. He had also done half the work needed for his doctorate in Islamic jurisprudence at the al-Azhar University. There, of course, he met fellow religious scholars from all of the Muslim world, including Afghanistan.

Like most of his contemporaries, Omar Abdel Rahman viewed the 1967 Israeli war victory over the Arabs as a new and even more serious case of what Arab historians called the 1948 defeat and loss of Arab Palestine: *An-Naqba,* The Disaster. The war jolted the blind preacher and innumerable other Arab and Muslim intellectuals around the world into a realization of the weaknesses of their societies and states in the face of the technologically superior West. Still a doctoral candidate at al-Azhar, but already entitled to use the titles of sheikh (religious teacher or scholar) and imam (prayer leader), Omar Abdel Rahman, on a sabbatical, was assigned by the state religious authorities to a little hamlet in the region of Fayoum oasis, an extensive green area to the south and west of Cairo. The hamlet was called Fidimin. By 1969 he had converted the Fidimin villagers with his fiery mosque sermons and lectures, into a center of activist political Islam. For using such terms of contempt about President Nasser – without naming him – as "pharaoh," "infidel" and "apostate," Sheikh Omar experienced his first two political trials. In 1969 and 1970, he spent eight months in one of Egypt's grim prisons.

In September 1970, at the time of the death agonies of Nasser, fatally ill of chronic diabetes aggravated by fatigue and heart failure following his successful mediation of the bloody civil war between King Hussein's Jordanian army and Yassir Arafat's PLO forces in "Black September" (as Palestinians call it), Sheikh Omar was traveling through the Fayoum villages knocking on doors. His message was, don't pray for the "faithless" Nasser. This was approximately as popular an activity in Egypt as an evangelist preacher's diatribes in towns of the American state of Georgia against President Jimmy Carter. Nasser's popularity with the ordinary folk of Egypt was immense, as the massive outpouring of grief, often crossing the frontiers of hysteria, at his funeral in Cairo in October 1970, soon showed.

By 1971, with Anwar al-Sadat well established in the presidency, Sheikh Omar had finished his first jail term, had completed his PhD at al-Azhar, and had begun to marry and produce offspring. (In 1993, US immigration authorities, seeking an excuse to end the liberal visa policies which the CIA had encouraged during his period of usefulness in recruiting for the Afghan jihad, were trying to base his possible deportation on the fact that he hadn't admitted polygamy. During that same year, 1993, he had two, possibly three, living wives – legal and admissible under the Islamic laws of Egypt – one daughter and nine sons. By then, two of the sons were leading units of the post-war Afghan terrorist and guerrilla groups in Pakistan and Afghanistan.)

Sadat, in power, soon began his famous turn to the Right in Egyptian politics. He released hundreds of interned and imprisoned Muslim Brothers and their fellow-travelers from jail. He cracked down on Communists and the liberal Egyptian Left, who, with the active supporters of the dead President Nasser, were now branded as enemies of the regime. In 1971, King Faisal of Saudi Arabia, who equated communism with Zionism and would soon support Sadat morally and financially in the secret preparations for a new war with Israel to liberate the territories lost in 1967, made an offer to the rector of al-Azhar, Sheikh Abdel Halim Mahmoud. It was an offer which the rector could not refuse: a hundred million dollars to finance a new campaign in the Muslim world against Communists and atheists, and to bring about Islam's triumph. Neglecting the implications of such a triumph, the CIA, in close liaison with the Saudi Arabian intelligence services under billionaire businessman Kamal Adham, offered support. This kind of Saudi–American cooperation would soon be shown in material terms in preparation for the coming holy war in Afghanistan.

Sheikh Omar, now rehabilitated by Sadat's administration and becoming known for both piety and political correctness, was sent back in dignity by the religious authorities to teach and preach in Fayoum, then to Upper Egypt; first to Al-Minya, then, in 1973, the year of the new war with Israel, to Assiut University, a hotbed of political Islam. It was here, as Mary Anne Weaver learned, that as a professor of theology, he began to interpret the doctrines of the charismatic Pakistani Islamist scholar, Abul Alaa al-Mawdudi, and of Sayid Qutb, former head of the Egyptian Muslim Brotherhood, linked to another alleged Brotherhood conspiracy against Nasser and executed in 1965. (Mawdudi, also, had been sentenced to death in Pakistan in 1953 for militant activities. He was amnestied and died in exile in the United States in 1979, the year the Afghanistan war began.)

Sheikh Omar emerged as an intellectual leader of the Muslim activists in Upper Egypt. Prudently, the blind cleric managed to evade the crackdown which the Egyptian authorities, alarmed by signs of formation of armed subversive groups, began in the mid- and late Seventies, by moving to Saudi Arabia in 1977.

The blind preacher made the theology faculty of the Imam Muhammad ibn Saudi Islamic University in Riyadh, the Saudi capital, his new base. There he taught hundreds of religious students. From there, with generous financial backing from the Saudis, he traveled from 1979 to 1982. These were the key formative years for the Afghan resistance movement, and the Sheikh was able to establish the friendships and contacts which, with American support, formed the international volunteer network of Afghani fighters.

An Arab diplomat who knew him told Weaver that he was "charming and beguiling, dangerous and duplicitous." An American diplomat in Cairo told me, "there is no doubt that he knew how to play upon the disagreements among the

Saudis, or his other benefactors." Those "other benefactors" were the Americans. But it was in Saudi Arabia that Sheikh Omar met the man who, at the time of writing is the most powerful man in the Sudan, and one of the most influential Muslim intellectuals in the world, Sheikh Hassan al-Turabi: brilliant, scholarly, elusive; profoundly opposed to American hegemony in the Middle East and the world. Of Sheikh Hassan al-Turabi, more later.

In 1980, after Sadat's peace treaty with Israel and the Soviet military push into Afghanistan, Sheikh Omar returned to Egypt. He was now flush with Saudi cash, and self-assured in opposing the relatively quietist politics of al-Azhar, which had trained him, and to the pro-American turn which Sadat's alliance with the religious establishment was taking. In Sheikh Omar's opposition to most of these policies, he made only one exception: Sadat's collaboration and that of Sadat's successors with the Americans in their war in Afghanistan.

Although, according to Egyptian court evidence, he had inspired Sadat's assassins, and had been arrested in one of the early security crackdowns ordered by Sadat preceding Sadat's murder, the Sheikh escaped – or was allowed to escape – from detention in mysterious circumstances. Following Sadat's assassination in October 1981, Sheikh Omar's territory in Assiut erupted in a major Islamist uprising, led by the Islamic Group. In the fighting and bloodshed, hundreds of policemen and militants were killed before government forces crushed the revolt.

In February and March of 1982, Sheikh Omar stood trial with Lieutenant Islambuli and the other defendants accused of Sadat's assassination. The blind imam was acquitted. In a later case with about 300 others, mostly members of *Al-Gihad*, accused of plotting to overthrow the government, he was acquitted again. However, between 1982 and his first trip to Peshawar, Pakistan, to aid the Afghan resistance, he spent about six more years in confinement, not for plotting but for his incendiary writings and sermons. These circulated on audiotape cassettes, like the tapes which the exiled Ayatollah Ruhollah Khomeiny used to send home to his followers in Iran during the last years of the Shah's reign.[11]

President Carter and after him President Ronald Reagan's ambitious and aggressive CIA director, William Casey, drew willing Egyptian governments and religious establishments into their crusade to rid Afghanistan of its Communist rulers and Soviet occupiers. Then, the Islamist adversaries of Sadat and his successor, President Husni Mubarak, began their own campaign to overturn Egypt's Western-looking parliamentary and presidential regime, to replace it with an Islamic theocracy. This campaign was well under way, long before the end of the American-backed jihad in Afghanistan, which Sadat and Mubarak had supported for their own reasons.

As the millennium and the twenty-first century approached, the Islamic activist movement in Egypt, stealing a few headlines with events like the massacre of 58 foreign tourists at Luxor, Upper Egypt, in November 1997, was challenging the basic premises of Sadat's compliance with Western wishes in 1979. These included formal peace with Israel, renunciation of political terrorism and violence and compromise with secular precepts of governance. This challenge was mounted with the planning, assistance and in some cases, as we shall see later, leadership, of the very men whom Sadat and his generals had sent to Afghanistan as volunteers. They and their understudies returned to Egypt as hardened veterans. They were determined to destroy Husni Mubarak's American-oriented and assisted regime, preparatory to installing the rule of the Koran. This was an unrealistic goal, in the light of Egypt's approximately six thousand years of existence as a relatively stable, organized state which had never been destroyed by centuries of occupation by foreigners.

Mubarak seemed to be getting the better of his native Islamists. Although sectarian strife between Muslim and Coptic Christian villagers developed in parts of Upper and Middle Egypt, planned terrorism by militant groups grew more rare. In the year 2000, Mubarak turned his attention more and more to maintaining Egypt's old predominant role in Middle Eastern politics, especially the so-called, US-sponsored "peace process." He prodded Israel's new Labor Party Prime Minister, Ehud Barak, and Barak's negotiating partners, President Hafez al-Assad of Syria and Yassir Arafat's Palestinian Authority. His aim was to help President Bill Clinton, in the waning months of Clinton's second and last presidential term, to broker a revival of the peace process which by late spring of 2000 appeared stalled on both the Palestinian–Israel and the Syria–Lebanon–Israel fronts.

Since the Afghanistan war began in 1979, Egypt has appeared to remain anchored to US policy: a mainstay, along with Israel, of a system of *pax Americana* in the Middle East; although the sluggishness and setbacks in the process of negotiating Arab–Israel peace under American auspices appeared severely to strain the chain between Cairo and the US anchor, after the murder of peacemaking Israeli Prime Minister Yitzhak Rabin in 1996 and the accession to power of uncompromsing Zionist hardliner, Prime Minister Benjamin Netanyahu. Israel was slow to follow up peace with Egypt in 1979 and with Jordan in 1994 with signed accords with Syria and Lebanon, or to implement peace agreements with the Palestinians. Nevertheless, the trilateral US–Egypt–Israel peace treaty signed in Washington by Presidents Carter and Sadat and Prime Minister Menahem Begin of Israel held firm. It might still hold on into the next century. Egypt has reaped the advantages of a deal, of which the Afghan war was an important component. These advantages, economic and military, may have spelled survival of the system which President Mubarak and his men inherited from Sadat, with Egypt receiving as much as $5 billion in US aid in some years.

Nevertheless, there is another vast shadow hanging over Egypt at the end of the twentieth century. It is not a direct legacy of the Afghanistan war, nor of the alliance between the US and militant Islam which helped engender that war and its aftermath. Many Egyptians – and not only the Islamic activists – do not approve the relationship with the United States, Israel and their Western friends and allies. There are vast gulfs among Egypt's diverse socioeconomic groups; from the postman or laborer for the state, who may earn less than the equivalent of $50 per month, to the technocrat or tycoon with foreign connections whose yearly earnings, after any taxes he pays, may be reckoned in millions of dollars. The unemployment and poverty which coexist with this system in Egypt continue to fuel both the unarmed political Islamist movement, and the armed terrorists, guided and inspired by the Afghan veterans and those trained by them. Their acts of murder, sabotage and public demoralization (like the temporary virtual destruction of Egypt's winter tourism in the 1997 Luxor massacre, with concomitant massive loss of jobs and income), have been, in frequency and sheer bloodiness, far behind those in Algeria. But the same pattern, with the same destabilizing aims, was present in both countries.

The Islamist movement in Egypt rejected President Carter's Camp David agreements, the 1979 peace treaty with Israel which followed, and the linkages with the United States which followed them, including the September 1993 Israel–Palestinian accords negotiated in Oslo for the autonomy of Gaza and Jericho. The Palestinians hoped these might eventually bring them an independent Palestinian state. The Islamist movement in the mid- and late 1990s in Egypt was taking its military cues from the Afghan veterans; its political guidance to some extent from Iran, and from the shaky, Islamist-backed military regime in neighboring Sudan, orchestrated by Sheikh Hassan al-Turabi. Spectacular attacks on foreign tourists like Luxor have lost Egypt untold hundreds of millions of dollars in tourist revenues, and perhaps in foreign investment as well. The more offenders are tried and condemned before military or state security courts to long prison terms or death, the more the Islamists try to respond with aggravated violence of the sort they and their forebears were taught to use in Afghanistan.

By early 2000, new sectarian violence strife threatened between Christians and Muslims, fanned by followers of Osama bin Laden who were tried in Jordan in April 2000. The kingdom was now ruled by Abdullah II, son of the late King Hussein who had died of lymphatic cancer in February 1999. Questioning of the suspects and the contents of a laptop computer belonging to one of them, Khalil al-Deek, an Arab-American computer expert trained in California before his apparent military schooling in the Afghanistan camps of bin Laden, indicated their intended targets included the Radisson Hotel in Amman. This, it emerged from court documents and interviews by the author in Amman, was considered by the conspirators a favorite of American and sometimes Israeli tourists who, as pilgrims, frequented several holy sites in Jordan that were also targeted: Mount Nebo, site of the prophet Moses' glimpse of the Promised Land and perhaps of his tomb, and ancient churches at Jesus Christ's presumed baptismal site on the Jordan river, at Madaba and at Bethany. The plan was to hit these sites, using a large cache of explosives found on a farm outside Amman, on or about New Year's Eve, December 31, 1999. Following the pattern followed in the terrorist massacre of foreign tourists at Luxor, Egypt, in 1997, the would-be attackers intended to rake the pilgrims present with automatic weapons fire. In March 2000, Pope John Paul II, on his historic pilgrimage to the Holy Land, visited the same sites in Jordan, before crossing to

Israel and the Palestinian territories. There was highest security protection for the Polish-born pontiff. John Paul II had been a terrorist target in Rome in 1981 and at the Roman Catholic shrine of Fatima in Portugal a year later. Former "Afghani" Ramzi Ahmed Yousef allegedly planned to kill the Pope in the Philippines in 1994.

During the same Christmas–New Year–Ramadan holiday period, as the twentieth century gave way to the new millenium, a far-flung group of men, mostly Algerians trained in bin Laden's camps or by his followers, attempted, as we will see in the final chapter, to bring explosives from Canada into the United States to create holiday-season mayhem there. In Lebanon, a week of fighting at the end of 1999 between Sunni Muslim insurgents, rumored to be led by disciples of bin Laden, and the Maronite-Christian-led Lebanese army, left at least 50 dead and over 100 wounded on both sides. Nothing like this has been seen in Lebanon since the Lebanese civil war of 1975–90.

However, moving backward through time in our narrative to the origins of the present situation in 1980, President Carter's envoys had neither the gifts of prescience, prophecy nor of miraculous foresight to appreciate what could happen during the generation to come. To enlist support of two other key players in combating the Soviet Union, those envoys next set out for Pakistan and China.

3   Zia al-Haq

"For the North," wrote Rudyard Kipling in 1888 of British India's Northwest Frontier, since 1947 part of Pakistan, "Guns always – quietly – but always guns."[1] For the administrations of Presidents Jimmy Carter and Ronald Reagan, and for General Zia al-Haq, Pakistan's military dictator and their partner in the jihad in Afghanistan, the gun-making, gun-running and gun-toting country of Pakistan's tribal northwest was the indispensable base to raise, train and launch an Islamic guerrilla army against the Soviet invaders.

As he flew onward from Cairo toward Islamabad, Pakistan's capital, in January 1980, Zbigniew Brzezinski already realized that the choice of Pakistan as a base for the coming proxy war was imposed, not only by the warlike propensities of the tribes spread through the Pakistan–Afghan border regions, but by the facts of geography; above all, by history itself.

Before Brzezinski's watch, Henry Kissinger had in the late 1960s and early 1970s realized and had begun to act on the strategic importance of Pakistan to the United States, in its Cold War with the Soviet Union. As the virtual foreign-policy brain of President Nixon, he used the close ties between the US administrations, especially the Pentagon and the CIA, and Pakistan's military rulers, to build entente and ultimately a strategic relationship with the other Communist superpower, China, the Soviet Union's great Asian rival and adversary. Within days of Brzezinski's initial pilgrimages to Cairo and Islamabad, President Carter's Defense Secretary, Harold Brown, was in Beijing. There he was to follow up on the careful work begun by Kissinger and Nixon in their earlier travels to China by securing China's assent and active help in the Afghanistan adventure. Pakistan, and much more discreetly, China, became two anchor positions in Washington's Asian game.

Independence from Britain and partition in 1947 left Pakistan, whose founder Muhammad Ali Jinnah aspired to create a Muslim state, worse off than India, its giant, predominantly Hindu, neighbor and rival. With only 23 percent of the land mass of pre-1947 India and 18 percent of the population, Pakistan found itself the poor neighbor. It had less than 10 percent of the industrial base of the two states together, and just over 7 percent of the employment facilities. It was mainly a producer of raw materials. The only way it could find the money needed to fund its strategic defense, without vastly increasing the size of its administration, was to seek foreign aid. This had to come from the capitalist West, for as a militarist, Islamicizing state, neither the Soviet bloc nor even the non-aligned bloc, then led by Pandit Nehru's India and Abdel Nasser's Egypt, could have accepted Pakistan into their ranks.[2]

One Islamic movement, also a political party, the Jamaat-I-Islami, Islamic Association, played a central role in trying to create a Muslim society, ruled by Muslim power, in Pakistan – making the country an even more propitious base at the end of the 1970s for an Islamic jihad against the Soviets and communism. Like the Muslim Brotherhood in Egypt and other Arab countries, Rafah or the Welfare fundamentalist party in Turkey; Dar ul-Islam in Indonesia; the Islamic National Front in the Sudan and others, the Jamaat played the central role it sought in Pakistan's politics. Like the other parties mentioned, it became heavily involved in the Afghan war and its aftermath, and like them has been profoundly affected by this aftermath.

The aims of the Jamaat, as elucidated by its founder, the Islamic revivalist Maulana Abul Alaa al-Mawdudi (1903–1979), were basically to restore to Islam, first in the Indian subcontinent, then in the wider world, the original teachings of the Koran and the Sunna (orthodox law of the majority Sunni Muslim faith). On this basis, the original socioreligious system established under guidance of the Prophet Muhammad, and his first four successors, called the "rightly-guided caliphs" would be restored. Later, secularist or revisionist developments in Islamic law, theology and philosophy would be rejected; as would be most of the institutionalized structures of modern Islamic states, such (for example) as the largely Western-style parliaments in countries like Egypt or Algeria, both countries formerly colonized by the West in which returnees from the Afghan jihad would, after 1989, lead armed Islamist insurgencies. Mawdudi also preached and wrote that the "gates of *itjihad*" (independent judgment, an important Muslim legalistic concept), open to thinkers and scholars in the earlier, golden centuries of Islam, had long been closed except to a select few.

Mawdudi, who was born in Hyderabad, Deccan, India, was a learned scholar and linguist at the age of 16 – his learning acquired not in the British colonial schools of the day, but in Muslim madrasas and other traditional schools in which his father insisted he be placed – and the editor of a series of Urdu-language journals and periodicals by the age of 17. His opinion about *itjihad* meant that a small elite, trained in both classical sciences of Islam and modern subjects, should have the power to make independent decisions affecting the society as a whole. Mawdudi's writings provided Muslims with access to the tenets still held by Islamists or, as some in the West prefer to call them, "Muslim fundamentalists" today. One is abolition of bank interest (now called "Islamic banking"). Another, spreading from Saudi Arabian and Pakistani origins outward into the wider Muslim world), is introduction of the *zakat* or obligatory alms tax for charity; Islamic penal and family laws (amputations, floggings and stonings being some of the more grisly punishments practiced by groups like the Taliban, a product of the Afghan jihad. The Taliban seek permanent power in Afghanistan's war-fractured society and beyond). A further tenet was strict socio-moral codes in sex and marriage roles. Birth control was to be prohibited in state-funded programs (one of the sins held against Abdel Nasser by the Muslim Brothers and their associates in Egypt). "Heretical" groups (such as the Baha'i nearly everywhere in the Arab world and in revolutionary Iran, or the Ahmadiya sect in Pakistan) were forbidden. Indeed, as Mumtaz Ahmed, one of Pakistan's leading commentators points out, the Jamaat program, which was to set the tone and the rules for so many other Islamic movements in the twentieth century, was much more a purely political movement than it was a religious or intellectual one.[3]

For Mawdudi, who has probably influenced twentieth-century Islamists more than any other single thinker or scholar, parochial Pakistani nationalism was as much anathema as British or Hindu nationalism. This made him indifferent to the ideas of Pakistan's famous founding statesman, Muhammad Ali Jinnah. As soon as the new state was founded in the summer of 1947, Mawdudi moved to Lahore, the city of his much admired scholar, writer and philosopher friend, Muhammad Iqbal. There, the Jamaat began work with 385 founding members, over half of them refugees from India. Jamaat began to campaign for a "pure" Islamic constitution for the new state. (Pakistan's name in Urdu means "Land of the Pure.") He supported the constitution adopted in 1956, even though it was largely a collection of secular laws for a theoretical parliamentary democracy, guided but not bound by Islamic ideology.[4] By the time the next constitution was written in 1973, the Jamaat, though its membership had grown and expanded to over 100,000, had only four members in parliament. Nevertheless, it played a major role in writing that constitution.This document preserved important parts of the 1956 one, but affirmed strongly that the president and the prime minister of Pakistan must be Muslims.[5]

The Jamaat's partnership with the military, which undoubtedly helped General Zia take power in 1977, paralleled to some extent Pakistan's strategic cooperation with the United States, though it lagged behind it somewhat in time. The US alliance with Pakistan could reasonably be said to have begun as early as 1951. By this time, during the first years of the Cold War, when the United States sought to ring the Soviet Union with a chain of strategic air bases and intelligence listening posts, policy-makers of the Truman administration had made up their minds that America's allies in Iran and Iraq (Iran under the young Shah Muhammad Reza Pahlavi; Iraq with a pro-Western regime and still under heavy British influence) could not successfully be defended against the Soviet empire of Joseph Stalin without the help of Pakistan. Bypassing in this case the "special relationship" with Britain and reliance on the British ally, US administrations established direct links with Pakistan. There, a military and civil bureaucracy, already beholden to Washington for early economic and military aid, was dominant in the new Islamic state by the fall of 1951.[6] Pakistan had a chance to win Washington's favor by supporting the United States' (officially the United Nations') cause in the Korean war. From June to December 1950, the new Dominion of Pakistan, as it was then called (emphasizing the British Commonwealth connection), Pakistan supplied UN forces in Korea with needed supplies of raw materials. On May 19, 1954, Pakistan signed a formal agreement with the US for military and technical assistance, supposed to be for defensive purposes only.[7]

From adoption of the 1956 constitution until Pakistan's first general elections on the basis of universal adult suffrage in 1970 – fully 24 years – the non-elected institutions of the army and the bureaucracy ruled the country, leaning on the unofficial but very real and solid partnership with the United States. To fully appreciate the compelling reasons for both Zia al-Haq and the Carter administration to launch the anti-Soviet holy war from Pakistan in 1980, it is important to realize how enduring and important this discreet, if not secret, US–Pakistani relationship had become by the 1970s.

Since 1950, as Seymour Hersh has noted in his studies of the developing nuclear standoff between Pakistan and India, Pakistan had joined the secret US network including the CIA and the National Security Agency (NSA), headquartered at Fort Meade, Maryland, for global electronic spying on the Soviet Union. This included watching and listening to signals from Soviet nuclear and missile tests in Kazakhstan and flying U-2 electronic reconnaissance flights. The famous flight of Francis Gary Powers, shot down by the Soviets in 1960, causing a serious crisis between Washington and Moscow in 1960, was based in Peshawar, Pakistan; later to become the main rear base for the holy warriors recruited for the 1979–89 jihad. A further joint activity of the US services and Pakistan's powerful Inter-Services Intelligence directorate (ISI) was surveillance of the tribes on adjacent Soviet, Afghan and Chinese territory, yielding background knowledge crucial in planning and waging the holy war of the 1980s.

Pakistan's first war with India over Kashmir in 1947 and the constant friction continuing over this territory led again to war in 1965. Kashmir aggravated Pakistan's lost war with India of December 1971 to hold East Pakistan, which with Indian military help became the new nation of Bangladesh. All these events helped in various ways to cement the US–Pakistan strategic partnership. Kashmir, as the only Muslim majority province to be retained within the Indian Union at partition in 1947, has remained to this day a constant irritant in Indo–Pakistan relations and the possible cause of a new war in South Asia which might be fought with nuclear weapons.[8]

Despite the old personal, pre-independence friendship between India's Hindu spiritual and inspirational leader, Mahatma Gandhi and Pakistan's much more secularly-inclined Muslim founder, Muhammad Ali Jinnah, each of the two nations has regarded the other as its hereditary enemy. In Cold War terms, for a generation before the Soviets invaded Afghanistan in 1979, the US perceived India, though officially non-aligned and neutral, as leaning toward Moscow. By the time of the first formal US–Pakistani aid agreement in 1954, Pakistan had joined the US-sponsored SEATO alliance (US, Iran, Turkey, Pakistan) and Washington had become its principal military supplier, partly as a *quid pro quo* for the intelligence facilities already described.[9]

Pakistan's facade of parliamentary rule was maintained until a military coup by General Ayub Khan in 1958 and the country's second constitution, which in 1962 installed a centralized, presidential government, following the 1958–62 period under martial law and Ayub as unchallenged dictator, combining the three august functions of commander-in-chief, chief martial law administrator and President of

Pakistan. Before and after the 1962 constitution, which reaffirmed the Muslim nature of the state, Ayub relied largely on the federal bureaucracy and, above all, the army, both of which were staffed at senior echelons by men from Punjab province. (Ayub himself was an ethnic Pushtu.)

Although Ayub continued to seek US support, even after the brief but fierce war between India, still Pakistan's enemy, and China, which the US would within a decade begin actively to court, there was some pressure from the Pakistani civilian intellectual establishment for better relations with the giant Communist Chinese state. Ayub began to smile in the direction of Beijing. At the same time, he tried to accommodate the wishes of those of his subjects who favored a swing to the Left domestically, and non-alignment in foreign policy. A brief and inconclusive war with India over Kashmir in 1965, and the Soviet-brokered peace agreement signed at Tashkent afterward, set in train events which led to suspension of American military assistance, advertising what one academic observer terms "the hollowness of the regime's foreign and defense policies." Domestic protest swelled into massive anti-government demonstrations by industrial workers, students, low-ranking civil servants and by the ulama, the Islamic scholarly establishment, between November 1968 and March 1969.

Under heavy pressure, Ayub gave in to the military establishment's urgent demand that he hand over power to General Yahya Khan, the army commander-in-chief. Yahya in November 1969 announced general elections, sidestepping the mounting tide of Bengali nationalism in East Pakistan and securing for himself the power to veto any constitutional document produced by the national assembly. Thus did Yahya Khan assure the continued dominance of the military and the bureaucracy, both predominantly Punjabi. However, in the elections held in December 1970, the (Bengali) Awami League and the rising Pakistan Peoples Party (PPP), led by a brilliant, demagogic populist lawyer-politician, Zufilcar Ali Bhutto, were the winners. The PPP was supported largely by Sindhi landlords (from Bhutto's native province of Sind), Punjabi farmers and a mixture of land-owning, middle-class and professional people from most districts of Pakistan. Bhutto fashioned a populist alliance; a curious mixture of Leftist, secular and landowning elements.

Ali Bhutto, whom this author met and interviewed in 1971, immediately after the defeat in war by India had brought about the independence of Bangladesh, seemed to have more than an inkling of the coming clash with the Soviet Union over Afghanistan. His political instincts were rather anti-military, and he was certainly far from the most pro-American politician Pakistan had ever known. Yet he wanted, above all else, big-power and if possible, nuclear status for Pakistan. Known for his anti-imperialist, anti-India and pro-China positions when he had served in Ayub's cabinet, Bhutto had disagreed with Ayub over the 1965 Tashkent accord, considering it gave too much away to India.

The power of Pakistan's military in politics was increasingly embodied in the rising potency of ISI, the military intelligence institution which increasingly meddled in politics, and which as an ally of circumstance of Washington would prove the driving force in the Afghanistan war of 1979–89. Despite Bhutto's wish to neutralize the army's role in public affairs, Bhutto resolved to have his cake and eat it too: with redoubled urgency following India's nuclear weapons test in the Rajestan Desert in 1974, Bhutto prodded, pushed and bankrolled his competent scientific community to develop such weapons for Pakistan. Protection of the highly secret program was confided to the army. At the same time, Bhutto tried to cut the military down to size. Some senior officers, whom he accused of "Bonapartist" tendencies, he removed. He restructured the military high command, abolishing the post of commander-in-chief and reducing the tenure of the remaining most senior officer, the chief of staff. A new constitution drafted under Bhutto's watchful eye made it illegal for the military to abrogate the constitution.

Aside from the disastrous military defeat by India in 1971, Bhutto further antagonized the army by calling it in to crush a tribal insurgency in Baluchistan. Part of that ethnic region lay across the border in Iran. It would play an important role, although one subordinate to the Northwest Frontier province, in planning and waging the Afghan jihad. The Shah of Iran's intelligence and military establishment was resolutely anti-Soviet. It was as anti-socialist as the Shah's American allies, seeing a sinister Soviet hand in efforts to destabilize the Baluchistan region and eventually obtain an outlet on the Indian Ocean for Russia. Bhutto was already regarded by some agencies in Washington as dangerously soft on the Soviet Union, and pro-socialist. So Iranian and Pakistani military both opposed Bhutto. All this helped to lead to his hanging by Zia al-Haq, with military approval, on April 4, 1979, and a new anti-democratic campaign by Zia and the military afterward.[10]

After Bhutto's disappearance from the scene, Zia discouraged most of the political parties. He began to extend total control by the military over civilian society. The Muslim League and the Jamaat-i-Islami, which had earlier supported Zia's regime, backed off from this support when Zia cancelled elections indefinitely. Zia then held managed local elections in September 1979, as the war clouds gathered over Afghanistan. Candidates could run as individuals only, not as party representatives. This made the twin goals of Zia and the growingly powerful intelligence establishment in the ISI, Islamization and militarization, easier, or so Zia and the spin doctors in the ISI believed. However, something went wrong with the control mechanisms, and the PPP, now led by Ali Bhutto's brilliant, Western-educated daughter Benazir Bhutto, managed to get many of its own into local bodies under independent labels. Zia was ruling in isolation (much as the military dictators in Greece did from 1967 until 1974, when the coup they staged in Cyprus and the subsequent loss of northern Cyprus to the Turkish army brought their downfall and democracy's return to Greece).

What was worse for Zia, and made him into an even more eager partner of the US for the Afghan jihad, was that the nuclear program had weakened his regime further, by worsening his relations with Washington. A congressional measure known as the Symington Amendment had suspended American military supplies.

The Western aid-to-Pakistan economic consortium was refusing to reschedule payments on Pakistan's multi-billion dollar debt. Zia "needed a good war", as several close observers of Pakistan have noted. Therefore the Soviet invasion of Afghanistan, which he perhaps sensed would be the last and biggest battle of the Cold War, he saw as a godsend.

Throughout the early decades of Pakistan's existence, the country's leaders had used Pakistan's strategic vulnerability to perceived Soviet encroachments – in Baluchistan; vis-a-vis Pakistan's neighbor and adversary, Soviet-backed India; in the pro-Soviet politicians and regimes in Afghanistan – as arguments to convince Washington to keep Pakistan under its military wing. The nuclear program had, it was clear to Zia, seriously endangered this support. He saw an opportunity to win it back in the joint project of repelling the Soviet invaders of Afghanistan.

Shortly after the Soviet invasion, Zia appointed a new chief of the ISI, General Akhtar Abdel Rahman Khan, who remained its director and, as such, the right-arm of Zia in the Afghan war until he died with Zia, US Ambassador Arnold Raphel and other senior Pakistanis and Americans connected with the war, in a plane crash in 1988. Akhtar's chief sidekick, Brigadier Mohammad Youssaf, who was directly responsible for the training and operations of the moujahidin from 1983 until 1987, greatly admired the bravery, steadfastness and devotion to Islamic principles of his chief, describing him as an "impressive [soldier] … with an immaculate uniform, three rows of medals and a strong physique. He had a pale skin and was intensely proud of the Afghan blood he had inherited."[11]

Akhtar Khan told his chief as forcefully as he could that Pakistan should back the Afghan resistance. This would defend Islam as well as Pakistan. The Afghan fighters would become forward defenders of Pakistan itself. If the Russians and Afghan Communists were able to get total control of Afghanistan, their next step, probably moving through Baluchistan, would be to threaten Pakistan. Akhtar (and the faithful Brigadier Youssaf) believed, with many of the senior American planners of the war, that there was need to defeat the Soviets in a major guerrilla war. Afghanistan could be converted into another Vietnam. This time the Soviets would be on the receiving end, instead of the Americans. Pakistan – doubtless with American and other outside help – must choose the military option, supporting the holy warriors with arms, ammunition, cash, intelligence, training and operational advice and support. The border areas of the Northwest Frontier province and Baluchistan would be sanctuaries for the refugees and bases for the guerrillas.

During Brzezinski's first meeting with President Zia in Islamabad in January 1980, the guiding rule of the alliance – that all arms supplies, finance and training of the fighters *must be provided through Pakistan and not directly from the CIA* – was dictated by Zia and agreed to by Brzezinski, with the approval of the top echelons of the Carter administration. How the supply operation was carried out was to prove fateful for the post-war spread of violence and terrorism in many areas by the moujahidin, as well as during the war's successful prosecution. The Americans, as former CIA senior officer Charles Cogan confirmed to the author,[12] soon learned that Zia meant what he said. He and the military commanders in the ISI were adamant: the ISI would take over the weapons supply to the Afghan warriors only if they kept absolute control over all stages of the operation.

Zia placed three absolute conditions for allowing shipment of the arms from Egypt, China and other points of origin, including the United States, through Pakistan to the holy warriors fighting the Russians. First, the countries concerned – the US, Egypt, Saudi Arabia, China and eventually Britain, France and even Israel, were to maintain *absolute silence* about the shipments. They would deny that they took place at all, repeatedly and whenever necessary. Second, arms and other war supplies were to be shipped to Pakistan by the fastest available means (hence the early airlifts from US "facilities" in Sadat's Egypt, where Sadat's full cooperation and commitment made possible both speed and secrecy, initially at least). Third, the shipments by air (as opposed to overland shipment from China and Iran, and the great bulk of shipments which came by sea to Karachi and other Pakistani ports), were to be limited to two planeloads per week.[13]

Although the Pakistani military stoutly insisted that they kept a rigid control over these shipments, the supply pipeline was cumbersome and vulnerable to corruption and diversion at most levels. Added to the nature of this Pakistani pipeline was the fact that the moujiahidin were divided into seven major groups or "Parties," as the Pakistani military and some of the CIA managers called them. The leaders, as we will see in more detail later, could only very rarely break down ethnic and tribal barriers and the personal jealousies in order to cooperate and coordinate their intelligence, sabotage and combat operations against the Communist enemy. British author and arms-trade specialist James Adams, who studied the war's progress, observed, "The mixture of Pakistani corruption and the Afghan aptitude for making money by any means produced an industry which had little to do with a holy war against the infidel Soviet invaders and a great deal to do with profiteering."

Adams reported that a typical case of 100 Kalashnikov AK-47 assault rifles, at that time the favorite of "freedom fighters", militias, bandits and terrorists from Kabul to Colombia, would be delivered from Egypt by ship, usually to the big port of Karachi. These rifles would be in brand-new condition. At least a third of them would be appropriated on landing by the Pakistani military, either to replace old stocks in their own armories or to sell on the black market. After transport across Pakistan in sealed army trucks (which, according to Brigadier Youssaf, moved singly rather than in strung-out convoys, so as to escape notice) or in railroad freight cars, weapons would be siphoned off at the point in the process where the supplies for the fighters were turned over to border regiments of the Pakistani army, for distribution under supervision of the ISI. Often, a fair amount, even the majority or all of certain shipments, would reach the leader of one of the seven main "parties" they were intended for. In many other cases, some of those handed over would then be stolen by other Afghans (later, by Arab or other foreign volunteers as well). Others would be sold by the Party leaders themselves. These were usually required to come in person to claim and collect the guns and munitions from the Pakistanis, before they reached the actual fighters.

Local tribal leaders demanded that members of any other tribe or band passing through his area should pay tribute, usually in cash or weapons – a practice noted by Rudyard Kipling, and many, many visitors to Afghanistan through the generations preceding and following him. US diplomats and intelligence officers on the scene acknowledged that sometimes the actual fighters were lucky if they got even 50 out of 100 guns sent to the Afghans, through the ISI, by the CIA and its allies. The diversion of everything from 12.7 mm. machine guns and RPG-7 87 mm rocket launchers to mortars, cannon tanks and armored personnel carriers (toward and after the war's end, even observation and combat aircraft, such as those reaching the Taliban movement in the 1990s), ensured that eventually, much of this equipment would reach the black market.[14]

Well before the final Soviet withdrawal from Afghanistan in 1989, the hardware of many of the Arab "Afghan" volunteers, and some non-Arab ones such as Turks, Iranians, Filipinos and Afro-Americans, were able to take weapons and munitions, as well as the CIA training manuals used with them, back to the wars they would fight at home in Algeria, Egypt, Yemen, Gaza and the West Bank; the Philippines; or in other areas where they were engaged in battle for Islamist causes, such as Bosnia and Kashmir.

The body supervising the war, more or less in cooperation with the CIA, which kept the presence of its own American officers to an absolute minimum in Pakistan or near the war fronts in Afghanistan, Pakistan's ISI, was actually a product of Pakistan's war with India in 1971. Prime Minister Ali Bhutto had created it after Pakistan's defeat and loss of eastern Bengal and the creation of independent Bangladesh. The ISI replaced the older Directorate of Intelligence Bureau (DIB). Its main initial task had been internal counter-espionage. Its director, N.A. Rizvi, was blamed for the unpardonable fault of having failed to predict the Bengali uprising against Pakistani rule which had helped bring on the 1971 war. A final ironic twist was that Rizvi's deputy, A.M.A. Sardar, chief of Pakistani intelligence for the former East Pakistan, defected to the Bengali insurgents – and eventually became the chief of independent Bangladesh's National Security Intelligence Agency (NSIA). Early on the ISI was charged by Prime Minister Bhutto in the 1970s, before his replacement and execution by Zia, with obtaining raw materials and technical knowhow for the Pakistani nuclear weapons program. In this, ISI had worked with the Pakistani Institute of Science and Nuclear Technology (PINSTECH) in Rawalpindi, later a main training and logistics base for the 1979–89 Afghan war, and for the new terrorist international which arose after the war.

The problem for Ali Bhutto, his daughter and one of his successors as prime minister, Benazir Bhutto, as for other Pakistani political leaders, is that the ISI has never been able to stay out of politics. ISI's Lieutenant General Ghulam Jilani appears to have played a major part in the conspiracy to prepare the coup which brought General Zia to power in 1977. After the Soviet invasion of Afghanistan, as we saw, General Akhtar Abdel Rahman Khan became the new ISI chief. He supervised a daunting variety of political and military operations, during the Afghan war decade, 1980–90. Under General Akhtar and the officer succeeding him, after Akhtar was killed with President Zia al-Haq and other senior Pakistani and American personnel in the still mysterious crash of Zia's plane in 1988, General Hamid Gul, ISI exercised supreme authority. It was not only a weapons distributor, trainer and sort of all-around political and military guru to the moujahidin. It was also a kind of political broker in Pakistan.

Outside Pakistan, ISI found itself cooperating with the Chinese against India; fighting the inroads and countering the siren song of the Soviet KGB, which encouraged separatism in the vast, mostly desert territory of Baluchistan. It was also both controlling and reportedly profiting from the fast-growing drug traffic which grew up with the Afghan war.[15]

It has often been argued by apologists of the Afghan war that US intelligence and policy-making bodies, as the decisions to begin the proxy war against the Soviets were made, lacked indications of the possibly dangerous consequences of total Pakistani control of the war. This was not true. Neither did the CIA and other agencies fail to take note of the implications for Pakistan's neighbors, especially India; nor did they ignore the possible consequences inside Pakistan and Afghanistan.

As we saw, India, feeling threatened by Chinese nuclear weapons, became in May 1974 the sixth country – after the United States, the USSR, Britain, France and China – to explode a nuclear bomb, in the Rajasthan desert. The "peaceful device," as the Indians insisted on calling it, had a reported yield of 15 kilotons, in the same range as the American bomb which devastated Hiroshima, Japan, in August 1945. Pakistan began to work at once to develop its own nuclear weapons. By the time Mrs. Indira Gandhi left the office of Indian Prime Minister in 1977, India and Pakistan were deeply engaged in an unacknowledged arms race. However, Mrs. Gandhi's successor, Prime Minister Morarji Desai, opposed this course. He publicly echoed statements by India's founding father, Pandit Jawaharlal Nehru, who totally rejected atomic arms.

The weakness of President Zia's internal position immediately prior to his agreements with the Americans on how the jihad was to be run was highlighted in a secret report produced for President Carter on September 26, 1979, barely three months before the Soviet seizure of Kabul. It questioned whether General Zia could even finish the year in power, so bad was Pakistan's economic situation. Among its main features were accelerating inflation, mounting debt and a huge balance of payments deficit. Pakistan, the report said, had asked for rescheduling of its huge international debt. It wanted more US aid to counterbalance the Soviet threat, but was determined to go ahead with the nuclear program, cost what it might. This and the complicated relations with Washington "may eventually undo the present improvement in relations with India [the heritage of Morarji Desai], which may be the best they have been in recent history."

The nuclear program continued, one US intelligence report asserted, "under the mask of research and development." The Pakistanis, it added, were dragging their feet in economic and military negotiations with the United States and other Western powers in order to gain time for their nuclear scientists. These were thought to be preparing for an early nuclear test. This was never to materialize until the Indians in May 1998 announced not one but *five* nuclear tests on their Porkhan test range in the Rajasthan desert. These included among other bomb types, "a thermonuclear device" (in other words, a hydrogen bomb). President Bill Clinton immediately implemented tough economic sanctions against India, trying to discourage Pakistan's government and military from testing their own nuclear bomb.

One prophetic section of the 1979 US intelligence analysis illustrates how well-informed was the Carter administration, on the very threshold of the Afghanistan war – prophecy later echoed by the US Drug Enforcement Administration (DEA) and which became self-fulfilling – about the vast threat to the West posed by the region's drug potential:

> Another problem in the US–Pakistani relationship is in the unchecked expansion of opium poppy cultivation in the tribal areas of Pakistan along the Afghan border. The output of the Pakistani area probably reached 400 tons last year. Combined with the production of neighboring Afghanistan, the total surpasses that of the "Golden Triangle" (the inaccessible Shan Plateau which ranges from northeastern Burma into Thailand, Laos and China) and Pakistani refining capacity is becoming increasingly sophisticated.
>
> The Pakistani writ of authority, never very strong in tribal areas, is now even less effective controlling opium production and smuggling because of the insurgency on the Afghan side of the border. In addition, the Islamic ordinance introduced in February [1979] banning all intoxicants paradoxically threw the narcotics control apparatus into a shambles when it removed existing enforcement mechanisms without providing new ones.[16]

Despite these clear warning signals of the impending boom in drug production and traffic, there is little or no evidence that either the American or Pakistani planners of the holy war thought much about this consequence, like so many others, of their campaign. In fact, initially on the instigation of French President Valery Giscard d'Estaing's chief of external intelligence, plans were at least discussed, and possibly deliberately implemented, to use drugs as a weapon in the war against the Soviets, as we will see in detail later in this book.

By February 1980 Brzezinski was able to travel again to Pakistan, after securing pledges of financial support in Saudi Arabia, which eventually would match the US government financial input "dollar for dollar." This time in Pakistan, Brzezinski met with General Akhtar, the ISI chief, as well as with President Zia al-Haq and with CIA station chief in Islamabad John J. Reagan. Brzezinski later gave associates essentially the same picture of General Akhtar that Brigadier Mohammad Youssaf sketched: a stolid, 55-year-old former artillery officer, an almost fanatically anti-Soviet soldier with some Afghan blood in his veins and so personally motivated to fight the invaders to the north.

By late winter of 1980, handmade weapons were in the hands of the holy warriors, already attacking the Soviets with hit-and-run tactics. These were weapons produced in the workshops of the proud Pushtu gunsmiths of the Northwest Frontier region. Sadat provided phony Soviet arms, including Kalashnikovs, rocket-launchers, mortars and anti-aircraft guns. Ways were also being found, at this early stage before the later arrival of the deadly US Stinger anti-aircraft missiles, to buy Soviet-patented SAM-7 anti-aircraft missiles in Poland.

By the spring of 1980, President Carter's CIA director Stansfield Turner was receiving reports about diversions of war material sent through the ISI. General Akhtar's policy was to observe a stubborn silence about this most of the time. When it became absolutely necessary to say something, someone senior in the military command or the government would issue an absolute denial. Meanwhile, Turner's CIA laid the foundations for a policy which would succeed in getting huge quantities of Soviet and Soviet-bloc arms for use by the Afghan holy warriors – and, unfortunately for the West, by their terrorist successors worldwide, once the war was over.

The Cold Warriors in Langley, Virginia, developed a top-secret program, unknown even to many of the most enthusiastic partisans of the jihad in other US government departments and in the Congress, to "buy, borrow or steal," in the words of *Los Angeles Times* writer James Risen, new, state-of-the-art war material, to supplement the older genuine captured Soviet weapons, supplied by Egypt, Israel and others, and also the false ones emanating mostly from Sadat's dream factory in Egypt.

This top-secret program, codenamed SOVMAT, was probably unknown even to President Zia al-Haq and the holy-war commanders in Pakistan's ISI. Part of it involved refining techniques developed by the CIA during the Indo–China wars, especially in Vietnam, in the 1960s and 1970s. Working with a vast array of phony corporations and fronts, the CIA under the SOVMAT program would buy weapons from East European governments and governmental organizations, such as the KINTEX trust in Communist Bulgaria, which had access to Soviet equipment as members of the Soviet-led Warsaw Pact alliance. Purchases and acquisitions under the SOVMAT program even included late-model Soviet tanks and advanced radar systems for Soviet fighter planes. Their acquisition and testing by the US military and the CIA facilitated development of counter-measures, such as improved anti-tank weapons used by the moujahidin, and probably the Stingers, even before they entered service in 1985 – only to escape the control of the CIA and ISI and find their way into the hands of such adversaries of the United States as Iran's Revolutionary Guards – of which more in a later chapter.

Quite early in the war, corruption and demoralization among Soviet units in Afghanistan eased the CIA's task. Some of its Afghan intermediaries purchased crates of new weapons, still in their grease and wrapping paper, from the quartermaster of the Soviet 40th Army in Kabul. Among these weapons were defensive flares, which Soviet pilots used to counter Stinger missiles, once these went into service. The CIA gave the flares to the US Army for tests to determine how best to wipe out any effectiveness they might have against Stinger fire. Officials running the CIA's SOVMAT program provided wish lists for CIA and ISI officers operating from Pakistan, who sent their Afghan mercenaries to ransack Soviet supply depots and search battlefields for the desired weapons and devices. Some Afghan fighters were taught in their CIA-managed training by the ISI in Pakistan to strip Soviet SPETZNAZ or special forces soldiers of their weapons, which were then handed in for study.

The CIA lured pilots from the Afghan Communist government forces to defect. In this way it acquired Soviet-built MIG-21 fighters, MI-24 and MI-25 attack helicopters and other aircraft, which were shipped to the United States. Aircraft downed by the holy warriors were stripped of their weapons systems and avionics. One of the classic cases of this tactic happened late in the war in 1988, when holy warriors shot down a Sukhoi-24 fighter-bomber. Its captured pilot happened to be Alexander V. Rutskoi, then a Soviet air force officer. Bartering, as they often did, with the moujahidin, the CIA succeeded in getting its hands on the Sukhoi jet, which had suffered little serious damage in its crash landing, by trading it for a Toyota pickup truck and some rocket launchers. Rutskoi refused the CIA's persuasions to defect. He returned home to Moscow, where during the Gorbachev era he became vice-president of Russia and a senior figure in the unsuccessful 1995 coup against Yeltsin.[17]

The ISI's preferred recipient of the vast inflow of arms, Soviet and otherwise, was Gulbuddin Hekmatyar, chief of the extremist *Hizb-i-Islami* and deemed by Zia al-Haq's men, with somewhat reluctant agreement by the CIA, as the most effective of the seven leaders of the seven main groups of moujahidin in fighting the Soviets. Later, he became a leader, trainer and an inspiration to the terrorists and guerrillas of the Afghan international. In the 1990s his picture appeared in such places as mosques used by the Islamists in Algeria and Bosnia.

Born in 1946, among the youngest of the seven senior commanders, Hekmatyar was educated at the Kabul Military School and University. He got a degree in engineering. In 1972 he was jailed by the then Afghan regime for anti-government (read anti-communist) activities. Later, the Communist Afghan regime of President Najibullah circulated scurrilous reports about his alleged homosexual life while a student and later. Brigadier Mohammad Youssaf was much impressed by his qualities as "not only the youngest but also the toughest and most vigorous of all the [senior] Leaders." He is, found Youssaf, a "staunch believer in an Islamic government for Afghanistan, an excellent administrator ... Despite his comparative wealth, he lives a frugal life. He is also ruthless, arrogant, inflexible, a stern disciplinarian, and he does not get on with Americans."

This was putting it mildly. Despite constant urging, cajoling and pressure from a variety of Afghans, Pakistanis and Americans, especially CIA officials, Hekmatyar kept his contacts with the CIA to a minimum. After President Ronald Reagan's election and William Casey's takeover of the CIA, he hardened this attitude to the point of publicly refusing to meet President Reagan during a visit Hekmatyar paid to New York in 1985 to address a UN meeting. This was regarded as an insult; biting the hand which by then was feeding the holy warriors to the tune of over a billion dollars a year. His argument, recalls Mohammad Youssaf, was that to be seen meeting Reagan would serve the KGB and Soviet propaganda. These insisted that the war was not a jihad, but a mere extension of US Cold War strategy. Moscow and its allies in the Najibullah regime in Kabul insisted that the Americans were paying the "rebel" Afghanis to fight other Afghanis, loyal to the Communist government, and their Soviet helpers. Hekmatyar wished to avoid providing public confirmation of this, according to Youssaf, who was convinced that this was a "grave error of judgement and that his action damaged the cause of jihad."[18] What it certainly did do, in the midst of visits to President Reagan, British Prime Minister Margaret Thatcher (an enthusiastic supporter of the jihad) and their senior aides by other, less uncompromising Afghan guerrilla leaders, was foreshadow Hekmatyar's critical future role as an inspirer of anti-Western terrorism.

In understanding how the anti-Soviet resistance shaped up under the watchful supervision of President Zia al-Haq into efficient, if competing, guerrilla forces; then, after the Soviets left, broke down into a congeries of well-trained terrorists, bent on destroying secular societies around the world and replacing them with "Islamic" ones, it is necessary to understand how the original resistance movements were organized.

When General Akhtar Khan assigned Brigadier Youssaf in October 1983 to head the Afghan bureau of ISI, the CIA was being run for President Ronald Reagan by World War II intelligence veteran and ex-lawyer and businessman William Casey. Youssaf and his boss General Akhtar had to keep explaining to Casey (who made at least annual visits to Pakistan during his intendancy), and to many of Casey's subordinates, that in supplying seven different Afghan political groups who were seriously fighting the Soviets, he was actually directing seven different wars.

There were two basic kinds of divisions inside the seven major groups: between Sunni and Shi'a Muslims; and between what the CIA and the American media liked to call the "moderates" (more correctly, traditionalist conservatives) and the "fundamentalists," or radical Islamists, of which Hekmatyar was the prime and most successful example, despite his aversion to displaying public gratitude to his American benefactors.

In the sectarian divide between Afghans, the Shi'a minority – perhaps 15 percent of the total population of Afghanistan when the war began in 1979 – had always looked to Iran for inspiration and support. Following the Iranian revolution and the victory of the Ayatollah Khomeiny over the Shah and the United States in 1979, the Tehran revolutionaries tried to unite Afghan Shi'ites under its control by purging and expelling the "moderate" Shi'a, who were not inclined to be too enthusiastic about the support for the regime of the ayatollahs in Iran. Most Afghan Shi'a are a tribal group called the Hazara, living in central Afghanistan. Tehran, through its Revolutionary Guards and other agents, tried to put young Afghan clerics, educated in the religious universities and colleges of Najaf in southern Iraq and Qom in Iran, and who resented the traditional power of traditional Afghan notables, under Khomeiny's domination. This did not succeed. Eight separate Shi'ite parties, all claiming to follow Khomeiny (and therefore receive Iranian largesse for their portion of the jihad effort), formed a coalition based in Qom. They managed to gather loosely under the banner of one of the seven major parties, called the Hizb-i-Wahdat (Unity Party) in the Hazarajat region of central Afghanistan. They stayed aloof from the other Sunni parties.

The Sunni–Shi'a sectarian rivalries and the Pushtun–Hazara ethnic hostility combined to prevent real Sunni–Shi'a cooperation in the jihad (just as the sectarian divide has prevented Sunni–Shi'a cooperation in most of the postwar international terrorist and guerrilla movements). There was a notable exception: HAMAS, a Sunni Palestinian group with roots in the Afghan jihad, active against Israel in the West Bank and Gaza, and Hizbollah, The Party of God (an Iranian-supported mainly Lebanese group, fighting the Israelis in south Lebanon and, according to not always well-verified Israeli reports, in certain terrorist actions in Europe and Latin America. Both certainly work to parallel purpose against Israel. They may also, at times, consciously coordinate their efforts and their missions.

The Sunni resistance parties in Afghanistan had their origin after the 1978 Communist coup in Kabul. The old Muslim Youth Movement split into three parts. The first was led by Hekmatyar. His followers at that time were already mainly uprooted ethnic Pushtuns, like Hekmatyar himself, of the Ghilzai tribal confederation. Hekmatyar's *Hizb-i-Islami* became the only one of the seven major parties to be led by a secular layman. The second splinter of the three, with, confusingly, the same name, *Hizb-i-Islami*, was headed by Mawlawi Younis Khalis, one of the few traditional clerics to join the more modernizing Islamist movement. His followers come mainly from tribal eastern areas. Although a man of over 70, Brigadier Youssaf praises Khalis' bravery for being willing to penetrate deeply into Soviet-held areas of Afghanistan on his own. The third broad group emerging from the split of the Muslim Youth Movement was the *Jamayat-i-Islami* (named the same as the Pakistani group), headed by former Professor Burhaneddin Rabbani of the Afghan State Faculty of Islam, ethnically a Tajik and linguistically the only native speaker of Persian among the Sunni leaders, and also a man of high culture who speaks six languages in all. Rabbani, far more moderate in his views, did not emulate Hekmatyar by opposing the United States and other Western benefactors in the jihad, nor did he recruit terrorists to fight in the West.

There was a fourth Sunni party. It was financed and inspired almost entirely by Saudi Arabia and its ultra-conservative Wahabi ideology, officially the founding ideology of the Saudi royal family. This was the *Ittihad* or union, led by another Afghan intellectual, Professor Abdul Rasul Sayyaf. This group was the core of an armed guerrilla band of several hundred men who, as we will see later on, moved from its Peshawar, Pakistan base to the southern Philippine Islands after the end of the Afghan war. Under the name of the Abu Sayyaf group, it operated on the fringe of the Moros Muslim insurgency. In the 1990s it was the most violent and radical Islamist group in the Far East, using its CIA and ISI training to harass, attack and murder Christian priests, wealthy non-Muslim plantation owners and merchants and local government in the southern Philippine island of Mindanao.

Of the seven major resistance parties, the other two Sunni ones were "moderate" or more properly, in the definition of French scholar Olivier Roy, "traditionalist." These were created in Peshawar, with benign attention from the ISI, after the 1978 Communist coup.Their followers and cadremen were a mixture of secular-educated younger men and most of the traditionally Islamic-educated ulama, or Muslim scholar-clerics. An umbrella was formed for the clerical networks: the *Harakat-i-Enqela*, not a radical organization and, unlike the groups of Hekmatyar and Khalis, not attractive to the Arab and other foreign volunteers recruited for the jihad. In consequence, far fewer of their adherents became post-Afghan war terrorists in the outside world. Most of the *Harakat* fighters were ethnic Pushtuns and Uzbeks. It advocated adoption of Muslim Sharia law, but rejected the idea of an Islamic revolution.

A favorite of American journalists covering the war, especially of *Soldier of Fortune* magazine, which idealized the feats of the moujahidin in glowing accounts, was the Islamic Front of Sayyad Pir Gailani, a layman and not a cleric; a man of private means who heads his own religious brotherhood; a tribal party which supported the restoration of the exiled King, Zahir Shah. A small party was the National Liberation Front, another favorite of the CIA and of American publicists, headed by a respected religious man, Sibghatullah Mujaddidi. Like Gailani, he has a largely Westernized family. In contrast to the stubborn, uncompromising Hekmatyar, Gailani and Mujaddidi appreciated their American backers so much that, according to Brigadier Youssaf, they visited the United States every six months or so, "all expenses paid." Finally, Mawlawi Nabi operated a small group of mainly ultra-religious men, with little fighting strength.[19]

During the first weeks of its proxy war against the Soviet invaders, President Carter's Cold Warriors, with the help of President Sadat in Egypt and General Zia al-Haq in Pakistan, had laid the foundation. What remained for Carter's men was to enlist China, the Communist but anti-Soviet giant to the north. The balance of power between the two Communist superpowers was delicate, and the situation throughout South Asia explosive. Although President Richard Nixon and his Secretary of State, Henry Kissinger, had begun an opening to China, with Pakistan's help, in 1972, there was nothing faintly resembling a formal Sino–US alliance. The crucial matter of enlisting Chinese aid for the Afghan holy war had to be handled quietly and discreetly. It might even have to be publicly disavowed. For these reasons, and because of the Pentagon's direct and official responsibilities, Jimmy Carter chose his quiet and infinitely discreet Defense Secretary, Harold Brown, to fly to Beijing.

4 Deng Xiaoping

During the opening years of the Afghan jihad, China joined the anti-Russian coalition. It did so for its own strategic reasons. It paid a terrible price during the blowback period after the war's end. That price was a renewed and spreading revolt of the Uighurs, the Muslim and Turkic-speaking peoples of China's far West, the vast province of Xinjiang, many of whom yearned for independence in their own Muslim state, after the fashion of the six ex-Soviet Muslim states of Central Asia which won independence with the Soviet empire's breakup during the early 1990s.

The decision of China to join the grand coalition against Russia in Afghanistan was, of course, a logical effect of its gradual rapprochement with the United States. This rapprochement had begun in earnest after Henry Kissinger's secret visit to Beijing, facilitated by Ali Bhutto's Pakistan government in 1971. However, public signs of the secret entente between Washington and Beijing were few and far between, until the start of the CIA's jihad against the Russians in Afghanistan.

President Jimmy Carter's taciturn Secretary of Defense, Harold Brown, was a sober, scholarly physicist by profession. He continued the tradition of near-silence about political and military cooperation with China, even during his trip to Beijing to enlist the Asian giant in the Afghan jihad on January 4 to 13, 1980.

As Brown discovered in Beijing, both the Chinese and American sides had done their preliminary homework well. This pleased Harold Brown, whose unflamboyant but incisive manner combined the zeal of Zbigniew Brzezinski with the outward mildness of Jimmy Carter. Brown was much less of a Lone Ranger than Brzezinski. Brown liked to rely on other people's expertise and teamwork, and to avoid the limelight. On his January 1980 voyage to the Middle Kingdom, Brown took with him a high-powered team of administration experts. These included a leading Cold Warrior of the Vietnam era, Robert Komer. There were also Asia veterans and arms-control experts such as George Seignious, who held the first-ever formal American discussion on arms matters with China's vice foreign minister, Zhang Wenjin.

At the time, Deng Xiaoping, very much a man of power and vision and an architect of China's hesitant but inexorable entry into the capitalist world, was vice-premier to Premier Hua Guofeng. After four days of talks with Deng, with Premier Hua, Foreign Minister Huang Hua and intelligence officials, Harold Brown emerged at a news conference. He confined himself to banal generalities, giving nothing away about China's decision to join the jihad. He had, he said, "found a growing convergence of views between our two governments on the outrageous and brutal invasion of Afghanistan by the Soviet Union." Each side would "take appropriate steps on its own" to counter the invasion. Brown refused to spell out what those "steps" were. He did acknowledge that while US arms sales to China were not discussed, "technology transfer" definitely was.[1]

Under persistent questioning by Pentagon newsmen Bob Clark and John McWethy immediately after Brown's return, the Secretary was just a bit more forthcoming, if extremely tortuous.

Yes, acknowledged Brown, right after reporting his trip to President Carter, the US and China had discussed "strategic cooperation," though not exactly a downright alliance. "We have parallel interests ...," he said, "and intend to take parallel action."[2]

The real, unpublished results of the visit, which had been well prepared by years of open and covert contacts between American and Chinese intelligence officials, were to be far more impressive than Brown's vague language disclosed. Both the US and China began to work against Soviet advances in Afghanistan, as well as Soviet aid to Vietnam. The victorious Communist regime in Vietnam had begun a campaign against Chinese influence in Cambodia and Thailand, something which Washington tacitly agreed should be fought against. In this sense, working with China in another part of South Asia was a new departure.

There was heartening news in the quiet exchanges which followed the Brown visit for hi-tech American arms merchants, and for the Pentagon's global strategy to "contain" the Soviet Union. The US would sell China a ground station for satellite reception. It would provide some "dual use" technology, especially communications and air transport equipment which had military as well as civilian uses. All of these items were on the list of items banned for export to the Soviet Union. Soon after Brown's return from Beijing, on January 24, 1980, the US Congress approved a most-favored-nation trade agreement with China. This was destined to become a subject of much controversy during wide-ranging debates, inside and outside the US Congress, over human rights and repression in China during the two Clinton administrations in the 1990s.

On May 25, 1980, after four months of covert American, Pakistani, Egyptian and Chinese aid to the CIA's jihad in Afghanistan, Geng Biao, Chinese vice-premier for security and secretary-general of the Chinese Communist Party's military affairs committee, came for a two-week tour in the United States. Brown announced that the Carter administration had authorized US firms to sell China a wide variety of "non-lethal" supplies, such as transport planes, helicopters and air defense radar. Sino–US deals for aid and American training of Chinese personnel followed. Military cooperation was further reinforced in September 1980. A Pentagon delegation visited Beijing, closely followed by a Chinese delegation to Washington led by Vice-Premier Bo Yibo. The emerging Sino–Pakistani–American axis, based on mutual aid to the anti-Soviet holy warriors in Afghanistan, was well and truly launched. So was a spectacular improvement in Sino–American relations in general.

One of Brown's central accomplishments in bringing China into the grand Afghan coalition was kept secret for years. This was the construction of two important US electronic intelligence posts in Xinjiang, the huge, problem-ridden Chinese province with an active and restless population of Muslim Uighurs, just barely touching the far eastern tip of Afghanistan. In the time of the Shah, which had ended with the Iranian revolution of February 1979 and the emergence of Shia Muslim power under the Ayatollah Ruhollah Khomeiny in Tehran, the United States had operated two critically important monitoring sites, codenamed Tracksman 1 and Tracksman 2. They monitored Soviet communications and missile telemetry emitted from the Soviet missile and space base at Tyuratam, in Central Asia. The Iranian revolutionaries seized both sites in early 1979, and they were lost, probably forever, to the United States. This loss had enhanced the importance, for tracking such matters as Soviet troop and material deployments for Afghanistan, of US and NATO intelligence sites in Turkey. This, of course, added in turn to the already vastly important strategic value to Washington of its partnership with Ankara, which had lasted since the start of the Cold War in the late 1940s.

One of the most important Turkish sites was at Pirinclik, eastern Turkey. It was used, among other purposes, for observing the proliferating host of satellites of many types and many nations, especially the Soviet Union, circling the earth. Pirinclik and other key Turkish sites had been temporarily shut down in the 1970s, when the US Congress embargoed American arms shipments to Turkey to show disapproval of the Turkish invasion and occupation of northern Cyprus in the summer of 1974. The embargo, which totally failed to influence Turkish policy on Cyprus or anything else, and which the Ford administration, after President Richard Nixon's resignation, perceived as highly damaging to American strategic interests, was lifted in 1978.

In the following year, as the Soviets deployed their forces against the growing resistance in Afghanistan, Turkey was linking renewed or continued operation of Pirinclik and other Turkish sites used by the United States to Turkish requests for new US military aid. Congress granted this aid in May of 1979. However, there has always been a question mark hanging over the future of the American installations in Turkey – especially in the 1990s, after the end of the Cold War – and with it many of the missile tests which an impoverished Russia and its former Central Asian Republics could no longer afford. These tests had been constantly monitored, from Pakistan, Turkey and elsewhere, by the gigantic, multi-billion dollar American electronic intelligence activity, the National Security Agency (NSA) at Fort Meade, Maryland. This was financed by a secret budget which dwarfed by far that of the CIA and all the other US intelligence agencies.[3]

The fragility of Iranian and Turkish intelligence sites, and the absence of earlier Pakistani ones, lent added importance to acquiring Chinese ones, especially when it was decided to support the moujahidin in Afghanistan. According to two French espionage specialists, intelligence contacts between the US and China, leading to construction of the Xinjiang sites, began shortly after the Sino–Soviet tension of the 1960s and resulting border fighting, especially in 1969. In Europe, the secretive, scholarly mandarin of American intelligence, General Vernon Walters, author of a book named *Secret Missions* and then deputy CIA director, met the Chinese military attache in Paris, Fang Wen. Soon afterward, there came the assassination of the Defense Minister, Marshal Lin Biao, on September 12, 1971, on orders of the supreme boss of Chinese intelligence, Kang Sheng. The official Chinese cover story about the death of Lin, presumed to be plotting against Chairman Mao, was that he crashed in a plane into the Mongolian desert while trying to flee to the Soviet Union. Actually, he appears to have been murdered by one of Kang Sheng's hit teams in a Beijing restaurant, together with close family members and friends.[4]

Lin Biao's demise had caused uncertainty about Sino–US relations. It was largely overcome by the momentous official visit of President Nixon, prepared in advance by Henry Kissinger, to Beijing in 1972. Within a year the CIA was able to open its first station there. It operated as part of the first US diplomatic mission which was headed by Ambassador David Bruce. For the CIA and Kang Sheng's operatives of the *Tewu,* the senior Chinese intelligence agency, this was a huge improvement over the clandestine contacts which Vernon Walters, and also Kissinger, had conducted with the Chinese in Paris, between November 1971 and May 1973. Later, Kissinger recalls, he held secret face-to-face meetings with veteran Chinese intelligence operative and statesman Huang Hua, one of Kang Sheng's top experts on Third World countries. These meetings usually took place in a "safe house" in Manhattan provided by the CIA. Kissinger recalls it was "a seedy apartment whose mirrored walls suggested less prosaic purposes."[5]

A senior Chinese intelligence operative began preparations for the future Chinese role in the Afghan jihad. This role would have serious consequences for China's control of Xinjiang and its Muslim population. The operative was Qiao Shi, deputy of *Tewu* supremo Kang Sheng. Qiao Shi, a veteran supporter of Mao, had been especially active in Eastern Europe during the 1970s, when the Sino–Soviet dispute still raged, promoting Chinese influence in countries like Albania (which expelled the Chinese in 1976), Yugoslavia and Romania. In September 1978, on the way home to Beijing from one of his Balkan missions, Qiao Shi stopped over in Tehran to see the Shah of Iran, who was ill with cancer and whose throne and authority were already under fire from a rising tide of popular, Islamist revolution.

Qiao Shi proposed to the Shah a new alliance to thwart Soviet expansion, especially in neighboring Afghanistan. Israel's foreign intelligence agency, the Mossad, had already brought the Iranians and the Chinese into contact. General Nasser Moghadam, who had recently taken over as head of the Shah's dreaded security and intelligence organization, SAVAK, met Qiao Shi. Agreement was reached to undertake a covert war in Afghanistan, apparently independent of CIA plans for the same country. Chinese agents began to move into position in Pakistan. Liaising with Pakistan's ISI was the Iranian ambassador in Islamabad, former head of SAVAK.

The best-laid plans of Tehran and Beijing were shattered by the Shah's overthrow in February 1979 and the Soviet onslaught in Kabul in December of the same year. Nevertheless, the Ayatollah Khomeiny's new revolutionary regime in Tehran still looked to Kang Sheng's Chinese intelligence like a possible ally against the Soviets. Qiao Shi and senior Chinese military intelligence officials decided to take aim at the Russians in Kabul. At the beginning of 1980, about the time of Harold Brown's mission to Beijing, a Chinese Muslim dignitary, closely allied with the Beijing regime, vice-president of the Chinese Islamic association, Muhammad Ali Zhang Jie, arrived in Tehran to negotiate with the Muslim clerics of Khomeiny. The China–Iran–Pakistan axis looked for a while to have some strength and consistency. The Iranians were assured by Chinese visitors that Deng Xiaoping would not hesitate in the future to supply arms for their struggle against Iraq's Saddam Hussein,[6] who attacked Iran in September 1980 and waged war until both sides were exhausted in 1988.

In Beijing, Chairman Mao's chosen successor, Hua Guofeng, with whom Harold Brown had finalized Sino–American cooperation in Afghanistan, would relinquish the premiership to Zhao Ziyang, another veteran politician, in September 1980. However, while Hua was still prime minister, the new CIA station chief in Beijing, reportedly David Gries, organized a visit for President Jimmy Carter's CIA director, Admiral Stansfield Turner. There followed talks to plan and prepare construction of the two top-secret US monitoring sites in Xingjiang, Qitai and Korla. The listening posts would perform such tasks as monitoring Soviet missile tests and communications, no longer possible after the Iranian revolutionaries closed down Tracksman 1 and 2 in Iran. The sites in Xinjiang would be manned by Chinese trained by Americans in SIGINT (Signal Intelligence) skills. The entire project would be placed under the CIA's Division of Sciences and Technology, directed by Leslie Dirks.[7]

The Chinese listening posts gave both Washington and Beijing a unique opportunity to eavesdrop on Soviet Central Asia. Politically, they gave the United States, the leader of the anti-Soviet coalition in Afghanistan, a choice asset in Chinese-controlled territory – although, as the Americans would soon more fully realize, that control from Beijing was contested by elements among the Uighur Muslim population of Xinjiang.

Qitai and Korla apparently continued their electronic spying operations until the end of the Soviet occupation of Afghanistan in 1989. This end coincided roughly with the crackdown in April of that year in Beijing's Tiananmen Square, when Chinese security forces crushed protest demonstrations and an incipient popular revolt by students and other dissidents. This inaugurated an era of bad feeling between China and the United States, both of which had disengaged (China first) or were disengaging from, Afghanistan by that time. There were some strong though unconfirmed indications that this bad feeling was a principal cause of the shutdown of Qitai and Korla.[8]

No indications at all have come to light that Americans or Chinese ever discussed the possible blowback on China of arming and training Muslim militants, especially the Muslim Uighur people of Xinjiang, to fight the Soviets in Afghanistan, on China's western back porch, so to speak.

During the jihad, Kang Sheng's Chinese intelligence services also cooperated briefly with West Germany in a curious, hybrid intelligence operation. West Germany's *Bundesnachrichtendienst* (BND) or Federal Intelligence Agency, was a direct participant. The BND (under such redoubtable directors as Klaus Kinkel, a Cold Warrior who after the post-Afghanistan collapse of the Soviet Union and East Germany, became one of unified Germany's most active foreign ministers), in the 1970s was working actively on many fronts with both the CIA and Israel's Mossad. As the Afghan arena heated up in the late 1970s, the Israeli service procured for the Germans, without public mention, a secret radio jamming and deception device, codenamed CERBERUS. It was probably not dissimilar to those Israel had used with great success in black operations against the Arabs, especially in the 1967 war. (Israel had confused Arab combat pilots with false orders purporting to come from their own Arab headquarters. It had even jammed and altered a crucial radiotelephone conversation at the war's outset between President Nasser of Egypt and King Hussein of Jordan.)

To test its effectiveness, the BND pressed CERBERUS into service along the Iron Curtain frontiers with the Warsaw Pact states, including East Germany. Bonn received from Beijing a request for technical assistance in China's own espionage operations against the Soviets, especially in and around Afghanistan. So the BND, then under Kinkel's management, decided on Operation Pamir (the name of the lofty mountain wall in the Soviet–China–Afghanistan–Indo-Pakistan regions). It consisted partly of installing a German-made reconnaissance radar in Chinese territory near the Soviet Union. With it, the Israel-supplied CERBERUS electronic-warfare system was also tested. It was then taken over and operated by Chinese personnel against Soviet electronics and communications.[9] Encouraged by the success of the combined system, the BND set up a series of front companies to cover delivery of approximately $25 million-worth of hi-tech electronic equipment to China. Critics in Germany who uncovered the Pamir operation charged that it was financed by West German defense ministry funds, a violation of existing German laws against transfer of sensitive technology.[10]

For the CIA and its Pakistani ally, the ISI, the logistical challenge of cooperating with China was how to get the Chinese weapons (like all of the other weapons from other suppliers) to the fighters themselves. One of the agreements secured by Harold Brown in Beijing was for US planes to fly cargoes of arms for the moujahidin through Chinese airspace. One of the persistent stories about the Afghan jihad is that the Chinese used the mountainous Wakhan peninsula, where Afghanistan and China briefly touch each other along a 40-mile border, which snakes its way through deep mountain gorges. The Wakhan's towering, icy peaks are mostly over 20,000 feet high, and thinly populated. All of the valleys are cut off by snow and ice for months in the winter. There is an Afghan proverb which says "even the birds can use only their feet" along the corridor's 120-mile length. At the time the Afghan jihad began, the 3,000 or so inhabitants, living in the valleys of the Hindu Kush mountain range and the edge of the Pamirs, were Muslim Kirghiz tribesmen. They were ethnically affiliated with the people of the then Kirghiz Soviet Republic, now independent Kyrgyzstan. These hardy mountain people also enjoyed occasional trade and other contacts with the Kirghiz and Uighur people next door in China's Xinjiang.

During early Soviet offensives in 1980, the Red Army halted traffic to the Chinese frontier, and simply annexed Wakhan to the Soviet Union. The Soviet puppet Afghan government of Babrak Karmal in Kabul signed the area away to Moscow in a formal document. Then it helped the Russians to push the Kirghiz people in Wakhan over the frontier into Pakistan, augmenting Pakistan's already critical problem of accommodating refugees of the Afghan jihad. Next, the Soviets proceeded to build small airfields and helicopter pads wherever they could find a patch of level ground, and fortified bunkers in the mountainsides. There a few troops could hunker down under the winter snows and await any disagreeable actions by the moujahidin or their Chinese supporters. In the summer, there was a somewhat larger Russian garrison of 1,500 to 2,000 men. It was placed under the Soviet military district of Murgab; in Kipling's time a buffer zone used by mountain units of the British Indian army.

All the actors in the Afghan jihad were also vitally interested in the Karakorum Highway, the ancient Silk Road of history. This passed between China and Pakistan, only about 35 miles from the Afghan border. Traveled by Marco Polo in the thirteenth century, the Silk Road was for many centuries the main East–West artery. Over it, pearls, silk, cinnamon, silver and above all books, people and ideas and doctrines, especially the Muslim religion, moved and were exchanged.

Russian sources have frequently claimed that the first Chinese arms for the Afghans were spotted as early as June 1979, six months before the Soviet invasion. If true, this may have been related to the Chinese understanding with the Shah of Iran, mentioned above. At any rate, in June 1979 Soviet intelligence sighted in Karachi harbor a Pakistani freighter, the *Rustam,* arriving from China. Moscow media reported that its 8,000 tons of arms and ammunition were taken to Peshawar (the classic route, by road and rail, later used by the ISI for the bulk of arms arriving at Karachi port). In Peshawar, the material was distributed, said the Russians "in the center of the saboteurs and bandits."[11] By early 1980, reported a White Book on outside intervention published by the Afghan Communist government in Kabul, China was "flying large supplies of arms and ammunition to the insurgents in Afghanistan."[12] Some of this material, which may have circumvented the filtering control of the ISI, made its way to training camps in Afghanistan belonging to the *Sholah-e-Javed* (Eternal Flame) organization, an Afghan resistance group with a strong Maoist complexion.[13] Arnaut van Lyden, an experienced Dutch correspondent, was asked to leave Pakistan. The cause, he told the author later, was that he reported with a bit too much graphic detail on the new Chinese mortars, machine guns, rockets and rifles, some still bearing their original Chinese army markings, which he saw in the Afghan camps of Peshawar and the border region.

In charge of the Chinese military training, both of the jihad volunteers in Pakistan, and of the Uighur Muslims trained in Pakistan, was the Military Intelligence Department of the Chinese People's Liberation Army (PLA) General Staff

Department. Intelligence experts in the West call it by its Chinese name, *Er Bu*, or Second Department. Its chief at the end of the 1980s, as the Afghan war wound down, was Major General Xiong Guankai, a veteran PLA intelligence officer, then in his late fifties. His personal assistant, Colonel Li Ning, was a Chinese military attache in London who in 1990 traveled to the United States to finish his graduate work at Johns Hopkins University's School for Advanced International Studies in Washington, DC. American and allied Special Forces officers involved in training the jihad volunteers were asked to return to South Asia after the war to track down men they had trained who had become involved in international terrorism. It is a reasonable assumption, though this is not known definitely, that men like Major General Guankai and Colonel Ling were pressed into service to track the Muslim fighters who, once trained and in some cases battle-hardened in the Afghan jihad, returned to lead the Uighur insurgency in Xinjiang by the early 1990s.

China's Second Department had already trained many volunteers from Maoist or other Leftist Latin American and African groups in the 1960s. Its input to the Afghan operation was its largest-scale operation of this kind, lasting from 1980 until 1988. This was almost, although not quite, the entire duration of the Soviet deployment. Moscow analysts claimed, probably with some degree of truth, that the CIA footed most of a bill of $400 million for the operation; a sum modest in comparison to billions of dollars provided by the CIA, Saudi Arabia and, as we shall see later on, private Arab financiers, through the ISI and directly.

The Chinese supply operation was well underway about a month after Harold Brown's January 1980 visit to Beijing. By February, at least six of the moujahidin groups were competing for the Chinese assault rifles, heavy machine guns, mortars and recoiless cannon. By September 1984, when Brigadier Youssaf's watch with the ISI was well under way, 107 mm and 122 mm artillery pieces were appearing at the various fronts in Afghanistan. One type was the 107 mm Type 63–1 12-tube rocket launcher, with lightweight alloy tubes.[14]

Brigadier Youssaf has high praise for the meticulous way in which the Chinese handled their supply operations. Until 1984, he adds, "the greatest amounts of arms and ammunition were purchased from China, and they proved completely reliable and discreet, providing [free] weapons as aid, as well as for sale." Then, in 1985, more and more of the arms arriving were from Egypt, purchased from President Mubarak's government by the CIA. In contrast to the businesslike and often new Chinese arms, the initial shipment from Egypt, Youssaf says, was rusty and sometimes totally unserviceable. Even some empty boxes arrived. The CIA also began providing Arab weapons captured in Lebanon by Israel, and rifles purchased in India.[15]

The CIA's most notable and important success was introducing the Stinger anti-aircraft missile, which would begin to turn the tide of the war in 1985, forcing Soviet attack aircraft and helicopter gunships to keep to ineffective high altitudes. Ironically, the loss of control of the Stingers by the CIA, and apparently by the Pakistanis as well, was a mighty contribution to the morale, if not the actual effectiveness, of the post-jihad terrorist groups and Iran's Revolutionary Guards, of which more later. In any case, Youssaf asserts that once Stinger instruction began at the ISI's main training camp at Ojhri, outside Rwalpindi, neither Chinese nor Saudi visitors were allowed. The only US Congressman permitted to visit the Stinger school once, in 1987, was Senator Gordon Humphrey, who had lobbied vigorously for the CIA to provide the Stinger for the jihad.

One of the most effective weapons provided by the Chinese was the 107 mm 12-barrel rocket launcher, mentioned above, and also known as the Multi-Barrel Rocket Launcher (MBRL). Youssaf reveals that a strong need developed for a single-barrel light rocket launcher, or SBRL, which one man could easily handle and move at night between hostile enemy outposts. This mobility contrasted with the MBRL, which had to be carried mostly on the backs of mules and was too heavy for one man to manipulate. To meet the need, the ISI took a tube from a partially destroyed MBRL. They demonstrated the resulting single-tube launcher to the CIA, which was enthusiastic. The CIA then convinced the reluctant Chinese, who had taken their older SBRL out of production, to reactivate the assembly lines in China. Youssaf ordered 500 of the SBRLs in 1985 and by 1987, as the war was winding down, the ISI had received 1,000.[16]

Pakistani sources have supplied no information on what happened to either the MBLRs or the SBRLs after the war. However, there is ample evidence that both have seen heavy and repeated use by the Afghan guerrilla factions themselves, including the post-1990 Taliban and their enemies, and the Kashmir guerrillas fighting Indian rule. The surviving inhabitants of Kabul, a capital ruined by the jihad and the internecine wars between the Afghan factions which followed, can attest to the terror and devastation spread by the repeated torrents of heavy rockets, mainly of Chinese origin, which the various factions have rained on the city, from the 1980s onward.

The PLA Second Department's training operation included, by 1985, the furnishing of about 300 advisors and instructors at camps in Pakistan. Locations included Muhammad Gard, near the Pakistani town of Nawagai; Shabqadar, 12 miles north of Charsadda; Lwara Mena, in the drug-running region of the Northwest Frontier province about 8 miles northeast of Landi Kotal, and at Faqirabad, near Peshawar. In 1985, China opened more camps on Chinese territory, near Kashgar and Hotan, in Xinjiang. Those selected for training learned use of Chinese weapons, explosives and PLA combat tactics, probably not unlike that which others were receiving from Pakistani, American and British Special Forces.

Until the late autumn of 1986, Soviet propagandists deliberately downplayed Chinese supplies and training for the jihad. The Kremlin wished not to endanger what it hoped, especially after Mikhail Gorbachev came to power in 1985 and began to hint at eventual Soviet withdrawal from Afghanistan, would be negotiations with China. It wished to solve the deep-seated and long-standing Sino–Soviet problems, which had almost led to war in 1969. Unlike the Russians, Afghan Communist President Muhammad Najibullah pulled no punches. He told a

Pakistani journalist that the Chinese had played "one of the most important roles in the war." Chinese military aid had exceeded $400 million in value. Other Afghan and private Russian sources claimed the existence of Chinese-provided training facilities for 55,000 "Afghans" – it is not clear how many of these were actually local Uighur Muslims or others, such as Uzbeks or other Central Asians – in the Xinjiang camps.[17]

The dangers China faced in the Afghan enterprise are apparent when one examines China's own ethnic and religious makeup.

By the time of China's 1982 census, when the Afghan war and Chinese assistance to the jihad were about two years old, Beijing would officially admit to only 14.6 million Muslims in China, probably a far too conservative figure. Islamists claim there are over 50 million in the 1990s. The nationalities include: Huis, Uighurs, Kazakhs, Uzbeks, Tajiks, Tartars, Kirghiz, Salars, Dongxiangs and Baoans.[18] In the sensitive Xinjiang region alone, which contains installations like the Chinese nuclear-weapons test site at Lop Nor and the two US-sponsored electronic monitoring posts, there are seven million Uighurs. They are Sunni Muslims. They make up 46 percent of the Xinjiang population, with 36 percent Han Chinese, one million or about 7.7 percent Kazakh and four percent Hui Muslims; two percent Tajiks (Shi'ites, like those in the former Soviet republic of Tajikistan, speaking a kind of Persian) and one percent of Kirghiz (mostly Sunnis, like the Kazakhs).[19]

For the Chinese, who have always considered their country "The Middle Kingdom," the center of the civilized world, non-Chinese were traditionally viewed as "barbarians." They were to be brought into conformity through what Harris calls *ji-mi* or appeasement, or through a process called *zhi-yi,* playing off one set of barbarians against another in order to control the actions of both (Persians against Arabs; the US against Russia, for instance).

This technique did not always work with the Muslims inside China, as the emperors of the Ch'ing or Manchu Dynasty (1644–1912) were to discover. Active resistance by the Muslims to Han Chinese central rule began in Gansu province, in northwest China, bordered by Mongolia. In the second half of the eighteenth century, a Chinese traveling scholar who had spent 20 years in Arabia's holy cities of Mecca, Medina and in Yemen, introduced a doctrine known as the "New Teaching." This stirred intercommunal conflict in Muslim areas. By the early nineteenth century, some 15 million Muslims in China were striving for self-rule. From 1818, there were several Muslim uprisings in Yunan province. The so-called Great Rebellion of Muslims in Yunan took place in 1853–73. In 1862–76 came the Tungan rebellion in Shaanxi, Gansu and above all in Xinjiang, where Muslims had begun to be affected by Anglo–Russian struggles called the Great Game. Yunan became divided into two competing Muslim kingdoms. One Muslim leader, Du Wenxiou of Pingnan Guo (Peaceful South Country) renamed himself Sultan Suleiman, after the fashion of the Ottoman Sultans. He sent his son to Istanbul to see them and to London in 1871, to plead vainly for help against the Ch'ing rulers. The fighting and destruction in what the Muslims were by now calling Eastern

Turkestan left deep scars and bitter memories. (The Uighurs and the vast majority of the other Muslims in these regions spoke Turkic languages.) As late as 1973, a major Muslim revolt in Yunan killed 1,700 people.

Closer to Afghanistan, Russia and the Muslim areas subjected to Russia by the czars, erupted in revolt in 1862–76. The chief rebel, with the very Turkic name of Yakoub Beg, was almost able to re-establish the rule of the Khojas, Muslim rulers of the fifteenth to seventeenth centuries. For a time, all central Chinese authority was expelled from the three provinces of Xinjiang, Shaanxi and Gansu. Yakoub Beg's 12-year kingdom, while it lasted, was centered in the Kashgar region. It was briefly recognized by Russia, Britain and Turkey. Russo–British friction arising from the "Great Game," the competition for influence between them, led to a tacit Russo–British accord that Xinjiang would serve as a buffer between the British and Russian empires. However, Yakoub Beg made a fatal error. It was one which today's Muslim insurgents, many of them trained in the CIA's Afghan jihad, should keep in mind if considering leaning too hard on modern Turkey, their linguistic and supposedly cultural motherland, for support. That error was to court and accept arms from Ottoman Turkey, Russia's worst enemy. The Sultan in Constantinople declared Yakoub an *amir al-moumineen* or Commander of the Faithful, a supreme religious title which challenged central Chinese authority. Later, the Turkic revolt had been suppressed by an imperial China. The Chinese rulers further weakened China by borrowing money abroad to pay for the military effort. The Ottoman Turks and the Ch'ing Dynasty then coexisted for a time – until both of them finally disappeared in the backwash of World War I.[20]

During the republic ruled by the Kuomintang, or Guomendang (KMT) party of Chinese founder and hero Sun Yatsen, following the revolution in Canton in 1911, Sun's leadership briefly took the Muslims seriously. It envisioned making them, using the generic name Hui, one of five "official nationalities" of China. During China's war with Japan in 1936, General Chiang Kai-Shek's KMT government gave Muslim morale in Nationalist China a boost. He conducted an official census. This showed 48.2 million Muslims, and probably gave the lie to the official Chinese Communist figures acknowledging only 16 million in the late 1980s, as the Afghan war against the Soviets approached its end, and the first signs of a well-trained insurgency, arising from veterans of the jihad, began to show in Xinjiang.

The foundations for this insurgency were actually laid between 1944 and 1950. The three largest ethnic groups of Muslims in Chinese-ruled territory: Uighurs, Kazakhs and Kirghiz, took advantage of the war with Japan in the east; the Soviet war with Japan's allies the Germans in the west, and the chaos which the almost simultaneous civil war between the KMT and the Communists, won by the Communists in 1949, brought to China itself. Together, these three main Muslim groups tried to create a shadowy "Republic of Eastern Turkestan." Its creators conceived of it as an independent state. The new Communist power in Beijing under Chairman Mao gradually turned its attention and its military power westward, to defeat the Muslims. Simultaneously, the Communist rulers attacked and annexed the Buddhist theocracy in Tibet, stirring armed resistance there which for a time in the 1950s, the American CIA surreptitiously supported. The 1979–89 Afghan jihad and the return of the warriors to western China, especially Xinjiang, breathed sparks of new life into the Eastern Turkestan liberation movement, as its Muslim leaders now call it. A second contributing factor was one more consequence of the Afghan jihad: the breakaway in 1989 and onward of the Muslim republics of the former Soviet Union in Central Asia.

The Chinese strategy seeking to muzzle, and finally to stifle, the Islamists by using the same tactics the Chinese used in Tibet, was the classic method of drowning their resistance in a tide of incoming Chinese settlers – as the French, British, Portuguese and indeed the Russians and others had done before them in *their* colonial possessions.

As the Afghanistan war wound down at the end of the 1980s, the human and military exchanges across the Pamir and Karakorum mountain barriers had begun to aggravate the latent stirrings of revolt in China's strategic Far West. In the second part of this book, we will see some glimpses of what has happened there during the 1990s.

Apart from this trouble between the Han Chinese central government and its Muslim subjects, what did China's support to the American-led holy war in Afghanistan really mean for China?

Throughout all this, China has had to tread cautiously. It has always had to weigh its overweening strategic consideration of meeting Soviet or Russian threats and India's rivalry and territorial claims in the Himalayas, against the need not to be seen as too cosy with the United States or Pakistan. This has been especially true on the broad stage of the Arab and wider Muslim world, where the United States' alliance with the State of Israel has remained anathema (China, after all, was one of the first and most genuine supporters of the Palestine Liberation Organization, with moral, diplomatic and armed support). Nor could China be seen to be acting in an openly divisive manner, such as favoring one Afghan faction over another.[21]

Finally, in the last analysis, the Chinese Communist rulers, like their imperial predecessors, found it undesirable to allow one "hegemonist" – the term Beijing often employed for the two super-powers of the pre-1990s period, Soviet and American – to win out completely, in Asia or the world, over the other. A strong United States, and, as developed especially during President Clinton's two administrations, a strong system of Western alliances which could counter Soviet expansion, was in China's interest. However, China had to continue to face the world, as it has since the Chinese revolution, as an opponent of big-power interference in the affairs of Third World peoples.[22]

As China confronted what it perceived as a direct threat to its own interests in Afghanistan in early 1980, it desired that the Soviets should be "contained" and mired, as the United States had been earlier in Vietnam, in an exhausting and unwinnable war which would bleed off its economic strength. As China gradually perceived, through the decade of the 1980s, that Moscow's waning effort in Afghanistan was not the threat it had believed it to be, its enthusiasm for what Chinese Foreign Minister Huang Hua had told Alexander Haig, President Reagan's first Secretary of State, in June 1981, should evolve into a "strategic relationship" began to diminish. This tendency was increased by China's growing prosperity and the visible crippling and imminent collapse of the Soviet Union.

5 Recruiters, Trainers, Trainees and Assorted Spooks

The training process could be compared to an inverted pyramid. Nearest to its tip were the cadremen and leaders; mainly Pakistani officers who would themselves become trainers, but also some Afghanis and other personnel. In the United States, they experienced tough courses in endurance, weapons use, sabotage and killing techniques, communications and other skills. They were required to impart these skills to the scores of thousands of fighters who formed the center and the base of the pyramid of holy war.

As seen from CIA headquarters in Langley, the training program followed Archie Roosevelt's principles, mentioned earlier. The CIA would be the overall manager. US Special Forces and a coalition of assorted allied specialists would train the trainers. Pakistan's ISI, in its schools and camps, would train the bulk of the moujahidin and send them into battle; often though not always under the same kind of ISI supervision applied to the distribution of weapons. A few British and American Special Forces veterans, men of the American Green Berets and the British Special Air Service (SAS), elected to go beyond the role of trainers chosen for them by the jihad's managers. They volunteered for scouting and back-up roles with the Muslim mercenaries trained by themselves, their colleagues and Pakistan's ISI.

President Jimmy Carter's administration took many of the basic decisions during its final year. These were amplified by President Ronald Reagan's men – especially his Director of Central Intelligence, William Casey. The Reagan–Casey team accelerated the process of reactivating US Special Forces. Their training missions, related to Afghanistan, as well as their operational ones in Central America and later in the Persian Gulf conflicts, took on new life in the 1980s.

Like the CIA itself, America's Special Forces had problems in its past which needed to be overcome. The exploits of the US Army's Rangers in World War II, from Omaha Beach in Normandy to the bitter battles against the Japanese in the Pacific islands, had made them heroes of the 1940s. After the war, they dropped from Army rolls until restored, by admirers with long memories, 35 years later, in the new American wars, covert and overt, in Southeast Asia. The Army's Special Forces, briefly popular with some of the American public in early phases of the Vietnam war during the Kennedy administration (1961–63), lost favor again in the 1970s as the war wound down and ended. It required the gung-ho, "go out and get 'em" attitudes, cultivated with regard to Afghanistan and elsewhere in the Reagan period, to repolish the legendary reputation of the Green Berets. This created disgust among rival formations, such as the US Navy's commandos, the SEALS (Sea–Air–Land teams). They felt their own exploits in Vietnam and elsewhere had been underpublicized, while the Green Berets got all the credit.[1]

The Green Berets – officially the US Army Special Forces – laid the direct groundwork for what was to be their main role in the Afghan jihad in Southeast Asia. This role was training "native" or indigenous guerrillas to fight communist forces. Before the mid-1960s, they were deeply engaged in Vietnam in what was called the "Civilian Irregular Defense Group" (CIDG). This involved training the Montagnard Rhade tribe, one of the minorities which the US tried to use against the Viet Cong, the Communist Vietnamese armies, by training them in weapons handling and guerrilla tactics. By late 1962, according to Major R. B. Anderson, a Special Forces commander and trainer, the CIDG program included 200 Vietnamese villages, 12,000 villagers armed by the Green Berets and 26 Special Forces "A" teams. (These were the Special Forces' basic operational unit, commanded by a captain and composed of 12 specialists trained in communications, weapons, engineering skills and medicine, as well as linguists.)[2] These were pre-established concepts adopted, with needed modifications, in "training the trainers" for the Afghan holy war.

Through the years since World War II, the US military's Special Forces' purposes had changed. From fighting and behind-the-lines derring-do when they were formally created in 1952, they had moved more and more to "civic action." This was a concept the French tried to apply in their colonial wars in Indo-China before and during the arrival of the Americans there. They tried again in Algeria, during the revolution this reporter covered there (1954–62). Civic action means trying to affect a country or a society through propaganda, psychological warfare, or "psyops" in American military and intelligence parlance, and other methods not always directly related to shoot-'em-up guerrilla operations.[3] This also became known, especially to cynical critics, as the doctrine of "hearts and minds," by aiding the "friendlies" even as you helped them fight the "baddies," such as fortifying, feeding and otherwise helping "friendly" households and villages, while you destroyed those presumed to belong to the enemy.

Once William Casey had taken over the CIA's directorship in 1981, and with Pakistan and other allies had turned his Muslim mercenaries against the Russians in Afghanistan, the Army Special Forces trained and used proxies with varying skills in all fields. Retired intelligence analyst and CIA consultant Russell J. Bowern observed that Casey revived the old concept, which Casey had applied in his own special ops with the wartime OSS (Office of Strategic Services) in Nazi-occupied Europe. "The idea," said Bowern, "was you had a job to do, and you go out and do the job, and you clean up the problems later."[4] In the case of Afghanistan, as Casey's associates and successors would discover, the problems would grow. There was no cleanup in sight by 1999, when the terrorist international and related drug mafias had spread around the world.

As distinct from recruiting for the jihad, in Pakistan and among the tribal areas inside Afghanistan, recruiting of foreign volunteers abroad was left by the CIA and Pakistan's ISI to Islamic religious and charitable bodies. Sometimes these were cover groups, organized directly or indirectly by the CIA for the purpose of recruiting; sometimes not. Deserving much more investigation and attention than it has had up to now is a vast, international Islamic missionary organization, headquartered in Pakistan but with branches and ramifications around the world, including North America. This is the Tablighi Jamaat, known to have recruited many North African volunteers (and probably, though the author lacks evidence), those in other countries and continents as well. Although almost unknown to non-Muslim Americans and Europeans, and even to many Muslims, the 1988 Tablighi Jamaat convention in Chicago, Illinois, during the last year of the Afghan war, managed to attract over 6,000 Muslims from around the world. The Pakistani scholar Mumtaz Ahmad believes this was "probably the largest gathering of Muslims ever in North America."[5]

The founder of the Tabligh was a Muslim scholar, Maulana Mohammad Ilyas (1885–1994). He worked in response to militant Hindu missionary efforts. According to Mumtaz Ahmad, his main purpose was to "purify" borderline Muslims "who had retained many of the customs and religious practices from their Hindu [dominated] past." Maulana Ilyas and his followers established a system of Islamic *madrasas* or secondary schools, and spread the Prophet's faith by word of mouth, especially in door-to-door proselytizing and good works of charity. Soon its influence had spread through India, organizing a system of religious learning, based on intense personal relationships and preaching, rather than on any body of theological writings or printed teachings. The influence of the Tabligh's strict orthodox approach is reflected in the austerity carried to fanatical extremes by the Taliban movement, although the Tabligh, unlike the Taliban, does not object to secular education, or, in general, to other "modernist" trends, provided they enhance the moral and religious character of the individual.[6]

How the Tabligh applied this personalist approach in helping the CIA and Pakistan's ISI, wittingly or otherwise, in recruiting young North African Muslims for the Afghan jihad has been a well-guarded secret, largely ignored by students of the war until now. Two Tunisians, one high in the power structure of Tunisia's authoritarian and secularist President, General Zine al-Abidine ben Ali, the other a senior but independently minded journalist, provided some of the details.

During the long rule (1955–87) of contemporary Tunisia's founder President Habib Bourguiba, he led his country to independence from France. Then, with the one-party, meritocratic rule of his political party, the Neo-Destour, women were enfranchised and given virtual professional and social equality; French-style state education established under the French protectorate which ended in 1955 was separated from religious training, and many other reforms were promoted which in effect made Tunisia a shining light of progress in both the African and Muslim worlds. There was little place in this small republic of less than ten million people for Islamism, let alone Islamist political parties, even though most Tunisians were Muslims, many of whom were shocked by some of Bourguiba's shock reforms, such as encouraging people who work to take daytime nourishment during the Muslim fast month of Ramadan. (Bourguiba in 1961 provocatively drank a glass of orange juice, at high noon on a sizzling summer day, before television cameras and the assembled ulama and other Muslim clerics in Tunisia's Muslim holy city of Kairouan.)

However, in response to the consciousness of religion which had begun to spring up in the Muslim world in and beyond North Africa and the Middle East, Tunisia's leaders began to notice, around 1986, that Islamists had begun to infiltrate both the university and colleges and the secondary school system. By then, 1,156, the majority, of *lycées*, French-style secular high schools of the type also common in Algeria (ruled by France until 1962) and Morocco (independent of its former French and Spanish colonizers since 1956) had their own mosques. Islamist-minded professors, teachers and students as well tried to persuade Tunisian girl students, who liked to wear jeans and high-heeled shoes, to cover themselves with a kind of chador-like garment, and even to assume the veil which most Tunisian urban women had long been encouraged by Bourguiba to discard. "The girls," my informant recalled, "would come home and sometimes with support of brothers, would try to persuade their secular parents to accept that they wear Islamic dress. Most parents, thoroughly secularized themselves, didn't accept. We had a generation gap and even conflicts over this."

By the mid-1980s, as more and more Arab and other non-Afghan Muslim volunteers were showing up in the training camps of the moujahidin in Afghanistan, the Tablighi Jamaat began to operate between North Africa and Europe. Its emissaries began discreetly to approach and proselytize young people, especially in the suburbs of Tunis and other Tunisian cities. They worked the schools, colleges – and the prisons. The Bourguiba regime had begun imprisoning real or suspected militants for the illegal Islamist parties, notably *En-Nahda* (Renaissance) which had gradually emerged during the late 1970s and the early 1980s. Islamists, often under Tabligh control, would appear as volunteer "chaplains." As such, they were given access to prisoners during Friday prayers. Released prisoners were taken in hand by Tabligh emissaries. Many were offered trips to Pakistan for free religious studies in Muslim monasteries, known as *ribats* in North Africa, or in seminaries in the Lahore area.

Usually, during about six weeks' religious studies, the new adepts were not offered military training immediately, or even briefed about the jihad against the Russian and Communist "enemies of God" in Afghanistan. This came at the end of the six-week period. ISI officers, usually in mufti, would then appear and offer opportunities for training in weapons, self-defense and "more advanced" subjects. Some of the Tunisians – there is no statistical information or detail here – accepted; others decided to stay on in Pakistan. Many were already on "wanted" lists at home, with family members or former teachers who had been arrested. Others accepted, and soon found themselves in the training camps, under the watchful eye of their ISI instructors. Perhaps occasionally, if among the thousands of Algerians, Egyptians, Sudanese, Saudis and others, an individual would stand out for his special skills, he would be singled out for attention by American or allied European visitors and travel to the West for special cadre training, though this was rare.

The En-Nahda party, with the Tabligh, organized trips to Europe for some promising young adepts. The typical destinations were France, through the port of Marseilles, or Germany, where active chapters of the Muslim Brotherhood operated among the resident emigres, especially in Aachen, Dusseldorf and other cities of the Ruhr region, and in Munich. The Brotherhood, sharing with the Tabligh a common interest in propagating Sunni Islam and in the anti-Communist crusade in Afghanistan, cooperated in the recruiting and ideological training of the new adepts.

In France, one of the key figures in the Tabligh recruiting network was a religious teacher from the southern Tunisian town of Gafsa, Sheikh Muhammed al-Hamidi. Like millions of other North Africans, he originally emigrated to France to look for work. He seems to have had sponsorship, or some other form of association with the Al-Zitouna Mosque, the leading traditionalist religious training center in Tunis. From Paris, al-Hamidi made his haj, or pilgrimage to Mecca, and then went to Pakistan. There the Tabligh recruited him for their work of spreading the faith in Europe. He returned to France, where this formerly poor North African emigrant was suddenly able to acquire a chateau, surrounded by ample parks and gardens. From the chateau, al-Hamidi operated as chief representative of the Tablighi Jamaat in France. Branches of the movement were soon opened in a number of mosques in the Paris region.

Meanwhile, in North Africa, mass unemployment and poverty in Algeria were generated by the sudden and catastrophic drop in the world price for oil, Algeria's main product. Serious trouble erupted in Tunisia when Bourguiba confronted and broke the challenge of mass labor unrest. All this created a situation propitious for the recruiters of potential moujahidin for Afghanistan. General ben Ali, who had commanded riot troops which broke the unions' power in 1984, was appointed Interior Minister in May 1996. Just prior to this, Bourguiba and his advisors had appeared conciliatory toward the Islamists. They had accorded the amir of the banned En-Nahda party (it was still known then under its French initials MTI, standing for "Islamic Tendency Movement"), Abdelfatah Mourou, a sort of semi-recognition. However, student unrest continued. There were some bomb attacks on government buildings. Ben Ali and the police clamped down ruthlessly, sending police to the university campuses in June 1986. A publishing house favoring Islamist books was closed down, 1,500 people were arrested, and a purge was begun of the civil service and the armed forces.

During roughly the same period, lawyers designated abroad by the Tabligh came to Tunis to plead for Islamists in court cases. Sheikh al-Hamidi was charged with trying to recruit mercenaries for the Afghan moujahidin and was later imprisoned for three years. Sentences of prison and in some cases death were passed on absent fighters in the holy war. Although the North African branches of Tabligh were set up as "cultural centers," both the Algerian and Tunisian governments uncovered their recruiting activities. They suspected them of generating local terrorism as well. In Algeria, terrorists were already striking at people who refused to support either the government or the Islamists. Many of upwards of 3,000 Algerians who went to train in Pakistan and fight in Afghanistan for the CIA were army deserters. When they returned to Algeria, they were already on "wanted" lists for desertion. Later in this book we will examine how the outlaw status they already suffered when they returned affected their leadership roles in the rising violence which was to engulf Algeria in a bloody tide. This happened after the military authorities blocked elections in 1991 which would have almost certainly brought the Islamists legally to power.

Grass-roots recruiting for the jihad in the United States was not handled directly by the CIA, despite its overall management of the program. Various local cover groups, often legitimate Muslim charities and mosque communities in cities such as New York, Detroit, Los Angeles and other large centers of Arab-Americans, shielded the CIA from direct recruiting. Such recruiting, and weapons training in America which followed, if directly run by the men from Langley, Virginia, would have been a flagrant violation of the CIA's charter, which forbids all domestic activity inside the United States. Surroundings for the induction and initial indoctrination of the future holy warriors were modest and humdrum. One was New York's Arab district, in Brooklyn along Atlantic Avenue. Another was a private rifle club in an affluent community of Connecticut. There were similar locations amongst the big Arab immigrant and Arab-American communities in Detroit and Dearborn, Michigan; Los Angeles and the Bay area of San Francisco.

In Brooklyn, the Al-Kifah Afghan Refugee Center, as it was formally called, became known to the group of Arabs, Arab-Americans and Muslim travelers from abroad who met and worked there, as the "Al-Jihad" center. This was because both recruiting and fund-raising for the Afghanistan jihad went on there. The funding came from charitable donations for Afghan refugee relief in the United States. Most probably, there were also hard-to-trace suitcases full of cash and anonymous bearer cheques or bank drafts, from the World Muslim League, the Tablighi Jamaat and other missionary and charitable organizations located in Pakistan. Often they were bankrolled by Saudi Arabian public and (later on, as the jihad wound down) private funds, such as those supplied by the multi-millionaire renegade Saudi construction tycoon, Osama bin Laden, of whom much more later in this book.

Key persons on the ground in the Brooklyn operation were a charismatic former Palestinian guerrilla, a founder of the HAMAS Islamic resistance movement in Gaza and the West Bank, named Abdullah Azzam. His New York agent, Mustafa Chalaby, ran the Brooklyn center. Both eventually met violent deaths. The now legendary Azzam toured the length and breadth of the United States in the early and mid-1980s recruiting for holy war, ostensibly only in Afghanistan. He was probably at least raising funds for HAMAS and its post-1987 revolt of the Palestinians against Israel in the occupied territories as well. Azzam was killed by a still mysterious car bomb in Pakistan in 1987. Suspects included Israel's Mossad intelligence agency; the Soviet KGB or its Afghan adjunct, the Communist Afghan

KHAD; the ISI or even the CIA itself, for whom Azzam by now had become a major embarrassment. With the start of the Soviet withdrawal from Afghanistan, his management of recruiting and training now had little or nothing more to do with the Soviets, and everything to do with guerrilla and terrorist ventures abroad.

Mustafa Chalaby was murdered in New York in 1991, in an unsolved case which probably involved disputes among the men of the Al-Kifah Center over use of funds. Sheikh Omar Abdel Rahman, the blind Egyptian prayer leader who recruited for the CIA, sent his sons to fight in Afghanistan, and with other suspects was convicted in the successful World Trade Center bombing of February 1993 and the subsequent, aborted conspiracy in June 1993 to bomb UN headquarters, traffic tunnels, bridges, FBI headquarters and government offices, as well as to assassinate pro-Israel officials and legislators. All frequented the office in Atlantic Avenue. Often they prayed in nearby mosques.

An investigation directed and aired on ABC News' Day One magazine program on July 12, 1993, showed details of Abdullah Azzam's recruiting activities, during which he visited no fewer than 26 American states. Some of the Brooklyn jihad workers, including El Sayyad Nossair, the accused murderer (who was finally not convicted of the murder, but only on an illegal weapons charge) of extremist Jewish Defense League leader, Rabbi Meier Kahane, trained as gunmen at the shooting range at the High Rock gun club in Naugutuck, Connecticut, just west of the highway north from Bridgeport to Waterbury in the same state. New York court documents show that recruits for Afghanistan were earlier trained in rifle shooting there. Nossair's course on the AK-47 assault rifle, the standard, originally Soviet weapon used by the moujahidin, was held as late as the summer of 1989. The Afghan war was nearly over by then, but as Pakistan's former Prime Minister Benazir Bhutto remarked on the same TV program, the dispersal of the fighters had already begun toward their new target countries: "They are all over the world," she said.[7]

Official and formal training in the United States had begun under the Carter administration in 1980. Even earlier, preparations had begun for the failed mission to rescue the American embassy hostages, a mission which collapsed when finally launched in April 1980. Chosen Green Beret officers, many of them seasoned veterans of Vietnam, took draconian secrecy oaths and then began the secret training assignments for the Afghanistan war. Many of them were already familiar with one of their most important training sites, Fort Bragg, North Carolina. This is the well-publicized base of the US Army's 82nd Airborne Division. It is also the much less-publicized site of the John F. Kennedy Special Warfare Center, a school of guerrilla and counter-guerrilla warfare which the author, as a newspaper correspondent covering the Pentagon, visited shortly before the Iranian hostage rescue mission in the spring of 1980. Colonel Charles ("Chargin' Charlie") Beckwith would lead the Iran mission on the ground and take the decision, backed by President Carter, to abort when everything went catastrophically wrong. Beckwith decided during the pre-mission training, when the Afghan adventure was still being organized, to move his elite Delta Force away from Fort Bragg to a smaller and more secure area. That area, which Beckwith called "Camp Smokey," was actually the CIA's Camp Peary. It would soon play a central role in training for the new holy war in South Asia.

Camp Peary, nicknamed "The Farm" in the American spy world, was and probably still is the CIA's main place of training for spies, infiltrators and covert operators of all sorts. Its very existence was classified secret until various visitors discovered it and began to write about it at the beginning of the 1990s. The Farm is a parcel of land about 25 square miles in area, just northeast of Williamsburg, Virginia, running between US Route 64 and the James River. Some of the future Afghan warrior-trainers, chiefly Pakistanis sent by the ISI, were probably able to see Beckwith and his men train on a model of the occupied American embassy compound in Tehran, rehearsing all their hypothetical moves once they got over the wall. Camp Peary was also where members of the CIA Career Training Program, many of them officers seeking advancement and new assignments in covert action in Afghanistan and elsewhere, studied and worked out. Subjects, which were imparted to the trainees for the Afghan war, included use and detection of explosives; surveillance and counter-surveillance; how to write reports according to CIA "Company" standards; how to shoot various weapons, and the running of counter-terrorism, counter-narcotics and paramilitary operations. There were also classroom courses in the all-important subject of recruiting new agents, couriers and assorted helpers. Paramilitary training also went on at another CIA-used Army Special Forces site, Harvey Point, North Carolina.[8]

Another Virginia site, used in the Afghan training program, and already known to Green Beret veterans of the secret and not-so-secret wars of the 1960s and 1970s in Indo-China, was Fort A.P. Hill, off the Washington–Richmond interstate highway. Like Fort Lee, Virginia, it had an authorized area for parachute jumping. There, pilots and other personnel were supposed to practice CARP (Computerized Airborne Point Release Flying). This was a skill which misfired in the operation on the Caribbean island of Grenada in 1983.[9] However, it was apparently used for supply drops to the Afghan fighters, and very effectively as well in the 1991 Desert Storm operation to free Kuwait from President Saddam Hussein's occupying Iraqis.

At Fort A.P. Hill and also at Camp Pickett, Virginia, Green Berets and US Navy SEALS instructed key Pakistani officers and, occasionally, visiting senior moujahidin (of Afghan or Pakistani origin, but apparently not Arab or other foreign volunteers), in infiltration techniques and ways of extracting friendly wounded, enemy prisoners or captured weapons from behind enemy lines.[10] Time and time again, these same techniques reappear among the Islamist insurgents in Upper Egypt and Algeria, since the "Afghani" Arab veterans began returning there in the late 1980s and early 1990s.

It seems to have been more difficult for American personnel to pass on some of the skills taught at Camps Peary or Pickett, or at Fort A.P. Hill to Egypt's Special Forces. Some of the Egyptian trainees were destined, in turn, to train Egyptian volunteers departing for the Afghan jihad. Others would be trained to pursue and kill them, when they returned to Egypt and took up arms against the Mubarak governments. US Navy SEAL veteran Richard Marcinko says he was one of a group of four SEAL teams spending six months in Egypt, trying to instruct Egyptian Army Rangers. They were, says Marcinko, only "moderately successful. No matter how hard we tried, it was almost impossible to teach the Egyptians about specialized operations ... We found their marksmanship unsatisfactory, their physical condition second rate, and their motivation non-existent." The reason, Marcinko claimed, was Egypt's military caste system which produced NCOs and officers who were softer, rather than harder, than their rank-and-file troops.[11]

The deadly skills which trainers of the Afghan holy warriors passed on numbered over 60. They included the use of sophisticated fuses, timers and explosives; automatic weapons with armor-piercing ammunition, remote-control devices for triggering mines and bombs (used later in the volunteers' home countries, and against the Israelis in occupied Arab territory such as southern Lebanon). The more successful aspiring guerrillas were inculcated with the Cold War principle that "brainpower replaces firepower" as the foremost fighting implement. They were also taught the tenet of Sun Tzu, the classical Chinese theoretician of the art of war: "to subdue the enemy without fighting is the acme of skill." In other words, use deception, ruse and evasion as much as possible to defeat him, rather than conventional, frontal-style warfare. Both the moujahidin and their mentors, Western and Pakistani, appeared to forget this in the latter stages of the war, when they adopted conventional warfare tactics. Although the Soviets were by then already retreating, senior moujahidin commanders were pushed by the Americans and Pakistanis to lay costly and often futile siege to fixed, fortified positions like those at Herat, which the Russian and Afghan Communist forces defended successfully, although they would have eventually yielded them without a fight when the general Russian withdrawal began.

Despite training given to the holy warriors in such techniques as how to stab an enemy sentry from behind or strangle him with a garotte, murder and assassination of senior enemy leaders, at least, were forbidden to the CIA by law. On December 4, 1981, President Reagan signed Executive Order 12333. This confirmed and made even more specific a prohibition Congress had insisted upon passing, following the CIA scandals of the 1970s, involving such bizarre measures as trying to assassinate Cuba's Fidel Castro with poison or exploding cigars. "No person," said Reagan's 1981 order, "employed by or acting on behalf of the US government shall engage in, or conspire to engage in, assassination."[12] On the face of it, this contradicted the curricula used by the Special Forces instructors. They taught their pupils such skills as strangulation, murderous karate chops and how to use a sniper's rifle with telescopic sights to eliminate a designated enemy officer.

One subject learned from the foreign instructors was "strategic" sabotage. Simple sabotage, in training manual jargon, "personalized, surreptitious interdiction by individuals and small groups to damage or destroy installations, products or supplies" was contrasted in training with "indirect" sabotage. The latter, in Afghan terms, would involve destroying crops belonging to a tribe or village committed to the Soviets, or otherwise reducing or degrading production controlled by the enemy state. This meant Najibullah's Communist regime in Kabul. This also became a favorite export of the holy warriors, who for example, tried to apply it to destroy industrial enterprises, espcially connected with oil and natural gas, benefitting the military regime or foreign investors in Algeria in the 1990s, without, as we will see later, notable success.

As American military analyst John Collins noted in 1987, it takes little expertise to pour epoxy on movable machinery or sugar into gas tanks. Quite another matter is "strategic" sabotage. This requires activists and organizers who can mobilize people and coordinate their actions in demonstrations, strikes, riots, boycotts, production delays and in other ways. In these activities, neither the holy warriors in Afghanistan nor the international terrorists and guerrillas, mostly fighting their own Third World governments after the Afghan war, have shown great success. A notable exception, of course, was the bombing by Arab "Afghani" veterans of the World Trade Center in New York City in February 1993. This crippled commercial activity in one of America's busiest business centers for days, as well as killing seven and injuring over 1,000 people. This was a pale prelude to the September 11, 2001 attacks which toppled the twin towers and ravaged surrounding buildings in the New York financial district and destroyed one portion of the Pentagon in Washington, killing a total of about 3,000 people.

One craft acquired in the Afghans' training where the alumni have shown real skill was in demolition and arson. This required detailed knowledge about explosives and incendiary devices (what kind, how much, where placed, how triggered). It was originally acquired from American instructors or others, like officers of Pakistan's ISI, who had benefitted from American instruction.

Since the backlash of the Afghan war in the spread of terrorism and the drug trade around the world began in the early 1990s, it has become fashionable among European commentators to put the burden of blame on the CIA and the various US administrations involved. In fact, and especially in the training process, there was allied involvement as well. However, it was really only Prime Minister Margaret Thatcher's British government which supported the jihad with full enthusiasm, however limited in practical and material terms. At the start of the Afghan war in the early 1980s, those two close cousins, Europe's peace and nuclear disarmament movements, were gathering strength in the media and in public forums. Mrs. Thatcher, an ebulliently middle-class, Oxford-educated grocer's daughter, had become prime minister in the spring of 1979, when the poisonous Afghan brew was beginning actively to bubble.

Turning her eyes at first westward rather than eastward (where she would first identify Mikhail Gorbachev publicly as a Soviet leader "you can do business with"), she had already anticipated the policies of Ronald Reagan in the United States. On the domestic British scene, she had advocated fiscal conservatism; the scaling down of taxes which "penalized success," and a cut in public spending on everything – except for the British military and the highly secretive British intelligence services. Mrs. Thatcher doggedly persisted in these policies. She saw her political fortunes decline correspondingly, until the Argentine military junta, ten thousand miles away, suddenly, in March 1982, hijacked the Falkland Islands. This act, regarded in Britain as virtual international piracy, presented her and her new friends, President Ronald Reagan and his CIA director, William Casey, with an ideal opportunity to inject the adrenalin of patriotism, tinged with some downright jingoism, into the tired veins of Britannia and, at the same time, rejuvenate the old but somewhat neglected "special relationship" with the United States.

From the beginning of the Afghan jihad, senior Britons and Americans in government consulted about it. However, before the British could officially step in and make their contribution to the training effort, both sides realized that before there could be real harmony over the proxy war in South Asia, however much Mr. Reagan and Mrs. Thatcher might wish for such harmony, the mess over US–British relations in Iran had to be cleaned up. In the spring of 1980, British firms were still selling arms to the Ayatollah Khomeiny's stridently revolutionary new regime. Howard Bane, who according to British writer on intelligence matters Stephen Dorrell, was the CIA officer coordinating intelligence on the failed American Iranian hostage rescue mission in April 1980, was exceedingly upset over these arms sales. When six staff members of the US Embassy in Tehran managed to escape being taken hostage with the others in November 1979 and asked for sanctuary in the British Embassy, they had been turned away. It was left to the Canadians, in their embassy, to save these Americans and send them safely homeward. The British Foreign Office also withdrew MI-6's veteran station chief from Tehran. There was no joy in Langley over this either.

The Falklands War re-knit these frazzled relations, paving the way for British help in training the Afghan holy warriors. In Argentina, the CIA had good human sources close to the ruling junta of generals, which had ordered the Falklands attack. In nearby Chile, the US National Security Agency (NSA), the worldwide American electronic spy agency based at Fort Meade, Maryland, had listening posts. On the orders of Casey, these and American satellites passed information on Argentine movements to Whitehall, enabling the British to read Argentine codes and ciphers. They also provided other intelligence, such as tasking American SR-71 Blackbird high-altitude spy planes to watch the Argentine war effort, although this was often ineffective because of nearly constant cloud cover over the South Atlantic.

More than this, the saga of the Stinger, one of the deadliest and most sought-after anti-aircraft missiles ever developed, as the Russians would soon learn to their grief in Afghanistan, began during the Falklands War. By night, a small group of American officials who, like William Casey, believed in all-out help to Britain, illegally (according to US law) delivered several of the Stingers to waiting British diplomats in a Washington, DC, parking lot. This violated a standing US government prohibition on transfer of hi-tech weapons to other countries, even friendly or allied ones.[13] Soon, the Stingers were shooting down Argentine fighter-bombers and saving the lives of British naval and ground personnel in the expeditionary force which Mrs. Thatcher sent to recapture the islands.

In return for this help, Casey sought and obtained British support for training and even some operations in the Afghan campaign. Because of the secretive nature of the British political establishment and the practice of sending warning "D notices" to editors or media executives contemplating a breach of secrecy, virtually requiring self-censorship, very little about this British effort ever leaked out during the 1980s. Much of it was coordinated by MI-6 men in Islamabad, notably Anthony Hawkes, an effective operative who served as that agency's station chief in Islamabad from 1984 to 1988. Hawkes liaised with the Americans and with Pakistan's ISI, the host service.

Apart from the the the determination of Prime Minister Thatcher, the "Iron Lady," to help the Americans in their anti-Communist crusade, the power center for British participation in the Afghan operation was at the heart of the highly secretive British intelligence establishment, and among veterans of Britain's elite Special Air Services (SAS), with a record of hard-hitting and usually effective covert action in places like Ireland, Oman and Malaysia. Of key importance was the Joint Intelligence Committee (JIC), part of the Cabinet Office.

The British public was largely ignorant or indifferent to Mrs. Thatcher's decision to follow the American lead in Afghanistan. One non-conformist in the House of Commons did speak out. Former Tory MP, the late Enoch Powell, scathingly referred to Mrs. Thatcher's "slavish" willingness to follow the lead of President Ronald Reagan, in Afghanistan and elsewhere. "How long," bellowed Powell, "will the UK continue to be dragged at the coattail of the disastrous misconceptions of American policy?"[14]

By the early 1970s, London had become a center of the arms trade as well as of the recruiting of already trained "soldiers of fortune" to serve both as trainers and in operational roles. Many of these had served in MI-6 or the SAS, or in irregular forces of other European states. There was a covert group of such personnel, available for hire, and known in London as "the Circuit" or sometimes simply as "the lads." There was a hierarchy of private security firms, as well as of individuals. At the bottom were lesser-known "lads" and smaller firms. These tended to do "dirty work" which the larger ones avoided. MI-5, the British domestic counter-intelligence service, and Scotland Yard's Special Branch kept close tabs on them, but rarely if ever interfered with their lives or activities. Important operations abroad, like the Afghan jihad, were cleared with the Foreign Office.

At the top of the private special operations pyramid were the especially well-connected companies. Officers and members usually had friends and relatives, if not at No. 10 Downing Street, then in the Foreign Office, the Ministry of Defence, or the security and intelligence services, as well as in London's City, the British equivalent of Wall Street; or in the leadership of the Conservative Party. This "old boy" network, of which my late friend Billy Maclean, a veteran of many covert campaigns in Oman, Yemen, the Gulf and elsewhere, was a member, functioned on a person-to-person basis, far more than most of the American Green Beret, SEAL or CIA veterans did. They used to do deals over lunch in London clubs, or at private weekend parties in English or Scottish country houses, as in the stories of John Le Carré. The most private firm of The Circuit had been Watchguard, formed by the bold and innovative World War II guerrilla warrior David Stirling, but no longer in business by the time of the Afghanistan war.

In 1973 the firm called Control Risks was formed as a subsidiary of Hogg Robinson, an important City of London insurance broker. Its initial purpose, according to members, was to advise Lloyds insurance syndicates on risks and premiums in kidnap insurance. This was a season of history when hostage-taking for financial and sometimes for political gain was coming into fashion in Latin America, Asia and the Middle East. By 1994, Control Risks had expanded to offer advice and help in 83 countries, with major offices in London, Washington and Melbourne. During the later stages of the Afghan jihad and afterward, it has been operating a computer-based information service and a data bank on international terrorism, a large part of which is traceable to the veterans of the Afghan holy war and the unholy wars which have followed it.

One outgrowth of Control Risks was the firm of KMS, now defunct, but according to private information from veterans, active in training small numbers of Afghan commando units. The initials KMS stood for "Keenie-Meenie Services." The name was a kind of insiders' joke for mercenaries who had served on the British side in the Mau Mau war in the 1950s in colonial Kenya. It was supposed to be derived from a Swahili word signifying something done covertly, or "slipping silently through the grass, like a serpent." KMS was formed in 1974; later revamped and named Saracen. Members boasted that it had trained and equipped "full-sized regiments" of mercenaries; though draconian secrecy oaths like those imposed on American Special Forces trainers prevented, under extremely severe penalties, its members from discussing its role in the Afghan jihad.

In 1977, KMS came under the control of former SAS Major David Walker and insurance broker Colonel Jim Johnson. Its true ownership in the offshore tax haven of Jersey, in the Channel Islands, was camouflaged, until exposed during the American Iran-Contra scandals in 1987. Walker, a graduate of Britain's elite Sandhurst military academy and Cambridge University, was a former Tory party councillor in Surrey, outside London. Jim Johnson, a former aide-de-camp to the Queen, reportedly helped David Stirling to organize secret British aid to the Yemeni royalists in the 1960s. Operations in Yemen were carried out by Billy MacLean, already a veteran of Allied covert operations inside Communist Albania, and others. Both Walker and Stirling were said to be millionaires. Both had direct access to Mrs. Thatcher in No. 10 Downing Street.

It was indeed KMS, along with individual SAS veterans, to which the main British role in training holy warrior cadre for the Afghan jihad seems to have fallen. KMS had a subsidiary called Saladin Security. This timed in well with the Saudi and Arab Gulf support for the holy war. Saladin, similar to that which the Vinell

Corporation of the United States was doing in training Saudi security forces, had gotten contracts to provide VIP-type bodyguard protection for Middle Eastern kings and emirs. In 1970, the British Secret Intelligence Service (SIS or MI-6) had helped to organize a coup to overthrow the ageing and avaricious Sultan Taymur of Oman by his son Qabus, still the ruler in 2002 of a stable and prosperous, British-oriented Oman. US Special Forces and the CIA had already helped the British "old boys" network to raise a mercenary army for Sultan Qabus to resist the Communist-backed Yemeni guerrillas of the Popular Front for the Liberation of the Occupied Arab Gulf (PFLOAG) in the 1970s. The Shah of Iran also sent forces, in a Safari-Club-like maneuver, to help in the final defeat of the guerrillas.

After the Shah's downfall in February 1979, President Sadat of Egypt, as part of his total cooperation with American efforts from North Africa to Afghanistan, replaced the withdrawn Iranian troops with some Egyptian units. In agreement with Mrs. Thatcher's government, Sultan Qabus of Oman also turned over to the United States the use of the big Royal Air Force base on Masirah Island, off the southeast tip of Arabia and later the air bases at Thamrit and Sib in Oman, as well as the Omani naval harbors at Matrah and Salalah. By the mid-1980s, supply flights on their way to Pakistan for the Afghan moujahidin were sometimes staged or refueled at these Omani bases.[15]

Earlier, a few SAS veterans had begun to train the moujahidin and Pakistan Special Forces. The chosen groups tended to be pro-royalist, like those of guerrilla leader Hadji Abdul Haq, who eventually traveled to the West on sponsored trips for audiences with both Prime Minister Thatcher and President Reagan. One of the senior Afghan trainers among the royalist holy warriors was Brigadier General Rahmatullah Safi, probably the most senior officer of the former royal Afghan army training for the jihad. He commanded training for the National Islamic Front of Afghanistan (NIFA) – one of the lower-profile groups among the seven major organizations. He claimed that 700 former Afghan army officers were included in NIFA ranks, and that he trained 8,000 men in the group's camps, apparently without control by the ISI.

General Safi, in his late sixties or early seventies during the war, had been schooled in the Soviet Union, Britain (probably by KMS or a similar organization) and in the United States. While serving in the royal Afghan army under King Zahir Shah, he founded an elite Afghan commando force of 1,600 men. He commanded it until the King's cousin, Prime Minister Muhammad Daoud, overthrew him and set Afghanistan on the slippery slope toward establishment of the 1978 Communist government and the 1979 Soviet invasion. He returned from what he described as a "comfortable life" in England to operate, probably in close liaison with British trainers.[16]

These trainers, including KMS personnel, chose to step out of the international limelight created by the publicising of the Iran-Contra scandal in the United States, disclosing that David Walker had directed paramilitary operations in Nicaragua on behalf of the anti-Communist Contras by KMS staffers. Walker and Johnson decided to leave day-to-day control of KMS and all its activities, including the training of Afghan fighters, to Lieutenant Colonel Keith Farnes and former SAS Major Brian Baty, both former officers of SAS' 22nd Regiment, called 22 SAS. A book called *Ghost Force* written by SAS veteran Ken Connor describes how selected Afghan fighters were smuggled into Britain disguised as tourists and trained in three-week cycles at secret camps in Scotland.

Training was facilitated by the blanket intelligence coverage of the South Asian war theater by the two senior electronic espionage organizations: America's National Security Agency (NSA), at Fort Meade, Maryland and Britain's General Communications Headquarters (GCHQ) at Cheltenham, England. Interception of Soviet and Afghan Communist communications, both tactical and strategic, gave the Allied planning staffs enough information to plan their training programs. For example, the monitoring of Soviet airforce aircraft and army helicopter communications with their home bases helped clarify which anti-aircraft systems – Oerlikon AA guns purchased by the CIA from Switzerland; SA-7 or similar missiles from captured Soviet stocks or Chinese supplies; ultimately the successful Stinger missile from 1986 onward – were working. Training programs were adjusted accordingly.

British intelligence input, and that of GCHQ in particular, was enhanced during the 1978–83 period, when British participation in the jihad was initiated and improved by Prime Minister Margaret Thatcher. This was partly due to the personal connection of GCHQ's director, a scholarly graduate of St. Edmund Hall, Oxford and London University's School of Oriental and African Studies named Brian Tovey (later knighted to become Sir Brian Tovey). The donnish Mr. Tovey shared, among other things, an interest in the Italian Renaissance with his close French friend and counterpart, Alexandre de Marenches. At the start of the Afghan war de Marenches headed the SDECE, the French external intelligence service, later re-christened the DGSE. They were firm friends. De Marenches would send Tovey copies of intercepts captured by the small (1,200 staffers as compared with GCHQ's approximately 10,000) French Groupe de Communications Radioelectriques (GCR). These intercepts showed significant variations in Soviet military air traffic to Afghanistan, enabling British intelligence to supplement its own intelligence collection resources and anticipate new Soviet tactics. The French intercepts and those of GCHQ and the NSA, from satellites in space and listening posts in Pakistan, China and Turkey guided the CIA, US Special Forces and the British trainers in what new Soviet moves the holy warriors must be trained to counter. In July 1985, for example, Soviet forces in Afghanistan received a new commander, General Mikhail Mitrofanovich Zaitsev. As Soviet commander in East Germany, Zaitsev was known to have thoroughly revamped training of the Soviet troops there. He put greater stress on individual initiative, encouraging junior officers to make decisions on their own. Jihad trainers accordingly modified their curricula to anticipate similar changes in the Soviet tactics in Afghanistan. Allied signal intelligence also learned that Zaitsev was increasing deployments of Soviet Special

Forces, the SPETSNAZ troops, in Afghanistan, probably to get some of the action away from their competitors in the GRU, the Soviet military intelligence service.[17]

The British training and operational efforts attracted enemy attention. In October 1983, Kabul Radio reported that a "British spy," Stuart Bodman, had been killed in Afghanistan on July 1 of that year. Other Communist reports added that he had been carrying equipment to transmit information to a US spy satellite and that he had been killed in a clash with guerrillas while trying to smuggle precious lapis lazuli stones into Pakistan.

The British Foreign Office denied all knowledge. On October 5, Communist reports monitored in Islamabad said six British nationals had been apprehended while "spying and smuggling." The Communist Afghan Foreign Ministry in Kabul named Bodman, Roderick Macginnis and Stephen Elwick, and claimed the other three were called "Tim, Chris and Phil." Soviet and East bloc journalists received a video purporting to show Bodman's body, his British passport and his driving license. It said the six Britons had entered Soviet-occupied Afghanistan in April 1983 to spy on a Soviet communications center and other targets. "Tim" was described as a British explosives expert sent to train the moujahidin to manufacture rockets and bombs, and to show how best to use them against Soviet and government forces. Nothing was said about the fate of the other five Britons.

The British authorities were mute on the subject. Two weeks later, the *Sunday Times* of London reported it had located the alleged dead spy, Stuart Bodman – playing darts in a pub near Gatwick airport, south of London. He turned out to be a 30-year-old warehouse worker who said he had never traveled further abroad than Jersey. "I don't know how they got my name ... the closest I've come to spies was when I caddied for Sean Connery" at a nearby golf club. He had once held a one-year passport, in 1972, but had burned it and had never held a driver's license. A check of births registries showed that the only 30-year-old Stuart Bodman in the UK was the one discovered playing darts.

Was the "Stuart Bodman" reported by the Afghan Communists, then, a "man who never was?"

The London *Observer* claimed to know on October 9, 1983, that "Bodman" had worked for the Americans, with the knowledge of MI-6. It said he was part of a five-man team, including former SAS men, sent to Afghanistan to collect Soviet weapons. The arms were then sent to military testing sites in the United States, Britain and France. The question remained: what was "Stuart Bodman's" real name? Someone had borrowed the name: the British passport office in London had indeed issued a ten-year passport to a man calling himself Stuart Bodman, obviously presenting phoney ID papers, and giving his age as 30. The mystery remained. However, this British operation left behind a well-publicized example for future international terrorists to follow. Many of the Afghan jihad veterans did follow it.[18]

Less unfortunate than the British team apparently was a three-man group of Americans, at least two of whom were trainers, led by Michael ("Mad Mike")

Williams, a veteran of World War II in Italy who was one of the first officers assigned to the 10ᵗʰ US Special Forces unit of the Army activated in 1952, and which then fought in Korea. Williams acquired experience in training and commanding foreign mercenaries and volunteers as commander in Korea of the 7ᵗʰ Battalion, 3ʳᵈ Partisan Infantry Regiment. This was composed of about 1,500 North Korean and Chinese defectors. Later, he served with the 77ᵗʰ Special Forces group in the United States and the 101ˢᵗ Airborne Division. Much of his time between 1964 and 1976 was spent as a mercenary in Africa, commanding the forces of another "Mad Mike," Mike Hoare operating out of Katanga. In 1976 he accepted a Captain's commission in the white Rhodesian army, was promoted to major and finally to commanding officer of One Squadron, Grey's Scouts, the mounted infantry which fought vainly to hold back the clock of African liberation and keep Rhodesia's last white ruler, Ian Smith, in power.

Retired US Army Colonel Robert K. Brown, an editor of the American old soldiers' favorite magazine, *Soldier of Fortune*, persuaded Mike Williams, Hunter Penn (another 101ˢᵗ Airborne veteran and a roper in rodeos in the American West), and Paul Fanshaw, who had survived 13 years in the French Foreign Legion, to form a private scouting party into Soviet-held territory. Hunter Penn had already served for three months with the holy warriors in the 18,000-foot Pamir mountains. He had a narrow escape there from the knife-wielding husband of an unveiled Afghan woman whom he had tried to photograph washing clothes in a mountain stream. The foursome flew to Quetta, capital of Pakistan's Baluchistan province. There they linked up with the fighting group of General Ramatullah Safi, whom we have already met. They crossed into hostile territory for several weeks of encounters with the Communists, living rough with Safi's fighters. All survived to tell the tale. All four improved their training skills in the process.[19]

France's involvement in actual training for the jihad (aside from the strong advice and moral support given to both the Reagan and Thatcher establishments by Alexandre de Marenches, the colorful chief of French intelligence) was very limited. This token effort during the administration of French President Valery Giscard d'Estaing may have been partly due to dissension inside the SDECE, the main French external intelligence service. One of Alexandre de Marenches's immediate aides had supported an unsuccessful coup attempt in 1980 against Colonel Muammar al-Qaddafi, the then hyperactive leader of Libya. Admiral Stansfield Turner's CIA apparently did not approve. It was still President Jimmy Carter's watch, not yet that of Ronald Reagan who would later call Qaddafi a "flake" and in April 1985 would order a large air raid against Libya by US Air Force and Navy planes. SDECE had tried in July 1977, this time with Egyptian Vice-President Husni Mubarak, who then ran Egyptian intelligence for President Sadat. Several days of air and ground attacks by Egyptian forces in eastern Libya failed to dislodge Qaddafi and probably strengthened him. This was one of the last, and least successful, efforts by members of the "Safari Club" of France, Sadat's Egypt, Saudi Arabia, the Shah's Iran and King Hassan's Morocco, to get rid of perceived adversaries of the West and its friends, in the period immediately before the Afghan war.[20]

After Ronald Reagan's friend William Casey had taken over the CIA in 1981 and de Marenches had yielded the helm of French intelligence to Pierre Marion, the choice of Giscard d'Estaing's successor President François Mitterand, there was a small flurry of French input to the jihad. French General Jeannou Lacaze, the dean of French Special Forces, visited Peshawar and met with the chiefs of Pakistan's ISI. France then committed some logistical support; probably fuel, communications equipment and ammunition.[21]

Some Frenchmen did offer the moujahidin medical training, and considerable medical care in the field. International medical groups, *Médicins Sans Frontières, Médecins du Monde* and *Aide Médicale Internationale*, with preponderantly French men and women doctors and paramedics, volunteered. Several trained Afghan medical personnel. One of these was Dr. Gilles Cavion, a physician from Metz, France. Geoffrey Moorhouse, a British writer and traveler in South Asia, encountered Cavion. The French doctor was in the company of Ahmed Shah Massoud, the moujahidin leader who distinguished himself as a brave fighter against the Russians. After the war he remained a bitter rival and adversary of Gulbuddin Hekmatyar. Massoud, contrary to Hekmatyar, was one of the very few holy warriors who understood and often warned that the anti-Communist zealots of the war period would turn into anti-Western zealots and terrorists after it ended.[22]

Discussion of the input of outsiders to training and operations in Afghanistan would be incomplete without mention of Iran and the State of Israel. Iran's major role in training and in supply is a matter of historical record. As for Israel, the evidence is much sketchier. At least half a dozen knowledgeable individuals insisted to the author, without citing proof, that Israel was indeed involved in both training and supply; in the latter case by imitating President Sadat's policy of furnishing captured and sometimes obsolescent Soviet weapons, taken from Palestinians or Arab armies. There is a record of similar Israeli supplies to Central American Rightist guerrillas.[23]

Whether or not units of Israel's elite special forces trained the Muslim warriors, who would soon turn their guns against Israel in Muslim organizations like HAMAS, is a well-guarded Israeli secret. Several Americans and Britons who took part in the training program have assured the author that Israelis did indeed take part, though no one will own to having actually seen, or spoken with, Israeli instructors or intelligence operatives in Afghanistan or Pakistan. What is certain is that of all the members of the anti-Soviet coalition, the Israelis have been the most successful in concealing the details and even the broad traces of a training role; much more than the Americans and British, despite the draconian secrecy oaths imposed on them by the Pentagon, Langley and Whitehall.

Of greater interest than what was possibly only a token Israeli role – which no Israeli government official would now want to acknowledge, now that Islamists around the world have turned so strongly against the Jewish state and against the

US-initiated Middle East peace negotiations – is the Iranian input to the Afghan jihad. Some tribal-type Iranian assistance, especially to Shi'ite groups such as the Hazaras, began even before the Khomeiny revolution in early spring of 1979. After the Iranian revolution, aid became official policy.

When I last visited the Shah's Iran as a newspaper correspondent in the spring of 1978, there was, as we saw earlier, already an official policy of opposing the Communists in Afghanistan. Ardeshir Zahedi, the Shah's son-in-law, Foreign Minister, and last Iranian ambassador of the Shah's regime to the United States, made this clear in several personal interviews.

The first big training center built by Khomeiny's revolutionaries after they took power in early 1979 was Manzarieh Park, on the southern slopes of Mount Towchal, dominating part of the affluent north Tehran suburbs. It had often been used in the Shah's time for Boy Scout jamborees. A carved stone statue of Lord Baden-Powell, founder of the Scout movement, stood beside the gate. If the Shah had not been overthrown, part of this vast area – 600 square miles in all – well-forested with cedar, oak and yew trees, would have become the Empress Farah University for Girls in 1981. Instead, by then it had been converted into the first and largest training center in Iran for the "export" of the Iranian Shi'ite Muslim revolution, including to Afghanistan.

In autumn 1980, Manzarieh was opened officially as a recreation center for wounded *pasdaran* or Revolutionary Guards. By February 1981, it was already an elite guerrilla and terrorist training center, with what Iranian author Amir Taheri describes as "175 hand-picked students, including nine Afghans and fourteen citizens of various Arab countries." The first camp commander was Sheikh Abbas Golru, of mixed Iraq-Iranian descent. He had formerly belonged to and was trained in the *Al-Saiqa* (Lightning) Palestinian guerrilla group, trained and led by the Syrian military. One student described courses to Taheri as "a mixture of theology and target practice," with little proficiency resulting in either.

The next camp commander was Nasser Kolhaduz, an alumnus of Palestinian guerrilla training in Lebanon. The Ayatollah Khomeiny, who disliked and mistrusted PLO Chairman Yassir Arafat and his entourage, would admit no Palestinians to training in Iran. He considered them a security threat. There were a few Syrian and North Korean guest instructors. Trainees were 15- to 18-year-old men; at first only those who had already served with either the Revolutionary Guards or the *baseej* units which later trained and sent Iranian teenagers to their deaths in suicidal "wave attacks" against the Iraqi army in the 1980–88 Iran–Iraq war.

The trainees, Afghans and others, included sons of well-off Iranian families. Some were studying in the United States or Europe at the time of the 1979 Iranian revolution. They had returned to Iran as volunteers. The Shi'ite mullahs at the camp often invited those who had spent time in the US to tell the rest about "the filth under which the Great Satan, America, is sinking" and how resurgent Islam would soon prove an irresistible force against it. At graduation on July 30, 1981, the Ayatollah Mahalati, who was the senior cleric responsible for the training and top Revolutionary Guard Commanders, sent over 100 "Blessed Ones" off to missions in Lebanon. Some went to fight secular or tribal adversaries in Iranian Kurdistan or Afghanistan's Baluchistan, now the main corridor of support for the Shi'ite Hazarat guerrillas fighting the Soviets.

Before Mahalati's unexplained death in 1985 and his succession as "coordinator for exporting the revolution" by Hojattolisam Mehdi Hashemi, a dedicated hardliner related to Khomeiny, at least fifteen other training camps had been established in Iran. It appears that Afghan volunteers were trained at all or most of them. In 1986 they included, besides Manzarieh, Saleh-Abad, north of the holy city of Qom. Others were at Parandak, about 20 miles west of Tehran, and Beheshtieh, about 12 miles northwest of the capital. Women guerrillas and terrorists, including those from Muslim countries, but also Irish, American and Lebanese women married to Iranians, were said to have trained there. (There were probably no Afghan women. Very few of these, Shi'a or Sunni, ever took part in the Afghan jihad.)

Eram Park, just outside Qom, was a former resort hotel converted to training Arabs and South Asian militants, including Afghans, Kashmiris and others. In the Gorgon Plain, about 400 miles east of Tehran, the Revolutionary Guards, with a nominal regular Iranian army presence, trained other recruits. French intelligence identified a camp at Vakilabad, 600 miles east of Tehran. This was used until 1984 to house Iraqi prisoners of war and later reportedly to train specialists in aircraft hijacking.

At such centers recruits including the Afghans were given fairly rigorous weapons, guerrilla and terrorist training. According to Colonel Taqi Barmaki, an Iranian Special Forces instructor at Saleh-Abad camp before 1985, cadets were told they would become "the spearhead of the Islamic conquest of the world."[24] This was the kind of dogma the Pakistani and Afghan trainers would soon be feeding the recruits for jihad in Afghanistan and abroad in their training camps.

Iranian aid to selected Shi'ite clients in the Afghan jihad was a matter of principle for the Ayatollah Khomeiny's men. Sadegh Ghotbzadeh, Khomeiny's Foreign Minister, was prompt to denounce the Soviet invasion. He repeated his critique of the Soviets in January 1980 and pledged all possible aid to the Afghan resistance movement. Ghotbzadeh was able personally to empathize with the training effort which would soon begin in Manzarieh and later in the other camps. He himself had undergone guerrilla training with the Revolutionary Guards and the Palestinians in the camps in Lebanon.

Iran's aid to the Afghans, mainly training, was selective. Its main interest was in the roughly 15 percent of the Afghan population who are Shi'as and who live in the central mountain fastnesses of Hazarajat, home of the Hazaras, a mainly peasant people who claim descent from the thirteenth century AD Mongols of Genghis Khan. There are also substantial Shi'ite Hazara communities in Kabul, the town of Ghazni and a few in Quetta and the Iranian part of Baluchistan. A second group, according to the eminent French scholar Olivier Roy, are the *qizilbash*. These are holdovers from the officialdom and army of Nadir Shah of Persia, who ruled Afghanistan in the eighteenth century. A third group, in the marshes and plains of the western province of Nimruz, are ethnically Iranians who speak Persian like those across the border. Small Shi'ite minorities live also in Herat, including some who belong to the Ismaili sect, considered heretics by the other Shi'a. For all these people, Iran was a religious rather than a political model. They neither influenced the Shi'ite clergy in Afghanistan very much; nor did many become international terrorists after the war.

Among the three main Sunni Islamist parties in Afghanistan, each of which developed its own guerrilla force, the Iranians, working mainly through the Revolutionary Guards, had some satisfactory ties with the most powerful two: Hekmatyar's *Hizb-i-Islami* and Burhaneddin Rabbani's more moderate *Jamayat-i-Islami*, but not with the mainly Pushtun *Hizb-i-Islami* of Yunis Khalis. The Shi'ite parties which did have different but fairly constant amounts of Iranian support were the rather feudally constructed *Shura-yi ittifagh-i-Islami*, mainly Hazara peasants led during the Afghan jihad by Sayed Beheshti. The *Nasr* movement was composed of radical Islamists, some of whom have turned up since in the international terrorist movement. They were led by a council. They used young Hazara recruits trained in the camps in Iran. The *Harakat-i-Islami* comprised moderate Islamists, led by Sheikh Asaf Muhseni. Its soldiers tended to be educated Shi'as from all the Afghan ethnic groups. The single group most in Iran's orbit was the *Sepah-I-Pasdaran* (Guardians of the Revolution or Revolutionary Guards), totally dependent on Tehran.[25]

A credible Israeli journalist, Samuel Segev, describes an Iranian effort, after the Iranian revolution, to get US arms supplies, apparently through an Israeli channel, for Afghan clients. He reports on conversations between President Reagan's security advisor, Robert McFarlane, and contacts in the arms business. The Israelis followed these closely, due to their role as intermediaries in the Iran-Contra arms deals between Tehran and Washington. During Colonel Oliver North's futile "chocolate cake" diplomacy trip to Iran in May 1986 to seek release of US hostages in Lebanon in return for Israeli arms deliveries, the Iranians assured North and his delegation that they were well aware of the Soviet threat. Iran was encouraging a Muslim religious revival in Soviet Central Asia. The Khomeiny regime assisted wide and illegal dissemination of the Koran – whether using the CIA's Korans, printed in Virginia, or Iranian ones, is not known – in the Central Asian republics. Yes, the Iranians said, we are training volunteers and arming them for the jihad. When Ollie North asked if the supply of American TOW anti-tank missiles would make a difference in the fighting, the Iranians replied that they were willing to set aside 200 TOWs for the Afghans out of every 1,000 the US sent in order to buy freedom for the American hostages.[26]

How the mainstream training of the holy warrior by Pakistan's ISI at the Ojhiri Camp during the war underwent a metamorphosis after the war and became terrorist training for the new international guerrilla brotherhood will be described later. Sustaining the war effort over a decade, providing the training, weapons, fuel, ammunition and other sinews of war throughout, was in some ways an even more complex problem than the training process was. The funding problem found solutions even more complicated than the problem itself. These solutions included a bizarre, often improvized mixture of "black" and therefore unaccountable budgets; "charitable" donations in the United States and Europe; the frantic profligacy of Saudi Arabians and other Arabs in the oil states in their efforts to support Islam in South and Central Asia against Godless communism; the reliance of the CIA and its allies on the crooked machinations of the biggest international criminal bank ever known; the fabulous profits of drug lords, and the usually unexceptionable generosity of US Congressmen with the funds of the American taxpayer. All of which we must next examine.

6 Donors, Bankers and Profiteers

"The sinews of war," said the Roman statesman Cicero, are "unlimited money." By the time the last Russian soldiers marched out of Afghanistan in February 1989, money measured in billions of dollars, to say nothing of over a million human lives, had been expended to win the war.

In the United States, official funding for the jihad got off to a slow start. The CIA and other concerned agencies were running into problems and constraints over how to use the Pentagon's large and secret funds, the so-called "Black Budget." One of the first requirements, connected with recruiting, was how to promise and to meet payrolls. Even when William Casey took over the jihad from Stansfield Turner in early 1981, there was still no clear picture of just how many zealots would flock to the Stars and Stripes, thinly camouflaged as the green banner of Islam. All of them would have to be paid. Edward Girardet, one of the most perceptive journalists covering the war, estimated in summer 1983 that there were already between 80,000 and 150,000 full-time guerrilla fighters. Their pay had to compete with what some had earned, or might earn, in more peaceful civilian callings. The figures for "regulars" did not include hundreds of thousands of Afghan and Pakistani civilians who functioned as part-time fighters. After several long visits to different fronts, Girardet determined that the resistance movement was operating, with varying efficiency, in as many as 300 different sectors throughout Afghanistan's 28 provinces.[1]

Although the CIA and ISI-managed logistical framework tried to supply and pay the guerrillas through each of the seven main political groups, in practice pay and logistics for fighters in the field often had to come directly from outside donors. Arab journalists who visited Arab volunteers in Pakistan and Afghanistan in 1980–85 discovered that a full-time fighter's pay, depending in part on where he served and how much fighting he saw – there was sometimes incentive pay for those engaged in especially hazardous sabotage or other covert operations behind Soviet or Communist lines – could range from $100 to as much as $300 a month; sometimes considerably more for commanders and their deputies.[2] For the majority of the young Afghanis, Pakistanis, Algerians, Egyptians, Filipinos and others, these were huge sums. After the war, when private Arab funds paid the new international guerrillas, both the old veterans of the Afghan jihad, and the new recruits for the unholy wars to be fought, in Afghanistan and abroad, took high salaries and fringe benefits, such as travel documents and ID papers provided by their commanders, as a matter of course.

Hadji Abdul Haq, the first moujahidin field commander to meet both President Reagan and Prime Minister Thatcher (he said he was more impressed by Thatcher than by Reagan), already wounded 15 times at the age of 29, found he always had problems raising enough money. Not only did his soldiers have to be paid, but fighters like himself often had to be bribed out of government jails – as when Abdul Haq's cousins paid a $7,500 bribe to get him out of the dreaded Pul-i-Charkhi prison. "You must understand," he told an interviewer, "that the [Afghan resistance's political parties] were very small then [early in the resistance movement]. Our organization in Kabul was very small. We were existing on what money we could raise in our home province of Nagarhar to buy ammunition and locally-made versions of the British Lee-Enfield rifle." Since neither Pakistani nor foreign trainers were on the scene at the time, Abdul Haq's impoverished fighters kidnapped a regular Afghan army captain, whom they didn't have to pay, and forced him to train them.[3]

Early in the war the Afghan Communist government and its Soviet mentors were already calculating how to compete with the vast resources of the West. Huda al-Husseini was one of the few Arab journalists to visit the Communist side. In September 1980 she reported in an Arabic-language magazine that the salary then being offered to the government militia was lavish by local standards (and by those of Miss Husseini's country, Egypt). At $162 a month it was more than that paid to a common soldier in most Muslim countries and was almost equivalent to the pay of a Pakistani army captain. A Pakistani military analyst who read her report added that she also highlighted that "handsome monetary inducements are offered to other tribal leaders for showing loyalty to the Kabul government and creating disunity among the tribes."[4]

By December 1980, when Admiral Stansfield Turner was ready to hand the CIA over to William Casey, one of Turner's briefing officers was able to estimate for Casey that the total cost of helping the Afghan resistance on a relatively modest scale, after only a year of Soviet occupation, had already reached $100 million. This turned out to be a pittance, compared to the hundreds of millions of dollars in costs, shared almost equally with the Saudis, accumulated in each year of the jihad until 1989. On January 15, 1980, in the first month of official aid, according to Washington journalist Bob Woodward, John N. MacMahon, the CIA's deputy director of operations, informed Casey that Saudi Arabia was already providing *more* funding than was the CIA.[5]

Although no government agency publishes any details about the US Defense Department's secret or "Black Budget," it is presumed by Washington insiders that this had to be an early and important source of American funds, especially before the Reagan administration and the Republican Congresses of the 1980s began to appropriate growing sums for the proxy war in South Asia by 1982. The Black Budget had existed ever since World War II. President Franklin D. Roosevelt created it to supply the then astronomical sum of $100 million to fund the Manhattan Project, which built the two nuclear bombs dropped on Japan. Subsequently, money had been siphoned surreptitiously from the Pentagon to create the CIA in 1947; the National Security Agency (NSA) in 1952; and the National Reconnaissance Office for overhead satellite espionage in 1960. However, until the Afghan jihad, the biggest covert war ever waged by the United States, became a responsibility of William Casey's CIA in 1981, annual Black Budgets had never exceeded about $9 billion a year.

From the first Reagan year to 1990, the Black Budget actually *quadrupled* to about $36 billion a year. Much of this cash was being used for secret weapons programs, some of which never saw the light of day, and some of which went to fund secret warfare in Afghanistan and Central America. There were enough well-publicized "black" operations, such as the secret arms sales to Iran, run by both official and freelance covert operators, that the administration's ability to keep them secret began to erode.[6]

To run the new covert wars, the Pentagon was allowed to launch a new US Army Special Operations Division. This began with an annual budget of about $100 million, but got off to a bad start. One of its senior officers, 35-year-old Lieutenant Colonel Dale Duncan, ended up with a ten-year prison sentence and a $50,000 fine in 1986, after a court-martial convicted him on charges of forgery, theft and obstruction of justice. One of Duncan's men "blew the whistle" on allegedly shady financing and accounting procedures of a classified Special Forces project codenamed Yellow Fruit. Its main purpose seems to have been to conceal from Congress and the media, and probably also from other executive agencies, details of covert overseas operations in Afghanistan and elsewhere and their financing. The operators of Yellow Fruit and similar programs reported to a group which the Pentagon never publicly acknowledged to exist: the Intelligence Support Activity (ISA), originally intended for secret missions such as rescuing or ransoming American hostages held in Lebanon in the mid-1980s, and possibly including Afghanistan.

One of the ISA's operations was trying to procure Soviet-made arms on the Iran–Iraq war front and elsewhere, for the Afghani fighters, supplementing the CIA's similar programs with Israel and Egypt. In 1982, the Deputy Secretary of Defense, Frank Carlucci, grew impatient with ISA's uncontrolled ways and finances. After various investigations came Duncan's court-martial and conviction. Despite pressure to disband ISA, President Reagan issued a secret finding authorizing ISA in 1983, in time for its futile efforts in 1984 to liberate former Beirut CIA station chief William Buckley and other US hostages in Lebanon.[7]

Mainstream Congressional funding was mainly the work of a handful of dedicated US Congressmen. They regarded the Afghan jihad as part of the global Cold War effort to get the better of the Soviet empire. They included Republicans Charles Wilson (D–Texas), David Dreier (R–California) and Bill McCollum (R–Florida), and the Republican Senator from New Hampshire, Gordon Humphrey,[8] who harassed the Washington establishment in 1984 and 1985 until Congress, with administration backing, increased appropriations and authorized giving the deadly Stinger anti-aircraft missile to Pakistan's ISI for the Afghan fighters.[9] McCollum also denounced – and pushed vainly for a solution to – the mystery of the fatal accident, or assassination, of Pakistan's President Zia al-Haq on August 17, 1988.[10]

President Zia and others aboard were all killed when a Pakistani air force C-130 suddenly dived and crashed, shortly after taking off from a military base where General Zia had attended the unsuccessful demonstration of a new US Army tank. Killed with him were American Ambassador Arnold Raphel, the US military attache in Islamabad and the chairman of the Pakistani joint chiefs of staff, General Akhtar Abdel Rahman who as ISI chief had run the support operation to the moujahidin, and several other senior Pakistani officers. More on this later in my narrative.

The single US Congressman who emerged as CIA Director William Casey's champion Congressional ally, especially for appropriating money, was Democratic Representative Charles Wilson of Texas, one of the most colorful American figures of the Afghan jihad. His responsibility, like that of Casey and Casey's subordinates, for both the victory over the Soviet Union and the chain of bitter consequences for the West and its allies which followed, will be for historians to determine. Wilson was a US Naval Academy graduate and Navy veteran who had succeeded in both business and politics in Texas, where he served in the Texas state legislature before his election to the US Congress. After long support for Right Wing and anti-Communist causes, such as the Somoza regime in Nicaragua, he discovered the anti-Communist crusade in Afghanistan, a venture on a vaster scale than anything he had seen in Central America. Always ready to promote the interests of the Texas defense contractors who supported him, he got seats on the powerful House Appropriations Committee and Defense Appropriations Subcommittee, which often has the last word on the Pentagon's budgets, including the huge and hidden "Black" portions.

Wilson made 14 separate trips to South Asia to promote the Afghan cause. He cultivated close personal relations with President Zia al-Haq. In 1982, he began intensive work in secret hearings of the Senate Appropriations Committee to inject more and more money into the Afghan enterprise. On one trip in 1983 he crossed into Afghanistan with a group of moujahidin. In early 1984, Casey's CIA had requested, and finally obtained, $24 million for the Nicaraguan Contras, a favorite cause for President Reagan; but had asked for only $30 million for the Afghans. Like Casey, Wilson was sure that Afghanistan was "the right war at the right time" and deserved much more funding than it was getting. He called the $30 million "peanuts," using the same expression his friend Zia al-Haq had used to express his disdain for the first official aid package President Jimmy Carter had offered during the last year of his administration.

Seeing for himself the crippling Soviet air superiority, Wilson realized that the SAM-7s, British-made Blowpipe missiles and the rather antiquated Soviet and Chinese anti-aircraft cannon used by the holy warriors were inadequate. Facing strong resistance to his advocacy of giving them the Stinger, Wilson first took the lead in proposing the Swiss Oerlikon rapid-fire anti-aircraft cannon, easily available to the CIA on the international arms market. "There were 58,000 [American]dead in Vietnam and we owe the Russians one," was one of Wilson's arguments. He got both a $40 million appropriation and approval for the Oerlikon purchase.[11]

Official US government funding, paid for by the patient and patriotic mass of US taxpayers, was not enough for President Ronald Reagan, nor for President George Bush (a former CIA Director) after him. Fortunately, they felt, the Saudi Arabian kingdom was matching US government funds, dollar for dollar. There was additional private Arab funding – millions and millions of dollars of it. In retrospect, the combination of public and private Saudi funding was decisive for the successful funding of the war. Gradually, the official Saudi government funding wound down with the war's end. It was replaced by private funding from multi-millionaire and multi-*billionaire* zealots like Osama bin Laden, seeking a global triumph of Islamism. The governmental funding was soon surpassed and almost forgotten.

Though not anything like the size of the contributions of bin Laden and other wealthy Arab supporters, the input of the failed Bank of Credit and Commerce International (BCCI), headed by the late Pakistani tycoon, Agha Hassan Abedi and Abedi's relations with eminent statesmen of the West, from President Carter on down, were of great importance to the success of the jihad. The BCCI connection seems to have been largely the work of William Casey. His successor as Director of Central Intelligence, Robert Gates, in October 1988, after the Bank of England's regulators had closed it down, branded BCCI "The Bank of Crooks and Criminals International."[12]

The creeping privatization of the jihad, for this is in fact what it was – not rogue governments, but rogue private financiers are responsible for much of the postwar political terrorism in the West – grew out of the Saudi–American alliance.

Some of the clues about the importance of BCCI and the Saudi and US operators in financing and privatizing the Afghan jihad were lying around Washington, New York and the Middle East during the last few years of the Carter administration. On February 11, 1979, just ahead of a blinding snowstorm, the author and other newsmen took off with Defense Secretary Harold Brown from Washington's Andrews Air Force Base for a rapid trip to Israel and Saudi Arabia. While we were in the air, the Shah's rule was crumbling in Tehran, and the ailing Muhammad Reza Pahlavi would soon be a fugitive, unwanted in most of his countries of refuge. When we arrived in Riyadh, Harold Brown and his staff were confronted by puzzled and angry Saudi officials, especially Prince Turki ben Faisal al-Saud, chief of Saudi intelligence. He had succeeded his uncle, Kamal Adham, in the job in September 1977.

How, asked the perplexed Saudis, had this been allowed to happen to the Shah? Wasn't America able to defend or protect its best allies? What and who was next on the list for destabilization or revolution? The Saudi royal family, guardians of America's biggest source of oil? The other states of the Persian or Arab Gulf? Afghanistan? Prince Turki's predecessor Kamal Adham had been a star player in the old Safari Club system, which had worked for a time. But now the Shah was gone; France and Egypt no longer seemed to be effective players. The system was no longer working. What to do?

It was several months before the Soviets moved into Afghanistan, and neither Harold Brown nor his boss President Jimmy Carter had real answers for the Saudis. One American who was looking for them was Raymond H. Close.

Shortly before my newspaper assignment at the Pentagon in Washington began in 1978, I had met in Beirut with Ray Close, a quiet, cultivated man. Close has been identified in many publications since then as the CIA's former station chief in Saudi Arabia. He retired in 1977, just about the time Kamal Adham's watch ended at Saudi intelligence, and Prince Turki's began. Close stayed in business in Saudi Arabia, sponsored by Adham, in National Chemical Industries, one of the many "royal" companies owned by a prince of the ruling House of Saud. Close has denied that he went to work "for" Adham. In any case, it was up to Prince Turki to handle the secret payments, already institutionalized in the old Safari Club enterprises. Soon – it is impossible to say exactly when – these included major cash flows to the more Islamist-minded of the Sunni Muslim Afghan resistance groups (as opposed to the Shi'ite ones which, as we saw, Iran preferred to help). The groups most favored by Saudi cash seem to have been those of Abdul Rasul Sayyaf (later, as it moved operations from Pakistan to the southern Philippines, known as the "Abu Sayyaf" gang), and probably Hekmatyar's fighters, as well as smaller Sunni Muslim bands. Collectively these groups came to be known locally as the "Wahabis," after the austere and orthodox Muslim sect from which the House of Saud had sprung. Even at this writing, when Saudi funds, for the most part private, continue to flow to fighters in Afghanistan's internecine conflicts as well as to those in Central Asia, Wahabi is the term applied to groups and to the funds financing them.

Kamal Adham and Prince Turki, with or without active cooperation with Ray Close, were in many ways the "godfathers" of Arab financing, before its privatization of finance in the Afghanistan operation. Adham was deeply involved in some of the BCCI's operations, at about the time the BCCI became one of the main paymasters of the jihad. Adham's plea of guilty to charges of conspiracy, unrelated to Afghanistan, before US Federal authorities in 1992, and his agreement to pay a fine of $105 million (a small fraction of his private fortune) and to disclose some of BCCI's labyrinthine global operations[13] may have saved both Adham and the CIA embarrassment. Disclosures about Afghanistan would have almost inevitably emerged during an extended trial. Adham's lawyers and associates had hinted that such disclosures might come, if no such plea bargain had been reached.

Adham's more or less graceful exit from the BCCI scandal closely coincided with charges filed by New York State and Federal officials against American elder statesman and advisor to US presidents since Harry Truman, 85-year-old Clark Clifford, and his law partner, Robert Altman. The counts included fraud, conspiracy and receiving millions in bribes relating to BCCI's penetration of the US banking scene. A jury acquitted them in 1993, despite the aggressive and tireless efforts of New York prosecutor Robert Morgenthau and his investigators. Clifford, Altman and the CIA all breathed more easily.

Sheikh Kamal Adham, as some biographers call him, was born in Turkey in 1929 to a Turkish mother and an Albanian father who took him to Jeddah, Saudi Arabia, as a one-year-old. His education included attendance at an elitist private English school, Victoria College, in Cairo. His introduction to the ruling House of Saud was through his half-sister, Iffat. She was the favorite wife of King Faisal, the shrewd and austere puritan monarch who reigned over the Saudi kingdom from 1964 until his murder by a young relative in 1975. It was the support of Faisal, as Crown Prince, which got Adham his appointment as first (and only) ethnic non-Arab as chief of Saudi royal intelligence. By this time, he was already a multi-millionaire through astute business deals, like a huge contract for offshore oil concessions between the Saudis and Japan's Arabian Oil Company, signed in 1957.[14]

During the 1960s, Adham's cultivation of Anwar al-Sadat, future President of Egypt, helped to pave the way for his future role as the first official Saudi treasurer of the Afghan operation. Adham benefitted from CIA help in setting up an important Saudi back channel to Washington. When President Nasser died in 1970 and Sadat succeeded him, Adham began to encourage Sadat to break ties with the Soviet Union and improve them with the United States. He was the emissary who on July 13, 1972, delivered Sadat's message to Henry Kissinger that Sadat was ready to talk to the Americans about what Washington could offer if Sadat went ahead with his scheme to expel the Soviet military presence, which Nasser had brought to Egypt. Sadat went ahead with this history-making move. It was a shock measure, marking the start of the Soviet retreat from the Middle East, and the beginning of America's return to it, decisively facilitated by Sadat and his eventual peace treaty with Israel. During the same period, Adham further strengthened his position in Cairo by becoming a business associate of Sadat's half-English wife, Mrs. Jehan Sadat, and other Sadat family members.[15]

At about the same time, Kamal Adham met Agha Hassan Abedi, the complicated and charismatic Pakistani who founded BCCI and its vast and ultimately fraudulent banking empire in 1972. Helping the Saudis and the CIA to finance the Afghan jihad was only one detail of Abedi's career. It was this help rather than his extraordinary life, which ended with a stroke at his home in Pakistan on August 5, 1995, at the age of 73, which concerns us here. However, it is worth recalling, with *The Economist* in its full-page obituary, that many people steadfastly refused to believe that Abedi was dishonest, despite his sentencing in absentia to eight years' imprisonment for fraud in the United Arab Emirates, and the legal actions by a New York prosecutor, who called him the mastermind of "the largest bank fraud in New York financial history." Abedi, after firmly anchoring his position in the Middle East and much of the Third World as a generous benefactor of many (and not only Muslim) charities and as a friend of many rulers, turned to the United States. He befriended President Jimmy Carter. Soon, Carter became an occasional passenger in Abedi's private executive jets. After yielding the Presidency to Ronald Reagan, Carter took Abedi with him on a trip to China, which lost both face and about $400 million in deals with BCCI, through trusting Abedi because he was a friend of

Carter. In 1991 the BCCI collapsed and many branches were closed by international regulators. Some $9.5 billion of the depositors' money was missing. Few, if any of either the minority of depositors who were drug traffickers and terrorists (including the notorious Palestinian, Abu Nidal), or the vast majority of over a million who were honest working people, especially Asians in the United Kingdom and the Gulf states, ever fully understood what had happened.[16]

The BCCI and Abedi, as he traveled and deepened his relationships with such eminences as Lord (James) Callaghan, British Prime Minister from 1976 to 1979 and Margaret Thatcher, looked especially attractive to CIA chief William Casey and his Cold Warriors. The CIA already had a history of using corrupt or criminal banks for its overseas operations. There had been the mysterious Nugan Hand Bank of Australia; Mercantile Trust and the Bahamas, and the Castle Bank which funneled cash to the CIA's anti-Castro operations in Cuba. BCCI held secret accounts in Switzerland, London, Miami and elsewhere. In these accounts, the Saudi government deposited secret funds for the Contras in Nicaragua, UNITA in Angola and apparently even support for General Noriega, the President of Panama.[17] Noriega was destined eventually to be captured in a major US Army operation against Panama at the end of 1989. He was imprisoned in a Florida jail for drug trafficking and other activities damaging to Washington's stature in the Western Hemisphere.

When the Bank of England's regulatory closing of BCCI brought the scandal of the bank into the public domain in July 1991, investigators for *Time* magazine, ABC News and other media discovered that BCCI had operated a "black network," a sort of "bank within the bank." It was involved in profitable commerce in arms, drugs and gold. The bank allegedly had links with intelligence agencies and arms dealers, and harbored accounts which Libya, Iran and Syria used to buy arms. *Time* and others alleged (though without proving it) that the black network had also funded joint efforts by Argentina, Libya and Pakistan to acquire nuclear weapons (Pakistan, at least, was well along this road by the end of the 1980s). In the US, the CIA and the DIA, the Pentagon's Defense Intelligence Agency, had also begun to use the bank for covert operations. New York prosecutor Robert Morgenthau complained that the Justice Department had been impeding Morgenthau's investigation of the bank's American connections and was asking witnesses not to cooperate with it. Justice had also hindered a major investigation by Massachusetts Senator John Kerry, and was asking witnesses not to work with Kerry, something Kerry confirmed. As early as 1984, the CIA sent a report on BCCI's drug-connected activities to various US government departments. It had followed this up with a serious look into links with terrorist groups like that of Abu Nidal. However, Justice, the Treasury and other Federal departments kept silent about what they knew.[18]

The CIA took the unusual step of flatly denying the media reports about CIA–BCCI links. The denial backfired. The British media and American investigative reporters for ABC News and others published a series of damaging revelations about CIA accounts in London branches of BCCI, chiefly the Cromwell

Road branch. These accounts were used to pay scores of British subjects and residents who worked as informants for the CIA. The *Financial Times* reported that Pakistan's finance minister had confirmed that the CIA used BCCI branches in Pakistan to channel money, presumably through the ISI, to the Afghan jihad. Further, it disclosed, the CIA and other US agencies used "slush funds" at BCCI branches to pay off Pakistani army officers and Afghan resistance leaders. The CIA issued a short statement promising to "investigate" the allegations. Soon, acting CIA director Richard Kerr admitted that yes, the BCCI did hold CIA accounts, the first such admission by the agency after months of stonewalling denials.[19]

BCCI's possibilities for assistance in the jihad seem to have come to William Casey's attention quite early. NBC News reported on February 23, 1992 that Agha Hassan Abedi had been meeting Casey secretly for three years in Washington's Madison Hotel. Senator John Kerry's investigating committee reported that a Senate aide who worked to supply the moujahidin with Stinger missiles and other weapons, Michael Pillsbury, kept up a close relationship with BCCI front-man Muhammad Hammoud.[20] Hammoud was a wealthy Lebanese merchant with many connections to the White House of President George Bush, the BCCI and First American Bankshares. This institution was implicated in American legal proceedings against BCCI officials as the US bank which Agha Hassan Abedi, at the height of his powers, was most interested in. Hammoud reportedly died in a doctor's office in Geneva, Switzerland, in May 1990. Some of BCCI's many adversaries hinted darkly that Hammoud met foul play because he knew too much about BCCI. According to one of the books about BCCI, he told a friend only hours before his death, "If anybody knew how dirty the Americans are in this BCCI business, they'd be surprised – they're dirtier than the Pakistanis."[21]

Norman Bailey is a former American National Security Council (NSC) official who monitored worldwide movements of money to track terrorist groups. He acknowledged that by 1984 he was completely aware of BCCI's involvement in laundering drug money, financing terrorists, arms deals and manipulation of financial markets.[22] BCCI took an even more direct role in the Afghan jihad. Their operatives took control of Karachi port, where so many of the arms cargoes consigned to the ISI for the Afghan fighters, arrived. They ran the Pakistani customs service through bribery and intimidation. BCCI even provided labor gangs and well-armed guards. While the CIA and Pakistan's ISI traded accusations about who was more corrupt, many of the guns getting through to the holy warriors – such as 60,000 rifles and 100 million rounds of ammunition withdrawn from service by the Turkish army – were totally unserviceable. An informant who testified in a court case on BCCI's involvement, claimed some BCCI men crossed into Afghanistan and personally delivered some of the guns. When they came under fire, or otherwise couldn't deliver, these BCCI operatives reportedly continued on into Iran. There they would sell the CIA-supplied weapons to the Iranians.[23]

In May 1998, after months of tortuous negotiations, an American television news team managed to establish contact and to interview in a mountain fastness in

Afghanistan held by the Taliban, the man whom the United States government and many of its allies considered to be the most dangerous international terrorist at large in the world. His name is Osama bin Laden, a multi-millionaire born in 1957. He built his fortune as a Saudi Arabian citizen, and became a leader and financier of the international terrorist network which grew out of the Afghan holy war. During the television interview in May 1998, bin Laden called for the murder of Americans and Jews, wherever they might be calling Americans "the biggest thieves in the world and the [worst] terrorists." He praised, and sometimes implied responsibility for, the World Trade Center bombing in New York in February 1993 and the debacle of US forces sent to Somalia in 1993–94. He expressed a desire by himself and his followers to drive Western, especially American, influence and interests out of the Arab and Muslim worlds. He vowed to drive the Saudi royal family from power and destroy it.[24]

The United States government had put a $3 million price on bin Laden's head, a measure which might prove awkward as long as he was being protected by the Taliban, who in turn were protégés of America's ally Pakistan. The story is essential to an understanding of how the Afghan jihad led directly to a number of terrorist outrages around the world, the multiplication of guerrilla operations resulting from the jihad and last but not least, the privatization of these operations through the personal financing of bin Laden and other players like him.

Knowing a little about the Yemeni origins of the bin Laden dynasty, which founded and made prosper one of the biggest construction firms in the world, helps to understand the international nature, both of the Afghan holy war itself, and the unholy guerrilla and terrorist wars and insurgencies which grew out of it.

The southern Yemeni coastal province of Hadhramaut, east of the big seaport of Aden, is a torrid land of picturesque, baked-mud, high-rise buildings which not too long ago were still constructed by hand. In past centuries, the trading ships of the Hadrami Arabs made the long voyage out to Indonesia and China. They brought back spices, incense, myrrh and frankincense from the Far East and the Indian subcontinent, centuries before the merchants of England and Salem, Massachusetts made their fortunes in the China trade of the nineteenth century.

Britain gave up its colonial grip on Aden and South Arabia in 1967, leaving the two independent countries of North and South Yemen in place of the old British-protected states and principalities in the South. Even before independence, a generation of Hadrami merchants, clerks and money-changers migrated north to seek their fortunes in Saudi Arabia. These fortunes – earned by dint of hard work and good luck combined – built or contributed to Saudi business and banking dynasties. Some of these now finance Islamic causes around the world through Muslim charitable institutions, private banks and foundations of various sorts. The Hadrami immigrants, makers and founders of these institutions, include a former counter clerk in a Jeddah money-changing booth, Salim bin Mahfouz. He owns the kingdom's largest and one of its most prosperous private financial institutions, the

Saudi National Commercial Bank,[25] once tied up with BCCI, but given a clean bill of health by Western courts and investigators after it broke these ties.

Muhammad bin Laden, father of Osama bin Laden, and founder of the formidable bin Laden construction dynasty, was another such Yemeni. Muhammad bin Laden emigrated to Saudi Arabia from the Hadhramaut as a very young man. He got a job as a bricklayer for ARAMCO, the Arabian–American Oil Company. He earned one Saudi riyal, about 20 US cents, a day. Like his fellow Hadrami immigrants, he deposited his riyals in a tin box. When he had saved enough to go into business on his own, he founded the bin Laden construction firm. He started modestly with small jobs, but soon moved into the big time by building palaces, in the early 1950s, for the House of Saud in Riyadh. Muhammad bin Laden's big chance, and that of his progeny – he fathered, with various wives, no fewer than 52 children – came when he won the contract to build a Medina–Jeddah highway in the holy province of Hejaz, after a foreign contractor had withdrawn.

Soon the bin Laden name was legendary in Arab construction, in the Saudi kingdom, the Gulf emirate of Ras al-Khaimah and in Jordan, for major road, airport and other infrastructure projects. The firm attracted engineering talent from all over the world and rapidly amassed a huge fortune. Sheikh Muhammad, as he came to be called, soon developed a reputation for piety as well as wealth, jetting as he did from one Arab construction site to another. He once had the unique experience of saying, in one day, morning prayers in East Jerusalem (before Israel's 1967 conquest of the holy city); noon prayers in Medina and evening prayers in Mecca. His reputation for piety soon rubbed off on the firm. By the time Sheikh Muhammad killed himself by crashing his own aircraft in 1966, the bin Laden conglomerate of companies was the biggest private contractor of its kind in the world, owning 90 of the largest Caterpillar excavators then in existence.

Despite its religious credentials, useful later when it would become a financier of the Afghan jihad, the firm was short on management knowhow. For a time, King Faisal appointed the owner of a smaller construction company to watch over its business affairs. However, by the late 1970s, one of Sheikh Muhammad's young sons, Osama, was running much of the business. Under his guidance, the group maintained its reputation for professional excellence and "can do" spirit in large projects. Osama bin Laden's inherited share of the family fortune was soon augmented by huge earnings.

By 1981, when CIA chief Casey and his Saudi associates, Kamal Adham and Prince Turki, were casting around for new sources of secret financing for the Afghan campaign, the bin Laden enterprises were all on a short list of possibly helpful families. Prince Sultan bin Abdul Azziz, the powerful Defense and Aviation Minister, told a high-level American business and investors' delegation, those firms "have all done great things for the kingdom."[26]

A standard and rather tardily-issued US State Department Fact Sheet on Osama bin Laden released in the summer of 1997 contains many interesting facts about his career as a master of Islamist and anti-American terrorism.[27] However, it omits the background facts which help to explain how early and close were his connections in the United States – making it easier for the Reagan–Casey jihad team to enlist his talents and his fortune in the jihad.

Adnan Kashoggi, another Arab tycoon who had pleased and helped to enrich the Saudi royal family, had begun to cooperate with the bin Ladens as early as 1953. In that year, Kashoggi was a young student at Chico State University, Nevada. His father sent him $10,000 to buy himself a car. He bought a truck instead and went into business by leasing the truck, complete with driver, to American firms operating in Saudi Arabia. Adnan Kashoggi's father was Dr. Muhammad Khalid Kashoggi, court physician to the royal family. One of Dr. Kashoggi's patients was Muhammad bin Laden, who needed some trucks quickly for his construction work in the kingdom. Adnan, still a student, arranged the deal with Kenworth Truck Co. in Bellevue, Washington state, from which he bought his own truck. Adnan Kashoggi soon received a $50,000 check from bin Laden, which helped with his expenses in America. Later, Adnan was to make a fortune as an intermediary in arms deals, notably as Saudi Arabian agent for the US Lockheed and Northrop Corporations, which paid him huge sums for easing billion-dollar aircraft sales to the kingdom in the 1960s and 1970s. Roy M. Furmark, a New York oil broker and old friend and client of William Casey, who had also done joint ventures with Kashoggi, introduced Kashoggi to Manuchehr Ghorbanifar. He was the Iranian middleman who became a central figure in the arms-for-hostages and funds-for-Contras deals with Iran, in which Kashoggi got involved. Kashoggi's own role in financing the jihad in Afghanistan is not clear, and may have been minor or non-existent. The author is unaware of any evidence that he financed postwar terrorism or guerrilla activities.

Not so with Osama bin Laden. As soon as the Soviets invaded Afghanistan in December 1979, he joined the moujahidin and soon took a leading role. "I was enraged and went there at once," he said in a 1993 interview with Robert Fisk of the *Independent* newspaper, one of the first journalists to spot him as a key mover in the jihad and that which followed. He set up a base at Peshawar, Pakistan, within easy reach of Pakistan's ISI but apparently not supervised by them. Through his own personal reputation as a pious Muslim who favored the cause of Wahabi Islamism, and through involvement of the bin Laden companies in construction and renovation work at the holy shrines of Mecca and Medina, he seemed to both Saudi intelligence and the CIA an ideal choice for the leading role he began to play.

Bin Laden began to pay, with his own and company funds, for recruitment, transportation and training of the Arab volunteers who flocked, first to Peshawar and then to Afghanistan, to fight in the jihad. According to Egyptian intelligence, his aid to the underground Egyptian Islamist groups in Egypt, including the *Gamaa al-Islamiya* and *Al-Gihad,* the killers of Sadat, began simultaneously with, or very soon after, his debut in Pakistan. By 1985 bin Laden had collected enough millions from his family and company wealth and from donations from wealthy Arab Gulf merchant families, to organize al-Qaida, the Islamic Salvation Foundation, to support the jihad. He established a network of al-Qaida recruitment centers in

Saudi Arabia, Egypt and Pakistan, through which he recruited, enlisted and sheltered thousands of Arab volunteers. Possibly he was assisted, though this is not clear to the author, by the Pakistani religious foundation Tablighi Jamaat, which was especially active, as we saw in the last chapter, in North Africa.

Many of those bin Laden recruited turned out to be zealous Muslims, like himself, and brave fighters. Some, however, were criminals, like those whom the Tabligh helped to undergo religious training in Pakistan, once they emerged from Algerian or Tunisian prisons. One Egyptian criminal was Muhammad Amer. He was an Egyptian Islamist who was among the non-Saudi Arab volunteers taking part in the big uprising and seizure of the holy mosque in Mecca in November and December 1979, just before the Afghan war began. Unlike many of the other attackers, who were beheaded by the sword, Amer was given the relatively lenient prison sentence of nine years. Egyptian intelligence claims that Osama bin Laden's network, on Amer's emergence from prison in Saudi Arabia, flew him to Peshawar. There, he joined a group of other Egyptian militants either nominally or actively involved in fighting the Russians. This group was led or influenced by Ayman al-Zawahri, a university-trained Egyptian professional man. He was the self-styled "amir" of an Islamist cell who escaped from Egypt and arrived in Peshawar some time after Sadat's assassination in 1981. In 2000, al-Zawahri, sending orders by fax and computer e-mail to the Islamist insurgents in Egypt from his various places of exile, especially Switzerland, was still one of the most feared men carried on the "wanted" lists of President Husni Mubarak's security and intelligence services.

Whether bin Laden was involved or not, one of the means the Egyptian Islamists used to raise cash was through counterfeiting and then laundering money. Muhammad Amer and another Egyptian volunteer, Al-Syed Muhammad Ibrahim, conceived with al-Zawahri the idea of printing massive quantities of false US dollars, Saudi riyals and Egyptian pounds to finance operations in Egypt and abroad. Egyptian intelligence claimed they had the support of Iranian elements, then under heavy suspicion by the US Treasury of counterfeiting great quantities of US 100 dollar bills. A sophisticated printing press was smuggled into Egypt and moved to a remote village, Bassous, where police raids were thought unlikely. The gang was discovered and captured, after engaging the services of a known professional counterfeiter who was already under Egyptian police watch.[28]

On the jihad scene in Afghanistan, Osama bin Laden imported through his companies bulldozers and other heavy equipment to cut new roads and tunnels. He built hospitals and storage depots in the Afghan mountains to transport and shelter the holy warriors and their supplies.

After the Soviet withdrawal in 1989 bin Laden returned for a short period to Saudi Arabia to tend to the family construction business at its Jeddah head office. At the same time, he continued to support militant Islamists who had begun to target the governments in Egypt, Algeria, Tunisia, Yemen, the Philippines and elsewhere. Already highly uneasy about his activities, Saudi security held onto bin Laden's passport during the 1989–91 period, hoping to prevent or at least discourage his contacts with extremists he had worked with, then with the full approval of the Saudi regime and the CIA (if not always with that of Pakistan's ISI), during the Afghan jihad.

In 1991, bin Laden and a number of Afghani war veterans loyal to him moved to Khartoum, the capital of Sudan. There he was welcomed by Hassan al-Turabi, the scholarly and prestigious leader of Sudan's National Islamic Front (NIF). When General Omar Bashir had seized power in a 1989 military coup, the NIF and Turabi were the discreet but muscular powers behind the Sudanese military regime. Since the early 1980s, bin Laden and his business associates had been watching for business and investment opportunities in the Sudan, which had been wracked by decades of civil war between the Islamic northern governments and the Christian and animist movements in the south. By 1990, before he moved to Khartoum, bin Laden had already started a number of business ventures.

Bin Laden made himself useful in the Sudan and increased his personal fortune at the same time by forming partnerships with wealthy NIF associates of Turabi. His company, called Al-Hijrah for Construction and Development, Ltd., built a needed new highway linking Khartoum with Port Sudan on the Red Sea and a modern international airport for Port Sudan. Bin Laden's trading company, Wadi al-Aqiq, Ltd., operating with his Taba Investment Company, obtained a near monopoly over Sudan's main agricultural exports: gum arabica, corn, and sunflower and sesame products. Here he operated with prominent NIF members. Another bin Laden firm, Al-Themar al-Mubarakah Agriculture Company, Ltd. acquired large tracts of land near Khartoum and in eastern Sudan. Together, again, with affluent NIF members, bin Laden capitalized a new banking institution in Khartoum, Al-Shamal Islamic Bank, dedicated to Islamic interest-free banking, investing $50 million in funds he controlled in the bank.

The work force of companies owned by bin Laden or under his control soon included hundreds, perhaps thousands, of militant Arab and other veterans of the Afghan jihad, seeking ways to avoid returning to their own countries. There, many faced prison sentences or even execution for crimes or for subversive political and terrorist activities. Bin Laden issued false passports and identity papers, as well as work contacts, to facilitate travel of the "Afghanis," as the veterans came to be called. In 1993, for example, he paid for travel to Sudan of 300 to 400 of them who were threatened with a crackdown by Pakistan, now under pressure from Egypt, Algeria and other countries they were by then targeting. A branch of the al-Qaida network grew up in Sudan to shelter and accommodate the new immigrants. Bin Laden continued to finance them and to continue the training many had already begun in Pakistan and Afghanistan, after the Soviet retreat.

Bin Laden's followers now began to work with other Saudi dissident groups against both the American military presence in Saudi Arabia and the Gulf, and against the Saudi royal family itself. His followers in the kingdom would mingle with and sometimes travel with pilgrims making the haj to Mecca and Medina, especially with those returning to Egypt or the Sudan or wanting to infiltrate there.

Egyptian intelligence, which had been concentrating on keeping the "Afghanis" out by maintaining tight checks on the Sudanese and Libyan borders, realized that they had been duped and that the leaks were coming from Saudi Arabia. In April 1993, President Mubarak made a special visit to Riyadh to complain about bin Laden's support for insurgent Egyptian Islamists.

In the same year, the Peshawar-based Islamist terrorist groups in Egypt increased their attacks on policemen, judges, Coptic Christians, foreign tourists and other human targets. At the end of May 1993, the Egyptian Interior Ministry, announcing the arrest of over 800 Islamist suspects and the dismantling of a major terrorist network, added that bin Laden was financing a new group called "Belonging to the Jihad." Bin Laden, said President Mubarak's men, had helped an Egyptian dissident named Magdi Salem to settle in Saudi Arabia, providing him with bin Laden company travel and work papers. When the Saudi authorities ousted Salem, he had returned to Egypt in 1991. There he seems to have worked under orders from the current *al-Gihad* leader, former Egyptian Army Lieutenant Colonel Abboud al-Zumor, coordinator of the successful murder conspiracy against President Sadat in 1981 who later escaped to Peshawar. Magdi Salem's task was to create new action cells in the Cairo and Nile Delta regions.

In Alexandria, Salem was directed to work with Fouad Daifallah. This man headed a local branch with the unoriginal and Iranian-sounding name of Hizbollah, the Party of God. Bin Laden, the Egyptian government claimed, provided funds after revolutionary Iran proved slow or reluctant to pay non-Shi'ite fighters (the Shia minority in Egypt is very small and without any religious or political clout. All of the dissident groups including Hizbollah were actually Sunni). Another investigation the Egyptians conducted with the Saudi authorities disclosed that bin Laden firms were channeling money to Egyptian Islamists to buy printing presses, weapons and other unspecified equipment.

By January 1994, according to US intelligence reports, bin Laden was financing at least three guerrilla or terrorist training camps for Egyptian, Algerian, Tunisian and Palestinian fighters, in cooperation with the NIF. A few Western reporters, including an ABC News team, who were able to visit one of the reported locations, found no sign of the foreigners but only of Sudanese NIF militia training. It was presumed, though not proven, that some of the foreign Arabs had put on Sudanese uniforms during the visits. Bin Laden's company, Al-Hijrah for Construction and Development, worked directly with Sudanese officials, the American reports said, to provide transport and supplies for the trainees.

In addition to his assets and construction projects, bin Laden helped his Sudanese hosts by facilitating purchases of Saudi oil for the energy-poor and dollar-poor Sudan at subsidized prices. He took a large house in Al Mashal Street, in the suburban quarter of Khartoum called Al-Riyadh, like the Saudi capital. This was conveniently located near the airport. Some 200 of his company staffers and some supporters and families from Peshawar arrived in the area, bringing money into the country. Following his arrival, messages flowed regularly between Washington,

Riyadh and Khartoum, asking General Bashir's government to scale down and end, if possible, bin Laden's support of guerrillas abroad. In 1993, a leader of Hassan al-Turabi's NIS seems to have assumed control of training and indoctrination of those in Sudan.

Osama bin Laden in 1994 began to focus on the ancient and troubled Arab country of Yemen, his father's country of origin. Yemen borders Saudi Arabia and has been embroiled in a serious territorial dispute with the Saudis ever since losing the region of Najran in a war with Saudi Arabia in 1933–34. In the summer of 1994, the conservative, Islamist-supported North Yemen government of President Ali Abdallah Saleh fought a serious armed conflict with the former British-ruled state of South Yemen. This has a much more secular society than the North. It was ruled in 1994 by self-styled socialists led by General Ibrahim al-Bidh. Bin Laden began to channel money, weapons and trained Afghani veterans into North Yemen. The South Yemenis began to provide President Mubarak's security services in Cairo with information they badly wanted on Islamist training camps in North Yemen. The Saudi royal regime, despite the seeming incongruity involved, was supporting and supplying the secular-minded South Yemeni regime in Aden against the North Yemenis in Sanaa, whom the Saudis considered more inimical to their interests. After a decade of cooperation with the United States and Saudi intelligence, during the Afghan war, then several years of Saudi waffling and equivocation, the royal family finally decided to yield to the urgent strictures of President Mubarak and the Americans. In a speech in early spring of 1994, Saudi Crown Prince Abdallah clearly proclaimed that hard-core Islamists elements, preaching violence and linked to Egypt's covert groups, were no longer welcome in the kingdom. Bin Laden's Yemeni activities during this general period, according to US government reports, included financing a group which in December 1992 attempted bombing attacks against some 100 US servicemen in Aden. The troops were billeted there to support UN relief operations in Somalia.[29]

On April 7, 1994, after a special visit by President Mubarak to complain about bin Laden to King Fahd, and a reported request to Interpol, the International Police Organization, by Yemen for assistance in apprehending him, the Saudi royal family went public. King Fahd announced that bin Laden was being deprived of his Saudi citizenship (a measure actually taken without publicity in February) for behavior that "contradicts the Kingdom's interests and risks harming its relations with fraternal countries" and for "refusal to obey instructions issued to him." A Saudi businessman told Youssef Ibrahim of the *New York Times* that the royal government had also moved to freeze Osama bin Laden's assets inside the kingdom, "though he was believed to control millions of dollars in foreign bank accounts." *The Times* report added that the decision against bin Laden appeared to signal to other less visible groups of Saudi financial tycoons to cut their ties with militant Islamic groups in Egypt, Jordan, Tunisia and Algeria. Such support, Ibrahim observed, frequently takes the guise of Islamic charity works, the building of mosques, or the starting of Islamic businesses that are used as channels to pump money into the militants' war chests.[30] Some of these funds, already flowing into Pakistan and Afghanistan since the decade of the jihad, were still being used as late as 1997 to finance the terrorist and guerrilla training camp at Kunar, Afghanistan. Egyptian security sources said the students at Kunar included members of the covert Egyptian insurgent groups. After the seizure in Pakistan in February 1995 and extradition to New York of the international arch-terrorist Ramzi Ahmed Yousef, later sentenced to life in prison for the World Trade Center bombing and other conspiracies, Pakistani investigators said that Yousef had resided at the bin Laden-funded Bayt Ashuhada (House of Martyrs) in Peshawar during most of the three years before his capture, of which more later.[31]

A few weeks after King Fahd's action against bin Laden, some newsmen covering the Middle East, including the author, received a fax message originating in London. It announced that Mr. Osama bin Laden had opened an office there. The fax bore his signature in English and Arabic, and that of a man designated in London as his office manager. From this time onward, bin Laden, who seems to have avoided even clandestine trips to London from 1995, became associated with the "Committee for Advice and Reform." This is a London-based Saudi opposition organization which in the later 1990s issued over a thousand pamphlets and tracts attacking the Saudi royal government and the House of Saud, often in violent terms. Bin Laden never publicly responded to the condemnation by his eldest brother, Bakr bin Ladin, who expressed in the Saudi media his family's "regret, denunciation and condemnation" of his younger brother's extremist activities.[32]

The royal family's worst expectations concerning Osama bin Laden's assistance to their Yemeni adversaries were realized. Since his arrival in Khartoum, and possibly earlier, bin Laden had helped a long-standing Hadhrami friend from Yemen, Tariq al-Fadli, to found the Yemeni Jihad movement in Sanaa, the North Yemeni capital. Jihad fighters were deployed in the Yemen conflict of June–July 1994 against the South Yemen socialist leadership in Aden. The Saudi rulers, perhaps because of this support, had expected that other bin Laden-supported Afghani veterans would also fight for the Islamist North Yemeni government, and that the North would win the war. Both expectations proved correct. The difficulty for Saudi Arabia was that it backed the *losing* side. Ironically, as we have seen, from an ideological point of view, it supported the southern part of Yemen, as the lesser of two evils, and in its manifest desire to keep the two disparate halves of Yemen weak and divided, and thus less of a threat to the House of Saud. To the disgust of the royal family's opponents, including the bin Laden organization, the Saudis stubbornly gave asylum, medical and housing facilities to the fleeing troops of the South which they had formerly called "Communists."

In North Africa, the ruling Algerian generals, as we will discuss in detail later on, found their most formidable opponents in the bloody civil war which has wracked that country since 1991 to be the "Afghanis." The returned Algerian veterans of the jihad were, as Algerian diplomats and government officials frequently asserted, battle-hardened and determined to impose Afghan fundamentalist models on Algeria's troubled and fractured society. Support for the Algerian insurrection came from Saudi and other foreign Arab charities, foundations and individual moneymen, including Osama bin Laden. In March 1994 the Saudi Interior Minister, Prince Nayef, visited Tunis. There he discussed with Tunisia's US-trained soldier-policeman President Zine al-Abidine ben Ali, the possibility of a "domino effect" on Tunisia from the Algerian turmoil. This was also a subject of concern to Algeria's Western neighbor, King Hassan II of Morocco. Ben Ali's talk with Prince Nayef resulted in a signed security agreement between Tunisia and Saudi Arabia to work together against Islamist political groups, like Tunisia's outlawed *En-Nahda*. This, as we saw in Chapter 5, had been implicated in recruiting for the 1979–89 Afghan jihad.

On the receiving end of largesse for Islamists, sent from Saudi Arabia and its Arab Gulf allies, especially the United Arab Emirates, were a number of mosques and Muslim community centers in Europe. These were private and "charitable" funds. One such center was a big mosque for the Muslim, mainly North African, community in Evrey, France. Contributors to the $6 million place of worship, where former Afghan veterans were made especially welcome, included the Islamic Development Bank in Jeddah, the Saudi financier and arms dealer Akram Ojeh, Kuwait's Minister of Religious Affairs and the Saudi Ambassador to France. Suspicious French investigators, probing terrorist bombings in Paris in the mid-1990s, tried to establish connections between this mosque and others to the Islamist militants, especially the Algerian groups. They either didn't find substantiation of their suspicions, or if they did, did not leak to the French media.

The author was told by a senior French diplomat that it was known that most of the funds collected in Saudi Arabia and the Gulf for Islamists in North Africa were chaneled through cover or dummy companies set in Switzerland, France, the Bahamas and the United States. Some of these firms, both camouflaged and legitimate, were said to be petroleum engineering enterprises or industrial management firms. The Algerian FIS and the so-called Groupe Islamique Armée (GIA), whose original leadership was mainly Afghan war veterans, was said to be involved. So was another Algerian group which used the name Hamas, like that of the Palestinian Islamist HAMAS though unrelated to it, also accused by French sources to own real estate in the United States, especially in Chicago and other large Muslim communities.

A further source of revenue for the post-Afghan war Islamist militants should be mentioned in passing. In the North African states of Algeria, Tunisia and Morocco, and in France, it goes by the name of "trabendo." This is a kind of polyglot word denoting contraband, trafficking and smuggling. The traffic in smuggled goods, especially in counterfeit "name brand" products, from phoney Rolex watches to "Lacoste" shirts made in Taiwan or Turkey, is known to provide millions to the Islamists each month.[33] In addition to taxes automatically collected by the Islamist organizations on this and other forms of black-market activity, in some ways a replica of the methods (other than drugs, our next topic), used in casual day-to-day financing of the jihad in Afghanistan in 1979–89, the legitimate businesses of Algeria, just as in the days of the 1954–62 war for independence from France, pay "voluntary" taxes and contributions to the Islamist war chest. In Egypt this is supplemented by robbery and banditry: armed attacks and armed robberies of banks, gold and jewelry shops and individuals. In Algeria, this kind of crime has been and still is a tradition, ever since Ahmed ben Bella, one of the chiefs of Algeria's revolution to evict the French, who became independent Algeria's first president in 1962, held up a post office in Oran, Algeria, to get cash to finance the initial uprising in 1954.

By the mid-1990s, US financial aid to the Afghan holy warriors was a distant memory. The fraudulent BCCI was no more. But the continuing, post-1989 jihad, in Egypt, Algeria, the Philippines, New York, Paris and other centers of the Muslim and Western worlds, was still being financed by Osama bin Laden and lesser players who had privatized world terrorism and made it into a major enterprise.

One of the biggest threats in this privatization process was the financing of the jihad and the violence which followed through the cultivation, processing and worldwide traffic in drugs. In the 1980s, a vast tide of drugs began to flow out of Afghanistan and Pakistan to Europe, the Americas and the Far East. By the late 1990s the flow, especially of opium, morphine base and even refined heroin, to say nothing of marijuana in various forms, had reached truly epic proportions. It sickened and killed millions, as did the cocaine from South America. Its impact was felt from the inner cities of America and Europe to the once rich "Tiger" economies of the Far East, as well as to the poverty-bound former Soviet republics of Central Asia and Russia itself. To the story of this plague, in many ways a direct consequence of the Afghan war which enriched drug merchants and their friends, but destroyed the lives of millions, we must next turn.

7 Poppy Fields, Killing Fields and Druglords

Using drugs to weaken your enemy or to stimulate your own army to fight with zeal recurs throughout history. In the medieval Middle East, the legendary Old Man of the Mountains, a thirteenth century Shi'a Muslim ruler in northern Persia, provided young disciples the delights of hashish-(cannabis) induced dreams of dalliance with luscious damsels; only to be awakened and told that to return to Paradise, they must carry out hits against his enemies. The young men became known as *hashisheen* or "Assassins." The epithet has stuck to political murderers, whether drug addicts or not, ever since.[1]

There is nothing new about the central role of drugs and druglords in modern Asian history. Start, for example, with China's Opium Wars of the nineteenth century. In June 1836, the then British colonial authorities had a monopoly on Bengali opium brought into China from India. A mandarin named Chu Tsun knelt before the Emperor of China, imploring him to outlaw opium. He reminded his lord that when the army went to crush a local rebellion in 1832, "great numbers of the soldiers were opium smokers, so that, although their numerical force was large, there was hardly any force found among them."[2] During the war between the Nationalist (Kuomintang) Chinese and the Japanese that raged before and during World War II, both sides sold large quantities of raw opium to each other, for profit and to weaken the adversary.[3] The American CIA cooperated with Nationalists in raising money through the drug trade in Burma, a main source, with Afghanistan, of the world's opium supplies.

Both the colonial French and the theoretically anti-colonial Americans used, and were in turn afflicted by, drugs, during the wars in Indo-China from the 1950s until the 1970s. Memories of this must have been uppermost in the mind of a certain big, burly mustachioed Frenchman. He appeared by appointment at the Los Angeles mansion of President-elect Ronald Reagan's advisor and friend, Alfred Bloomingdale, one day in December 1990. This was to be the the Frenchman's first meeting with Reagan, whose anti-Communist and anti-Soviet views he fully shared.

The big Frenchman was Count Alexandre de Marenches, head of France's secret foreign intelligence service, the SDECE (later the DGSE). We have already met him as a founder and mover of the anti-Communist Safari Club of the 1970s and its proxy wars. He had accurately predicted the Soviet invasion of Afghanistan.

Despite some serious problems between the French agency's men and American drug-enforcement officials, de Marenches had good access to the Washington of the Reagan era. General Vernon Walters, just promoted from his old post as US defense attache in Paris to become deputy director of the CIA, was one of de Marenches' oldest friends. He put in a good word for the robust French spy chief.

This assured him of a good reception by President-elect Reagan in Los Angeles.[4] The two men sat down to study maps of Afghanistan. Before he left, de Marenches warned Reagan that the rank-and-file staff of the CIA, where a mutual friend, William Casey, would soon take over as chief, was not to be trusted. "These are not serious people," de Marenches said. They couldn't keep secrets, he added. It was too easy to spot their officers and agents. Usually they were under highly transparent cover as diplomats in American missions abroad.

Soon after his inauguration in January 1981, Reagan saw the Frenchman again. This time it was in the Oval Office of the White House. De Marenches had a concrete suggestion for a Franco–American venture to revive the old alliance and counter the Soviet threat in Afghanistan. He called it Operation *Moustique* or Mosquito. You know," he told the President, "how much trouble a mosquito can cause a bear. If you're not in a position to shoot the bear yourself, you should consider this method."

De Marenches continued that he was in contact with a bunch of bright young journalists. They could produce a perfect specimen of a convincing but false Red Army newspaper. Other friends could print Bibles in the Cyrillic alphabet, and in languages of the Central Asian Muslim Soviet republics. They could be put around in Red Army barracks and do a lot of damage to spirit and morale. There was another thing: "What," he asked Reagan, "do you do with all the drugs seized by the DEA [the US Drug Enforcement Administration], the Coast Guard, the FBI, the Customs?" Reagan responded that he didn't know. He supposed they burned them. "That's a mistake," the Frenchman said. " Take all those confiscated drugs and do as the Vietcong did with the US Army in Vietnam. Supply them on the sly, to the Russian soldiers." In a few months, he explained, they would be demoralized and their fighting ability would be gone. De Marenches added, according to his published memoirs, that a few trusted people could do all this at a cost of only about one million dollars, truly a bargain in subversive warfare.

After very short reflection, Reagan, according to his French visitor, replied that this was a great idea. No one had suggested anything like it to him before. He picked up the phone and told William Casey. The two should meet and discuss Operation Mosquito. When de Marenches met Casey two days later and explained the plan, the Frenchman recorded in his memoirs that Casey "loved it ... he leaped from his chair and sliced at the air with his fists." Although Casey knew there would be problems with Congress, he was eager to go ahead. Would, could, France carry it out if the CIA put up the cash? Yes, de Marenches agreed, but only on condition that no Americans were directly involved. "Your compatriots," he told Casey, "don't know how to do this type of work. They're likely to get a pile-driver to crush a fly, rather than turn a mosquito loose to make life impossible for a bear."

By the French spymaster's account, planning then began. Pakistani operatives and Afghans would handle the distribution of the black propaganda material – phoney Russian newspapers with demoralizing articles and exhortations to desert the Red Army; Christian Bibles – and hard and soft drugs for the "Russkies."

Casey had an afterthought. Wouldn't Pakistan's ISI be involved? "We need the Pakis," he mumbled, with the habitual intelligibility which made him hard to understand. "I'll take care of that," said de Marenches. "But I have another condition. This kind of operation is very delicate. I want to be sure that France won't be mentioned in published articles. I want to be sure that I'll never see my photo in the *New York Times* or the *Washington Post,* along with a little item about what I'm doing." Sorry, Casey retorted. Washington leaked like a sieve. Casey couldn't promise anything of the kind.

According to de Marenches, the joint Franco–American project was dropped: in other words, France withdrew, after having provided the idea. However, the fake issues of *Krasnaya Zvezda* (Red Star), the Soviet army newspaper, did appear later in Kabul.[5] So did large quantities of hashish, opium straw (a dried poppy product used in the area to make mildly narcotic "tea") and packets of heroin, all made easy for the Soviet personnel to buy for nominal prices or "find" as free gifts. There were even small quantities of cocaine, not produced at this early time in the South Asian war boom in drugs, in laboratories in Pakistan or Afghanistan. Later, a massive traffic grew in cocaine from South America to Asia.

The question of whether Operation Mosquito's drug aspect was ever deliberately implemented is part of a larger, extremely important issue: was there a concerted, US-conceived or supported plan to spread drug addiction into the Soviet army, and from there, into Soviet and post-Soviet Russian society, where it has acquired gigantic proportions at the end of the 1990s?

There were absurd contradictions of American policy in the "Golden Crescent" drug states of Afghanistan, Pakistan and Iran, during the 1980s and 1990s. Quite simply, the left hand did not know (or when it did, could not control) what the right hand was doing. President George Bush in 1987 and President Clinton during his two administrations in the 1990s both declared "war on drugs." But the drug wars' multi-billion-dollar budgets seemed unable to cope with the floods of drugs out of South Asia in the wake of the unholy wars in Afghanistan. The CIA and its allies, in order to help finance the proxy US–Soviet war, tolerated the rise of the biggest drug empires ever seen east of the giant Colombian cocaine cartels. While the US Drug Enforcement Administration (DEA) and other agencies were spending billions of dollars to stem the tidal wave of narcotics from South Asia, the CIA and its allies were turning a blind eye or actively encouraging it. In dollar costs, the jihad effort surpassed expenditures for the White House and DEA drug-prevention programs, and so helped to cancel them out.

Russian chroniclers of the Afghan war often report how addiction among the Red Army forces compared with that suffered by the Americans in their anti-Communist crusades in Indo-China. There, the CIA encouraged drug traffic to compensate local tribes helping to fight the Communists. British author Brian Fremantle enlisted support of the Reagan White House, the DEA, the US Customs Service and other national, United Nations and East bloc agencies to produce an authoritative book, *The Fix.*

After debriefing Soviet and Afghan officials and moujahidin, Fremantle concluded that guilt for the Red Army's drug addiction lay not only with their Western adversaries. Afghan fighters on both the Western and Communist sides would regularly take time off from fighting to go home and cultivate their poppy and hashish crops, both seasonal enterprises. Survival of their families often depended on it.

Fremantle, like other visitors to the area in the 1990s, found that the Afghans had so successfully exploited their opium and marijuana crops that the drug habit took hold of many officers and men of the Soviet occupying forces. By the mid-1980s, this caused the Soviet high command to limit the service of some units and personnel in Afghanistan to nine months. Even this rapid turnaround policy hadn't prevented addiction from growing and spreading among the ranks. It also aggravated the incipient social problem at home by speeding the return to Russia of more and more of the addicted soldiers.

The returnees spread drug dependency to the homes and streets of Moscow, Leningrad, Kiev and other Soviet cities. It was not uncommon to find young soldiers swapping ammunition for drugs with the very people they were fighting, the *dushi* or "ghosts," their name for the phantom-like guerrillas who would hit them mercilessly without warning in the dark of night, then fade away into the landscape.

The Indo-China wars brought first French and then many American military and civilians into contact with hard and soft drugs for the first time. Soldiers and civilians brought drugs and drug habits back home to their civilian families and societies. So it was with the Russians and other Soviet soldiers in Afghanistan. Hashish, called *anasha,* became a novel delight for them. Another was called *plan,* an opium derivative, refined only half a step toward morphine base, the substance from which narcotics laboratories manufacture heroin. In the case of Red Army draftees from the Central Asian republics, there was an old pre-war hashish habit. The war accentuated it, as it did alcohol addiction: nearly everyone from private to general drank vodka regularly.[6]

A team of Russian military historians, officers who served in the Afghan war, worked military reports into a remarkably candid book called *War in Afghanistan.* Members of the team, especially Lieutenant Colonel Yuri Shvedov, answered the author's questions with equal candour. Did the CIA consciously continue Operation Mosquito's narcotics plan after French intelligence had bowed out? Shvedov responded that "there certainly was circumstantial evidence for some kind of systematic program. It was easy for our personnel to find the hash, the opium, and yes, sometimes the heroin. It was very sad. We realized what you Americans went through in Southeast Asia."

High on the Russian suspect list in early drug operations was the National Islamic Front (NIF) of Afghanistan. Sayad Ahmed Gaylani, called "Effendi Juan" by compatriots, headed the NIF. He was a wealthy Afghan aristocrat, supporter of the exiled king, Zahir Shah. Gaylani had a strong bent for business. In 1952 he married a woman of the royal dynasty, the Durranis. He wisely invested profits from holding the sales franchise for Peugeot cars in Kabul. At the same time, he kept the religious prestige attached to his descent from the Qadiriya brotherhood, one of the mystic Sufi orders of South Asian Islam.[7]

The Soviet intelligence report on Gaylani's NIF found that it "has significant financial resources. Besides the aid from various foundations in the USA, Western Europe and Arab countries, it makes profit on selling drugs and exacting taxes from the population." Simultaneously, the Front carefully cultivated its image among Western journalists "of a respectable, reasonable, credible political facade."[8] Afghanistan, the report went on, had always exported opium, especially rich in morphine, up to 20 percent in strength. Areas of poppy cultivation were inhabited by "militant tribes" where government control was "purely symbolic." Before the war, most opium was smuggled out of the country, not consumed within it. However, the Soviet account observed, American information media in 1978–79 downplayed Afghanistan as a country involved in drug trafficking, because "the USA decided to use the structures of the narcomafia and the smugglers to topple the people's [communist] power in Afghanistan." Smugglers and their sponsors, said this Moscow narrative (without directly implicating the Pakistani military or ISI), were used to create the illusion of a large-scale rebel movement early on. Later, the smugglers tasted the glory of being "freedom fighters" and "their trafficking was termed 'a battle for religion.' This satisfied both the smugglers and the CIA." The Soviets believed that in 1980 most American DEA personnel in the region had been replaced by intelligence officers, "some of whom used the pretext of the fight against the narcomafia to set up infrastructure for the secret war against Afghanistan."

By then, all close observers of the war knew that the drug smugglers carried weapons into Afghanistan and took drugs back with them. Heroin laboratories began to spring up in the rear of the various Afghan battlefronts. Prophetically, the Russian historians quote an unnamed DEA agent as telling an equally anonymous American newsman that the moujahidin were earning money to buy weapons "which they would use to expand their activities. Can you imagine the price we'll pay for that? That means thousands of new drug addicts; death and crime increase. We are facing a new wave of narcomania."[9] The Russians quote newspaper accounts appearing in Kuwait (a country which, unlike Saudi Arabia, prudently avoided heavy support for the Arab volunteers in the jihad) about Afghan refugee camps in Pakistan "turning into centers of narcomania." Leaders of the Afghan "gangs," as the Russians called them, had their men smuggle and sell drugs in Pakistan and further abroad under the pretext of the need to finance the jihad.

The Soviet account quotes the American Left–liberal magazine, *Rolling Stone*, reporting on a powerful narcobusiness network, including vast new fields of opium poppies on both sides of the Afghan–Pakistan border, created during the jihad. It was "complete with well-planned routes and a whole network of dozens of factories" to process the opium into morphine base and heroin. "Western experts" [names and nationalities unspecified] supervised creation of the labs in camps of

Gulbuddin Hekmatyar's group. However – and here, interestingly, the Russian view of the wartime drug traffic diverges from the Western one – "the real 'King of Heroin,'" said Shvedov's Russian team, "is considered to be Gaylani who has far surpassed Hekmatyar in narcobusiness and controls the overwhelming majority of the operations of the opium mafia." The CIA, the Russians added, was working closely with both Hekmatyar and Gaylani.

The Russian account then follows US media reports, attributing to the "big Seven major moujahidin groups an annual opium production in 1989, at the end of the Afghan war, of over 800 tons, or more than twice the annual national production of Pakistan and Iran combined."[10]

As rebel tribesmen grew opium poppies in Afghanistan and Pakistan, Musto (Dr. David Musto, a Yale University psychiatrist and member of Washington's Strategy Council on Drug Abuse) and a colleague wondered whether the US was "erring in befriending these tribes as we did in Laos when Air America [the CIA's notorious 'proprietary' charter airline] helped transport crude opium from certain tribal areas?" The flood of new heroin from South Asia, they found, was on the streets "more potent, cheaper and more available than at any time in the last twenty years … this crisis is bound to worsen."[11]

President Carter's DEA discussed the threat at a special conference at John F. Kennedy airport in New York in December 1979, at the very beginning of the Afghan war. The DEA intelligence chief reviewed for the assembled DEA agents the "new Middle East heroin threat," which was growing. Gordon Fink, one of his deputies, mentioned the DEA's "concern and frustration … due mainly to lack of control and intelligence in … Pakistan, Afghanistan and Iran." Special Agent Ernie Staples, fresh from the region, acknowledged that due to unfavorable "political situations," the DEA's best defense, interception near the cultivation areas, had collapsed. Processed southern Asian heroin was capturing the European market. Wholesale heroin prices were falling in Europe. Purity of the heroin was reaching new heights, with 500 deaths from drug overdose in West Germany alone. The Marseilles Corsican syndicates were already operating new heroin laboratories to process the morphine base and sometimes raw opium, arriving through Turkey and Syria. DEA agents from main American cities, such as Chicago, Boston and Newark emphasized the mafia's growing role in distributing the heroin in the US through the "pizza connection" of Salvatore Sollena, using a chain of pizza parlours. In New York, Black syndicates in Harlem were moving from the import of Southeast Asian heroin to that sent by aspiring Afghan and Pakistani druglords. This had already captured about half of the New York City market. Hepatitis cases from contaminated needles were up. The Washington, DC central DEA office reported that the flow of heroin from New York had caused "an increase in overdose death statistics."[12]

With President Reagan and CIA Director William Casey, a new era began. On January 21, 1982, the US Federal Bureau of Investigation (FBI) which had largely avoided drug matters, was plunged squarely into them. Attorney-General William

French Smith announced that the FBI, instead of the DEA, would henceforth control anti-drug campaigns inside the United States. This effectively ended hitherto secret cooperation between the two services. It moved the DEA, which was struggling to control drug trafficking both inside and from outside the United States, further away from the main power centers in the Afghanistan war: President Reagan's National Security Council (NSC) and Casey's CIA.

Casey was now able secretly to engineer an exemption, sparing the CIA from a legal requirement to report on drug smuggling by CIA officers, agents or other "assets." Attorney Smith granted exemption in a secret memorandum on February 11, 1982, two months after President Reagan had authorized covert CIA support for the Nicaraguan anti-Communist Contra army. Investigative work in Washington in the late 1990s has disclosed that Casey realized that the CIA would face a serious legal dilemma if federal law continued to require it to report drug smuggling by its agents. On March 2, 1982, Casey thanked Smith for the exemption which, Casey wrote, helped to protect intelligence sources and methods.

After many details of CIA knowledge, if not control, of large-scale cocaine traffic from South America became public, President Clinton's administration in 1995 quietly rescinded the CIA narcotics exemption. The Contra-cocaine issue arose again in 1996 with investigative articles by a reporter for a California newspaper. Despite CIA denials, the Agency's inspector-general, Frederick P. Hitz, compiled a two-volume investigative report. He admitted that the CIA did indeed know about Contra drug trafficking and covered it up. The second volume reportedly was even more damning for the CIA, but at this writing it hasn't been released. It probably contains details of the South Asian drug operations as well, because the authority given Casey in February 1982 stayed in effect for the duration of the Afghan jihad.[13]

In the 1970s and even earlier, the region had been known to young Europeans, Americans and others as a good place to buy cannabis cheap, and to find harder substances too. Before the 1973 coup in Afghanistan, from 5,000 to 6,000 hippies or "flower children" were estimated to live in Kabul.[14] Young drug afficionados learned there that the familiar marijuana, which some American states were imitating countries like the Netherlands and "decriminalizing," was only the mildest narcotic product of the cannabis plant. This, according to a United Nations definition, was the "cannabis leaf, sometimes mixed with [the plant's] flowering tops in order to increase the drug's potency." On the other hand, "hashish, a far more potent form of cannabis, is the separate resin of the cannabis plant, whether crude or purified, obtained from the flowering tops." Hashish is also used to describe "compacted blocks of flowering tops of cannabis." Even more powerful in its hallucinatory effects is cannabis oil, an extract of the tops and the resin. It has a high concentration of the active substance in all parts of the ubiquitous cannabis weed, called tetrahydrocannibinol, or THC for short.[15]

What especially interested Ronald Reagan's Attorney-General in his visit to the Northwest Frontier drug country was neither the varieties of cannabis nor his surrender to the CIA of immunity from prosecution of its personnel involved in drug trafficking. He was anxious to see, in this forbidden backwater of the druglords' realm, the actual heroin which was killing thousands of Americans, Europeans and others each year. More and more of this heroin, he knew, because he read the DEA reports, was flowing from the poppy fields and laboratories of this region. The American Embassy and the DEA station in Islamabad arranged for him to focus on a famous village, Landi Kotal, already in 1982 – and it remained so into the 1990s – a center of the traffic in narcotics and in weapons.

North of Landi Kotal in Afghanistan, the men of Hekmatyar, Gaylani and other notables of the jihad were by this time doing the seasonal harvesting, for which they were allowed time off from fighting, of the poppy crops. Poppies are normally planted on irrigated land where there is also sufficient rainfall, as they require ample water. In eastern Afghanistan's Khash valley and the Keshem district of Badakshan province, the poppy fields are rain fed. The opium poppies normally compete with wheat grown during the same season, although the cash earned by raising the poppies is often fivefold that for wheat. In lower altitudes the poppies are sown in winter; higher up in the spring. Poppies are a short seasonal crop, allowing for two harvests a year in many parts of Afghanistan and Pakistan. They are usually followed by the planting of maize or corn; more rarely by cannabis or cotton.

At lower altitudes, the full- or part-time poppy farmers sow their fields normally from mid-October to late April; higher up, from the beginning of April to the end of August. Poppy blooms are either purple, red or white; and are often mixed in color. As soon as the petals fall, the bulb-like capsules appear at first bright green, then turn grayish. Harvesting of the opium resin or gum is done a few days after defoliation. It normally lasts two weeks. During this time, guerrilla fighters or trainees – especially, after 1996, in the northern parts of Afghanistan not controlled by the Taliban – are usually able to take leave to do their profitable work.

The capsules are scratched in the afternoon and the resin collected to prevent the loss of the milk, called *sheera,* on the next morning. Each pod or *ghozah* is incised two to six times, with an interval of two to three days before scraping. Opium resin is collected from small surface incisions on the capsule. The resin collected is called *apeen* or *taryak*. Yields of raw opium vary but normally weigh from 15 to 20 kg. per hectare (2.47 acres). As a UN drug report dourly observes, harvesting and weeding the poppies is labor intensive. It takes already scarce workers away from raising needed food and other tasks. Land used for poppies, as for cannabis, "cannot be used to grow previous food crops and as such contributes to the net deficit in food supplies in Afghanistan."[16] This is one big reason why Afghanistan is filled with unproductive land and underfed people at the end of the twentieth century.

Once the farmers have scraped off the poppy sap, which congeals and changes to a dark brown-blackish color, horses or mules carry it on their backs (unless the farmer himself is lucky enough to have a Toyota pickup truck, or belongs to a clan which owns one) direct to the nearest cooperating refinery. Here it is immediately converted to morphine. Compact morphine "bricks" are easier to handle than messy bundles of raw opium (which are smelly and so easily detected by sniffer dogs, or even human customs inspectors). Traffickers therefore prefer to convert the opium to morphine as quickly as possible. Conversion is done by first dissolving the opium in drums of hot water. Lime fertilizer is added to the hot, steaming solution. This precipitates out the organic wastes and leaves the morphine suspended near the surface. After removing residual waste matter, the morphine is put into another drum; heated, stirred and mixed with concentrated ammonia. The morphine solidifies. It drops to the bottom of the drum and can now be filtered out as chunky, white kernels. Once dried and packaged, the morphine base has only about ten percent of the original weight of the raw opium from which it was extracted.

Transforming morphine base into heroin is more complicated. Before the Afghanistan war period, Hong Kong and Marseilles were the heroin-refining capitals of the world. By the end of the 1990s, processing laboratories existed almost everywhere that opium poppies are grown, and in some other places near them: Southeast and Southwest Asia, Turkey, Iran, South America and, since the breakup of the Soviet Union at the end of the Afghan war, in the Muslim republics of Central Asia, the Caucasus and East European countries, especially Romania. The refining process comprises five stages. In chemical terms, the principle is chemically to bind acetic acid to the morphine molecule. This generates a substance which is converted into heroin powder. Ten kilograms of morphine can produce an equivalent amount of No. 3 or No. 4 heroin, ranging from 80 percent to 99 percent pure. To carry this out, a "precursor" chemical, as drug enforcement experts call it, named acetic anhydride is necessary. In Asia, acetic anhydride used to be trafficked mainly from India to Pakistan and then Afghanistan, but the Afghan war and postwar periods and their resulting drug profits have seen new precursor sources appear since the mid-1990s in Central Asia, the Far East and Europe.

How the refined heroin reaches Europe and the United States used to, and still does, involve elaborate webs of deception, networks of transport, ruses and variable routes, couriers and payoffs. By the time the Afghan fighters got into the business, sometimes with the established Pakistani traffickers, some of the usual routes ran through Baluchistan's bare deserts into Iran, Turkey, Syria, Egypt, Greece, Nigeria, Italy, France, England, Ireland, Germany, Belgium and the Netherlands – to say nothing of Denmark, Norway, Sweden and Finland. Since the Afghan and post-Afghan war profits began to flood into the pockets of the South Asian druglords and the mafias which work with them in the West, many new routes have been added to the old ones. These run through Eastern Europe, especially the former Yugoslavia since the Balkan wars which began there in the early 1990s; and the Muslim republics of former Soviet Central Asia. The results of these multiple new laboratories, smuggling routes and trafficking centers are dramatic and tragic for the West. From slight production before the Russians and the CIA began the war in 1979, the so-called Golden Crescent countries of Pakistan and Afghanistan have grown into the largest center of heroin production, consumed elsewhere as well as locally, in the world. By UN and other estimates, this amounted by 1997 to around

500 tons of pure white heroin powder. Its wholesale value in the United States alone was about $50 billion. US State Department narcotics reports point to a glut in supply, with world production in the late 1990s *ten times* its level in the pre-war years of the 1970s. This, despite huge expenditures on interdiction and other means of control. In both the United States and Europe, notably in the United Kingdom, heroin has made a spectacular comeback in the latter half of the 1990s. Formerly, most heroin was sold at only four percent purity. By 1998, the average purity of street heroin was 65 percent. Smoking and injecting this purer product is catching on among middle-class users. The British Home Office warned on August 3, 1998, that schoolchildren in smaller English towns, as well as London, Liverpool and other big cities, were being supplied with heroin at or near their schools and homes.[17] Heroin deaths, in the time lapse since the Afghan war ended, are up 100 percent in most of North America. The story is similar for Pakistan, the host country of the jihad: a disastrous 1.7 million addicts estimated in 1997, up from virtually none before the 1979–89 war. The UN Drug Control Program (UNDCP), according to its December 30, 1999 news release, found that Afghanistan had become the world's top opium producer. By February 2000, new UN figures estimated that the shattered country was producing 70 percent of the world's opium crop. The UN estimated the 1999 production at 4,600 tons, over 3,000 tons in 1998. Although Pakistan's own production of opium for export of 800 tons in 1979 had fallen to only 25 tons in 1998 and was forecast to drop to 5 tons in 1999, addicts in Pakistan by the year 2000 consumed 130 tons of drugs, mostly imported from Afghanistan. Social workers found around 200,000 *child* heroin addicts in Pakistan. By January 2000, more than one million addicts, including 80,000 children, lived in Karachi alone.

Our story, almost unknown except to two or three enterprising European investigative authors who have literally risked their lives in its pursuit, involves one central character, Hadji Ayoub Afridi. He is a dark, mustachioed chief of the Pushtun clan of the Afridis. They have lived for the past 2,000 years along the Khyber mountains, connecting Pakistan and Afghanistan to Central Asia. This route has seen the passage of the armies of Alexander the Great, Byzantine kings, Mongol Khans and Queen Victoria's regiments. Most recently it is the scene of the twentieth century's unholy wars between Soviet and Russian armies, and those of the anti-Communist West, allied with militant Islamist mercenaries.

Landi Kotal, where US Attorney-General William French Smith beat his hasty retreat without viewing the Afridi-controlled heroin laboratories in 1982 along the 10-mile long nerve center of the Khyber road, is the center of a heroin-producing empire. This empire's drug profits first supported the jihad against the Communists; then, even before it ended, was extending its operations into Europe, Asia, Africa and the Americas.

Hadji Ayoub Afridi, in his mid-sixties by 1995, had become the monarch of all he surveyed in Pakistan's Khyber Pass area. His clan or nuclear "family" (in the Sicilian sense), the Zakhakel, controls the region of the Khyber Pass and the crucial frontier post of Torkham, on the Khyber road between Pakistan and Afghanistan.

When the Russians arrived in Afghanistan in December 1979, he began to do business with them. Then Pakistan's ISI, needing him for the transport of arms and all manner of supplies to the moujahidin, soon won his full cooperation. Although proof in the public domain is lacking, close observers concluded that much of Afridi's fortune came from moving opium or even heroin from Afghan laboratories back down into Pakistan in the same trucks or caravans which had carried the arms northward. Another important product which the Pakistani drug clans move southward from production laboratories in Central Asia is acetic anhydride, the "precursor" chemical essential for conversion of opium and morphine base into heroin. French investigative author Stephane Allix, a leading European expert on drugs, was told that the ISI used proceeds of its narcotics transactions to finance anti-India guerrilla operations in Kashmir and Pakistani nuclear weapons programs, as well as the jihad in Afghanistan.

In any case, Afridi used his fortune to build himself an immense marble palace in his bastion of Landi Kotal. To the few journalists, politicians or other critics who dared to ask where he got his fortune, he would respond that he earned it selling china and crockery and in "international trucking."

By 1994, Afghanistan had become the leading world producer of opium. Afridi and some other members of the Zakhakel clan were multi-millionaires. At the beginning of March 1995, Hadji Ayoub Afridi traveled to Singapore where he knew Prime Minister Benazir Bhutto was visiting, and to whom he wished to propose a deal. In Singapore's Hyatt Regency Hotel, Afridi met members of her entourage. Hadji Ayoub knew he was on the list of individuals compiled by the American DEA and Justice Department as "extraditable"; men and women whose arrest and transfer to the United States for trial were the subject of sealed and often secret warrants. To avoid such a fate, Hadji Ayoub sought a deal with Benazir Bhutto: help him get off the American "wanted" list, in return for a thorough cleanup of the drug scene in the key Khyber and Afghan zones the Afridis controlled.

Prime Minister Benazir Bhutto, without meeting Afridi in person, let him know she didn't want to hear about it. So Afridi pursued private, parallel contacts he had already made with the American DEA station in Islamabad, especially with DEA Agent Gregory Lee. Afridi called a *tamzin*, or council, of clan and tribal leaders. The meeting drafted and sent to the US government, probably through Gregory Lee, a proposal to "cleanse" the Northwest Frontier region of drug laboratories, stockpiles of drugs and to end the transit of opium, in return for guarantees of legal immunity or safety. Most of the Afridi clan were rich enough by now to retire more than comfortably, and not seek additional compensation for their cleansing efforts.

Afridi made an offer through New York attorney Steve Goldenberg to a Brooklyn, NY prosecutor, who was apparently building a case against him for extradition. If charges were dropped, Afridi would *personally* see to a general cleansing of the drug scene in northwest Pakistan. Goldenberg wanted to arrange a meeting between Afridi and New York law-enforcement officers on "neutral" ground, such as London. However, Gregory Lee's arguments for a deal with the DEA prevailed.[18]

It was a cold mid-December day in 1995 in downtown Peshawar, the main center of the Afghan veterans' international terrorist and drug-trafficking networks. Two nephews and assistants of Hadji Ayoub Afridi summoned foreign journalists in Peshawar to the fortress-like Afridi palace in Peshawar's university district, not far distant from the ISI's guerrilla training center outside nearby Rawalpindi. The assembled newsmen were astonished at the announcement: the boss had surrendered to his hunters. Afridi, 63, had "fallen ill," and withdrawn to Tirah Valley, the heart of Afridi tribal territory near the Khyber Pass. Here he had collected a handful of faithful followers. He crossed the snowy mountains to the Valley of Nangarhar, Afghanistan, in territory still free from the encroachments of the already advancing Islamist zealots, the Taliban. Apparently following the terms of a deal reached with Gregory Lee of the DEA, Afridi got a safe-conduct from the then Afghan government in Kabul before arriving there by truck. From the Afghan capital, already falling into ruins from the internecine fighting rending the country since the Soviet evacuation in 1989, provided with an Afghan passport already containing an American visa, the Khyber tycoon flew to Dubai in the United Arab Emirates. There he boarded a regular flight to New York. One of his family members told a questioning journalist, "he's innocent and he'll prove he's done nothing wrong."

Afridi evidently felt that he was escaping, not from the frying pan into the fire, but from imminent ruin of himself and his clan in Pakistan. After his faithful service to the CIA and ISI in the Pakistani jihad, a merciless war had begun between the Afridi clan and General Naseerullah Babar, then Pakistan's Interior Minister and the strongman of the current government of Prime Minister Benazir Bhutto. Babar, probably on Benazir's orders, dedicated himself totally to bringing Afridi down. In 1993, the Benazir Bhutto government cancelled Afridi's mandate in parliament and he lost his seat there. Other members of his clan were declared unfit to be candidates. The Interior Ministry's Anti-Narcotic Force filed a complaint, resulting in confiscation by a special court in Peshawar of all the assets of Afridi and 17 other members of the clan. All were condemned under a 1977 anti-smuggling law. Commented General Babar: "These guys don't like to be incarcerated."

Hadji Ayoub Afridi himself was still at large, but he faced tough choices: capture by Babar's forces, followed by a grim jail confinement to await trial in either Karachi, Lahore or Islamabad and possible, if not probable, murder in prison; or he could give himself up to the persuasive blandishments of Gregory Lee of the DEA and face a regular trial in New York. This was the option Afridi finally chose.[19] Afridi, unfortunately for him, did not understand the vagaries of the American legal system, let alone the complex politics of justice in New York.

Afridi arrived at New York's Kennedy airport on the night of December 12–13, 1995 from Dubai, in the company of a DEA agent. According to the account of a wealthy New York attorney who became his friend and defender, a lawyer awaited him and he moved to a luxury Manhattan hotel. At the time he firmly believed that the DEA would see to it that he was released on bail and that he faced no more than perhaps a few days' inconvenience. He scarcely realized that the sum of the drug offenses he was charged with could land him in prison for life. On December 15 he appeared at the DEA offices in New York. Then he found himself appearing before a Federal judge in Brooklyn who remanded him to pre-trial confinement in the Manhattan Correctional Center. The judge read to him the charge of having in 1986 supplied hashish (not opium or heroin, though these were reputed to be the commodities in which he had dealt on behalf of Pakistan's ISI and their CIA colleagues) to another person. This other person had then smuggled it into the United States, said the charge. Afridi had been the subject of an international arrest warrant since 1988.[20]

Afridi pleaded innocent. He had come to the United States of his own free will, to clear his name. But the Brooklyn district court was adamant: no deal, and no bail. He was to be held in preventive detention in the dismal Brooklyn Correctional Center until his trial. The general charges, as opposed to the relatively mild specification about hashish sounded grim: drug trafficking, fraud, laundering of drug money, customs violations, smuggling and forgery of documents.[21] After about a year and a half of appeals and other efforts by his sympathetic and wealthy attorney and friend, Ivan Fischer and a defender, Steve Goldenberg, he finally went to trial in July 1997. He got a five-year sentence. This was lightened in circumstances which are unclear. Hadji Ayoub Afridi was now a broken man who had lost a lot of weight, as well as any faith he had earlier in the US government, whose agencies he had served so well during the Afghanistan war, and in American justice.

According to what Stephane Allix says Fischer told him, Afridi's other lawyer, Steve Goldenberg, decided to prosecute the DEA agent, Gregory Lee, who had brought about Afridi's capture, on grounds of a flawed arrest and legal proceedings.[22]

While Hadji Ayoub Afridi sat slumped in a prison cell in New York, his native Pakistan, between 1995 and 1998, saw deterioration of relations between US and Pakistani police and drug enforcement personnel. It was worse than what went on at the other end of the drug trail, in the United States, between the DEA and American justice authorities.

To set the stage for what she hoped would be a successful visit to the United States, and in search of ways to turn back on the nearly dried-up taps of Western investment and American military aid, Prime Minister Benazir Bhutto in early 1995 set out on an apparent anti-drugs crusade of her own. She repeated earlier public statements, largely for foreign consumption, that the American and Pakistani military conduct of the Afghanistan war had dropped her country and people into the pits of street violence, drug addiction and general poverty and misery. This, she said, was scaring off needed foreign investment. "It is the drug barons," she said at a ground-breaking ceremony for a $50 million Disneyland-like Adventure Land

Park in Lahore, "who can't see our government attracting huge foreign investments and improving the quality of the downtrodden classes."

She added harsh words for the Pakistani Islamist groups, including the Afghan war veterans, who resorted to street violence: "Those who throw bombs in mosques are not Muslims; they are *kafir*," (unbelievers), she proclaimed, referring to over 1,000 people who had died in ethnic and sectarian violence in Karachi during the previous 14 months. Narcotics dealers, she said, were financing the warring groups and "hiring guns to create fear" to deflect the pressure which her government was trying to apply against them. Two US diplomatic staffers had just been shot dead by an unidentified gunman and a bomb had exploded in a Shi'ite mosque, leaving another 12 dead.[23] All this happened during the visit to Singapore when, as we saw, Bhutto's aides had spurned Afridi's efforts to make a deal with her.

During the next few days, Bhutto's government tried to prove they were serious about cracking down on drugs. Some 2,800 men in armored vehicles of Pakistan's paramilitary Frontier Corps raided one of the remote Khyber valleys – Afridi country. There the government claimed it had dismantled 15 heroin laboratories and seized 6.3 tons of heroin. If true, this would be a world record for heroin seizures anywhere, and equal to the total amount of drugs of all kinds seized in Pakistan in 1994. At the time, the United Nations Drug Control Program (UNDCP) had just reported that, at about 120 tons of heroin a year, Pakistan had with Burma become the world's largest heroin distributor.[24]

In the United States in April 1997, the DEA arrested a senior Pakistani air force officer, Farouq Ahmed Khan. The charge was that he had smuggled two kilograms of heroin into the United States aboard a Pakistan Air Force Boeing 707. He was arrested while trying to sell the drug to an undercover agent running a "sting" operation at a MacDonald's restaurant in New York. Pakistan's narcotics cops launched their own investigation and apprehended, as *Time* magazine reported in December 1997, another air force officer in a Karachi hotel. He was allegedly running a small trafficking operation which included Farouq Ahmed Khan. Pakistan then made a surprise arrest which looked like revenge against the DEA. On April 28, 1997, the police seized one Ayaz Baluch, a trusted Pakistani employee of the American DEA and charged with drug trafficking and "anti-state activities." A senior Clinton administration official commented: "It seems he was arrested for carrying out his responsibilities as an employee of the DEA" – which would fit in with the old antagonism between the DEA on the one hand, and the CIA–ISI alliance on the other.

Throughout the second half of the 1990s, the single most crucial factor in the flow of drugs out of the Golden Crescent countries of Afghanistan, Pakistan and Iran has been the conquest of most of Afghanistan by the extreme Islamist movement, the Taliban. Their ambiguous attitude towards narcotics – proscribing their trafficking, sale and use on religious grounds, while tolerating and even profiting from their export – has, on balance, kept the narcotics flowing from Southwest Asia to all parts of the globe, especially the West.

To understand how the Taliban influence the Asian drug scene, one has to first try to understand the Taliban themselves, and the circumstances of their birth. The civil war that followed the 1989 Russian withdrawal from Afghanistan of the defeated Russians saw a constant struggle for control of the capital, Kabul. It was fought for three years between the two strongest parties to emerge from this war. One was the moderate Islamist faction, led by Burhaneddin Rabbani, who headed several postwar Afghan governments and his military chief, Ahmed Shah Massoud, the very successful field commander of moujahidin. The other party was the Islamist alliance headed by Gulbuddin Hekmatyar.

While these two main groups fought over Kabul, Afghanistan's hinterlands were run largely by their parties and partly by outsiders; warlords and druglords who belonged to none of the original seven parties which had fought the CIA's jihad against the Russians. However, local control was largely held by local commanders. They levied and collected "taxes," sometimes simply exacting road tolls from travelers and on goods shipments passing through their fiefs. They punished violators and adversaries; sometimes with a kind of rough justice; often with refinements of cruelty and corruption. One abuse which weighed most heavily on people all over Afghanistan had begun during the jihad – roadblocks where gunmen stopped travelers and shook them down for money every few miles. One journalist from Peshawar, Pakistan, Rahimullah Yusufzai, as reported in *The Economist* in October 1996, counted 24 "checkpoints" where money was extorted on a three-hour drive from Spin Boldak, in the Khyber region, to Kandahar. All this made normal travel and commerce more difficult, drove up prices of everything from onions to opium, and angered ordinary people.

In summer 1994, road bandits halted a convoy on the road north of Kandahar. The convoy's owners happened to be top-drawer, influential Pakistanis who demanded that their government do something. It couldn't intervene directly. Instead, officials – unclear whether they were ISI officials from the outset, or whether the ISI's control came only later – encouraged a group of Afghan students in the *madrassas* or religious schools to organize for militant action against the bandits. The guiding organization was the Islamist Jamiat-i-Ulema Islam, with outposts along the Afghan border.

About 2,000 of the students, who soon came to call themselves Taliban (which can mean simply "students" but is sometimes translated by the more romantic term, "the Seekers"), went to Kandahar and freed the convoy from the bandits. A legend sympathetic to the Taliban, and possibly true, recounts that two girl refugees, prisoners of a local commander and ill-treated by him, were freed by the Taliban. They then went on to capture Kandahar, the second largest Afghan city. There they were welcomed by most Kandaharis. This was because this original group of Taliban were Kandaharis themselves. The local strongman, a follower of Ahmed Shah Massoud, happened to be corrupt and thoroughly hated. Compared with past armed bands the Kandahar population had known, the young students behaved in exemplary fashion. When they cleared the gunmen from the roads, they merely disarmed them instead of killing them. They then sent them on their way, saying, in effect, go and sin no more. Through this, the pristine Taliban movement became associated with peace, order and Islamic law; at first without the excesses and distortions in the abuse of women and use of cruel punishments which marked their later "enforcement" of Muslim law codes.

The Taliban, by now the recipients of aid of various sorts from the Pakistani military, moved northeastwards from Kandahar and in February 1995 conquered Gulbuddin Hekmatyar's base outside Kabul; the base he used to shell Kabul with rockets in his efforts to dislodge the Rabbani government from power. Later, Hekmatyar allied himself with the Taliban. Failing to capture Kabul this time, they moved to the northwest to capture Herat, a city where they were less popular. People of Herat speak Persian. They are well-educated, liberal and traders in outlook. Many women were well-educated and followed fairly liberal employment practices and dress codes. The Herat people regarded the invaders as Pushtun peasants. They were stunned and shocked when a young man said to have shot two members of the Taliban was hanged from a crane – a practice the Taliban later adopted in other parts of Afghanistan – in the presence of the assembled public, while loudspeakers blared Koranic slogans.

In late summer of 1996, the Taliban moved decisively on Kabul, capturing Jalalabad on September 12. On September 26, 1996 they captured the capital and swiftly realigned all of the political forces in Afghanistan and in the entire region. Their repressive, even sadistic policies, to deny women the right to work, attend school or even go out of their homes uncovered or without the escort of a male relative; their eventual banning of television, music, enforcement of public prayer and obligatory beards for men; forbidding the playing of football in shorts and a huge list of further proscriptions, had already antagonized large segments of people under their control, who began to realize the price they had to pay for the peace and order they had welcomed so much. However, it was the public castration and execution of Afghanistan's last Communist, President Najibullah after they had entered Kabul, which especially repelled the international community, and made it difficult for them to win recognition, except from their mentors in Pakistan, Saudi Arabia and later, the United Arab Emirates.

Since his fall from power in April 1992, Najibullah had lived in the sanctuary of the UN office in Kabul. Many Afghans had virtually forgotten him, as well as his responsibility for countless tortures and executions of his opponents in the past. The fall of Kabul gave the Taliban effective control of all but about the northern one-third of the country. The Taliban were predominantly Pushtuns, and their ethnic adversaries, the non-Pushtuns, now rallied in opposition. The president whom the Taliban chased from power in Kabul was Burhaneddin Rabbani, a Tajik. The new anti-Taliban alliance after the fall of Kabul came under the command of an Uzbek, Abdul Rashid Dostom, a former general in Najibullah's army who had changed camp after the Soviet withdrawal. Dostom, while not recognizing Rabbani as president, cooperated loosely with him and his military commander, Ahmed Shah

Massoud in an alliance. This anti-Taliban alliance also included the Shi'ite group, Hizb-i-Wahdat, led by Abdul Karim Khalili who represented Iran's firm opposition to the Taliban. Afghanistan was now effectively polarized, as the leading American academic expert on Afghanistan, Barnett R. Rubin has pointed out, between Pushtun and non-Pushtun forces.

There was even greater polarization in geopolitical terms. Pakistan's ISI and Saudi Arabia; the former with arms and logistical support; the latter with its seemingly inexhaustible supply of money which had flowed during and since the CIA's jihad against Russia, supported the Taliban advance. Many regional observers believed that the US did too, after such senior American envoys as Ms. Robin Raphel, divorced wife of US ambassador in Islamabad Arnold Raphel, who had died with President Zia al-Haq in the crash of Zia's plane in 1988, met with Taliban representatives. This alarmed Russia, the Central Asian republics and especially Iran. Since the birth of the Taliban in 1994, the Central Asian regimes feared that the Taliban would sweep northward into Tajikistan, intensifying an already vigorous civil war there and threatening the former Soviet borders. These had now become the security frontiers of the post-Soviet Commonwealth of Independent States (CIS). Then as later, Iran feared the Taliban as a Sunni Muslim (and therefore anti-Shia) force which would exclude the Shia from power, and especially as part of a US strategy to encircle and contain Iran.[25] Tehran and others in the region, including Indian officials in Delhi, believed and still believe as the new century began, that the United States deliberately allied itself with Pakistan and Saudi Arabia in these efforts, using the Taliban in the same way as they had used the moujahidin in the 1979–89 Afghan jihad against the Soviets.

In reality, this was at best both an oversimplification and an exaggeration. The US State Department and those CIA or other agencies' officials who would comment at all on the Taliban consistently denied official US support for the Taliban. They used lack of diplomatic recognition by Washington as one of their main items of evidence. Washington's best-informed analysts understood that the Taliban were, indeed, a Pakistani creation. One seasoned American observer returned from one of his frequent visits to Afghanistan to tell the author, "the Taliban began, essentially, as a kind of experimental Frankenstein monster [the same had been said by thoughtful observers of the Taliban's immediate predecessors and kinfolk, the moujahidin]. They were created in the laboratories, so to speak, of Pakistani intelligence, the ISI – *in order to produce a counter-force to Iran and Iranian Islamism, which would be even more repugnant and unacceptable to the West and Russia than the Ayatollah Khomeini' successors in Tehran.*"[26]

To better understand the Taliban's ambiguous policy toward the flow of drugs which the 1979–89 jihad against the Soviets had helped to generate, it is first desirable to give a closer look to the genesis of the Taliban movement, and those who supported it.

As we saw, the first Islamic students in the movement had galvanized, as Dr. Barnett Rubin observes, resentment of ethnic Pushtuns against corruption of the former holy warriors' leaders, and domination of the Kabul government by Tajiks and other non-Pushtuns. The generals and colonels of Pakistan's ISI, with or without concurrrrence of their erstwhile allies and mentors in the American CIA, saw in the Taliban a means of re-establishing Pushtun hegemony. This would mean that ethnic Pushtuns on both sides of the frontier might drop their historic plans to unite in a single Pushtun nation, or at least would not focus these revindications on Pakistan. Even more important – and here the Pakistani goals converged with those of SOCAL, a giant American oil company which has its eye firmly on the energy resources of Central Asia and hopes to build a trans-Afghan pipeline from Central Asia to the Indian Ocean to pump them out – was the hope that the Taliban, once in control, would be a security blanket. It would be able, they conjectured, to secure the truck highways and eventually routes for oil and natural gas pipelines, so dearly desired by SOCAL and other international groups. These trade and energy routes would run through Pakistan, America's ally, rather than through Iran, her adversary ever since Khomeiny's overthrow of the Shah in 1979. Encouraging for the likes of the ISI and SOCAL was that while one route northward was blocked by fighting in Kabul, the Taliban succeeded in opening another route. This led through their bases in Kandahar and Herat, which they captured in September 1995, to Turkmenistan, rich in oil and gas.[27] In 1993, Pakistan and Turkmenistan had signed an agreement to jointly develop their energy resources and build a pipeline between the two countries. UNOCAL, based in California, signed a protocol with the then Turkmen government to explore the feasibility of building a pipeline through Afghan territory to Pakistan. The one-year study cost $10 million for a huge energy project worth $18 billion, to transport Turkmen oil and gas by pipeline to the Indian Ocean. This would bypass Iranian ambitions to channel Turkmen energy. However, with the decline of the Taliban's support in the West, including UNOCAL, the project appeared frozen if not dead, by 1998, after Iran and Turkmenistan finalized an agreement for a short gas pipeline from Turkmenistan across their common frontier.

A further objective of both Taliban and Pakistan is the recovery of natural gas from northern Afghanistan's Shibergan province, pumped northward to Russia through Uzbekistan. This resulted from a deal signed between Moscow and the pre-invasion Afghan secular government in 1977. Afghan estimates of the resources in the Shibergan gas fields run to 1,100 billion cubic meters. Export of the gas continued throughout most of the 1979–89 war, despite periodic sabotage orchestrated by the CIA and Pakistan's ISI, and carried out by specially-trained moujahidin groups. Under the contract, which continued in force between Afghanistan's government in Kabul (under Taliban control since 1996) and the Russian government in Moscow, Russia imported two billion cubic meters of gas each year. Some of the gas, but only minimal quantities, was sold locally in Shibergan and also in Mazar-i-Sharif, which the Taliban captured from its opponents on August 9, 1998. The overwhelming bulk of gas was pumped northward for Russian use. When they captured Mazar-i-Sharif, the Taliban accused General

Dostom, chief of the anti-Taliban coalition, of "squandering" the Russian revenues for the gas for his own personal use. In exchange for keeping the gas flowing to Russia, a Taliban newspaper charged, "Dostum received weapons and military supplies from Russia in order to retain his hold over the norrthern areas, and fight against the Taliban."[28] It remained to be seen whether in the course of consolidating their control over all of Afghanistan, the Taliban would retain the old contract with Russia, summon it to pay arrears from all the years Moscow was paying Dostum, and ask what rates, if any, it would pay in the future.

During the first two years of the Taliban's ascendancy, 1994–96, the US government indulged in excessive wishful thinking that they would curb or even end the plague of drugs from Afghanistan. This wishful respect for the Taliban's supposed good intentions was based in part upon their growing military power: their Saudi and Pakistani benefactors saw to it that by October 1996, they had fielded an army of fully 25,000 men, complete with tanks, armored vehicles and fighter aircraft; mainly old MIGs held over from captured Afghan government stocks, recycled in part through Pakistan's ISI. They were able to recruit former Afghan military personnel in Pakistani refugee camps who were veterans of service as fighter pilots, tank drivers and technicians in various fields by offering them high salaries paid in US dollars.[29]

The Taliban attitude toward drug cultivation, production and trafficking has proven to be a curious mix of religious principles, ambiguity and expediency. On August 26, 1996, the Islamist Sharia radio station in Afghanistan announced that the Taliban had banned the production, taking and sale of both heroin and hashish. Nothing was said about the cultivation of opium poppies, the main earner of revenue in the areas of southern and western Afghanistan where the Taliban seemed to have firm control by then. However, to the perhaps wishful officials of the United Nations International Drug Control Program (UNDCP), who had been urging the Taliban to impose an absolute prohibition, the broadcast seemed a hopeful sign. For years, UNDCP had been struggling to stop heroin production in the Golden Crescent. It saw the Taliban's new jihad as an opportunity. The deposed Kabul government of President Burhaneddin Rabbani, now heading the anti-Taliban coalition, had endorsed UN conventions forbidding production, but had no means to enforce them. The trouble was that the men and women of the UNDCP put too much faith in the literal power of sharia, Islamic law, which relies heavily on interpretation. The agency enlisted Islamic scholars to support its case against drugs. However, Taliban leaders, on the rare occasion when they would discuss it at all with outsiders, insisted that the Taliban alone had authority to interpret the law. In fact, until its military victories in the summer of 1998, when it overran Mazar-i-Sharif and most of the other bastions of the opposition along the northern frontiers, it had made no clear ruling about heroin.

Stephane Allix, already cited above, is an intrepid, 30-year-old French traveler and journalist who has gained real expertise concerning the flow of drugs westward from South Asia. He acquired this expertise by traveling himself the routes taken by the drug traffickers through South and Central Asia, and by interviewing hundreds of drug growers, merchants, traffickers and law-enforcement officials of all descriptions in the region's different states and in Europe. Allix recorded the results of his investigations in a lively and informative book published in Paris in 1998, *La Petite Cuillere de Scheherezade* (Sheherezade's Little Spoon). Questions about Taliban narcotics policies and practices were uppermost in his mind when he met Mullah Muhammad Omar Akhunzadeh, the nearly "invisible" leader, as Allix calls him, of the movement. Mullah Omar was born in country where the peasants cultivate opium, the Maywand district of Kandahar province of Afghanistan. Allix found him to be a tall, thin man of rather elegant appearance, with an "almost inaudible voice, broad beard and a turban." The Taliban leader had been injured three times in battles of Afghanistan's unholy wars. Allix found him to be suffering from what Allix called the "Ignatius de Loyola Syndrome," because that early Jesuit ideologue, like Mullah Omar, was "using his injuries as a means of access to God," a kind of self-righteous martyrdom while still alive and leading his soldiers. Mullah Omar offered Allix no more enlightenment on drugs than he had to other Western visitors who very rarely had access to him.

Basically, concluded Allix – and concurring with him are many drug-control officials of the UNDCP and national drug-control and law-enforcement agencies – that despite the Taliban prohibition of drugs, the movement cannot escape the fact that drugs and the drug culture are fundamentally rooted in the still overwhelmingly tribal Afghan society. By 1999, this society had suffered 14 years of war, followed by four years of social and economic chaos. This had encouraged continuation and expansion of the opium cultivation, which the generals, warlords and intelligence officers had so richly rewarded during the 1979–89 jihad. Following the capture of Kabul in 1996, Mullah Omar and the other Taliban leaders realized that they might be able to exploit their very genuine, religious-based opposition to drugs to offset Western hostility, aroused by such practices as placing women in a kind of permanent purdah; floggings, stonings to death, amputation of fingers, hands, and feet as punishments; and even the public live burial (by bulldozing layers of rocks onto them) of men convicted by the Taliban courts of sodomy.

On November 9, 1996, Giovanni Quaglia, the UNDCP director in Islamabad, received a letter from the Taliban Foreign Minister, Mullah Muhammad Ghaus. It stated a rather self-evident truth: "the struggle against production, refining and traffic in narcotic substances is possible only through regional and international cooperation." This was the first Taliban statement concerning drug *production*, as opposed to trafficking or use. Quaglia told Stephane Allix and other journalists that it was unquestionable that Taliban capture of the Jalalabad and Nangarhar regions in early September 1996 had given them control of the majority of opium production zones. Quaglia added hopefully that the Taliban appeared ready to cooperate with the UNDCP in substituting other crops for the opium poppies. If this indeed turned out to be true, "the problem could be settled within ten years."[30]

However, it had long been clear to those among the Pakistani officials anxious to curb the drug traffic – often the same ISI and other officials concerned with keeping governments in Kabul weak and unstable, so as to keep regional Pakistani hegemony strong – that two conditions were necessary to suppress drugs. First, there had to be internal and external peace and security. Second, Afghanistan had to have one strong central power in Kabul with real authority everywhere. Neither condition, of course, has been achieved since the Soviets invaded in 1979 and the holy war against them was begun.

One of the drug trails to the West begins in Nangarhar province of Afghanistan, where the largest local bazaar where the opium farmers market their wares is in the village of Khanikel, not far from the frontier with Pakistan. Buyers come from miles around, including Pakistani territory, and purchase 100 to 150 kilos of raw opium at a time. Often they only view samples, and the final deliveries, resulting from negotiations, run into tons. The Afghan poppy farmers pay to the local Muslim cleric, the mullah, a tax on each transaction called the *zakat* or *ouchar*. This is a tax at the source, amounting to about 10 percent of the value of the sale. Since they took control, the Taliban have centralized all tax collection, including the tax on opium. The Taliban which Stephane Allix observed supervising these matters in the Dar-e-Noor area appeared not to be real zealots or genuine religious students. They were too lax, and came from another part of the province. Beyond the frontier, in the Dir Valley in Pakistan, Allix found what had been a center of intense poppy cultivation now switching to raising peas and onions. A joint project of the Pakistan drug control authorities and a UN agency, plus the recent arrival of electric power in the region, had made it easier to get the replacement crops to market. A farmer in the area could earn three times as much with peas as he had formerly from opium. This was because trucks provided by the UN program could get the vegetables to market much more expeditiously than the former opium crops, carried by human couriers and by mules.

In the northern Afghanistan region of Mazar-i-Sharif, which had opposed the Taliban and successfully repulsed their earlier attacks until their conquest of the whole of northern Afghanistan in August 1998, the hashish crops are said to be of the best quality in the world. The so-called Friendship Bridge across the Darya river to Uzbekistan at Khariaton, where the last Soviet troop convoy left Afghanistan at the end of the holy war on February 15, 1989 – the day celebrated by the CIA with a party at their headquarters in Langley, Virginia – is a bridge heavily involved in drug trafficking. Opium, morphine base and heroin as well as the local hashish cross to Uzbekistan. Chemical precursors used for heroin production, precursors produced in Central Asia since the early 1990s, cross in the other direction. The Uzbek authorities, in deadly fear of Taliban invasion or incursions, hermetically sealed the bridge in the summer of 1998, as they did during previous, less permanent Taliban advances.[31]

Allix found huge fortunes being earned by traffickers in and around Mazar-i-Sharif, before the Taliban came to stay. The "businessmen" from nearby Uzbekistan,

Pakistan and more distant Russia and Turkey made extensive contacts there for their drug export operations. The bosses of heroin laboratories founded since the Soviet withdrawal in 1989 have facilities to move tons of acetic anhydride and other precursor chemicals which supply the labs in Afghanistan. In February 1995, 15 tons of acetic anhydride were seized in one control operation by the Russian-controlled Uzbek narcotics police in Yermez, across the border from Mazar-i-Sharif, where giant portraits of General Dostom, the Uzbek warlord who ruled the area before the Taliban takeover of 1998, symbolically dominated the city's streets and squares.[32]

Further east, Allix found that the Badakshan region of Afghanistan was producing about 60 tons of opium annually, only 2.5 percent of the Afghan total but enough to supply France's heroin addicts for a year. There are two main opium routes out of Faizabad, the provincial capital. One leads toward Tajikistan, the other toward Pakistan over the Dora mountain pass, 4,500 meters high. Dominating both routes and controlling the traffic on them in 1998 was a local strongman named Hadjmuddin Khan, an ally of the intrepid former anti-Soviet and subsequent anti-Taliban fighter, Ahmed Shah Massoud. It is mountain country where people walk behind their donkeys and mules on very bad roads, although some of the more successful local drug farmers and traffickers drive new Toyota "four by four" pickup trucks. Since Iran and Pakistan both tightened border controls, the drug routes northward into Central Asia have been opening up.

Several Western investigators who have been able to penetrate the area found that one of these drug routes, into Tajikistan, was being used to smuggle uranium and other dangerous contraband southward toward Pakistan. In this region, Allix met a tailor who was a regular buyer of opium from peasants. He was paying $50 a kilo and reselling the opium after carrying it by car to a place called Khawahan, for about $150 a kilo. He was making a profit of about $30,000 on each trip. His monthly earnings as a tailor were about $8.00.[33] There are innumerable similar cases of sudden enrichment of little people all along the drug trail from fractured Afghanistan, to the drug-ridden societies of the West.

UNDCP, DEA and other investigators have found evidence of many heroin laboratories during the late 1990s in Badakshan province of Afghanistan and in the nearby Shinwar region of Pakistan. In Taloqan and Mazar-i-Sharif, before capture of both by the Taliban, highly refined heroin (up to 70 percent pure) sold for between $3,000 and $5,000 a kilo. At the Tajik frontier, Russian border guards of the 201st Russian division try to keep out both the Taliban and other Islamist fighters from Afghanistan and, theoretically, the drugs. However, travelers report that some Russian officers on the Tajik–Afghan frontier were "in the game;" i.e., taking kickbacks from the drug smugglers on shipments allowed into Tajikistan.[34]

Blocked from entering Central Asia for a time, Allix flew to Pakistan and found that customs inspectors at Islamabad airport were discriminating against some airline passengers. Dark-skinned ones, whom they seemed to think were more suspect – perhaps because of the involvement of Nigerians and other Africans in the drug traffic – were often forced to lie down and be X-rayed by a baggage machine. This sometimes detected heroin-filled condoms swallowed by the drug couriers, a technique favored for years by the cocaine smugglers from Colombia. In the Northwest Frontier Province, opium was in the later 1990s no longer as easy to find as it was when President Reagan's attorney general visited the region more than a decade earlier. You now had to go to known villages and caves in the back country to find it. Hashish, however, was sold freely in the tribal areas, where the government of Prime Minister Nawaz Sharif, Benazir Bhutto's successor, was struggling to establish more central government control. About six miles from Peshawar, it was on sale in sewed-up goatskins. It was as easily available as sugar or flour.

One of the reasons for Iran's extreme hostility toward the Taliban is drugs. Before the opening of the Central Asian routes and the Iranian clerical regimes' crackdown on the transit of drugs from Afghanistan in the 1990s, huge and heavily armed drug caravans, using camels and trucks, used to cross the deserts from Afghanistan and the Baluchistan region of Pakistan to reach Iran. During the intense hostility between Washington and the revolutionary Iranian regime, there were frequent American statements accusing Iran of poor enforcement and lack of cooperation in halting international drug trafficking. However, both the UNDP and Interpol have praised Iran's efforts. In 1989, anticipating the new post-Afghanistan war floodtide of drugs flowing westward, Iran in January 1989 passed tough anti-drug legislation. It included an obligatory death penalty for anyone caught with at least 30 grams of heroin or five kilograms of opium. From then until March 1998, more than 3,000 drug smugglers were executed and hundreds of thousands of addicts jailed by the Iranian ayatollahs. Over the same period, Iran reported its drug seizures averaging about 160 tons of various narcotics each year. To combat the social problems caused by rising addiction, the Iranian government spent $350 million to cut off the drug transit routes in the eastern frontiers, and to build walls and fences along its desert and mountain borders with Afghanistan and Pakistan.[35]

In Dushanbe, Stephane Allix talked with the president of Tajikistan's State Commission for Drug Control, Rustan Nazarov, who is closely supported by the UN anti-drug programs. Nazarov proudly announced seizure of 3.5 tons of opium on Tajikistan's frontiers in 1997. From that year onward, there were persistent reports of a big heroin laboratory in Kunduz, Afghanistan, directly across the border from the Tajik town of Nijni Piandj. Smugglers move the heroin from there to Dushanbe, to Uzbekistan and to a big trafficking center called Khojent, northern Tajikistan (called Lenininabad in the Soviet time), where there is both a railway line and an airport. It is located in the Fergana Valley, a fertile region where many crops including opium are raised, and which also happens to be a historical center of Islamist activity. The inhabitants were among the fiercest opponents of the Soviet colonization of Central Asia. On the frontier with Tajikistan, the Afghan dealers sell opium at $110 for a kilo. It is resold inside Tajikistan for $150. At Dushanbe, the capital, the price doubles to $300. By the time it reaches Khojent, it fetches $700.

An organized drug mafia in Dushanbe sells opium locally, but the bulk of the shipments go onward to Uzbekistan and finally Russia. In 1997, Kyrgyzstan, Tajikistan and Uzbekistan signed a cooperation agreement with the UN to fight drug trafficking.[36]

The Taliban conquest of northern Afghanistan in the late summer of 1998 highlighted two roles for Uzbekistan, another former Soviet republic. One was in the defense of Russia's southern flanks against what was seen in Moscow as the threat from militant Islamists – a kind of revenge for Russia's futile and disastrous invasion of Afghanistan in 1979. The second role which history seemed to be assigning to the 15 million Uzbeks was to act as a hub for the drug traffic toward the West and Russia, which had developed in the wake of the unholy wars on Uzbekistan's southern side.

As the Taliban's bearded young warriors captured all of their main objectives in northern Afghanistan, and in August 1998 reached Hairaton, on the 90-mile Uzbek border with Afghanistan, the Uzbek government of President Islam A. Karimov in Tashkent completely sealed off that border. Frontier troops, with enthusiastic Russian backing, were alerted and there were persistent rumors in Tashkent of an imminent arrival of Russian troop reinforcements in the former Russian dominion. The Taliban advance had unquestionably brought Uzbekistan and Russia closer together, after a long period when the Kremlin had been losing its influence in Central Asia. In May 1998, Uzbekistan, Tajikistan and Russia set up an alliance to combat religious extremism, incarnated for them by the Taliban, as successors of the CIA-supported moujahidin of the 1979–89 war. In early August, when the Taliban fighters captured Mazar-i-Sharif and moved toward the old Soviet frontiers, General Anatoly Kvashin flew to Tashkent with Russian First Deputy Foreign Minister Boris Pashtukhov. Russia and Uzbekistan together called on the Taliban to halt their advance and reserved the right to take "all necessary measures" to protect the borders of the Commonwealth of Independent States (CIS). Tajikistan, with close ethnic ties to the ethnic Tajik general Ahmed Shah Massoud, commanding remnants of the anti-Taliban forces, has experienced, along with its plague of drug trafficking, a bloody civil war, almost since its independence from Moscow. It was perfectly natural that President Rakhmanov should appeal to the CIS – read Russia – to strengthen border security and to the United Nations to help negotiate a peaceful end to the unholy "civil" war in Afghanistan. It was also expectable that, as things turned out, President Saparmurad Niyazov of Turkmenistan, the third ex-Soviet neighbor of Afghanistan and Iran, should say little. In the past his Turkmen government had refused to condemn the Taliban. This was mainly due to the planned natural gas pipeline from Turkmenistan through Afghanistan to Pakistan. Whether Niyazov could successfully keep his neutral position remained to be seen.

None of the three northern neighbors had recognized the Taliban as a legitimate government in Afghanistan, and in the past, helped their enemies. In July 1998 the Taliban leader, Mullah Muhammad Omar Akhunzadeh, felt called upon to warn Uzbekistan and Tajikistan not to allow any opposition bases to take root in their countries.[37]

Clearly, the drug barons in Uzbekistan and its surrounding states might have much to fear from any further advance of the Taliban into their domains. In Tajikistan, according to UN reports, the opposition apparently financed its anti-Taliban operations inside Afghanistan in part by selling opium and its by-products. In Afghanistan, the leader of the ethnic Uzbek (and equally anti-Taliban) militia, General Rashid Dostom, was suspected of earning huge profits by exporting drugs via Uzbekistan. In 1997, Uzbek television showed much footage of drug raids by Uzbek authorities in which huge quantities of opium and heroin were seized on trains between Tajikistan and Uzbekistan, hidden in sacks of jute and plastic bags. The seizures increased in size in 1997 and 1998. The Uzbek boundaries are permeable to drug smugglers because of the tangled national frontiers between the Tajik, Uzbek and Kirghiz republics drawn by Soviet dictator Joseph Stalin. These frontiers placed pockets of national minorities of neighbors in each country. Also, national capitals are always close to neighbors (Tashkent, for example, is only seven miles from the border of Kazakhstan). The capitals are also cut off by international borders or often insurmountable mountain barriers from their second largest cities. This makes it impossible to patrol all of the tangled frontiers.

The two leading trading centers for the drugs smuggled out of Afghanistan and Pakistan are Osh in Kyrgyzstan and Samarkand in Uzbekistan. Some of the opium collected in Samarkand is sent for refining to Chechenya, Russia's rebellious vassal state in the Caucasus, and across the Caspian Sea. Drugs gathered in Osh are sent to Tashkent, enriching some customs officials enormously and enabling them to buy palatial homes costing up to $500,000 and Mercedes or other limousines worth upwards of $30,000 – although the most senior state officials draw salaries of $150 a month or less. Chimkent, a rail station and river port for trade with Russia, is a sort of Tashkent annex in Kazakhstan. Business activities there are apparently controlled by three top Uzbek businessmen. A plant for legal pharmaceutical products in Chimkent was officially closed down after the collapse of the Soviet Union, but was at last reports still operating under new private management – rumored to be drug mafia men. No one, from UN officials to journalists like Stephane Allix, have been able to check. Security fences, walls and guards keep anyone from getting close to it.[38]

The Russian daily newspaper *Konsomolskaya Pravda* on May 5 and 12, 1996, published exposés about a major drug trafficking ring between Afghanistan, Uzbekistan and Chechenya involving "senior officials" of those states. The story was never denied by anyone in authority, and it named Russians and Chechens linked to the KGB and General Rashid Dostom. The general was the one-time ally of the Russians who then changed sides and fought with the CIA and Pakistan against them, after they withdrew support from the Najibullah Communist regime in 1991. The reports said opium was collected in the southern Afghan province of Helmand, a major cultivation area, and sent across the border to Termez,

Uzbekistan, from where it was airlifted to Samarkand by General Dostom's own helicopter force, each carrying two-thirds of one metric ton at a time. Dostom's partner in Uzbekistan was said to be a top official of the narcotics police.

Since the end of the Afghan war Uzbekistan has been used for transit of precursor chemicals. Tightening of international controls and an informal 1994 control accord between Iran and Pakistan led the druglords to seek new suppliers in Central Asia, and more recently, in East Europe. Chemicals are shipped to the heroin refineries through Central Asia. Examples cited by the UN and an extremely well-informed private French think-tank on drugs called OGD, short for General Drug Observatory, were seizures of chemicals by Uzbek authorities in 1996. On August 30, 1996, they confiscated 33 tons of acetic acid, enough to make 22 tons of acetic anhydride which could serve to produce between seven and ten tons of heroin, On September 28, the Uzbeks found another 7,200 liters of finished acetic anhydride, also bound for the heroin laboratories in Afghanistan.

In Central Asian cities like Tashkent, Almaty, Kazakhstan or Ashkabad, the capital of Turkmenistan, addicts, especially young people, have since the Afghan war become users of semi-finished drugs, unmarketable in Western Europe, but sold by local drug pushers. Many of these people, whom American "born again Christian" fundamentalist groups are trying to recruit and win away from the drugs, are envious of the "fever of conspicuous consumption," in the words of one European observer of the area, "gripping the *nouveaux riches* who revel in dream cars, girls on tap and 100-dollar discos. They are a sitting target for purveyors of unexportable drugs." Opium, locally called khanka, sells for $4 a ball. It is diluted with alcohol or an ampule of the drug Dimidrol, then injected. Small-scale Uzbek gangs, operating in Tashkent and also in Tajikistan, sell ampules of a synthetic opiate called Norphin at $40 for a ten-pack of 2-milliliter shots. The ampules come in boxes with a taped-on label: "Norphin, manufactured in India by Unichem Laboratories." The cost price is 105 rupees a pack.

In Uzbekistan, Azerbaijan and elsewhere, the privatization of former socialist state enterprises has become tied to the laundering of drug profits. Some 45,000 private companies were created in Uzbekistan in 1995. A reporter from the French OGD organization spoke with a small employer named Anwar, who employed only a dozen men, but had to register five companies in order to operate his real business. In Uzbekistan, a company can have no more than the equivalent of between one and three dollars (150 soms, the Uzbek currency unit) on hand in cash. Anything over this has to be banked within 48 hours. The banks still operate under the old socialist rules of the Soviet era. They monitor deposits, manage expenditures and charge up to 40 percent interest on cash flows. This guarantees that the state retains control over "private" business. Anwar therefore created five companies, sitting on the board of all five but owning only one. His group is called Cascade Limited. He always has bills outstanding between one company and another, keeping enough cash flowing through them that doesn't need to be banked because it never stays in one firm for more than two days. Anwar, of course, has a clever accountant. These practices are operated on a much larger scale by the big-time "barons" of the Central Asian economies. A university professor who had grown weary of trying to survive on a threadbare salary of a few dollars a month and who joined one of the "barons" showed OGD's man a stack of bills owed to a company in Tatarstan, the homeland of the Tatars, whom Stalin deported to Siberia during World War II, in the Russian Federation. They represented 11.7 million Uzbek soms for 12 tons of motor oil, or $5 million wholesale at the exchange rate then prevailing. When the OGD private eye expressed surprise at the exorbitant price, the accountant showed him blank pre-stamped bills in the names of Kazakh, Turkmen and Russian companies, and blank receipts ready to be filled out by hand.

Many companies operate from private houses. Some are ostensibly travel agencies, selling luxury holidays in the Maldive Islands, Greece and Turkey where Uzbeks who have made some money buy into real estate in the south coast resort of Antalya. Others organize charter flights of prostitutes to the Arab Gulf states. Many sell passports stamped with necessary exit visas for $500 apiece, $100 of which, in 1996, was going to "understanding" interior ministry officials.[39]

The Republic of Kazakhstan is another key arena for trafficking and marketing of the drugs flowing out of postwar Afghanistan. It became independent when the Soviet Union dissolved on December 26, 1991. The reigning Communist party chief, Nursultan Nazarbayev, was elected president unopposed. In legislative elections on March 7, 1994, criticized by international observers as unfair and corrupt, his ex-Communist party won an overwhelming victory. On February 14, 1994, Kazakhstan qualified for a respectable role in the US and Russian-supervised "new world order," proclaimed earlier by President George Bush, by dismantling its Soviet-era nuclear-tipped missiles pointed at the United States, and adhered to the 1968 Nuclear Nonproliferation Treaty. Washington duly promised new aid. Nazarbayev's term of office was extended to December 2000. Socialism began to be discarded by legalization of private land ownership in December 1994.

One reason why Kazakhstan has become such a satisfactory work area for the drug smugglers, traffickers and marketeers, is its diverse ethnic structure. The last census in 1994 showed 42 percent of the population to be Kazakhs and 37 percent Russians. Its remaining nationalities include communities of Germans, Turks, Ukrainians, Chechens, Bulgarians and others, many of whom were originally exiled to Kazakhstan by Stalin, who had a mania for deporting people from their own homes in the Soviet Union to distant lands.[40] A similar situation also exists in Kyrgyzstan. In both countries, each national and ethnic community tends to take on a special task in the drug trade: drug addiction in Almaty, Kazakhstan's principal city, is growing fast. The laundering of drug money, through purchase of land, houses, Mercedes and other big luxury cars, has become a major industry. In the division of labor, the Chechens tend to run the heroin laboratories, while Bulgarians and Turks manage local marketing and onward transport toward the streets of Europe.

Drug income is laundered through cotton culture, mining, construction of hotels (like the Hyatt Hotel in Almaty, sold to local operators by Marco Polo, the Austrian chain which operates hotels in Moscow and other cities of the old Soviet Union and Poland). Banks quickly appear and equally quickly vanish. Many work with banks in Switzerland and offshore banks in the Caribbean. A Korean community resident in Almaty has been active in finance and shipping of drugs. Fifteen tons of acetic anhydride, the heroin precursor chemical, sent by Koreans outward and probably intended for the heroin laboratories of Afghanistan or Pakistan, were seized at Termez on the border in February 1995.

One of the most active "legitimate" firms is Transworld Enterprises Ltd., which in 1998 had a letterbox in Dublin but was controlled by the Chorny Brothers, who come from Bokhara, Uzbekistan. They developed excellent contacts with Boris Yeltsin and when he came to power, they gradually moved into the control of aluminum, chrome and iron ore mining and refining in Russia, according to Allix. In 1994, they moved out of Russia to Israel, after some pressure from law-enforcement agencies in Russia. They operate in Kazakhstan with an entrepreneur named Alexander Marchkevitch, who set up a huge network with large investments and using many cover firms. They are said to control a plant at Chimkent, on the road between Almaty and Tashkent, which during the Soviet era produced legal pharmaceutical products, including opiates. After the Soviet collapse, huge quantities of opium were reported to be stored there which, Allix was told by local informants, could produce heroin on an "industrial" scale. No one, including visitors from TACIS, the economic cooperation program of the European Commission in Brussels, has been permitted to get even near it, let alone visit.[41]

Railroad lines from Central Asia connect with Kazakh and Turkmen ports on the Caspian Sea. From those ports, opium, heroin and hashish move to Azerbaijan and Georgia; then into Turkey and across the Black Sea to Romania and into Moldova, both of which harbor many heroin laboratories. The trans-national nature of the newer drug trade out of South Asia was well illustrated by seizure of a Tajik truck driven by Kazakh drivers, bound for Moscow, on the Tajik–Uzbek frontier, coming from Dushanbe. It carried 250 kilos of opium and a few kilos of heroin. There were also a few grams of hashish – for the use of the drivers.[42]

Next along the narcotics trail westward from Afghanistan lies the Republic of Turkmenistan, population about 4,200,000 on an area of 185,000 square miles, 80 percent of which is the desolate desert of Kara Kum. Smugglers and other travelers have the saying, about the Kara Kum, "you can get in, but you probably won't ever get out again." Turkic tribes have inhabited the habitable parts since the tenth century. Czarist Russia conquered it in 1881 and colonized it as Russian Turkestan, which joined the Soviet Union as a constituent republic called Turkmenistan in 1925. It declared independence on October 27, 1991, even before the Soviet Union officially broke up. Its huge reserves of oil and natural gas, especially the latter, place the Republic in a much better economic position than its poorer and more populous neighbors. In 2002 the supreme ruler since independence was still

President Saparmurad Niyazov, an authoritarian figure who, like his Tajik, Uzbek and Kazakh neighbors, still relies on Russian security troops to protect him from internal and external foes. His honorific title is Turkmenbashi, Father of the Turkmens, and his portrait has become a cult object, displayed everywhere. A new rail line has connected Turkmenistan with its southern neighbor Iran. This quickly became a new route for Golden Crescent drugs moving toward Europe.

The economics of the West-bound drug traffic illustrate the relative importance of Turkmenistan in the post-Afghan war drug trade. According to a UN drug expert, 10 percent of Afghan production passes through Central Asia. This would represent roughly 300 tons of raw opium, which would make 30 tons of heroin. A kilo of opium sold for about $1,000 in Almaty, Kazakhstan, could end up only in Moscow or St. Petersburg, because of the established trafficking channels. In Russia, this opium would more than treble in value. However, if the same kilo of opium were sold in Turkmenistan, it would fetch only the same amount, about $1,000 and thus earn no profit whatsoever. This single kilo of opium would not profit the heroin merchants, because it takes ten kilos of opium to make one kilo of heroin. At $2,000 per kilo of opium, this would bring the price of a kilo of heroin to around $20,000. Since in Romania, where there are thriving heroin laboratories, heroin sells for significantly cheaper prices, the opium arriving for refining in Turkish or Romanian labs cannot be coming from Kazakhstan or Uzbekistan. It comes from Turkmenistan. Criminal groups bring it from the northern Afghan frontier. The opium produced in Afghanistan costs between $150 and $200; the heroin between $3,000 and $8,000 per kilo, depending on quality.

Turkmenistan offers the same kind of advantages for the traffickers which Iran offered before it began to clamp down on trafficking. It has a long frontier with Afghanistan, and a direct route of export to the laboratories. For Iran, the ideal country to export to was Turkey; whereas for Turkmenistan, the best markets and next transit countries westward are the Caucasus countries and Romania. UN statistics, probably provided mainly by Turkmen law enforcement agencies, show only minimal seizures in 1997; only about 100 kilos of heroin intercepted, plus about 50 tons, in two separate seizures, of acetic anhydride precursor. The chemicals were bound for a firm in Herat, Afghanistan, and the shipments were made to look as though meant for the leather industry there. The acetic anhydride came from a firm in Moscow which turned out to be only a PO box number. One shipment came in a liquid tank; another from Uzbekistan. Turkmen drug control officials said the heroin laboratories supplying heroin seized in their country came from the north and the extreme south of Afghanistan, especially Nanghahar province, where the Taliban were said to be knowingly levying a tax, profitable for them, on the fabrication of the heroin, plus transit fees on the merchandise leaving for Pakistan.

The railroad line in Turkmenistan to the Afghan frontier crosses that border at Towraghondi. Containers loaded onto trains that use it often have double bottoms or sides, and 12 tons of hashish were seized in 1997 in such a container. A firm in Kandahar, Afghanistan, Muhammad Essa and Company, according to Stephane

Allix, sent a container with a double bottom to Slovakia and drugs were detected in it before it left Turkmenistan. A rail link leads through Turkmenistan to the Turkmen port whose Soviet name was Krasnovodsk, renamed Turkmenbashi after the all-powerful Turkmen ruler. In Ashkabad itself, a kilo of opium worth about $200 on the Afghan frontier jumps to a value of $800 to $1,000; while the kilo of opium worth between $3,000 and $8,000 jumps to $15,000. No wonder, a visiting Western journalist mused, that the streets of Ashkabad, like those of Almaty, Bishkek or Tashkent, were teeming with new Mercedes and BMW cars.[43]

8 Russia: Bitter Aftertaste and Reluctant Return

Noon in Moscow, mid-winter 1994. White snow, black ice and struggling traffic outside. Inside the posh restaurant, steamy windows, warmth, snug chairs, gleaming crystal on spotless white table cloths. Few foreigners at the tables, but plenty of Moscow's *noveaux riches*: members of the Duma, the post-Soviet Russian parliament, many of them with private incomes; actors, actresses, successful artists; high officials and, doubtless, some of the *rekittery* (pronounced much like the American word it mimics and signifies: racketeers or mafiosi); theatrical producers; probably some high-class tarts and call-girls (hard to tell the players apart here without a program or personal acquaintance); assorted but affluent Bohemians.

Somehow dominating the scene was the huge, gaunt and muscular man seated at our table, cinema actor and director Vladimir Ilyin. A powerful nose and jaw under a bare, bald forehead, sweeping back finally to a crown of hair falling to his shoulders. The physique of an active athlete; eyes with a steely but humorous glint, reflecting bemused intelligence.

While ex-ballerina Irena Rachashavskaya, ABC News' Moscow bureau research specialist and myself rather self-consciously but dutifully consume an expensive lunch, our guest lunches on a couple of bottles of beer. "I had a sandwich at the studio; too much work today." He waves aside our ineffectual protests. Ilyin, a presence commanding attention, talks to us. He passes rapidly over his Brezhnev-era and pre-Brezhnev career as a Russian cinema idol. The Afghanistan war began and "sometime, I went into the army," he affirms. He was selected and trained for the elite SPETZNAZ forces and served in Afghanistan for nearly five years.

It was sheer hell, he acknowledges. "The war itself was already hell enough …" Worse was seeing what it had done to some of his buddies in SPETZNAZ. It had been bad enough fighting the *doushki* or "ghosts," the elusive holy warriors on the enemy side. Those buddies, Ilyin remembers, could not rid themselves of the war, even when it ended. They took its burdens home with them. "What burdens?" was the obvious question. Ilyin stretched out his arms, the sinews of a weight-lifter showing under a clinging, silk shirt, his palm turned upward. "Drugs, weapons, the habits of violence," he responded.

Wanting, most probably, to purge his soul of his own war experiences, and at the same time share them with wider cinema audiences, he had set up a California office. It was called the Hollywood Moscow Connection, in Woodland Hills, not far from Los Angeles.

In Ilyin's film, the hero bears the film's name, "Stinger" – after the deadly American anti-aircraft missiles which did much to defeat the Soviets in Afghanistan. After 13 years there, the last few spent trying to induce Red Army comrades taken hostage by the moujahidin, but who converted to Islam, to return to Russia with him, Stinger sets out in the film scenario through the high mountains across Chinese territory. The time is supposed to be the near future. Russia and nearby areas have fallen under the sway of an evil dictator, Merlan. With two American companions, one of them a former intelligence operative, the other a *Time* magazine correspondent, Stinger and a few other brave souls finally triumph over the bad guys supporting Merlan. Our hero re-enters a Russian society fractured, like the former Soviet empire collapsing around it, and moving swiftly into an unknown future.

The tale of the Stinger film contains some paradigms for the impact of the Aghanistan war on the nation and society which was forced to wage it. One of the many themes it suggests, the progressive demoralization of the Russian armed forces, which accompanied their impoverishment, and how many of its individuals turned to big-time crime, Ilyin disclosed in a candid moment, toward the end of our lunch. I asked him whether any of his fellow SPETZNAZ veterans had gone abroad after the war, to seek their fortunes, as it were.

Ilyin grinned broadly. He took another sip of beer. "You bet they did," he chuckled. "I could give you – but I won't – the names and locations of four of my army buddies now in America. All of them have found their fortunes. They're bigtime gangsters."[1] They, were, in fact, members of the huge syndicate of Russian organized crime which spread across North America and Europe after the end of the Afghanistan war and the collapse of the Soviet Union.

Many of the embittered veterans, *Afghantsi* as they were called in Russia, returned to find silence, indifference or even the jibes of their fellow countrymen; experiences much like those of innumerable American veterans of Vietnam when they came home. The bitterness was doubly difficult to bear, because they had shared with the American Vietnam veterans another traumatic experience: they had failed against an enemy which was, despite the largesse of their CIA suppliers, woefully under-equipped in relation to themselves, the Russians, but which was totally and stubbornly determined to win. The Red Army, according to official figures, had suffered around 14,000 dead and missing between 1979 and the withdrawal of half of the remaining 116,000 Soviet troops in Afghanistan by August 15, 1988. The remaining half were pulled out by February 15, 1989; the day of the senior CIA officers' little victory party at Langley, Virginia. The worst single year had been 1984, with 2,343 dead, including 305 officers.[2]

At home in Russia, the returned *Afghantsi* began to organize and lobby for the defense of their rights and their dignity. They formed clubs and even vigilante groups, to keep up old wartime comradeships and civic spirit. The new freedoms of the Gorbachev era brought about a cascade of unprecedented public criticism of the war itself, and of the decisions taken by the tiny oligarchy around Brezhnev, to launch it in 1979. The first man who dared to declare that the whole adventure had been a costly and tragic mistake was a former speech writer for Nikita Khruschev, the much earlier Communist reformer. This occurred at a television roundtable in June 1988, just two months after the signing of the Geneva accords.

A columnist for the very official newspaper *Izvestia,* Alexander Bovin, observed that sending over 100,000 troops into Afghanistan was a leading example of the excessive use of force in Soviet foreign policy.

Artyom Borovik, a journalist, author and former soldier who had written graphic reports about demoralization of the Red Army in Afghanistan through drugs, interviewed the former Soviet commander-in-chief in Kabul for the weekly magazine *Ogonek*. He disclosed that the army command had not supported directives of the Brezhnev politburo to invade Afghanistan until it was forced to by being overruled. Borovik depicted the stark horrors of the war for the Red Army soldiers: ambushes by night, the spectral, unseen enemy; the smell of charred flesh in the ruins of a downed Soviet helicopter. President Mikhail Gorbachev personally gave the censor the green light to publish Borovik's unprecedentedly frank and brutal account. Borovik's editor, Vitaly Korotich, described for *New York Times* correspondent, columnist and author Hedrick Smith how he had called General Sergei Akhromyev, chief of the general staff, on a hotline phone given to Korotich by Gorbachev, to get permission to send a reporter to the front. Gorbachev had decided to prepare the Soviet public for the withdrawal from Afghanistan. As Hedrick Smith observed, "he was manipulating the press just as surely as American presidents do – but in ways the Soviets were unaccustomed to."[3]

With the new freedom of expression came a general realization among Russians and their non-Russian subjects in the disintegrating empire of how the Afghanistan adventure and its accompanying suppression of truth had hidden the parlous plight of Soviet society. Alexander Solzhenitsyn, in his Vermont exile until 1984, wrote in 1990 of how "Time has finally run out for communism." During the 70 years of Communist rule (which, he might have added, was culminated by the Afghanistan disaster), Russia had lost a third of its people to war and the executioners of Stalin and his successors. Its peasant class and its agricultural resources, rivers and lakes and clean atmosphere had been destroyed by mismanagement and waste of resources and by industrial pollution. Families had been destroyed and women subjugated. "Our health care is utterly neglected, there are no medicines, and we have even forgotten the meaning of a proper diet. Millions lack housing, and a helplessness bred of the absence of personal rights permeates the entire country."[4]

The angry *Afghantsi* veterans launched new crusades. Many became instigators or founding members of lobbies for proper health care, preferred treatment as consumers and, like the Vietnam veterans in America, Australia and elsewhere, for more understanding from the folks at home. Along with the other new associations of professional people came reformist officers of the armed forces. They formed an organization called Shield.[5]

Afghantsi had their angry say at a historic meeting of the Congress of People's Deputies, unprecedented in its efforts to constitute a democratic forum, which opened in Moscow on May 25, 1989. Liberals and reformers wanted an open agenda and open debate. The old ex-Communist power establishment, however, wanted only to go through the motions of electing Gorbachev as the legislative chairman, in effect Soviet president, and of selecting 542 members of the still-existing permanent legislature, the Supreme Soviet. Andrei Sakharov emerged as a champion of the reformers and radicals. He was impatient for rapid democratic change and for smashing of the old, corrupt bureaucratic structures. On April 9, 1989, there was a brutal crackdown on spreading anti-Russian nationalism, this time in Tiblisi, the capital of Georgia. Troops commanded by Russian Colonel-General Rodionov, a people's deputy to the congress, crushed a Georgian nationalist demonstration. Rodionov became one of the main targets of the radicals.

On June 2, 1989, the radicals turned their frustrated wrath on Andrei Sakharov, the nuclear physicist, called "the father of the Soviet H-bomb," and the best-known of all the Soviet dissidents. Sakharov had solemnly and repeatedly accused the Soviet forces of abuses, atrocities and criminal involvement with drugs and smuggling in Afghanistan, all well-substantiated charges. The Soviet Old Guard, as Hedrick Smith observed, was determined to humble the reformers and radicals, even those of Sakharov's stature, on national television as anti-patriotic. First to attack Sakharov was Sergei Chervonopisky, a 32-year-old former major in the Soviet airborne troops. He had lost both legs fighting the moujahidin. He was one of 120 Afghanistan war veterans in the congress; a delegate from the Ukraine. Chervonopisky took on Sakharov for asserting in an interview with a Canadian newspaper, the *Ottawa Citizen,* that Soviet combat pilots had sometimes fired on Soviet ground troops to prevent them from being taken prisoner. The general, a Ukrainian, denounced Sakharov for an "irresponsible, provocative trick," for trying to discredit the armed forces and trying "to breach the sacred unity of the army, the Party and the people." Many speakers followed his lead. One was Marshal Sergei Akhromyev, former chief of the general staff, who accused Sakharov of deliberately lying.

Amid hoots, catcalls and insults, Sakharov took the podium. He repeated to the assembled congress that "The Afghan was a criminal adventure … a terrible sin. I came out against sending troops to Afghanistan and for this I was exiled to Gorky." He expressed pride in his exile and affirmed, "I have not apologized to the Soviet army, for I have not insulted it. I have insulted those who gave criminal orders to send troops to Afghanistan."[6]

Sakharov went on to urge dismantling of the KGB and other repressive apparatus of the Communist Party. Eventually Gorbachev cut off Sakharov's microphone. After Sakharov died in 1990, his posthumous memoirs disclosed wide differences between his scholar's reasoned objections to the Afghanistan war and Solzhenitsyn's deep-seated, religious and almost visceral aversion to nearly everything the Soviet Union had done on the world stage, including development of Sakharov's H-bomb.

Demoralization of the Soviet armed forces in the Afghanistan war worked its way up through the ranks. It bred drunkenness and drug addiction (with or without the assistance of the CIA) among the troops. But it also worked its way from the upper ranks downward, and laterally outward into Soviet and post-Soviet civilian society.

It fostered avoidance of military service by young men who dreaded being conscripted, after reading and hearing accounts of the horrors of Afghanistan. At the top, advocates of change emerged from the war. One was a political officer in his early thirties, Major Vladimir Lopatin. He published a series of insubordinate criticisms of the civilian leadership under Gorbachev. Real change, Lopatin asserted in many public forums, was hindered by "the almighty Trinity: the military-industrial bureaucracy, the nomenklatura [privileged elite] of the Communist party and the senior generals."

A decade after the last departing Soviet troops crossed the Amu Darya river bridge from Afghanistan, those Russian "peacekeeping forces" in 1998 were back. This time they were secretly, not openly, engaged in the turmoil which they and the Americans and Pakistanis had left behind in Afghanistan. The new Russian mission concerned, to a large degree, the quest and the safeguarding of the oil and gas reserves of Central Asia. More, they were attempting to reassert Russian political influence in its former empire. Most of all, perhaps, President Boris Yeltsin's crumbling state machinery, beset by the worst economic crisis since World War II, was determined to stem the tide of Islamism which the advancing Taliban were carrying with them to the old frontiers of the former Soviet empire.

Without committing troops for the second time in a generation to the quagmire of Afghanistan, where it had lost so many soldiers and so much prestige during the nine-year occupation, Russia in 1998 was supplying heavy weapons, training and logistical support to the foes of the Taliban, grouped loosely in the Northern Alliance, struggling to hold the northernmost tier of Afghanistan's mountains. In doing so, at least until the United States retaliated for the killing of nearly 300 people and wounding of thousands of others around US embassies in Nairobi and Dar es Salaam in August 1998 with cruise missile strikes against Osama bin Laden's training camps, the Russians found themselves loosely allied with Iran in countering the Taliban. Actually, Iran was supplying equal amounts, or more, arms, fuel and other resources to the anti-Taliban forces than the Russians were. Facing Iran and the approximately 25,000 Red Army troops on the mountain frontiers were also Pakistan and Saudi Arabia, the foreign creators and benefactors of the Taliban.

Worst of all for the demoralized and underpaid Russian soldiers, whose younger men were mercilessly hazed, harassed and sometimes seriously injured by the bullying of their seniors, they were again facing their old enemies, the moujahidin. The Northern Alliance was led by none other than Ahmed Shah Massoud, once one of the toughest and most effective leaders of the CIA's jihad against the Soviets in 1979–89. "Massoud," recalled a US intelligence official to James Risen of the *New York Times*, "was the pointed end of the stick, the man we went to when we really wanted something done against the Russians." Only this time, neither the CIA nor the US government, despite their vexation with Osama bin Laden's international terrorist network, appeared to stand behind Massoud in his fight with the Taliban, who were sheltering bin Laden.

Standing behind the new Russian covert involvement in Afghanistan in 1998 were Moscow's strategic interests in South and Central Asia, as well as Iranian interests which partly overlap with the Russian ones.

The Northern Alliance was the last buffer, as the Russians saw it, between the Taliban and the Afghan border with the Central Asian republics. Meanwhile, the continuing civil war in Afghanistan had one attraction for the Muscovite strategists: it prevented Western oil companies from building pipelines across Afghan territory. Russia fears that Islamism will spill over the borders from Afghanistan into its remaining sphere of influence in the Muslim republics, which as we have seen, are already ridden by drug trafficking and organized crime. The Shi'ite Muslims of Iran see the Sunni Muslims in the Taliban movement as bitter rivals and adversaries. Both Iran and Russia want to ensure that many of the planned pipelines to ship Caspian oil to the world's markets cross Iranian or Russian territory. This gave both of them an incentive to block such plans as that of the US firm SOCAL and other Western companies to build pipelines across Afghanistan to the Indian Ocean ports.

A measure of how the 1979–89 Afghanistan war and the Soviet Union's subsequent breakup weakened the Russian defense establishment is that Ahmed Shah Massoud acknowledged that he received much equipment from the Russian Mafia arms merchants, rather than the Russian army or Defense Ministry. Western intelligence officials admitted this, but insisted that both the governments in Moscow and Tehran were involved. The arsenals in use in 1998, from jet fighters to some fairly up-to-date tanks and armored vehicles on both sides, could not be operated without foreign assistance. Both the Northern Alliance rebels and the Taliban were using surplus weapons left over from the 1979–89 war; the need for spare parts, regular maintenance and training forced both sides to solicit outside help. The main rear supply and logistics base of the Northern Alliance in the late summer of 1998 appeared to be an air base in Tajikistan, where 20,000 Russian troops were based and Moscow's political writ still ran.[7]

In their postwar deployments in South Asia, the Russian army's officers and enlisted cadres had to keep in mind the bitter lessons of the 1979–89 war. Ethnic conflicts had rended the Red Army before and during the war, and these conflicts survived into the postwar decades. In the invasion of December 1979, the high command mobilized reserve units stationed near the frontier. At least two of the divisions first sent to Kabul by land and air were made up of non-Russians; Central Asian Muslims mustered in what was called "castrated" units, fleshed out with recent draftees. Many of the conscripts had spent their earlier service in non-fighting units, using picks and shovels or working on the railroads. As their initial commander, Marshal Sergei Sokolov, discovered, the Asian troops not only lacked training and experience, but were politically undependable. They shared racial and Muslim religious and cultural links with the Afghans they had to fight. Many spoke the same languages. This led not to better fighting spirit, but to the opposite: collaboration. Central Asian soldiers were seen passing ammunition, and even personal weapons to the locals, and buying, in the local bazaars, Korans – some of which had probably been printed, as we saw, by the CIA in Virginia.

By the end of March 1980, the Soviet high command had realized its mistake in sending in the Central Asian troops. It pulled them out and sent home the Muslim reservists. Subsequently, most of the Soviet troops sent to Afghanistan were Russians, Ukrainians or other non-Muslim Slavs, considered militarily more proficient and politically more reliable. By mid-November of 1980, mobilization for the Afghanistan war was augmented by another for service in Poland, then under severe threat of a total Soviet occupation and subjugation which never came about. Whereas Turkic-speaking Azeris, many Uzbeks, Kazakhs and Uighurs, all Muslims, were initially mustered from local populations for Afghanistan, the Politburo in Moscow authorized the mobilization of the European non-Russian ethnic groups: Carpathians, Balts and Byelorussians, for the expected intervention in Poland. Many reservists never answered the call and could not be located. Many who did show up had to be housed in tents. In the winter chill, others deserted and headed for home, prodded by the merciless bullying of their seniors. There were so many deserters, as later in Afghanistan, that in some cases the military authorities gave up efforts to track and punish them. By the late 1990s, when reinforcements were again being sent to South Asia to contain the perceived threat from the Taliban, annual desertion estimates reached five figures.

As the Afghanistan war wound down and ended in the late 1980s, the ethnic fracturing of the Soviet Union itself spread from a number of fault lines, one of the biggest being Afghanistan itself. During the Afghan civil wars following the final fall of the Communist Najibullah government and the entry of the moujahidin into Kabul into April 1992, the various Afghan factions cooperated with their ethnic cousins north of the borders. At a conference in Davos, Switzerland in February 1994, the growing instability in much of South and Central Asia resulting from the war was aired in talks among Pakistan's then Prime Minister Benazir Bhutto and the presidents of Turkey, Uzbekistan, Kazakhstan and Turkmenistan. The latter three states shared a bond of similar language with Turkey itself.

Uzbekistan's president, Islam A. Karimov, objected to Ms. Bhutto's argument that the rise of militant political Islam, awakened by the Afghanistan war, was not a real problem for the region. Karimov antagonized the Pakistanis by demanding more attention from them and the United Nations to saving Afghanistan from the internal wars now destroying it. He also depicted Pakistan as an "instrument" of the Islamists. Uzbekistan, meanwhile, was maintaining relations both with the leading ethnic Uzbek warlord in Afghanistan, General Rashid Dostom and with the exceedingly radical, Pushtun CIA creation, Gulbuddin Hekmatyar, who opposed the Tajik President Burhaneddin Rabbani. By this time, Uzbek units were also fighting side by side with Russian troops. They were both defending the ex-Communist government of nearby Tajikistan from Islamist ex-moujahidin, now attacking across the border from Afghanistan, and menacing that government in Dushanbe. As a senior diplomat from Uzbekistan assured me in Washington DC in November 1994, Pakistani and also Saudi Arabian money was still buying fuel for Islamist fires in the ex-Soviet republics, and even inside the Russian Federation itself.[8] This trend continued on into 1998. The United States found itself in a dilemma. Its Pakistani and Saudi allies were still financing the radical Taliban, who sheltered its proclaimed enemy, Osama bin Laden. Suddenly the US found itself at least temporarily allied with its old adversaries, Russia and Iran, against the Taliban.[9]

The violence, bullying and ethnic persecution in the armed forces, as in civilian society, all helped to prepare the ground for the explosion of organized crime and Mafia-type violence which swept over Russia in the 1990s. This crime and violence was exported to much of the rest of the world, especially Western Europe and North America, where the term "Russian Mafia" became almost as familiar to Americans and Canadians as did household names like John Dillinger and Al Capone in earlier decades. The main ingredient of this crime in Russia itself was the drug culture. This, as we saw in the last chapter, grew out of both the addiction and smuggling in the armed forces during the Afghanistan war, and spread into Russia along the narcotics trails from Central and South Asia. However, the drug culture, which by this end of the twentieth century has taken as firm a hold on society in Russia and its former colonies as it has in the West, also has older and deeper roots.

In traditional Soviet Communist mythology for internal use, drugs were a social problem only in the West, although occasionally government or government-inspired literature would make bland references to "old traditions," meaning use of opium and hashish in Central Asia. These official and officially-inspired accounts always insisted that opium poppies were grown only for "licit" use by the pharmaceutical industry. The poppies were supposed to be produced on collective farms under the eyes of virtuous and incorruptible security men, who guarded the morals of their charges, as well as their fields. It was also acknowledged that some poppies were grown in backyards in the Ukraine or Byelorussia (not, mind you, in Mother Russia herself) in order to make that favorite of Mom's home baking, poppyseed cake.

Arkady Vaksberg asserts that experts he knows of, "using their own independently derived (and thus presumably more reliable) figures, confirm that in the middle of 1990, there were no less than four million people regularly using drugs" in Russia, and that the number was constantly growing. At that time, the Soviet militia and customs service were seizing no more than 10 to 20 percent of all drugs in circulation, or about 30 tons at the most.[10]

By 1997, as United Nations and independent organizations noted, organized crime had largely taken control of both the export and domestic trafficking and marketing of drugs in Russia. The delay was apparently due to the fact that the Russian "mob" was busy ransacking and looting the former state-led economy. They were emptying the treasuries and cash-boxes of the Communist Party and the state enterprises. They removed the billions of US dollars and other hard currencies they had stored in suitcases and trunks to be laundered in Switzerland, London, Paris, Cyprus, New York and many other destinations. When the initial pillage was over, the Russian organized crime groups turned their attention increasingly to drug trafficking on a major scale.

The main seizures of drugs in Russia by the late 1990s were of hashish, much of it in transit toward Western Europe, and opium poppy straw. Seizures of hashish were mostly destined for the Netherlands, where the drug's sale is quasi-legal in small quantities. Lithuania and Estonia receive small shipments by rail, although in 1996 Baltic officials began to intercept large shipments from trailers carrying containers from commercial cargo ships. The hashish arrives in Russia mostly in private automobiles from Kazakhstan, Kyrgyztan and Turkmenistan. Hashish from Afghanistan and the rest of the Golden Crescent states comes mostly by plane in false-bottomed baggage on commercial flights between Russia and Central Asia. In 1995, hashish was still transferred onto planes heading for Zurich and Geneva. Beginning in 1996, hashish arrived in the Moscow area, probably to be repackaged and shipped by road to the Netherlands.

On the ever-growing domestic market for drugs in Russia, competition from Ukrainian pushers and dealers has been increasing. Raw opium, morphine base and other "raw" materials, as well as their transport, have come into the hands of a single group of "businessmen" investing in the drug trade. In the Far East, the Russian customs service and the organized crime department of the FSB (the former KGB) are fighting Chinese smugglers who have expanded into the port city of Vladivostok and other Pacific coastal areas by distributing drugs conditioned into pills. These pills are mostly derivative of the drug ephedrine, which has many therapeutical uses in medicine, especially in respiratory diseases. The drug is produced in massive quantities in northern China. Inside Russia, major criminal organizations have moved into control of the domestic market. Even government and NGO (non-governmental organization) assistance to addicted inmates and street dealers, consisting of smuggling drugs into detention camps and prisons, is under mafia-type control. LSD and other synthetic drugs are on the increase. Russia's overworked anti-drug squads have great difficulty identifying these substances. In April 1996, Moscow post office employees discovered 500 LSD "hits" conditioned as a booklet of stamps in a packaged book. Plentiful quantities of LSD and the drug called Ecstasy were openly available in Moscow night clubs, especially before the economic crash of the summer of 1998 which drastically reduced the affluent clientele. Azerbaijan nationals who used to deal in fruits and vegetables have switched to dealing drugs in the streets and market-places. The Central Asians, in their turn, were being displaced from 1997 onward by Africans, especially Nigerians, who have established efficient and well-concealed networks for selling heroin and cocaine in Moscow's student living areas and university residences.

One of the most tragic aspects of the drug scene in Russia, as in the Western world, has been drug use among children, especially young girls. In the St.

Petersburg area, 15 to 30 percent of school pupils use drugs, such as hallucinogenic mushrooms gathered in forests outside the city for sale to high school and university students. Another consequence of youthful drug addiction in Russia, well-known in the West, especially through growth of intravenous drug use, is propagation of the AIDS virus. According to Professor Vadim Pokrovsky of the Scientific Methodological Anti-AIDS Russian Center, a million people were expected to be HIV positive by the beginning of 1998. All of Russia, even isolated areas in northern Siberia, are affected. Professor Pokrovsky estimated the actual number of cases at the end of 1997 at around 10,000.[11]

Closely allied with the druglords in post-Soviet Russia are the arms merchants, both international and local. In the years following the Afghanistan war, they have nurtured what was, when the war ended in 1989, a healthy infant into a monstrous adolescent, growing as the new century approached at a breakneck speed into a malevolent adult. It is closely linked with regional conflicts like that in separatist Chechenya in 1994–96 and other regional conflicts inside and around the Russian Federation. The growth of the arms trade in Russia has, since the Afghan war's end, been related also to the rise of terrorism.

The story of the Stinger anti-aircraft missile, the namesake of producer Vladimir Ilyin's film, is classic. It contains a major lesson for any government which, like that of the United States, gives one of the deadliest weapons in its arsenal to mercenaries or proxies, and then provides training in that weapon.

The first American Stingers were in the hands of the Afghan guerrillas by the summer of 1986. They shot down their first Soviet helicopter in September of that year. Over the next ten months, the moujahidin fired nearly 190 missiles. Under what was at first careful watch by their US Special Forces instructors, with Pakistan's ISI supervising the training and benefitting from it, they achieved the very high kill rate of 75 percent. Soon, Afghan government pilots flying the sophisticated Soviet attack helicopters were monitored complaining on the radio that their Soviet "advisors" no longer dared to fly with them. The guerrillas were able to trap their enemies inside a few cities and major military camps.[12]

As US enthusiasm for the weapons increased, controls over them gradually slackened. As a US intelligence official in Washington told the *Washington Post*, "we were handing them out like lollipops." By the time of the Soviet withdrawal in 1989, the CIA was already engaged in frantic efforts to buy back the missiles. Pakistan's ISI apparently kept a fair amount. Local guerrilla commanders, said observers on the scene, would have sold their mothers if necessary to buy them back. Inside Afghanistan, a former Pakistani officer compared the buyback efforts to a "fish market with everyone running around trying to get hold of Stingers because everybody in between had a stake." Missiles which cost the US Army about $35,000 each in the mid-1980s were selling, by the early 1990s, at up to $100,000 each on the black market. Most Afghan commanders wouldn't give them up at any price.

Outside Afghanistan, the Stinger appeared in the Persian Gulf during the Iran–Iraq war. On October 9, 1987, the Pentagon acknowledged that spare parts for the missiles had been found in an Iranian boat belonging to the naval branch of the Iranian Revolutionary Guards. Pentagon sleuths eventually discovered that two aides of Gulbuddin Hekmatyar had sold up to 16 Stingers in May 1987 to Revolutionary Guards for about one million dollars. A Russian report cited capture by Iranian border guards of an Afghan truck convoy carrying Stingers, some of which were sold to official Iranians and ten more to drug smugglers anxious to ward off helicopters trying to watch and cripple their transnational trafficking. The price was said to be $300,000 each.[13]

During the latter years of the Bush administration, the CIA requested and got from Congress an initial $10 million for Operation MIAS (for "missing-in-action Stingers.") The amount was pathetically insufficient. As the ex-Soviet republics began to break away from Moscow's control, and in some cases like that of Azerbaijan and Armenia, to fight one another, the Stingers began to fetch premium prices on the black arms market.

One of the first post-Afghanistan war dramas involving this traffic in Stingers developed in the stubborn little warrior state of Chechenya, a reluctant member of the Russian Federation which fought for its independence from Moscow in the 1990s. About 9,000 square miles in area, it had before its war with Russia, which surrounds it completely, about 1.2 million inhabitants. About 280,000 of these were Russians and 735,000 native Chechens. The Chechens are among the oldest peoples of the northern Caucasus. They are mainly Muslims of the Sunni or Orthodox persuasion, and have waged holy wars against the hated Russians, regarded as colonizers, for about 300 years, with some interruptions. About a fifth of the population emigrated to the Ottoman Empire in 1858. In 1942, Soviet dictator Joseph Stalin, suspecting the loyalties of the Chechens (as he did those of the neighboring Inguish people, the Crimean Tartars and other non-Russian nationalities who longed for independence and fought or sympathized with the German invaders in hopes of winning it), had the Red Army shell Chechenya's mountain villages. He deported the survivors, especially the people of Grozny, the capital, to Central Asia.

The Chechens, warlike men wearing sheepskin hats, used to tell visitors they loved their guns better than their wives. They had elevated weapons to almost godlike status. A Chechen shooting party, hunting either animals or a rival mountain clan, compared in bellicosity with many an Afghan clan, and would make a National Rifle Association outing in the US look like a Quaker Sunday-school picnic. Soon after Chechenya's unilateral declaration of independence from Moscow in 1981, as Mikhail Gorbachev failed to hold the old Soviet empire together, a Chechen named Rossian Outsiev, 28 years old, found himself in London in possession of millions of US dollars. These had been provided by the generous oil revenues of his little state. (Grozny, in fact, had at that time become the only capital in the Caucasus or Central Asia with a local Rolls-Royce dealer.)

Outsiev's official mission, ordered by Chechenya's godfather-like president, a former Soviet airforce general named Joukar Dudayev, was to arrange for printing of banknotes, postage stamps and other attributes of nationhood for the state, just declared "independent" by Dudayev (but recognized by no one, including other republics of the Caucasus). Outsiev plunked down $1.1 million in cash for a penthouse apartment in London's Baker Street. He spread huge tips among waiters in restaurants, gambling casinos and call-girls. He would even rent whole gambling halls in London hotels for his private use. Sometimes, he and his 20-year-old brother, Nazerbek, would host several prostitutes in one night in his Baker Street flat.

A few people who kept an eye on Outsiev soon realized his real purpose was to buy Stinger missiles, hundreds if possible, on the active London arms market. The Stingers were for Muslim brothers-in-arms of the Chechens: the Azeris of Azerbaijan, in their war with Christian Armenia over the disputed mountain territory of Nagorno-Karabakh; surrounded by Azeri territory but with a predominantly Armenian population. Outsiev made one fatal mistake. He hired an Armenian, a certain Gagic Ter-Ogannisiyan, as his translator. Ter-Ogannisiyan, a loyal Armenian, soon realized what Outsiev's real mission was and informed Armenian intelligence. Immediately, it became known in Armenia's capital, Yerevan, that there was a real threat developing to Armenia's meager, Soviet-supplied (and partly Russian-manned) airforce. Swiftly, Yerevan delivered the order: kill Rossian Outsiev, to block the Stinger sales. Together with an Armenian gunman, Ter-Ogannisiyan shot the two Outsiev brothers dead in their London apartment in February 1983. Both were arrested. Ter-Ogannisiyan was convicted of the murder and jailed for life.

One night in May 1993, gunmen murdered Mrs. Karen Reed, 33, as she opened the door of a home she shared with her sister in Woking, Surrey, England. British police concluded Mrs. Reed had been mistaken for her sister, Ms. Alison Ponting, the wife of the other killer of Outsiev. Because the Russian, Armenian, Chechen and other assorted mafias had already imported their brand of crime to London, the two women had been given a panic button linked to the local police station and told not to open the door to strangers. This time, Mrs. Reed opened the door without using the button. The Chechen mafia had sworn revenge for the murders of Russian Outsiev and his brother. Much earlier, even before Ms. Ponting's husband was jailed, she received death threats. Later she was arrested, but not charged, for trying to import a phial of snake venom from the United States. It was speculated that the two murderers were trying to obtain the means to commit further killings – or commit suicide.

Ms. Ponting worked at Bush House, London headquarters of the BBC, when her sister was murdered. She was then a producer with the BBC's Russian and Ukrainian service and had met her husband while touring Armenia in 1988. Another man, Nikritsch Martiossian, accused of complicity in the murder of the two Chechen brothers, shared a house with her after arriving in Britain. He was found hanged in his cell while awaiting trial. He had told police detectives, after confessing to the background of the murders, that "the KGB" would never forgive him: "By talking about these murders I am signing a death warrant for my family," he told them.[14]

In many ways the 1979–89 Afghanistan jihad was responsible for President Boris Yeltsin's decision no longer to ignore Chechenya, as Mikhail Gorbachev had done, and to brand it "the bandit state" and its president, Joukar Dudayev (later killed by a computer-aimed Russian air-to-ground missile) as "the Qaddafi of the Caucasus." Russian intelligence considered that Grozny, the Chechen capital, had by 1993 become a center fueling ethnic conflicts in nearby Georgia and from Abkhazia to the nearby South Ossetian region. Chechenya's international criminal networks, arising after World War II, stemmed in part from the need to survive in a rugged land of people who had survived the terrible experience of deportation to Central Asia by Stalin. The Afghanistan war gave them a tremendous impetus, and by the late 1980s, branches of the Chechen mafia extended not only to the London arms market but also throughout continental Europe and North America. They dealt in drugs as well as arms.

When the Red Army soldiers began to come home from Afghanistan, many bearing guns, other military gear and drugs, Dudayev's men began to work with the spreading Islamist organizations. Grozny became known to the Afghan veterans as a major haven for the Arab veterans in transit from Afghanistan and Peshawar to Europe and the Mideast. This role apparently strained the good relations Dudayev had earlier set up with former benefactors of the holy warriors, such as Saudi Arabia. Following a visit to Riyadh and a meeting with King Fahd, Dudayev accepted a Saudi suggestion that he appoint Shamsuddine Yussef, a Jordanian businessman of Chechen origin, favored by the House of Saud, as Chechenya's foreign minister. Since then, relations between Riyadh and Grozny have chilled, because of Dudayev's connections to pro-Iranian and other groups disliked by the Saudi royal family. Nevertheless, in the name of Muslim solidarity, Saudi Arabia raised its voice against Russian military campaigns aimed at crushing the Chechens.

At first, Dudayev's propitiation of local Islamists, especially a Chechen branch of the Muslim Brotherhood called the Islamic Path party, went too far for many of his countrymen. They approved of independence from Russia, but did not want their nation to become an Islamic republic. From April 1992, Grozny experienced continuous domestic crises. After dissolving a rebellious parliament, Dudayev formed a new government, while the parliament proclaimed its own, rival cabinet. Finally, in December 1994, President Boris Yeltsin and his advisors lost patience. They began a bloody and ill-fated military campaign to subjugate the Chechen state, dethrone Dudayev and end the self-proclaimed independence of the Chechens.

US and Russian investigators mulled over whether Arab and other Muslim Afghan veterans had helped Dudayev obtain Stingers. Frantic efforts to acquire them were going on around the world. Four US investigations in the early 1990s halted Stinger purchases by agents of the Medellin drug cartel: Iran; the Irish Republican Army (IRA) and the Croats who seceded from the old Yugoslavia and set up an independent Croatia. Authorities in Italy broke up another ring trying to get missiles to Croatia. In Bosnia-Herzogovina, an inconclusive investigation seemed to show that a Stinger had brought down an Italian cargo plane in 1992. A kind of Stinger mythology grew; to the point that when almost any aircraft anywhere in a conflict zone was downed by ground fire, Stingers were blamed, often wrongly.

What most concerned Boris Yeltsin's government in Moscow, however, was not myth but reality. Fighting began in earnest in May 1993 between moujahidin attacking across the Afghan border into Tajikistan and Tajikistan's Russian garrisons, now on the defense. Tajik rebels allied with the Afghans brought down a Sukhoi 25 fighter-bomber with a Stinger. In Georgia, Muslim Abkhazian separatists shot down three Georgian airliners in early 1993, killing 126 people. Abkhazian leaders bragged to newsmen that they had obtained Stingers through the Russian military – presumably from stocks seized in Afghanistan. In any case, the Russian defense industry, good at copying American and other foreign technology, was already producing a plausible replica.[15]

Serious hostilities erupted between Chechens and the Russian army in December 1994. In Moscow, Yeltsin's political opponents and many thoughtful Russian citizens warned against involvement in a "new Afghanistan," where their army would get involved in another nightmare guerrilla war with locals confident that they were fighting for their freedom. There was another serious possibility: the stubborn Chechens, with or without Stinger missiles or other modern weapons, would take inspiration and perhaps even direct battlefield help and advice from some of the same Arab and other Muslim Afghan guerrilla veterans who defeated the Red Army in the 1980s. The Russian high command recognized that post-Afghanistan war perils in the Caucasus revolved around that area's historic role as a mixing tank, where potent, ethnic explosions were likely and frequent. Those which occurred in the mid-1980s were already, in the 1990s, spreading conflict in this easternmost region of Europe.

In September 1999, a wave of massive terrorist bombings of apartments for civilians and military housing closely followed Muslim rebel incursions into Chechenya from its Russian Federation republic neighbor, Daghestan. Russian federal forces repulsed the incursion. But the bombings left 292 civilians and an unknown number of Russian soldiers dead. Hundreds of people were wounded. The Kremlin administration of President Boris Yeltsin blamed Chechens; Russian politicians and generals swore revenge.

The Russian army immediately launched a new invasion of Chechenya. Moscow analysts blamed Osama bin Laden for financing and inspiring the rebel leaders. The two main ones were Shamil Basayev, who in the earlier war had taken Russian civilians hostage (and who was reported captured himself by the Russians in the early spring of 2000, though details were sketchy); and a fighter calling himself Amir al-Khattab, or simply Khattab, a Saudi associate of Osama bin Laden. Russian and Western analysts agreed that on such as Basayev and Khattab, the influence was paramount of the austere and wealthy Wahabi religious sect, dominant in Saudi

Arabia, and which worked closely with Saudi intelligence against the Russians during the Afghan war, and, quite possibly, after it.

President Boris Yeltsin's resignation and the takeover first as acting, then as elected President, by former KGB officer Vladimir Putin in the spring of 2000, paralleled a fierce and wasteful new military campaign against the Chechen rebels, who had humbled Yeltsin's Russia in 1993–94. By February 2000, Grozny had been destroyed again and evacuated by most rebels, who withdrew into their southern mountain redoubts to wage a new and classic guerrilla campaign. Russian Colonel Vladimir Kruglov, a paratroop officer and Afghan war veteran, told the London *Daily Telegraph* of January 17, 2000 that the rebels "use the same methods [as in Afghanistan]; they are financed by the same people and some of their leaders are the same as well." General Gennady Troshev, relieved of his command in early January, but back in charge after the Russian re-conquest of Grozny, most of whose population joined over 500,000 Chechen war refugees in the misery of camps in Ingushetia and other neighboring regions, said of the rebels: "They approach, open fire and then hide. And the next morning, they smile at you in the streets." Word for word, that quote could have come directly from the diary of a soldier or Soviet war correspondent during the Afghanistan campaign.

As the new Chechen guerrilla war raged on in the southern mountains, the European Union (EU) states first dithered, then in April 2000 suspended Russia's voting rights in the Council of Europe. President Putin, still in early 2000 a popular leader fighting a popular war, found as summer approached that high Russian casualties – again the parade of coffins and broken, mutilated wounded, shown on foreign and sometimes Russian TV – was weakening that popularity. Russia was becoming more of a pariah in the West. She found herself at odds with human rights groups and others who, in Western Europe and in and around the American Congress, placed democracy and human rights to Russia above new trading or financial concessions in the IMF and other world financial institutions.

With its deep valleys and high mountain passes, the Caucasus has always been a corridor of passage between the Eastern and Western worlds. The East–West routes snake around the mountain peaks, much as the trade and invasion routes between Central Asia and Afghanistan do. Adolf Hitler and his generals discovered in 1941–44 to their grief a truth long known to geographers: these mountains are one of the severest military obstacles in the world. This became clear to the Wehrmacht when it unsuccessfully tried to rescue the beleagured German invasion forces in Russia and to reach the Middle East oilfields through the north. The Caucasus marked the eastern demarcation line of the Persian, Roman, Byzantine and Ottoman empires, and a southwestern frontier area of the Soviet empire, which collapsed with the Afghanistan war. Its mountain barriers not only make it difficult for Muslim Turkey and Iran, and the Arabs of Syria and Iraq to help fellow Muslims in any battles with Russians. It also blocks direct communication of Central Asian Muslims with the Turks, Iranians and Arabs.

The concerns of President Yeltsin and his advisors and their allies in the CIS states stemmed from their primal fear, revived in 1998 by the perceived threat from the Taliban, that an Islamist offensive starting from Afghanistan and Tajikistan would destabilize all of Central Asia and the Caucasus.

Since the victory of the Khomeiny Islamist revolution in 1979, the Soviet KGB had waged war where they could against the Islamists, fearing contamination from Iran. In 1992, after the moujahidin veterans captured Kabul, the most violent of all the civil wars in the former Soviet empire erupted in Tajikistan. It was feared that Uzbekistan might be the next "domino" to fall. The Russian military feared the Islamist movements could threaten Russia itself, given its Muslim population of over 12 million, 800,000 of whom lived in Moscow itself by 1992.[16]

Another Russian consideration in its unsuccessful 1994–96 effort to subjugate Chechenya was trying to maintain the Russian army, historical heir of the old Red Army, as an obedient and cohesive fighting force. The survival or downfall of General Pavel Grachev as defense minister was also at stake. The shadowy memory of more than 13,000 men killed in Afghanistan haunted those who opposed new military campaigns. A further issue was the future constitutional shape of Russia and its "Near Abroad" in Central Asia and the Caucasus. A new Federation treaty, supposed to unite the 88 separate regions of the Russian Federation, some ruled by old hardline Communists, was drawn up by Yeltsin's men and signed in 1992. The greater freedom it gave them was not enough for many. One-third of the dissidents in the rebellion of the Duma, the Russian parliament, against Yeltsin in October 1993, when loyal military units shelled the Duma in Moscow, were regional bosses.[17]

The immediate, direct impact of the Afghan jihad veterans was felt in both Chechenya and Nagorno-Karabakh, as well as in Tajikistan. In the late summer of 1993, Gulbuddin Hekmatyar, the former darling of the CIA and Pakistan's ISI, was observed recruiting Afghan mercenaries to fight in Azerbaijan against Armenia and its Russian allies. The recruits were paid the equivalent of a dollar a day; slightly more than their Afghan "wage" of $10–$20 a month for this particular group. They were promised a bonus of $5,000 each upon completion of their contracts. Gaidar Aliev, the veteran former Communist leader of Azeri politics, confirmed that an agreement had earlier been struck with the Azerbaijani Popular Front, in which his influence predominated. Under its terms, Afghans or former fighters in the jihad who were by now unwanted in Pakistan could earn money fighting the Armenian Christians. By this time, Hekmatyar, having sided with Saddam Hussein during the Gulf war of 1991, had lost his former Saudi financial support, and was apparently not on the payroll of Osama bin Laden. Therefore he needed funds, and this way he could continue his dream of "exporting" the Islamist revolution and earn money at the same time by providing mercenaries for the Azeri forces.

According to the Russian Foreign Intelligence Service, from September 1993 some 1,500 Afghan veterans had entered Azerbaijan. They played an important role in the recapture from the Armenians of Goradiz, a town southeast of the Nagorno-

Karabakh capital, Stepanakert. They did this by attacking the Armenians from behind, along the Iranian border. By summer 1994 their numbers had swelled to 2,500, most stationed on the southern front along the border, and used primarily, due to their superior weapons skills, as assault troops in mountainous regions. A kind of autonomous Afghan command in Baku coordinated their operations. Their presence strengthened Moscow's propaganda position: Russia could credibly insist that it had to resume control over all of the external borders of the CIS states. After suffering high casualties in battles with the Armenians, the Azeri "Afghan brigade" was dissolved in 1994. The fighters that remained next turned to sabotage and terrorism.[18]

Some of this terrorism involved a series of bombings in central Baku in 1993 and 1994. In February 1993 a bomb exploded aboard the Kislovodsk (central Russia) to Baku train, killing 10 people and injuring 13. In February 1994 a bomb exploded aboard the same train as it stopped at the central Baku train station, killing 3 people and injuring over 20. Further bombs exploded in a subway tunnel in central Baku killing 7 and injuring 47 in July 1994, and in other parts of the Azeri capital. In February 1996 a Russian military court convicted three Armenian intelligence officers, arrested in Russia in 1995, of having organized the Baku bombings. In April and May of 1996, Azeri authorities arrested 20 members of a Lezgin national movement called "Sadval" (Union). The Lezgins are mostly Sunni Muslims, influenced by the Afghan jihad, whose homeland is split between the Russian republic of Daghestan and northern Azerbaijan. Their goal, like the Pushtuns in Afghanistan and Pakistan, is to unify their historical homelands into one independent Lezgin state.

Azerbaijan, now a Mecca of Western oil and gas firms eager to extract and market its huge energy resources, has also had its share of anti-government terrorism, some of which seemed to be organized by disaffected Afghan war veterans. After the disbanding of the "Afghani Brigade," they turned to violence against their former paymasters. There were four reported coup attempts against President Gaidar Aliev – in October 1994, March 1995, July 1995 and one that had been planned in early 1997. Plans to blow up a bridge over which President Aliev was to pass and other plans to shoot down his plane with a Stinger missile were discovered. No group or individual ever claimed these attacks or attempted attacks.

The war between Armenia and Azerbaijan over Nagorno-Karabakh lasted in its acute phases from 1988 to 1994. Besides the direct action of the Afghan Brigade on the Azeri side, there was terrorism inside Armenia which smacked of Afghani activity, though little direct proof of this was evinced. From 1993 to 1995, for instance, a series of bombings of trains, rail lines and gas pipelines disrupted Armenia's fuel and supplies coming from Georgia, in defiance of Azerbaijan's embargoes against Armenia. In May 1995 the Armenian government branded the attacks "acts of international terrorism" by "agents of the Azeri government." The Armenian–Azeri conflict spilled over into Georgia with a number of terrorist bombings, including several in Tbilisi, the Georgian capital, in which civilians including children were killed.[19]

The Kremlin's senior planners had plenty of reasons to fear the backlash of the Afghanistan war in Chechenya. Immediately after the collapse of the Soviet Union in 1991, Grozny, the Chechen capital, became a transit point for the Afghan veterans, especially the Arab ones. In August 1995, a spokesman of the Russian Federal Security Service reported that units from Afghanistan and Jordan – which has a large and influential Chechen community in residence – were fighting on the side of Chechen President Joukar Dudayev. There were said to be about 300 foreign mercenaries at that time, out of a total Chechen guerrilla force of 6,000. Dudayev had begun recruiting Muslim mercenaries during a trip to Turkey, Turkish-occupied northern Cyprus and Bosnia-Herzogovina. Later he acknowledged that Chechen volunteers were fighting with the Bosnian Muslims in the Bosnian war.

As a pilot officer in the former Soviet airforce, Dudayev had at first declared that he was fighting for a secular and democratic state; the Russian intervention of 1994 in fact hastened the "Islamization" of the war there. The conflict gave rise to terrorist activity in Chechenya itself and spillover activity in neighboring Ingushetia, Daghestan, North Ossetia, and in Russia proper, including Moscow. The most spectacular incident was the June 1995 seizure by Chechen fighters of the Russian town of Buddenovsk, in which over 100 people were killed and several hundred taken hostage. Shamil Basayev, the leader of the seizure of the Buddenovsk hospital and a right-hand man of Dudayev, was reported by the Russians to have been trained in Afghanistan by none other than the disciples of Gulbuddin Hekmatyar.

A diffuse anti-Russian terrorist organization in Chechenya was believed by Moscow to have links with Pakistan and Saudi Arabia, though it was also supplied with arms, stolen from or sold by the Russian military. Aided by the Hizbollah organization in Iran and in Lebanon – Dudayev visited Lebanon at least once – Afghan war veterans and Iranian volunteers entered Chechenya through Daghestan and Azerbaijan. One Chechen commando unit, headed by Salman Rauyev, married to a daughter or niece of Dudayev, after failing to capture the Kizlyar power station in Daghestan, guarded by the Russians, repeated the feat of Basayev at Buddenovsk by seizing a local clinic in a Russian town called Pervomayskoye. The 250 Chechen partisans, entrenched in the village, repeatedly repelled attacks by Russia's elite SPETZNAZ troops, of Afghanistan fame. Mikhal Barsukov, chief of the Federal Security Service in charge of the special units, admitted that the Chechen fighters were "a very serious unit, very well-trained, very well-prepared." – possibly by Pakistan's ISI and the American CIA during the 1979–89 jihad, or afterward by the jihad's many alumni.

The Chechen war, which ended with withdrawal of the Russian forces from the exhausted and devastated country in 1996, aroused attention and sympathy among fellow Muslims elsewhere. In Turkey, the Islamist Welfare Party sponsored training camps for Islamic fighters, until a crackdown on the party and its leader, the portly Necmettin Erbakan, by the fiercely secularist Turkish army in 1996–98. A Turkish Fascist youth group, the "Grey Wolves," was recruited to fight with the Chechens. One group under Muhammed Tokcan, an ethnic Abkhazian who had fought with

Shamil Basayev in Chechenya and Abkhazia, hijacked a Black Sea ferryboat, the *Avraziya,* to show solidarity with the Chechen cause. Moscow exploded in rhetorical anger against Turkey, stressing that it had repeatedly warned Turkey against allowing the existence of training camps for Muslim extremists on its territory – one of a long list of grievances stemming from centuries-old Russo–Turkish enmity. There were several terrorist attacks against Russian targets in Turkey.[20]

The political and military battles in the Caucasus and Central Asia which followed the Red Army's withdrawal from Afghanistan carried over, along with the corruption at the top of the military hierarchy which began in Afghanistan, into Russia itself. It also spread among the Soviet commands in eastern Europe, especially East Germany, into the post-Soviet era. By the late 1990s, senior Russian generals, once a well-disciplined and discreet group who had unquestioningly accepted orders from Communist political superiors, had become a quarrelsome bunch. Often, they questioned basic orders from Moscow. In December 1994, for example, two deputy Russian defense ministers, General Boris Gromov and General Georgy Kondratiev, opposed the orders of President Yeltsin and his National Security Council for the campaign to subjugate Chechenya. General Gromov even said he would join other Russian parents in resisting efforts to send their conscripted sons to fight in the Caucasus. "His words," reported *The Economist,* "have the conviction of experience: he was commander-in-chief of Soviet forces in Afghanistan."

Most exposed to criticism was the top general in this potentially mutinous army: Defense Minister Pavel Grachev, who in 1998 was a 48-year-old paratroop general. He commanded the troops under Yeltsin's orders during the attempted anti-Yeltsin coup by leading the attack on the Duma building in Moscow, stronghold of the coalition of Russian nationalists and ex-Communists who tried to overthrow Yeltsin. After a bomb killed a Russian journalist investigating corruption in the armed forces in East Germany and elsewhere, Grachev came under heavy fire in the Russian media. Late in November 1994, when the first heavy Russian–Chechen hostilities flared, Grachev was a target again. An opposition group trying to depose Chechen President Joukar Dudayev was repulsed by Dudayev's partisans. Some of the prisoners taken by Dudayev's men were regular Russian soldiers, masquerading as freelance mercenaries. The commanding general of the elite Russian Kantemir division resigned to protest the abuse of his men in the bungled operation. Defense Minister Grachev at first pretended he knew of no Russian involvement in Chechenya. He abandoned the pretense only when it became clear that the Russian air force had attacked Chechen targets.

Equally insubordinate, but gifted with political prescience and a strong will to succeed Boris Yeltsin as Russian president, was General Alexander Lebed, a hopeful in the Russian presidential elections of the year 2000 (or sooner, if Yeltsin had left the scene before his elected term was up). Lebed had also served as a decorated paratroop battalion commander in the Afghanistan war, which he bitterly criticized after its end. He became commander of the Russian Fourteenth Army in another breakaway region, Transdniestr, in Moldava, next door to Romania. General Lebed declared his admiration for Chile's former military dictator, General August Pinochet. He said he, Lebed, would make a better defense minister than Grachev. A poll found that 70 percent of the Moscow garrison agreed, and were willing to say so. Among General Lebed's declared supporters were the commander-in-chief of ground forces, General Vladimir Semyonov and air force commander-in-chief General Pyotr Deynikin. General Grachev lost support through persistent stories of corruption among officers who had served in Afghanistan, Central Asia and Eastern Europe. In the presidential election campaign of 1996, Yeltsin won re-election over his Communist challenger Gennady Zyuganov and against Lebed, who had in the meantime been forced to resign from the army for criticizing Grachev's policies in Chechenya and elsewhere.

Lebed won a seat in the Duma in the December 1995 elections and then ran for the presidency in 1996. His authoritarian and sometimes anti-Western rhetoric appealed to voters and he reached the second round of voting before being defeated by Yeltsin. Yeltsin fired a number of senior aides and advisors, including Grachev and in August 1996 gave Lebed the responsibility for ending the war in Chechenya. Lebed traveled immediately to Grozny to meet both the Russian military commanders and the separatist leaders (Dudayev had already been killed by a Russian missile in April 1996). Soon, Lebed negotiated a ceasefire which included an agreement to defer a final decision on Chechen independence until the year 2001. Yeltsin became alarmed by Lebed's growing prestige and fired him as security chief on October 17, 1996, saying he was not a team player and was getting too pushy about his aspirations to the presidency. Lebed campaigned sporadically throughout 1997 and 1998 as head of his Russian Republican Party, constantly urging Yeltsin to resign because of his poor health and what Lebed and others called his addiction to alcohol and incapacity to make crucial decisions when they were needed. During the new Chechen war of 1999–2000, after Vladimir Putin's accession to power, Lebed's star seemed to fade.

During the Afghanistan war, the boundary between grumbling dissent and open mutiny had very rarely, if ever, been crossed in the old Red Army. Under the postwar blue, white and red flag of Russia, new civil conflicts, repressive campaigns and some real military ones spread across the expanse of the Russian Federation and the former Soviet empire. Unpaid, sometimes starving young recruits who were constantly bullied by their seniors fueled mass desertions, and held out the likelihood of mutinies, or worse, to come.

So it was that as the new millennium approached, with Russian troops again confronting militant Islamism in formats like that of the Taliban, the leaders in the Kremlin were still struggling to limit or control the damaging consequences of Leonid Brezhnev's foolish Afghanistan war. Meanwhile the Arab and other Muslim veterans of that war were triggering, fueling and fighting other, decidedly unholy, ethno-religious wars, fought in the name of Islam, inside countries far distant from Russia's frontiers.

9 The Contagion Spreads: Egypt and the Maghreb

On November 17, 1997, an Egyptian Islamist gunman named Medhat Muhamad Abdel Rahman, who Egyptian security officials say was trained in the Afghan guerrilla camps, led five others in the mass murder of 58 foreign tourists and at least four Egyptians on the banks of the Nile river at Luxor, Upper Egypt. The attackers, who horribly maimed about 20 more survivors, all perished in the following pursuit and gunbattles with police and at the hands of the enraged tourist guides and townspeople of Luxor. These became a frenzied lynch mob.

The legacy of this atrocity, unprecedented in Egypt in its ferocity and magnitude, was the virtual ruin of Egypt's tourist industry for at least a year. This meant a halt in the livelihood of millions of Egyptians employed in tourism and the hotels, transport and food industries and the many other industries serving it. Tourists in Egypt, until this case of mass murder on the Nile, had been bringing in over $3 billion a year – approximately equal to one year's American economic aid to President Mubarak's public and private development programs. It also dealt a severe blow to further foreign investment in Egyptian tourism, the effects of which lasted about a year, but only too real to Egypt and its people. Above all, it was a numbing psychological blow to Egypt's own society, already caught between the rock of its tolerant, secular traditions and the hard place of belligerent Islamist terrorist violence. Once again, Egyptians had cause to reflect on the consequences of President Anwar al-Sadat's enthusiastic and, for him, fatal embrace of Islamism and the holy war in Afghanistan.

The manner of the mass killings, which according to survivors and newsmen like the London *Independent* newspaper's Robert Fisk who arrived on the scene soon afterward, recalls in some respects accounts of throat-cutting and disemboweling which took place during the 1979–89 Afghan jihad – tactics which had been so rare as to be almost unknown until then in Egypt.

There was double irony in the terrorists' choice of the site for this holocaust. On October 12, 1997, the same Temple of Queen Hatshepsut was the scene of a lavish open-air performance of Verdi's opera *Aida*. Seats cost from $200 to $350 each – many times the salary of an average Egyptian worker or employee. President Husni Mubarak and his wife led the list of guests of honor in evening dress. They included Sean Connery (alias James Bond, Secret Agent 007), who was heard by a German reporter to comment after the performance, "It's fantastic here, and absolutely safe." The production was a belated celebration of the 126th anniversary of *Aida*'s first performance in Cairo in 1871. Egypt's ruler, the Khedive Ismail, in the heyday of Egypt's Westernization, commissioned the opera to mark the festive inauguration of the Suez Canal.

Intelligence reports warned of a serious threat that terrorists would attack and disrupt the performance. The warnings were kept out of the media, but the security authorities heeded them and sent massive police reinforcements, uniformed and in plain clothes, to defend the spectacle, which passed without incident. Unfortunately, the precautions were relaxed and the reinforcements disappeared immediately afterward. The incredible laxity of security caused President Mubarak, who visited Luxor on November 18, the day after the attack, to fire Interior Minister Hassan Alfi. It led to the trials and convictions to prison in 1998 of six senior Egyptian police officers, all generals and colonels.

The alert before the operatic extravaganza had ample grounds. During 1996 and the months of 1997 before the Luxor attack, at least 150 unarmed civilians had been killed by armed men believed to belong to *al-Gama'a al-Islamiya* and led in several cases, according to Egyptian police, by Afghan war veterans. In February 1997, for example, ten civilians, all Coptic Christians, were killed by four *Gama'a* gunmen who attacked a church in the village of Abu Qurqas in Minya province. This attack prompted the (later disgraced and dismissed) Interior Minister Hassan Alfi to revive accusations that Iran and Sudan, as well as the Afghan veterans, were behind such attacks, which Iran and Sudan both vehemently denied. On December 23, 1997, the newly arrived US Ambassador to Israel, Edward Walker, told Israeli Foreign Minister David Levy that Iran was involved in teleguiding the Luxor massacre, according to the *Jerusalem Post* of December 24. There was no confirmation.[1]

The Cairo government intensified efforts to persuade Britain, Germany, Switzerland, the United States and other Western countries to extradite to Egypt for trial militants who were accused terrorists in Egypt, many of whom had sought and obtained asylum or residence in the West. A consultative chamber of the Egyptian parliament debated a long working paper on "The Foreign Dimensions of Terrorism." Resolutions called for tough measures against foreign states sheltering wanted terrorists. Foreign Minister Amir Moussa repeated his demand for an international conference on fighting terrorism. The murder of the Copts at Abu Qurqas, Moussa said, was aimed "not to ignite sectarian strife. The target was the security and stability of the Egyptian people."

Egypt's senior Muslim clergy reacted swiftly to head off sectarian strife. The Grand Sheikh of al-Azhar Islamic university, the Mufti of Egypt (the country's highest Muslim spiritual advisor) and Waqf (Religious Endowments) Minister Mahmoud Hamdi Zakzouki all traveled to Abu Qurqas to offer condolences to the bereaved Christian families. But despite such conciliatory moves, in March 1997, 13 civilians including at least nine Coptic Christians were killed in two separate attacks in Rezbet Dawud and Naga' Hammadi, both villages in Qena province, Upper Egypt. In mid-September, nine German tourists were killed in another attack at their bus in front of the Egyptian Museum, just behind the Nile Hilton Hotel in central Cairo.[2]

In Egypt, army officers, ever since the "Free Officers" led by Muhammad Naguib and Gamal Abdel Nasser deposed King Farouk and took power in 1952, have been the decisive force in governance. The army's role, especially during President Sadat's enthusiastic support for the Afghanistan war of 1979–89, took the Egyptian military into an uneasy partnership with the American CIA in support of Islamic extremism. This may prove crucial in charting Egypt's future. The fate of Cairo's continuing partnership with Washington, which Sadat began by launching the 1973 war with Israel and then by calling upon US Secretary of State Henry Kissinger for help in pressing a stunned and shocked Israel to give up its occupation of the Sinai Peninsula, looks like remaining the key determinant of Egypt's fate in the twenty-first century.

President Nasser's fateful decision to leave some of the best forces in his Soviet-equipped and trained army in the political and military morass of the Yemen war helped bring about Israel's crushing victory over Egypt and Syria in June 1967. Egypt emerged from the war almost without any air force, and with its ground forces decimated. Without the superior Western equipment Israel possessed, and with only one in 60 Egyptian officers possessing a university degree in 1967, the Egyptian military stood at its lowest level since the defeat of King Farouk's forces by the new Jewish state of Israel in 1948–49. Between 1971 and 1973, under President Sadat's leadership, and even without the defensive Soviet air and missile shield which Sadat discarded when he expelled the Soviet military in 1972, the armed forces achieved tremendous qualitative improvements, enabling them to achieve the all-important initial success of the 1973 war, in crossing the Suez Canal and breaching Israel's much-touted Bar Lev defense line in Sinai. The improvements were in equipment (then still Russian, for the most part), training and education levels. By the late 1990s, Egyptian officers still regarded the 1973 war as a great victory, despite its indeterminate outcome and American diplomatic intervention to extricate an Egyptian army trapped in Sinai by Israel's own crossing of the Canal in late October 1973. It was Egypt's demonstrated ability to challenge and damage Israel's military superiority which inspired pride in the military. This enabled Sadat to negotiate from a position of moral strength at the ensuing Camp David and Washington peace talks.

Since the US–Egypt–Israel peace accords, the US Congress has been as generous to Egypt in sending military aid as it was to the Afghan moujahidin in the 1980s, voting an average of $1.3 billion in annual defense procurement credits since 1979.

After much of the older Soviet equipment had been sent to the Afghan guerrillas and the new American equipment, from hand guns and automatic rifles to transport and fighter aircraft had begun to arrive, the Egyptian officers were gradually acquiring Western training and expertise in Western Europe and America. Nevertheless, a cadre of older officers remained primarily Russian-trained. This created some intra-service difficulties. For political reasons, especially the desire to limit US influence in the armed forces, which some officers blamed for drawing Egypt into the Afghanistan adventure in the first place, the brightest officers are often tested for loyalty to the Mubarak government. One result has been that US-trained officers find that their promotions to higher grades are held back or sparingly granted.

President Mubarak retains supreme authority over the 440,000-strong army, navy, air force and air defense units. Conscripts are enrolled at a rate of about 80,000 per year. They usually serve three years of active duty and remain on reserve rolls an additional nine years. Mubarak also depends upon a 300,000-strong paramilitary Central Security Force (CSF), staffed with conscripts. The CSF was formed in 1977 after food riots which erupted when President Sadat temporarily removed government subsidies on basic foods and other commodities, and the police were unable to cope with popular uprisings which the army had to put down. Mubarak has tried to build up the CSF as a counter-force to any possible future subversion or rebelliousness in the army. In 1986, a rumor concerning the amount of time conscripts would have to spend in the CSF, including the tourist police, led to a riot and a purge of 20,000 radical members from the ranks. The regular armed forces again had to be called in to end the rampage.

The government has long suspected infiltration of the CSF by extremist elements like those in the army who in 1981 had conspired against Sadat, then killed him and whose survivors escaped to Afghanistan. When Major General Raouf Khayrat, a 20-year undercover agent for the CSF was murdered in 1994, it was thought that the general's well-guarded identity could have been betrayed only by very senior officers of the agency. The heterogenous makeup of the CSF and the low pay of its rank-and-file foot soldiers made it a tempting target for the Islamist extremists. Of Islamists arrested in the 1970s, 80 percent were college or university graduates. By the mid-1990s, these figures had dropped to 20 percent. Young people most disadvantaged by unemployment or low wages in civilian life are more likely to accept the lead of Afghani veterans or other activists and become Islamist insurgents. Low pay and poor treatment of the CSF and also of regular army enlisted men make them prime recruits for extremist groups.

Extremism has never been absent from the Egyptian armed forces in modern times. Best organized was the Muslim Brotherhood, existing since 1928, and partly responsible for the successful Nasser–Naguib Free Officers' coup in 1952. Today's Brotherhood, as we saw, although it has been important in the all-pervading incursion of Islamism into Egypt's civil and cultural society, is one of the least radical of about 50 Islamist groups. President Sadat's assassination by Lieutenant Colonel Khaled al-Islambuli in October 1981 and Vice-President Husni Mubarak's succession to the presidency initiated a long period of mistrust between the military and civilian leaderships. After the assassination, the military tried to purge extremist elements, including the Special Forces officers who had trained volunteers for Afghanistan in Sadat's time and who had acquired some of the Islamist ideology of the moujahidin. Conscription, however, soon brought new Islamist recruits, since they came largely from the lower-income groups in the society which filled out military ranks. Islamist recruits are purged as soon as recognized, and the government's witch-hunting mentality goes as far as exempting relatives of suspects from the draft.

In August 1993, shortly after the start of intensive Islamist terrorist activity, two army cadets and a reservist were tried along with 50 civilian members of the "Vanguards of the New Jihad," a group held responsible for trying to kill the interior minister with a bomb in August 1993. "Vanguards" are former *al-Gihad* members, some of whom fled to Peshawar and Afghanistan after Sadat's assassination. Many returned, often under the auspices of Osama bin Laden, to resume the struggle to turn Egypt into an Islamic theocracy, with the specific goal of accomplishing this by taking control of the armed forces.

During the 1990s, opposition has risen to President Mubarak, himself a clean and uncorrupted leader, but who has often been accused of tolerating corruption around him. In November 1993 the CSF uncovered a plot to assassinate him, after a *Gama'a al-Islamiya* member was captured during a raid. He admitted that the group planned to assault the president's plane at the Sidu Baranni airport, and that one of Mubarak's residences, to be used for a meeting with Libyan leader Muammar al-Qaddafi, was also a target. Several members of the group, including two soldiers, were condemned to death in a secret military trial and executed by firing squad a short time later.

Many Egyptian voices in the military as well as in civilian life, have warned that the government could correct many social and economic injustices by observing the social aspects of Islamic law more strictly. General Saduddin al-Shazli, a hero of the 1973 war against Israel but who fell out with President Sadat over the latter's unwillingness to order a full offensive against Israel in Sinai at the moment, early in the war, when the Egyptians held the initiative, rebuked the establishment in these terms: "If Islamic groups are calling for the implementation of Sharia, this is no crime. The government must respond to those demands because it is not the demand of the Islamic groups only, but the demand of a large sector of the people."

Shazli's remarks, made after he had served three years in prison for publishing top secrets about the 1967 war in his autobiography, were considered prophetic by some Egyptians. Shazli warned that as repression escalated into civil strife, as he believed it would, the government could not win a war fought on religious grounds. To combat this kind of thinking, the Mubarak regime has insisted that civilians charged with terrorist activities may be tried in military courts, which work faster than civil ones. The president retains ultimate power to confirm or commute death sentences. Since 1992, many harsh sentences, noted by Amnesty International and other international organizations, have been meted out. Defense counsels generally have little access to their clients and are given litttle time to prepare their responses to long and detailed charges of terrorism and terrorist planning.[3]

In its 1998 report, Amnesty International repeated detailed allegations of torture, abuses and arbitrary trials and capital punishment found in its previous reports during the decade of the 1990s. "Thousands of detainees," said Amnesty, "continued [in 1997] to be held in prisons where conditions amounted to cruel, inhuman or degrading punishment." It detailed deprivation of medical care and "disappearances" of some prisoners who were never seen again after their arrests. "The death penalty continued to be used extensively," the report added. At least 55 people were sentenced to death [in 1997], including four in absentia. Thirteen of them were civilians sentenced by military courts, two in absentia, after grossly unfair trials, and five others, two in absentia, were sentenced by Emergency Supreme State Security Courts, which allow no appeal. In October, four people were executed. They had been sentenced to death by a military court in January in a case involving 19 defendants – 18 Egyptians and a Palestinian – all alleged members of *al-Gama'a al-Islamiya*, for allegedly bombing two cinemas and killing a security officer.[4]

An attempt to outlaw the Muslim Brotherhood in 1995, when the organization was being tarred, justly or otherwise, with responsibility for the actions of many of the dissident Afghan war veterans, brought on a major political crisis. Muslim Brothers, many of them respected lawyers, doctors and other professionals, were routinely arrested for "conspiring against the government and violating the constitution," even if there was little evidence against them. Commentators compared these developments with the situation in Algeria, where a government crackdown on the Islamic Salvation Front (FIS) was stirring the coals of political revolt and mass violence into white heat. On November 23, 1995, 54 Brotherhood members were given three- to five-year prison terms, some at hard labor, for "belonging to an illegal organization and propagating its aims." After closure of the Brotherhood's Cairo headquarters, most members and sympathizers became even more militant in their actions, and the declaredly non-violent Brotherhood entered into serious contacts with the extremist groups.[5] Shortly after this came the summer 1995 attack on President Mubarak in Addis Ababa, Ethiopia, which the government blamed on *al-Gihad* members, some of whom it said found asylum and shelter under the wing of Sudan's Islamist-controlled military government, during a period when Osama bin Laden was living in Khartoum and working closely with the power behind the Sudanese military, Islamist Sheikh Hassan al-Turabi. The issue remained an open wound between Egypt and the Sudan.

A *New York Times* analyst as long ago as July 4, 1995 called "Cairo's corrupt and self-perpetuating military autocracy, now in its fifth decade of rule, no longer offers hope for democracy or a better life to millions of desperately poor Egyptian peasants." Under these conditions, which are growing more rather than less urgent, the militant variety of Islamism which the Afghanistan war helped to spawn will try ruthlessly to exploit this vulnerability, a situation which Western and Egyptian policy-makers alike must soberly and honestly confront.[6]

Before moving westward from Egypt to examine the consequences of the Afghanistan war in the Maghreb or Arab North African states of Algeria and its neighbors, the gradual Islamization of Egyptian civil society, another post-Sadat phenomenon, deserves mention. In May 1993, as the Islamist terrorist offensive was gathering speed, a kind of Islamist cultural counter-revolution was also beginning.

Dr. Nasr Hamed Abu Zeid, a professor of Islamic studies who commuted to his teaching job at Cairo University daily in a battered Volkswagen Beetle, was astonished to read in his morning newspaper that he was an accused apostate. Dr. Abdul-Sabour Shahin, a prominent Muslim cleric and professor of linguistics, had brought criminal charges against him in a court in Giza, one of Cairo's largest districts which includes the site of the Pyramids. Dr. Abu Zeid was accused of apostasy, abandoning his faith in Islam for criticizing in his writings the retrograde beliefs, as he saw them, of the Islamists in Egypt.

Since Sharia courts were abolished in Egypt by Gamal Abdel Nasser's military regime, all law in Egypt except family law had been largely based on secular principles. Many went back to the Napoleonic code-based laws introduced into Egypt by Muhammad Ali in the early nineteenth century, following Napoleon Bonaparte's brief but influential occupation of Egypt. In an initial trial, the Giza court rejected the prosecution's demand that Abu Zeid be forcibly divorced from his wife, Ebtehal Younes, a well-educated and widely-traveled daughter of an Egyptian diplomat, 15 years younger than Abu Zeid. But on appeal in a second trial, another, Islamist-minded judge and two other judges in June 1995 found, in a ruling totally without precedent, that Dr. Abu Zeid's writings proved him to be an apostate who had convicted himself. Therefore, he had lost the right to be married to a Muslim woman and it ordered him to divorce Ebtehal. Within hours, a fax had arrived at foreign news agencies from *al-Gihad* in Switzerland, ordering that Abu Zeid be killed. Six days later, several al-Azhar scholars called on the government to execute Abu Zeid unless he repented. On July 26, 1995, Abu Zeid and his wife fled to Leiden University in the Netherlands, where they chose to live, fearing for their lives – although without the wide publicity given to Anglo-Indian author Salman Rushdie for the death-threatening fatwa or religious decree ordering his death by the late Iranian ruler, the Ayatollah Khomeiny.

Another notorious case is that of Youssef Chahine, an Egyptian filmmaker who enjoys great esteem throughout the Arab world, and whose films have also won awards in the West. He was threatened with prosecution for a film treating in an allegorical mode the persecution of the twelfth-century Islamic scholar Ibn Rushid, known in Western literature as Averroes. Chahine, awarded in 1997 the lifetime achievement award at the Cannes Film Festival, said he had never, in his 40 years of work in the Egyptian cinema, experienced anything like the intellectual McCarthyism perpetrated by the Islamists since the Sadat era.[7]

President Chadly Benjadid, like Houari Boumedienne before him an army general, but unlike Boumedienne, who was a graduate of Cairo's al-Azhar Muslim university, not an Islamist, tried to use the crisis to impose needed and overdue reforms. Many Algerians believe that his fatal misstep was legalization of the FIS, which he apparently believed he could co-opt into a coalition government which would also include the army and the FLN. On December 26, 1991, using its network of mosques and Islamic charities, and led by vocal veterans of the Afghan jihad who had returned from the East, the FIS won a plurality of 189 in the parliament in the first round of voting, building on its earlier successes in local elections. In January 1992, the military intervened to cancel the decisive second round and in February 1992, imposed martial law.

Algeria soon began its tragic descent into an abyss of terror, violence and destruction. The veterans who had fought in Afghanistan began to trickle home. Some of them brought with them the CIA training manuals used by Pakistan's ISI. Instructions in them were already being applied by the Islamist terrorists in Egypt, especially the assassination of policemen and judges. This began to happen in Algeria, and by the end of 1992 had reached a rate of up to ten policemen murdered a day. Military trials were reported by the official news agencies, as in Egypt. Also similar was the reporting of those captured or killed by the police, or who disappeared or died mysteriously in police custody. All were called "terrorists," whether charges had been leveled against them or they had passed a trial, or not. Neither the Egyptians nor the Algerians appreciated such comparisons with each other. Foreign journalists or human rights investigators who drew them were unwelcome.

For this author and other newsmen who covered the 1954–62 Algerian war for independence, it was impossible to avoid such comparisons. What has been happening in Algeria from 1992 onward (and which paralleled many similar events in Egypt) grimly replicates many aspects of the anti-colonial Algerian war with France. My own experiences as a young freelance journalist in Algeria, which began in 1956 did not, however, prepare me or colleagues for the savage new war between the Islamists and the established military order in Algeria. This war was not caused by the backlash from the homeward bound Algerian "Afghanis," but it was aggravated and accelerated by them.

In fact, the Algerian Muslim personality – which the Islamist extremists of the 1990s are trying to revive and impose in a totalitarian Islamic state, unlike any which has ever existed in Algeria – was bruised, crushed and all but exterminated during the generations of *L'Algerie Francaise* or French Algeria; the expression used to denote the legal fiction that Algeria was a province of metropolitan France. Algerian nationalists of the early and middle twentieth century, until the beginning and middle phases of the 1954–62 revolution, were interested mainly in legal equality; in becoming real Frenchmen and Frenchwomen with the same legal rights as those across the Mediterranean in metropolitan France. These people faced a terrible dilemma. Until the FLN victory in the revolution and the advent of independence in 1962, an Algerian, either of the ethnic Arab Muslim majority, or of the large ethnic Berber Muslim and small Jewish minorities (there was also a tiny handful of Christian Berbers, mostly converted as orphan children by the French Roman Catholic orders) could escape from the humiliating colonial status of "native" (*indigene*) in only one way. He or she had to be naturalized as a full-fledged French citizen. Millions of Algerians, through the generations since the Cremieux Decree, chose this solution and emigrated to France during the twentieth century.

Many roots of the current catastrophe in Algeria are found in the systematic suppression of Islam and of Muslim culture in the colonial past; a circumstance exploited by the new Islamists of the 1980s and 1990s. In 1901, only 3.8 percent of Algerian Muslim children of school age, as opposed to 84 percent of the European settler minority, went to school. Though the French compulsory secular education laws were applied to Algeria, the Muslims were mistrustful of the French schools. An Algerian working for the French administration as a professor wrote that Algerian Muslim parents who sent their children to French schools believed the French teachers were fanatics – like the White Fathers of Cardinal Lavigerie in the predominantly Berber Kabylie mountain districts in the nineteenth century – who tried to convert their Muslim pupils to Christianity, and succeeded with many orphans.

Muslim intellectuals regarded with suspicion the "evolved" (*évolué*) or "Frenchified" Muslim minority. After about 1920 this group gave rise to the nationalist movement throughout "French" North Africa (chiefly the Destour Party in Tunisia, the Istiqlal Party in Morocco and the North African Star (*L'Etoile Nord-Africaine*) founded by Algerians in France in 1924). The conservative Algerian ulama or religious intellectuals considered *évolué* Arabs, with European-type educations, as actual or potential collaborators of the colonial regime. That, of course, was exactly what their French overlords had intended them to be.

The madrasas or traditional Muslim secondary schools began to play a central formative role in Arab nationalist thought. They became nuclei of political resistance – not unlike the role of the religious schools in Pakistan, Afghanistan and other parts of the Muslim world. However, since they were supposed to be training "loyal" French civil servants, mainly for religious posts, the French administration protected them from attacks by the European colons or settlers. Towns and cities where the main madrasas were located (Algiers, Oran, Constantine and Medea) became centers of Islamic thought and eventually, of nationalist sentiment. This continued through the war for independence, 1954–62.

After 1962, as old-fashioned secular nationalism gradually gave way to Islamism, they became, in post-colonial Algeria, centers of militant Islamist thought and action. It was therefore no accident of history, for example, that Medea, in 1994, became a center of guerrilla operations by the militants of the Islamic Salvation Front (FIS) and the more violent, anti-foreign and anti-Christian, Armed Islamic Group (GIA).

That the central role of the CIA's Muslim mercenaries, including upwards of 2,000 Algerians, in the Afghanistan war of 1979–89, was the history of France's use of Algerian Muslim troops to fight her own wars, was ironic. It tore at the very soul and fabric of Algerian society. It began with the French war against Prussia in 1870. Algerians (as well as Tunisians and many Moroccans) served again in Europe in World War II. In the Indo-China wars of the French, which preceded those of the Americans, the Algerian soldiers absorbed the revolutionary guerrilla tactics of one of the most successful guerrilla commanders of all time, General Vo Nguyen

Giap of Vietnam, the nemesis of both the French and American expeditionary forces. To these lessons in the art of guerrilla warfare, the CIA and ISI-trained Afghan veterans brought their own refinements in the cruel and savage tactics of the GIA; the Islamic Salvation Army (AIS), the "military" branch of the FIS, and other smaller groups. They joined and helped to lead the offensive against the Algerian military establishment and government. These, in 1992, frustrated the hope of the Islamists of legitimate accession to power through free national elections by suddenly and brutally canceling those elections.

Some historians, most of them French, have deprecated the role of Islam and its political expressions in North Africa's anti-colonial struggles. They upgraded instead the importance of Marxist, socialist concepts in Algeria. The Islamic factor, however, was always there. That its strength was rarely adequately recognized helps to explain the helplessness of both Algerian society and Western observers in trying to understand the violence which erupted in the new Islamist upheaval which began in 1992.

Ottoman rule over Algeria began essentially in 1529 AD, and was basically a colonial regime. From an early date France traded with the Regency of Algiers, as it was called, importing leather, coral and grain. Most governments in Paris managed to maintain good relations with the Porte in Constantinople, the Regency's masters. France bought from the Regency leather, coral and other products on credit. When the French merchants were slow about paying, the ruling Dey, Hussein, slapped the French consul with a fly-swatter. The government in Paris sent the French fleet and a force of marines to bombard and occupy Algiers on July 3, 1830. Hussein fled to Italy and his force of janissaries embarked for Turkey. The new French colonial masters, who began the conquest of the "useful" agricultural plains and hills, north of the Atlas mountains and the Sahara desert beyond, discovered a population of three million, divided into tribes and clans which the French discovered they could manipulate to accentuate tribal divisions. The arriving French settlers proclaimed there was no such thing as an "Algerian people," but only a collection of rival clans.

Led by Islamic clerics and a warrior chief with a first-rate intellect, the Emir Abdelkader organized armed resistance to the French in western Algeria. He and his tribesmen fought tenaciously and stubbornly, but were never able to enlist either the Sultan's forces in neighboring Morocco (which had never come under Turkish sway) or the Berber tribesmen of the Kabylie mountains. In 1847 Abdelkader surrendered personally to the Duke of Aumale. Imprisoned in Amboise, France, Abdelkader was allowed to choose Syria, another Turkish possession, as his place of exile. His name became a legend in nineteenth-century Syria and Lebanon for halting a civil war there between the Maronite Christians and the Druze people, saving the lives of thousands in the process. The rest of the story was a steady advance of the settlers, as we saw, in their efforts to claim all of the country's choice land and agricultural and mineral wealth.

American, British and to a lesser extent Free-French forces invaded North Africa in "Operation Torch," in November 1942, in a major episode of World War II. The allies replaced the Vichy regime and fought the Germans and Italians in Tunisia and Libya. This deeply influenced the young Algerians who would later lead the FLN in its anti-colonial war. One major uprising, with hundreds, perhaps thousands of Algerians killed by the French security forces and army, erupted in the Constantine area in 1945. It had become clear that the vague promises of self-determination promised at the Casablanca Conference of President Roosevelt, Prime Minister Churchill and the Free French did not include either Algeria or the French protectorates in Morocco and Tunisia.

More years of war followed until independence. Appropriately this took effect amid scenes of mass rejoicing, which this author covered in Algiers on July 3, 1962, just 132 years after the first French colonial expedition attacked Algiers. About one million people, three-quarters or more Algerians, had perished during the war. Some 2,055,000 Algerians, one Algerian in every four, was forced by the French army into "regroupment camps" where they were forced to live in almost concentration-camp conditions. This was the last major uprooting by the French of the Algerians from their native farmlands, and the biggest of all. In 1962 a million "pied-noirs," the term the European settlers gave themselves, departed for a France where few of them had been born and even fewer knew anything about the 50,000 "harkis," Muslim mercenaries who fought for the French army and were executed, many by having their throats cut for their "treason." Algerian Muslim emigration to France doubled from half a million to one million a year. Millions more Algerians moved for good to the cities and their outskirts, deserting the land and creating huge *bidonvilles* or shanty-towns around and outside the cities. Marginal areas of the cities, where mostly the "poor whites" of the former pied-noir population had lived, became urban slums peopled by Muslims.[8]

These post-independence urban slums provided much of the manpower for the Islamist revolt which began in 1992. Among the basic reasons for this revolt was the total failure of the single-party FLN governments, always allied with the powerful army, which grew in power after 1962, to give most Algerians a better life. There were three presidential regimes: those of Ahmed ben Bella (1962–64); Colonel Houari Boumedienne (1964–78) and Colonel Chadli Benjadid (1978–92), before the Islamist uprising followed the canceled elections. None of these regimes lived up to promises made during the revolution to grant women equal rights and to permit religious freedom.

From the 1954 Aures mountain uprising onward, the so-called "historic chiefs" of the revolution and founders of the state in 1962, displayed a curious kind of schizophrenia about religion. In all of their public policy statements, such as a revolutionary charter of May 1956, the FLN leaders solemnly proclaimed: "Algeria, conscious of its economic, cultural and political vocation, will be a democracy which will admit diversity of races, religions and opinions." At the same time, FLN propaganda, especially that directed to Arab and Muslim states, from the beginning spoke of a jihad or holy war, in terms similar to those the Afghani moujahidin and their Algerian and other Muslim recruits used. The FLN's official newspaper, edited and produced in Tunis, Cairo and sometimes Rabat, was called *Al-Moujahid* (The Holy Warrior). It was published in both French and Arabic. It glorified, especially in the Arabic edition, Algeria's "national Islamic culture" and the "need to realize North African unity within its natural Arab-Muslim framework." Little was said about women, except for vague statements assuring "our sisters who fight with us" of their equality.

At the same time, FLN diplomats and publicists like Muhammad Yazid, who was married to an American woman from New York and who spent years lobbying for Algeria's cause at the United Nations, did their best to reassure Algeria's Christian and Jewish minorities that the war for liberation was not a jihad or religious war; nor was it an "outlaw" movement as official French government doctrine and much popular or tabloid journalism painted it. (One of the favorite French newspaper terms for rebel guerrilla fighters in Algeria, Morocco or Tunisia in the 1950s was the North African Arabic term, *fellagha*, or "bandit.") In an open "Letter to the French" in 1956, just before a campaign of urban terrorism in Algiers which was snuffed out by heavy resort to torture of suspects by French security, the FLN affirmed it had "nothing to do with … Muslim religious fanaticism [leading to] revival of a vast and conquering Arab empire."

During the eight-year independence war, Islam had played a large role, though this was often obscured from Western eyes. Mosque attendance increased from 1955 on, especially in rural districts. The French authorities systematically blocked literature and periodicals from the Arab and larger Muslim worlds. Millions of Algerians began to take an interest in their neglected Arabic language by listening to short-wave radio broadcasts from Cairo, Damascus or elsewhere. Official Arabic and Kabylie (Berber)-language broadcasts by the French authorities were largely ignored. French development of Algerian television during 1960–62, the last two years of the war, partly offset this – but only among the tiny minority of Algerian Muslims – not more than a few hundred – who could afford this expensive plaything of the Europeans. Mosques, sometimes safe from police informers, became centers to spread news and propaganda for the cause – just as they have in the new Islamist insurgency of the 1990s.

In education, Algeria's Association of Ulama succeeded in opening some new schools during the early war years, such as Dar al-Hadith College in Tlemcen, historically a religious center. It began classes in 1956. General de Gaulle's accession to the French presidency in 1958 and the first secret, then finally overt moves toward a negotiated peace between France and the FLN, brought no relaxation of the tight French strictures on financing of mosques and the Muslim prayer leaders. The Muslim clerics, one French official told me in 1961, "pretend to keep out of politics, but they are really the very heart of the rebellion."

The *Khutba* or political sermon, usually delivered in mosques on Fridays, was forbidden before independence – and revived with full force in the 1990s, especially after the start of the new civil war when former Afghan fighters, often dressed in Afghan clothes, would flock to the mosques and listen to prayer leaders who wore the same garb. During the war the FLN assassinated members of the religious hierarchy considered to be collaborating with the French administration. Again, this was replicated during the insurgency of the 1990s, after the Algerian volunteers who had fought in the Afghan jihad had witnessed how the moujahidin would murder clerics considered to be working with the Communist Afghan government and therefore the Russians. Similarly, the Islamist HAMAS organization in Palestine, some of whose leaders were also Afghan veterans, would kill Palestinian clerics considered to be cooperating with the Israeli occupation authorities in the West Bank and Gaza. This intensified with the outbreak of the Palestinian *intifada* or uprising from 1987 on.

The FIS, the first political magnet attracting the returning Afghan veterans, was formed at the mosque in Bab al-Oued, a poor quarter of Algiers, under supervision of the mosque's imam or prayer leader, Ali Belhadj, who became the deputy leader of FIS. Its chief became Sheikh Abbas Madani, who did a year in prison in the 1980s for denouncing the ruling FLN as "anti-Islamic." The two operated in duet: Madani provided intellectual sustenance, while Belhadj preached fiery, populist sermons. Belhadj generally represented more extremist views. The FIS resulted from the merger of four smaller Islamic groups. Significantly, one of these was the local chapter of the South Asian pan-Islamic Jamaat al-Tabligh, whose role in recruiting young North Africans for "religious instruction" in Pakistan, which often led to military training for the CIA's Afghan jihad, we have already noted. The Tabligh propagandists worked assiduously among younger working-class and unemployed Algerians to spread their message that adherence to a strict and puritanical Islam was Algeria's only hope.

Financing for the FIS came initially from Saudi Arabia. This began to fall off as early as late 1990 and was cut entirely – to be replaced, Algerian security officials believe – by largesse from Osama bin Laden, who facilitated the return of the Afghan veterans with false passports and sometimes company work papers. The official Saudi aid ended partly because the Riyadh government was deeply upset by a trip Madani made to Baghdad after the August 1990 Iraqi invasion of Kuwait. He met President Saddam Hussein and announced support for any moves to defend Iraq against "aggression."[9]

John-Thor Dahlburg is a *Los Angeles Times* correspondent who was able to report from Algeria in the mid-1990s, before it became difficult to obtain visas from the military government and critically risky for all journalists to work there. Dahlburg documented the start of the armed uprising in a palm-bordered oasis near the Tunisian border called Guemar, on November 29, 1991. A gaunt, bearded chieftain, who resembled the Hollywood stereotype of an Islamist, led the attack on a border guards' barracks. He was Aissa Messaoudi, known as "Tayeb al-Afghani," or "Tayeb the Afghan." He had become an active FIS member after his return from Afghanistan's post-1989 unholy wars. Tayeb and his squad caught the young border guards asleep. Using the same tactics employed against Russians in Afghanistan, they hacked their victims to death with knives and swords. Some were burned with blowtorches. The attackers seized 30 weapons from the armory and fled into the desert. Algerian army units soon tracked them down and arrested them. "Tayeb the Afghan" was tried by a military court in the Saharan town of Ouargla. A firing squad executed him.

Many observers view the Guemar butchery as the birth of the Armed Islamic Group, or GIA. This soon became the most brutal and ruthless of the armed bands ravaging rural Algeria and some of its towns as well. The GIA's initial cadre was composed partly of Afghanis like "Tayeb" and partly of older men like Larbi Bouyali, killed in a battle with the army, who had fought the French in the independence war of 1954–62. In the final three years of the Afghan war, 1986–89, the Pakistani Embassy in Algiers issued 2,800 visas for Algerian nationals heading for Pakistan, many of them recruited by the Tabligh. Somewhere between 600 and 1,000 Algerians with combat experience in Afghanistan returned home, either traveling officially with help from bin Laden or similar "private" supporters of jihad, or sneaking across the Moroccan or Tunisian desert or mountain borders. Sociologist Mahfoud Bennoune states flatly that "the nucleus of the terrorist movement in Algeria had combat experience in Afghanistan."

In the opening months of the uprising, the Afghan returnees shared their military expertise with the organizers of the GIA. Some of these had, as early as 1985–86, attended summer camps created by various Islamist groups on the Mediterranean coast and in the mountains of Algeria, learning martial arts and a literal interpretation of the Holy Koran. The returning "Afghans" added guerrilla tactics, ambushes, demolition and all of the other tactics and methods originally imparted from the CIA through Pakistan's ISI in the Afghan and Pakistani training schools and camps. They were so lionized, Dahlburg reported, by restless, alienated young Algerians that some teenagers and youths began to don Afghan-style clothes in imitation of them. In June 1991, when serious anti-government rioting erupted in Algiers streets, the "Afghanis" and their acolytes appeared in the front ranks of the rioters, chanting Islamic slogans and wearing black scarves. A former university student who had frequent contact with the returnees reported that they didn't look Algerian at all: "They wore turbans, didn't eat at the table but on the floor and with their hands. They used twigs instead of toothbrushes and put kohl [black makeup] around their eyes."

To FIS members who were trying to play the peaceful political game by preparing for elections, the Afghan returnees said , "Listen, it's not your method that will give you power. The right way is what we did in Afghanistan, where we broke the Soviet union into pieces," reported Abdelaziz Belkhadem, a former speaker of the Algerian parliament. One of the initial GIA leaders, a man of about 30 named Si Ahmed Mourad, called Jaffar al-Afghani, tried to impose savage tactics on outlying branches of the spreading movement. Men under his leadership are credited with killing the first of several hundred foreigners to die in the civil war – two French surveyors. Jaffar's special savagery and his orders to kill intellectuals, including journalists, women and even children in rural raids to intimidate the mass of the nonpolitical or indifferent rural population, caused one of the first serious splits in the GIA. Some of his rivals apparently tipped off his whereabouts to the army. During the holy fast month of Ramadan in 1994, an army unit surrounded Jaffar and nine followers as they took the *iftar*, the traditional fast-breaking supper after sundown, and killed them all.

One of the most important Afghani veterans, whose influence predated the 1992 insurgency, was Kamreddine Kharban. Depending on which source you credit, he was either a Soviet-trained Algerian force pilot trained to fly MIG fighter jets, or an air force mechanic trained to service them. In 1983, he left the Algerian military and Algeria and turned up in Peshawar, Pakistan. Here, he and another Algerian volunteer in the anti-Soviet war who stayed on for post-graduate training, so to speak, named Bounoua Boudjema, known as Abu Anes, discussed with Osama bin Laden and another Islamist support group called the Islamic Rescue Organization, the raising of an "Afghan Legion" to lead the struggle to turn Algeria into an Islamic state. Boudjema strengthened his links with the Peshawar-based Isalmist guerrilla establishment by marrying the daughter of the charismatic Palestinian, Abdallah Azzam, one of the ideological founders of HAMAS and whom the CIA used as a recruiter for the Afghanistan jihad in the United States.

Kamareddine Kharban was by this time a member of the exiled executive committee of FIS. The additional training he received in Pakistan seems to have broadened his horizon beyond that of Algeria. His former air force career in Algeria and training as an officer combined with the Peshawar experience to make him a desirable military advisor for the Bosnian Muslim army. He began to travel to Bosnia and also to Tehran. At the time when the US component of NATO in Bosnia was turning a blind eye to Iran's airlift of military supplies to the Bosnian Muslims, Kharban attended a conference of Islamic organizations in Iran. Soon afterward, Israeli-made Uzi and Scorpio submachine guns began to turn up in both Bosnia and Algeria in the hands of pre-GIA insurgent groups, like that of Mustafa Bouyali. Shortly after Bouyali's death, Kharban returned to Algiers to preach in a suburban mosque in the neighborhood of Belcourt, called, with irony and black humor by some, "Kabul." This became a base for the early GIA covert guerrilla cells of men like Tayeb al-Afghani after the creation of the GIA. This happened especially during the June 1991 riots in Algeria.[10]

During those riots, when many Algerian Afghan veterans made their way home, Algerian security forces caught numerous Muslims of other nationalities, either with weapons or passing out leaflets on behalf of the FIS. At the end of June, the security authorities arrested scores of Sudanese and Pakistani nationals deployed from another mosque in the Algiers suburb of Al Harrach. When President Chadly Benjadid met with leaders of the newly-formed FIS – well before the fateful canceled elections of January 1992 – some of the earlier Islamist prisoners were amnestied. Others fled to Pakistan or Afghanistan. One was Abdelkader Benouis, who soon moved to Saudi Arabia where he became involved in fund-raising, probably with the bin Laden organization, for the Algerian insurgents. In May 1993, Benouis was sentenced to death in absentia in Algeria, together with two sons of the FIS leader Sheikh Abbasi Madani. The sons were named Usama and Iqbal. Also sentenced was Rabah Kebir, the active FIS spokesman in Germany. German authorities later detained and jailed Usama Madani and Rabah Kebir.[11]

Benouis had left Algeria in 1992 and found refuge in France, which expelled him to Pakistan in August 1992. From there, he was tracked to Belgium, then to Britain. There he became one of the Islamist exiles whom the Algerian, Egyptian and Tunisian governments refer to as terrorist leaders, demanding their extradition in 1998 from the reluctant Labor Party government of Prime Minister Tony Blair.

After a rash of terrorist bombings, apparently by Algerians, in France in 1995 and especially after the hijacking of an Air France Airbus on Christmas Eve 1994, French authorities and some French commentators tended to blame Afghan veterans. In the hijacking three passengers were killed in the initial clash at Algiers airport. It ended in Marseilles. French commandos stormed the plane and killed the four Algerian air pirates, leaving 25 injured passengers, crew and police. This seems unlikely to have had an "Afghan" connection. The moujahidin who fought in Afghanistan were not trained by their CIA or Pakistani mentors in hijacking, and nothing similar happened during the 1979–89 Afghanistan war.[12] By 2000, according to French analysts with whom the author spoke in the spring of that year, the GIA appeared to have split into "national" and "international" fragments. The "internationalists," evidently weary of slaughter and bloodshed in their own country, turned to terrorism abroad, with apparent support of Osama bin Laden's networks. Individuals like Algerian Ahmed Ressam, captured by US customs officials on December 14, 1999 at Port Angeles, in Washington state, as he tried to smuggle explosives in a car from Vancouver, Canada, into the US for intended bombings at the Christmas–New Year–millennium celebrations, and Ressam's alleged accomplices detained in the US and Canada, were associated with this GIA "international" group.

Before examining more closely an art in which the moujahidin were carefully schooled – sabotage of sensitive installations such as oil and gas pipelines or refineries – it is worth mentioning that the Algerian government authorities and many ordinary Algerians blame the Afghan veterans for introducing into Algerian society "marriages of convenience," a "self-awarded license," as John-Thor Dahlburg calls it, to kidnap and rape women as the supposed privilege due holy warriors, and which is widely reported from Afghanistan's unholy internecine wars of the 1990s. An Algerian judge told Dahlburg that "the most abominable crimes" were committed by the Afghan returnees. "I've had 40 'Afghans' [appearing before me in court] and only two, I think, actually took part in the fighting. But a certain number were trained by our Pakistani friends to handle explosives, whether for operations in Afghanistan or elsewhere is an open question. They say, 'We believe that God told us to kill.'"[13]

Large-scale and successful sabotage operations against Algeria's crucial and largely Western-financed and operated oil and natural gas installations have been few and far between. However, the relatively few sabotage incidents of this type may reflect the tactics used successfully against the Soviets in Afghanistan and inside neighboring Soviet territory during the Afghanistan war. These tactics were taught by Pakistan's ISI and proudly acknowledged by Pakistani Brigadier Mohammad Youssaf in his book, *The Bear Trap*. The first "professional" sabotage operation against oil installations in Algeria during the Islamist insurgency was a successful fire-bombing and killing raid against an oil base of the Franco-American drilling company, Schlumberger, in northeastern Algeria in October 1994. This, and the murder of a British oil worker and other foreigners in October 1994 caused Schlumberger and other firms, including BP and the Italian Agip, to withdraw their staff from Algerian work sites and fly them back down to Algeria for short work periods. The big American companies, in particular Anadarko, tended to keep their expatriate staff in Algeria, but only inside fortified and well-guarded compounds, where all their material wants were met without the need to venture out to nearby towns or cities.

In early December 1997, however, an Algiers court condemned 13 members of the GIA to up to 15 years in prison for attempting to burn down Algeria's largest oil rig sometime in 1996. They had tried to set fire to the Hassi Messaoud desert platform, situated in the desert about 300 miles southeast of Algiers. Two men were convicted in absentia. Another six, suspected of belonging to a local (non-GIA) Islamist ring in the eastern city of Annaba, were acquitted. All of those accused, including some former employees of Algeria's national oil company, Sonatrach, pleaded their innocence. Like many other defendants in many other trials, they accused the police of using torture to extract their confessions.[14]

There are powerful economic reasons why in general, the CIA Afghan sabotage training was the slowest of all the types to backfire against American and other Western oil interests in Algeria. The political leadership of the FIS and probably even some of the most radical of the GIA leaders, must realize that oil and gas are Algeria's lifeblood and key to the future prosperity of any Islamic-type state and society they might succeed in erecting in the future. The attempted sabotage at Hassi Messaoud was especially portentous for Algerians and their Western associates in the petroleum business and its associated banks and other financial institutions. The Hassi Messaoud oil field was discovered by the French in 1956, during the independence war. Since then, the rich oil- and natural gas-bearing zones around Hassi Messaoud have grown to thousands of square miles, comprising the Saharan regions of Hassi R'Mel, Amnas-Edjele at the Libyan frontier, and another zone under heavy development in the late 1990s around In-Salah, at the extreme southern confines of the Algerian Sahara, about 700 miles south of Algiers. Algeria's oil reserves were estimated in 1998 at nine billion barrels; those of gas at five trillion cubic meters. In 1997 the government earned about $14 billion in revenue from oil and gas, about 95 percent of its total income.

One reason, Algerian government officials and apologists say, why the atrocious massacres of men, women and children in villages and tribal areas close to Algerian army or gendarmerie posts in the mid-to-late 1990s could not be prevented was that the bulk of the regular army was deployed to defend the heavily fortified energy sites. By 1998, the Algerian national energy company, Sonatrach, had signed joint-venture contracts with 24 foreign firms, the largest of which were with France's Total and America's Anadarko. At Arzew, on Algeria's western Mediterranean coast, Sonatrach, the French firm, Air Liquide, and Air Products of the United States, have built a helium production plant near the earlier liquid natural gas (LNG) plants. These had serviced gas tankers hauling gas to Europe and the United States. Military units, equipped far better than Soviet ones defending refineries and pipelines attacked by the Afghan holy warriors in the 1980s, use radar, electronic surveillance and helicopters to protect the installations and the Western technicians and engineers serving them.[15]

Though neither their companies nor the US government like to publicize their role or their presence in war-torn Algeria, the 500 to 600 American engineers and technicians living and working behind barbed wire in these protected gas and oil enclaves in Algeria may be one of the main reasons why Osama bin Laden or other international manipulators of terrorism were unable, or unwilling, to strike at this principal US interest and investment in North Africa. This little-publicized but heavy US commercial involvement in Algeria began in earnest, not when the French oil companies were forced by Algerian independence to withdraw from their monopoly positions after 1962, but rather in 1991 – ironically, at the dawn of the Islamist insurgency. In December 1991 the Algerian state opened the energy sector on liberal terms to foreign investors and operators. About 30 oil and gas fields have been attributed to foreign companies since then. The main American firms involved, Arco, Exxon, Oryx, Anadarko, Mobil and Sun Oil received exploration permits, often in association with European firms like Agip, BP, Cepsa or the Korean group Daewoo.

As soon as an oil or gas field becomes commercially productive, production and proceeds are shared with the state firm, Sonatrach. Algeria's oil production, about 800,000 barrels per day (bpd) in 1997, was estimated to rise to one million bpd by the year 2000. Most contracts are drawn in such a way that Sonatrach's share will diminish and those of the foreign firms increase. The US firms of Arco and Anadarko accounted in 1998 for one-third of all production. Four foreign firms are involved in developing new gas fields. They are the Europeans BP and Total and the Americans Exxon and Arco. Algeria's 1997 production of about 33 billion cubic meters of natural gas is expected to increase substantially by the turn of the century. Two trans-Mediterranean gas pipelines are to go into service then. Algeria's reserves of natural gas, estimated at five trillion cubic meters, put it in eighth place in the world. The majority of oil and gas exports go to nearby Europe. Though American firms in Texas and Boston, Massachusetts, were major customers in the 1960s, the main clients in the late 1990s are France, Belgium, Spain and Italy.

Europe takes 80 percent of Algerian oil exports; the United States only 10 percent, with the remainder to Canada, Africa, South America and the Far East. The consequence of this is that the growing share of American operating companies in Algerian oil and gas development will increase dependence of the economies of the European Community on these firms,[16] implying an ever-growing Algerian stake in their security. This may be the only question on which the military governments of Algeria and the Islamist rebels see eye to eye. It seems to be in the interests of no Algerians to rock the boat.

Early in 1998, there was a fresh wave of especially bloody massacres in rural areas, attributed by the government to the GIA. Many Algerians and outsiders blamed government "death squads" or local militias with private blood feuds to settle. There was overwhelming pressure from Amnesty International and a number of other human rights organizations for outside intervention. Some of them suggested that the United States ought to exercise pressure on the government of General Liamine Zeroual to allow such intervention – by limiting US imports of Algerian oil and natural gas. The US State Department's soft-spoken spokesman, James Rubin, put paid to this idea on January 5, 1998. There were no such plans, he said. "I have not heard in the discussions that we've [United States] had ... that these tools would be necessarily in our interests to implement," he told journalists at a daily briefing. The Algerian government should, he added, do more to protect its civilians while respecting the rule of law. It should allow international investigators to visit. In 1998, visiting missions of United Nations and non-governmental human rights organizations did succeed finally in making some limited observations and interviewing a few Algerians, selected by the military government, in the summer of 1998, with inconclusive results.

The direct impact of the Afghanistan war on Algeria's civil war receded while its long-term influence lingered throughout the 1990s. The unhappy country's future seemed tied more and more to the ambitions and aspirations of its military rulers, the heritage of its eight-year war for independence which lasted the longest. Paramount in this story of military rulers who have given lip service to democracy without permitting it to exist has been the rise and decline of the head of state from late 1995 until early 1999, General Liamine Zeroual. His victory in the presidential elections of November 16, 1995 seemed for a brief time to promise an era of reconciliation with the Islamist revolt. He declared "war" on the "terrorists." At the same time, he proclaimed a policy of *rahman* (reconciliation) toward repentant armed militants and promised new legislative elections at an unspecified date. His 61.06 percent of the popular vote and the rate of voter participation which, despite Islamist threats to voters, was a startling 75.69 percent, held out hope. FIS leaders, including Rabah Kebir in Germany, offered dialogue. Extremists, including the GIA, however, stepped up their attacks. GIA fighters in particular increased assaults on unveiled women, teachers and their institutions of learning, journalists, writers, entertainers including actors and musicians – a tactic which, far more even than in Egypt, deprived society of its means of expression, cutting off its cultural oxygen, as it were. Some 600 schools and several universities were burned down. Once again there was a clear and dramatic parallel with Afghanistan, where the Taliban and some of their ideological forebears, viewing schools as breeding grounds for Marxism and Westernization, did the same. Women's emancipation, which is certainly a vital prerequisite for social modernization and democracy, is viewed by the Islamists in Algeria, Afghanistan, Sudan and other Muslim countries of the late twentieth century as an immense threat to cultural "identity." Even under FLN rule in Algeria, the 1984 family code, though offering the FLN's traditional lip-service to women's equality, tried to reduce women to dependent status in society. The Islamists view re-imposition of the kind of subordinate role the Taliban have imposed on Afghan women as a means of gaining total control over that society. FIS leader Sheikh Abassi Madani declared in 1989: "A female should emerge from home only three times in her life: 'when she is born, when she is married, and when she goes to the cemetery.'"[17]

Even during President Zeroual's first year of office in 1996 it was clear that the domestic economy, regardless of the growth of foreign income from the export of oil and natural gas, was eroding and sinking under the attacks of the Islamists. Taxes were uncollected. Normal civil and legal procedures were largely paralyzed. A "brain drain" took hundreds of thousands of talented and qualified professionals, men and women, abroad. Criminality and the drug trade soared, buoyed on the rising black market and "trabendo," or semi-legal smuggling. All of these social tendencies continued and worsened through 1998. Zeroual had studiously avoided promising any specific reforms and these did not materialize. He opened negotiation with some of the legal and, some Algerians would say, "tame" opposition parties, but did nothing serious with the FIS. Through a succession of civilian prime ministers too numerous to enumerate here, it became clear that the two main schools of opinion within the ruling military concerning the Islamists – the "exterminators" or all-out repressors, were at serious odds with the "accommodationists," who sought avenues of negotiation with the insurgents.

In late 1997, President Zeroual's military government scored a minor victory. One of the smaller Islamist groups called the Islamic League for Dawa and Jihad (preaching and holy war), with the acronym LIDD, announced a truce in October. At the same time it demanded immediate freedom for FIS leader Sheikh Abbasi Madani, in house arrest in Algiers, and of his deputy Ali Belhadj, still in prison. The LIDD, whose leadership included a few Afghan veterans who had not gone over to the GIA, had distanced itself from the GIA in November 1995 and concentrated its hundred or so fighters in the area of Medea, south of Algiers. Soon it became apparent that its unilateral truce was coordinated with a call for a truce made by the armed wing of the FIS, called the Islamic Salvation Army (AIS) on September 21, led by Sheikh Madani Mezrag. The AIS more or less observed its own truce from October 1997 onward.[18]

At the same time, President Zeroual traveled to Saudi Arabia to replicate Egyptian President Mubarak's appeals to the Saudis to cut off all public and private aid to the Islamist insurgents, including that provided by the likes of Osama bin Laden. Without giving details, King Fahd agreed to help. In return, President Zeroual apparently assured him of Algerian support for the Kingdom's policies on the Arab–Israel "peace process," already in serious trouble, and in the wider Middle East, including the Persian Gulf.[19]

During the opening weeks of 1998, a phenomenon which Zeroual and his fellow generals had apparently neglected or ignored in their efforts to plan their way out of Algeria's predicament, began to be recognized. This was the gain, in both monetary and political terms, by the extremist GIA from prosperity based on energy exports. When the civil war erupted in 1992, economic prospects looked bleak indeed. Then, in 1994, thanks to some perspicacious Algerian and World Bank negotiators, Algeria's foreign debt of $8 billion was rescheduled in a way which released billions of dollars, about 75 percent of its annual oil and gas export revenues, for the security forces' budget, enabling a huge recruiting drive and the tripling in size of the paramilitary anti-terrorist force, gendarmerie and part-time armed "village guards." At the same time, public enterprises, often under physical attack by the GIA, were privatized and became profitable, creating both new jobs and consumer benefits. An example was a cement factory at Meftah, Algeria, nearly reduced to rubble by terrorist attacks. The remains were purchased and rebuilt by private firms which expanded operations and provided cement for thousands of new units of public housing for the poor. In such ways, Zeroual's administration was enabled to restructure large sectors of the economy, with the approval and help of the IMF and foreign investors. A new middle class of private entrepreneurs emerged, enlarging the military regime's power base – something the Communist regime in Kabul in the 1979–89 Afghanistan war had never been able to do.[20]

Would the resignation of General Zeroual from the presidency, announced by him in September 1998 for February 1999, 18 months before the end of his constitutional five-year term, help to pacify the troubled country? Francis Ghiles, an expert observer of Algerian affairs, described and analyzed the feuding within the ruling military which brought about Zeroual's exit. Three months of bitter feuding within the army high command preceded Zeroual's announcement. However, the root cause was years of serious disagreements between President Zeroual and his closest political ally, General Muhammad Betchine. The opposing group included the chief of staff, General Muhammad Lamari and the national chief of security, General Tewfik Mediene. Behind the scenes were the men whom Ghiles calls "the real king makers" in Algeria: Generals Khaled Nezzar and Larbi Belkheir. Nezzar was defense minister when the fateful 1992 elections which nearly brought the Islamists to power legally were canceled.

After the murder of the "clean" President Muhammad Boudiaf, an FLN veteran of the independence war brought back from exile in Morocco by the military in 1992, Nezzar joined a collegiate presidency which ran the country until General Zeroual's election to the presidency in 1994. General Larbi Belkheir, the right-hand man of President Chadly Benjadid until Benjadid's resignation at the start of the insurgency, was a former interior minister. The Lamari group, known as advocates of "eradication" of the Islamists through ruthless and total repression, have generally enjoyed support from the US, France and other foreign countries with heavy investments in Algeria. President Zeroual, on the other hand, made repeated if ineffectual efforts to broker a compromise with "moderate" Islamist parties like the Algerian Hamas party, and even with moderate elements of the FIS. Economic and financial interests, resulting from the privatizations and the IMF-approved economic policy, also come into play in the controversy between the two groups, who feuded openly in an otherwise tightly controlled Algerian press. Sinister events occurred, including a mysterious car accident in the desert of another general close to Zeroual, and the murder of the commander of the coast guards, which some observers believe were connected to the intra-military feud.

On April 15, 1999, Abdelaziz Bouteflika, a veteran of the 1954–62 revolution against France and a former foreign minister, got 70 percent of the popular vote and was elected president. His six rivals had all withdrawn the day before. Bouteflika was clearly the choice of leaders in Algeria's political, military and affluent business establishments. During 1999 he offered a series of amnesties to the Islamic rebels. Only the FIS and its armed wing seemed to respond, through individual surrenders. The government managed to collect some arms, mostly from them. On January 14, 2000, AFP reported from Algiers that the GIA had rejected any dealings with the government, while a GIA splinter group calling itself the Salafist Group for Preaching and Combat (GSPC) was preparing to surrender. It never became clear that they did. Skirmishes with the security forces occasionally reached the proportions of pitched battles. Massacres of villagers, travelers and other civilians continued through the spring of 2000, though on a reduced scale.

Neither Tunisia nor Morocco, Algeria's immediate neighbors, suffered a backlash from Afghanistan comparable to Algeria's. Tunisia did indeed undergo an Islamist revival, snuffed out by an authoritarian president with US training and a military and police background. Morocco's monarchy, scarcely touched at all by either recruiting or any repercussions of the Afghanistan war, used both the carrot of limited democratization and the stick of effective police repression to foreclose any chance of an Islamist uprising in the 1990s. The start of the rising in Algeria with the Guemmar attack in 1992 led both neighbors to seal their frontiers and to more coordination between the three regimes to control Islamist activities.

The first significant groups, as we saw in Chapter 5, to arise in Tunisia under President Bourguiba in the 1970s were encouraged, just as the Americans encouraged the Saudi, Afghan, Pakistani and other Islamists during that period, in order to contain "Communist" movements and ideas. The Khomeiny revolution in Iran in 1979 sent shock waves throughout North Africa. The Pakistanis, especially the recruiters of the Tablighi Jamaat, made it easy for young volunteers to get a Pakistani visa and an air ticket to join the religious training courses in Pakistan. These courses preceded military training for those who chose to join the anti-Soviet jihad. However, at home in Tunisia, those young Islamists who didn't go to

Afghanistan were never permitted full, overt legal political activity, as we saw in Chapter 5. The condemnation of the Islamist leader Rashid al-Ghanushi to life in prison and others to death in absentia in 1987 helped to bring on Bourguiba's removal from power and his replacement by American-trained President Zine Abidine ben Ali in November 1987. Ben Ali's early relaxation and honeymoon with the Islamists ended in November 1989 when the Tunisian Education Minister, Muhammad Sherfi, proposed bringing back old school textbooks about Islam, used in the Bourguiba era and stressing retrograde aspects. He charged that the new books approved by the Islamists taught Tunisian children "obscurantist" doctrines. The Islamist response was that the Minister's proposal insulted Islam. It demanded his resignation, unleashing agitation in the high schools and universities against him.

New unrest erupted across Tunisia. On May 18, 1991, only weeks after Tunisians of various political persuasions had vociferously opposed the ben Ali government's support for the US and its allies in the Gulf War against Iraq, ben Ali announced discovery of an Islamist conspiracy to overthrow the state. Government supporters leaked news about the supposed role of returned Afghan veterans, though public proof of this was not presented. Ghanushi, traveling on a Sudanese diplomatic passport arranged for him by the power behind Sudan's Islamist military regime, Sheikh Hassan al-Turabi, denied his involvement. After a new series of trials and revelations about police torture and other abuses, a civilian court in August 1992 handed down milder verdicts than the prosecutor had demanded. There were no death sentences, only prison terms. Charges which the court declared proven included trying to overthrow the state and storing caches of weapons for this purpose. President ben Ali was to have been murdered by a Stinger missile, presumably brought home by Afghani veterans, fired at his aircraft on takeoff or landing. There were a number of acquittals. Several of the military suspects, tried in absentia, had already fled to Spain and taken asylum there. Ghanushi and other Islamist political leaders were again sentenced in absentia. The main leaders present in Tunisia of the En-Nahda (Renaissance) party, as it was called, Sadok Shourou and Habib Ellouz, were jailed.

Since then, ben Ali and his governments have brushed aside Ghanushi's protestations of moderation from his chosen place of exile in the United Kingdom, and refused to legalize any radical Islamist group. This, they argue, has preserved civil peace in Tunisia (with the exception of some minor anti-tourist terrorist incidents at the end of the 1980s) and kept Tunisia a haven for three million or more foreign tourists yearly and for foreign investors. They argue, as do Algeria's generals and most French governments, that an Islamist party, once democratically elected to power, would permit no further democratic life. Ben Ali seems to have advised Algerian President Chadly Benjadid, in vain, not to legalize the FIS. The generals who threw Benjadid out of power and canceled the Algerian elections in January 1992, did indeed follow ben Ali's advice.[21]

Although the smallest of the five members of the Union of Arab Maghreb States which also included Morocco, Algeria, Mauretania and Libya, Tunisia was economically the most successful among them. Its good economic performance might help to account for the significantly lower level of radical Islamist activity than existed in Algeria, or Egypt. There was in the 1980s and earlier 1990s an even lower level in Libya. This was partly because Colonel Muammar al-Qaddafi had combated the Islamists in his country from the time he seized power in Libya in a coup in 1969. From time to time, as in several speeches in April 1993, Qaddafi indicated he was considering imposing some aspects of sharia law in Libya. But like King Hassan II of Morocco, he discouraged proselytization and recruiting in Libya for the CIA's holy war in Afghanistan. Only a few Libyans – perhaps fewer than 300 – seem to have taken guerrilla training or to have seen combat in Afghanistan. On the other hand, during the last few years before the Soviet withdrawal from Afghanistan, rumors difficult to evaluate indicated Qaddafi had given some of the largesse he had so generously handed out to terrorist and liberation groups around the world to Gulbuddin Hekmatyar's extremist Afghan organization. Whenever disorders or violent opposition to his rule erupted in Libya, as it did in the eastern parts of his country in the later 1990s, travelers reaching Egypt would insist that Islamist groups had identified themselves as the authors. However, there is no reliable evidence known to this author of any involvement by the returned Afghan veterans.

The Kingdom of Morocco, traditionally aloof from Eastern Arab and Islamic influences of various sorts, remained largely so from late twentieth century Islamism. However, the few available sources indicate that by 1987, the lure of the Afghan jihad had attracted several hundred young Moroccans to leave their country under various pretexts – there was firm official objection to their overt recruitment and departure for Peshawar. Usually, they would make their way through a European capital or Saudi Arabia, whose ruling family and intelligence service were strong friends with King Hassan and his regime. Ultimately they reached the training grounds and in a few cases, the killing fields, of the holy war in South Asia.[22]

Sometime in early 1993, there appears to have been an attempt to create a unified Morocco–Algeria Islamist command, located inside Morocco near the Algerian border. This was foiled when the watchful Moroccan security services in May 1993 arrested Abdul Haq Layada, an Algerian Afghan veteran. He had formed a small cell-like organization called, after an earlier Egyptian Islamist revolutionary group, *Al Takfir wal Hijra*, roughly translated as Deliverance and Flight, a Koranic reference to the Prophet Muhammad and his followers and their movements which gathered headway in Arabia.

According to the prosecutor of an Algerian special court in September 1993, Layada was secretly extradited from Morocco to Algeria and he was in custody there. This followed weeks of anti-Moroccan polemics in the Algerian media which charged that Layada's presence in Morocco proved the Moroccan monarchy's support for the Algerian Islamists. Layada had such a high opinion of himself and his own capacities that he bragged, while still in custody in Morocco, that he was the "national amir" of several guerrilla units and had 600 men under his direct command. Layada boasted that a rival group called Al Jazara, led by three Afghan veterans who in turn commanded other Afghan veterans, was negligible in the "armed struggle" compared to his group.

Morocco's own home-grown Islamists exist, but they labor under a major disadvantage. Morocco's kings, like the forebears of their Alaouite dynasty (no connection with the Alawite Islamic sect in Syria, to which President Bashar al-Assad belongs), claim direct descent from the Prophet Muhammad. Therefore family members, like those of King Hussein's Hashemite family in Jordan, bear the title of *shorafa*, the Arabic plural of *sharif*. Kings preserve the additional title of *Amir al Moumineen*, or "Commander of the Faithful." The Moroccan kings or sultans, as they were often called then, acquired the title in the anti-colonial wars from the sixteenth century onward against the Portuguese, Spanish and finally French invaders of Morocco. To Morocco's simpler folk, pious Sunni Muslims, the title is God-given, and empowers their king to a higher degree than any other North African ruler. This made it easy for politicians, practicing the forms if not the substance of parliamentary rule in a constitutional monarchy and multi-party system, to cobble together a loyalist "Party of the King." This competed with the traditional and mildly Islamist Istiqlal (independence) party and the "socialist" parties to Istiqlal's Left. A leader of one of these, the Union of Socialist Forces (USFP), Abderrahman Youssefi, a thoroughly honest attorney of great integrity who was jailed in the 1960s for opposing the king, became prime minister of a coalition government formed in Rabat in July 1998. This was a new step in Hassan's limited but forward-looking experiment in parliamentary democracy.

The all-pervasive police watch the Muslim clerics, and any students, teachers or others including any returned Afghan veterans, extremely closely. Police and judiciary deal swiftly with any outspoken criticism of the king or the monarchical system. In 1974, two years after unsuccessful attempts by young cadets and officers in the army and air force to overthrow Hassan II, an individual close to the Muslim Brotherhood, a foreign entity in Moroccan society, named Abdallah Yassin, wrote an open letter to the king. It was entitled "Islam or the Deluge." It warned that either Hassan must convert to the kind of traditional Islam upheld by the Muslim Brothers, or he would cease to reign. Yassin's reward was three and a half years of prison, then several months reclusion in a psychiatric hospital. After his release, Yassin tried to publish magazines and start organizations with an Islamist flavor. Each time he ended up again in jail.

Muhammad Abdelkrim Muti was a trade union leader belonging, curiously, to the socialist USFP, but he also managed to be a member of the Muslim Brotherhood. With government approval he founded a group called "Islamic Youth," which opposed the fashionable "Maoist" Leftist movements which attracted some young Moroccans in the 1970s. Eventually he was accused of complicity in the then unsolved murder of a well-known Leftist, Omar Benjelloun, on December 18, 1975. He had to seek refuge in Saudi Arabia, especially after Moroccan Leftists accused him of acting as an instrument of the police in Benjelloun's killing. When

King Muhammad VI, Hassan II's son, assumed power upon his father's death in August 1999, he kept Youssefi as prime minister, but fired his hardline Interior Minister, Driss Basri. He began a series of reforms, aimed at raising literacy and educational levels; reforms aimed at taking the wind out of the Islamists' sails, for the first time even naming a woman as a royal counselor.

In general Morocco, like its ally Saudi Arabia, still possesses such traditionalist groups. But in both kingdoms, political power and religion are concepts already so closely engaged that the Islamists have a tough time getting a hearing for their arguments in favor of a total marriage of religion with politics.[23] The situation is different in states like Algeria and Egypt, where legal systems and social mores were originally fashioned along more secular lines. There, the lure of the Islamists and the susceptibility of the state and society to extremists like the Afghan veterans, and others like them, has proven far greater.

10 More Contagion: The Philippines

"Fair Philippine Islands, jewel of the sunny Orient," begins the English translation of the Philippine national hymn. Anyone singing these words on the islands at the dawn of the twenty-first century must have paused to reflect on their sad irony.

Although shock waves from the repercussions of the 1979–89 Afghan jihad had spread throughout some of the Far East with only indirect effect, one of the seven main fighting groups in the jihad had moved by about 1990 to the Philippines, with a very direct impact. By summer 2000 the Abu Sayyaf group and its allies were undoing the peace efforts exerted by the government in Manila with the larger Muslim separatist groups, by kidnappings, bombings, burning and pillage in the southern islands. Abu Sayyaf had, in fact, made a small but quite lethal contribution to pushing the southern Philippines into an abyss of virtual civil war, with repercussions felt throughout Southeast Asia and much of the Pacific region.

To understand how a relatively small group of Afghan veterans could help to destabilize this huge East Asian nation of nearly 70 million people living on the 860 inhabited islands of the 7,170 islands in the Philippines archipelago, we must again delve briefly into the history of Western colonial imperialism. Like the Spanish and Portuguese conquests in Latin America, the French in North Africa and to a lesser extent the Italians and British in parts of Africa, the Spanish conquest of the Philippines in 1565 by the conquistador Miguel Lopez de Legazpi aimed at converting the inhabitants to Christianity. As usual the cross and the sword were linked, with the sword of Spain's Christian soldiers going on before the cross.

The Spanish churchmen-soldiers, like their European contemporaries and successors in Africa, found a majority local population of polytheists. Also as in Africa, there was a strong, faithful Muslim community, some of them living as far north as Manila. So the priest-conquerors from Spain brought to the islands in the fifteenth and sixteenth centuries a religious system which they had to superimpose on this unpromising base, where polytheistic spirit-worship prevailed (and still prevails even today in some of the Filipino uplands). Where there was a dual presence of Islam and polytheism, shamans competed with imams, the Muslim prayer-leaders whom the Spaniards of that era, like many mistaken Christians today, persisted in calling "Muslim priests," although Islam neither ordains nor recognizes any sort of priests.

Philippine Catholicism, although today officially a majority faith (84.1 percent, according to a 1995 census, as against 6.2 percent independent Philippine Church members and only 4.6 percent Muslims), nevertheless fights a rear-guard action against Muslim insurgents in the southern islands. This is a Catholicism deeply influenced since the Spanish *conquistadores* by the policies, internal biases and

strategies of the friars of the various Catholic religious orders, especially the
Augustinians, Franciscans, Dominicans and, quite naturally, the Jesuits. These
were the only "white men" dedicating their lives to converting and ministering to
Spain's Pacific Ocean colony before it was lost to the United States in the
Spanish–American War of 1898. The friars and priests divided their island domains
into distinct territories. They learned many of the local languages, vernaculars and
dialects (today the Philippines officially has 988. English, the colonial heritage of
pre-World War II American rule, is the language of everyday business and
administration). Since most of the secular colonial bureaucrats from Spain intended
to live away from the motherland no longer than was necessary to accumulate
comfortable fortunes, the Catholic friars assumed the robes of Crown representatives and implementers of government policies in the countryside. This incestuous
relationship between church and state weakened Madrid's hold on the colony when
in the late nineteenth century nationalist revolt raged in the islands. Filipino priests
seized churches and established the Independent Philippine Church (*Iglesia Filipina
Independiente*).

After US President Teddy Roosevelt and his "Rough Riders" had driven Spain
from Cuba and his "Great White Fleet" had ejected the heirs of the *conquistadores*
from the Philippines in 1898, a new occupation, an American one, began. Now it
was the turn of American Protestant missionaries. Like those already swarming over
much of the world from the Caribbean to Egypt and China, Korea and Japan, they
arrived in their droves in the Philippines. They built churches and began to spread
American culture. Gradually, in the twentieth century, English replaced Spanish in
official business and commerce. Decades before the arrival of the Ford motor car
and McDonald's fast-food restaurants, missionary and secular schools taught the
"natives" English with an American twang, whether their own language was
Tagalog, Cebuano, or one of the hundreds of other tongues. Only the Japanese
occupation, which lasted through World War II from 1941 until 1944–45, put a
temporary brake on this educational and acculturation process.

The rise of Islam from a minority religion to the status of a powerful and (from
the viewpoint of the secular rulers of Christian faith in Manila) potentially
threatening force, went hand-in-hand with the evolution of Philippine relations
with the Middle East. Now, in the twenty-first century, these relations have become
a crucial focus of the archipelago's international relations. The main aspect of
these relations is three-fold. First, an overseas labor market, especially in the
Arabian Peninsula and Gulf countries; for both skilled and unskilled workers –
the often-exploited and long-suffering Filipino housemaids, barmaids and even
school-teachers and engineers – are all-too-familiar figures in host countries from
Saudi Arabia to Cyprus. According to 1998 statistics published in Europe, money
sent home to the islands by Filipinos and Filipinas working abroad amounted to $6.5
billion, out of a Gross National Product (GNP) of $82.1 billion.[1]

The second main ingredient in the heady brew comprising interaction between
the Middle East and the Philippines is oil dependence. Like the rest of the Far

East, and indeed the world, the Philippines need reasonably priced oil. The oil price shocks of the 1970s and 1980s and, to a lesser extent, fluctuations of the 1990s generated crises in the economy. There were inflammatory strikes by the drivers of the "jeepneys," jeeps converted to carry passengers in Filipino cities and towns, and a mainstay of public transport in Manila. Every Philippine government, from the time of dictator Ferdinand Marcos up to the present, has been keenly aware of the need to propitiate Middle East oil producers. They have also been aware of the impact on those relations of the way in which Manila dealt with the rising movement of the Muslims, called the Moros, in the southern islands.

The third ingredient was Moro Muslim separatism. This interacted intimately with oil dependence and labor conditions for the Filipino contract workers in the Arabian Persian Gulf states. Moro separatism was limited largely to the southern islands – southern and western Mindanao, southern Palawan, and the Solo Archipelago, where in 2000 some of the extremist activity by Abu Sayyaf and its larger and older colleagues, reinforced by Afghan war veterans, was centered. The majority of the Moros belong to three out of a total of ten language subgroups: the Maguindanaos of North Cotabato, Sultan Kudarat and Maguindanao provinces; the Maranaos of two provinces on the island of Lanao; and the Tausugs, mainly from Jolo Island. (It was to Jolo that the Abu Sayyaf group kidnapped a group of European tourists who were diving in the turquoise waters of a Malaysian island resort in April 2000. Here, the piratical expedition evidently enjoyed the sympathy and support of the Jolo locals.)

The same Tausugs were the first group ever to adopt Islam, when Arab and other missionaries arrived there in the first centuries after the Prophet Muhammad's death. The Tausugs, proud of their ancient orthodoxy, are critical of the more recently Islamicized Yakan and Bajau peoples for their lack of zealotry in keeping Muslim tenets. In the 1980s, however, such differences tended to fade and be outweighed by their growing consciousness of belonging to the *Umma*, or worldwide community of close to a billion Muslims. This, and shared cultural, social and legal traditions, made it easier for CIA affiliates to recruit Filipino Muslim volunteers for the Muslim jihad in Afghanistan and for the hardened and well-trained survivors of the jihad to return home. Some joined the ranks of the transplanted, Filipino version of the Abu Sayyaf movement. Others joined other indigenous Moros movements.

Moro society was built around a sultan, who is both a secular and religious leader. Ranged under his general authority were *datu*, communal chieftains whose power was measured by the numbers of their followers. The *datu* were feudal overlords. In return for labor and tribute, they provided their communities with help in emergencies and support in disputes with followers of a different chief. In a kind of court called an *agama*, not totally unlike the *majlis* or meeting used by Middle East Muslim rulers to settle disputes and hear petitions for favors, a *datu* exercised his authority. He might have as many as the four wives allowed by the Koran. He might enslave other Muslims in raids on their villages or take them in bondage for debts. He could also demand revenge for the death of a member of his community, or for injury or insult to his pride or honor.

By the 1980s, when the Moros national liberation movement began to emerge and to take the forms it would have by 2000, the *datu* continued to play a paramount role. In many Muslim regions of Mindanao, they administered Muslim *sharia* law through the *agama*. Rather than raid other villages – a practice which began to return with the advent of Moros insurrection in the 1990s – they concentrated on accumulating wealth through agriculture, trading and smuggling. This wealth was used to extend aid, employment and protection for less fortunate neighbors – in a similar manner to which the rival clans in Afghanistan or the Hizbollah Shi'ite movement in Lebanon operated. Although today most Moro *datus* cannot afford more than one wife, polygamy was allowed, in the fashion followed in traditional Muslim societies elsewhere, as long as the *datu* had sufficient means to provide for more than one wife.

The first Philippine governments following independence from the United States in 1946 – an independence which President Harry Truman and congressional and popular sentiment in the United States felt the islands had earned through overwhelmingly siding with the American war effort against the defeated Japanese – abolished the machinery which the pre-war US administration had used to deal with minorities. This machinery operated to move people from the densely-populated towns and cities of central Luzon to the wide-open spaces of Mindanao. During the 1950s hundreds of thousands of new settlers, in the majority Christians of northern tribes, were settling in Muslim areas. Moro society reacted angrily to their influx. Land disputes were at the center of the rising friction. Christian migrants to the provinces of North Cotabato and South Cotabato on Mindanao island complained that after buying land from one Muslim individual, his relatives would refuse to recognize the deal and demand more money. The Muslim residents insisted that Christians would obtain land titles through government agencies run from Manila, which were unknown to Muslim residents unfamiliar with the system of land tenure.

In the early 1960s many of the future difficulties between Manila and the Muslim insurgents were anticipated by a series of uprisings for political and land gains in central Luzon by the Communist Hukbalahap guerrillas, nicknamed "Huks" by the US counter-insurgency teams called in to help fight them. (In 1947 the United States had obtained – and retained until 1992 – important military base facilities in the Philippines, notably Clark Field, a huge airforce base, near Manila.) With this American help President Ramon Magsaysay subdued the Huk guerrillas in 1954. In 1968 President Ferdinand Marcos (and his notorious wife Imelda, who had more pairs of shoes in her wardrobe than a medium-size Filipino village had people) faced another Huk rebellion in Luzon, again brought on by the urgent need for land reform. The following year Marcos suppressed this with a vigorous military offensive mounted by government forces. The federal troops operating in Luzon had the advantages of much shorter supply lines and better logistics than they had operating in the southern jungles and mountains against the Muslims.

The influx of Christian settlers also spread distrust and resentment through the public educational system. Most Muslim residents saw the public schools as establishments created to spread Christian teachings, in the style of the old missionary schools of the colonial era. By 1970, a Christian terrorist organization called the *Ilagas* ("Rats") began operating in the Cotabata provinces. The Muslim *datus* countered by forming Muslim armed militias. Christians named a new militia the "Blackshirts." In Lanaos province, a Muslim band called the Barracudas began fighting the *Ilagas*. When the Manila government despatched troops to restore order and peace, the Muslims accused them of siding with the Christian settlers. The dictatorial Marcos finally declared martial law in 1972. What Manila has tried to deal with as a sectarian and criminal insurgency by Muslims has raged, with few long periods of relative peace, ever since.

To replace the old American colonial institutions, in 1957 the Philippine government set up a Commission for National Integration, later replaced by the Office of Muslim Affairs and Cultural Communities. The governments and their Filipino nationalist supporters tried to plan for a united country where Christians and Muslims alike would be offered farm subsidies and other economic advantages by the government. Muslims would be assimilated and, as a 1991 US Library of Congress Study says, "would simply be Filipinos who had their own mode of worship and who refused to eat pork."[2]

Many Christians and many more Muslims were dissatisfied with this concept. The Muslims saw it as a thinly disguised version of assimilation. Even so, Muslims were exempted from government laws, heavily influenced by Roman Catholic doctrines, prohibiting divorce and polygamy. In 1977 the government tried to codify Muslim law on personal relationships and to tune Muslim customary law to accord with Philippine public law, a bit like squaring the circle.

At the end of the 1980s came the resignation and subsequent death in Hawaii of Ferdinand Marcos, and the turbulent presidential term of office of Corazon Acquino, widow of Benigno Acquino, the opposition leader murdered by Marcos' gunmen at Manila airport in 1983. The next president was Fidel Ramos. He had been Mrs. Acquino's choice as successor and was elected in 1992 when she refused to stand for re-election. One of Acquino's accomplishments in office had been the 1990 conclusion of an interim peace accord with the Moros. This established a Muslim Autonomous Region in Mindanao, giving Muslims in the region limited jurisdiction in some aspects of government, but not over either the crucial subjects of national security or foreign relations. This was expanded in 1996 to a full-scale accord between the Manila administration and Nur Misuari, leader of the emerging Moro National Liberation Front (MNLF).

Misuari, whom the government tried unsuccessfully to enroll as a mediator with the Abu Sayyaf kidnappers during the crisis of spring 2000, had lived in the West and Arab capitals. He has especially close ties with Libyan leader Colonel

Muammar al-Qaddafi, who played a constructive role in several interim peace deals negotiated between the Moros and Manila governments. In the 1996 accord, the MNLF was given four provinces to run autonomously in exchange for peace. The accord had more or less disintegrated by the time of the hostage crisis in 2000, due to lack of financing and poor performance of the MNLF in running the autonomous region. Konrad Muller, a former Australian diplomat, commented in the *International Herald Tribune* (May 9, 2000) that this poor performance was compounded by "corruption, poor accountability for public funds, lack of transparency, a bloated bureaucracy, simple incompetence. When a vote is held [in 2001] on expanding the autonomous region, just one more province is likely to join; a far larger domain was once expected. Front officials accuse Manila of bad faith."

Into this boiling cauldron of Muslim disaffection, the returning Filipino veterans of the 1979–89 Afghanistan war, many of them well trained by their CIA and Pakistani mentors, began to filter back to the Philippines. During the 1990s, the larger and relatively more moderate MNLF of Nur Misuari splintered and produced a smaller, much more aggressive group calling itself the Moro Islamic Liberation Front (MILF), advocating full secession of the Islamic south from the rest of the Philippines. In 2000 its head was a Muslim named Salimat Hashim. He regards the break of East Timor with its former Indonesian occupiers as a model, and calls for a UN-sponsored plebiscite on the future of Mindanao. Significantly, the armed MILF forces were said to number 15,000 including a cadre of 600 Afghan war veterans. In mid-January 1999, the MILF leadership declared the 1996 peace accord with Manila null and void, and launched what often appears to be a full-scale war of secession in Mindanao, proclaiming that they would name their independent state "Bangsa Moro." On January 26, 1999 President Joseph Estrada, a former actor, elected in June 1998, proclaimed a general offensive against the MILF. Commentaries at the time recalled that the civil strife had, up to the time of the 1996 agreement, killed 100,000 people in the southern islands; a war which reached far greater proportions than the earlier anti-Communist campaigns against the Huks.

The problems for Estrada developed on the constitutional front as well. On August 20, 1999 tens of thousands of Filipinos demonstrated in Manila against constitutional changes planned by Estrada. Among other changes was a concession to foreign investors, allowing them to control up to 40 percent of Filipino enterprises, as well as ownership of real estate in the same proportion. The opposition political parties feared that Estrada would use the civil warfare with the Muslims in the south as a pretext or cover for further constitutional changes, such as extending the presidential term of office beyond six years, leading to a reversal to the totalitarian excesses of the Marcos era.[3]

John Pilger – an Australian journalist and recipient of many awards for his fearless and often caustic critiques of Western, especially American and British, policies around the globe – comments on social and political inequalities in the Philippines in his 1998 book, *Hidden Agendas*: "One Filipino child is said to die every hour, in a country where more than half the national budget is given over to paying just the interest on World Bank and IMF loans." Addressing the Burmese opponent of the Myanmar (Burma) ruling military junta, Aung San Suu Kyi, Pilger says: "Look at [former President] Cory Acquino in the Philippines. She ran a campaign similar to yours, and she ended up [after being successfully elected] having to pay half her country's budget in debt repayments. And her plans for her people were shelved."[4] The Philippines' foreign debt in 1997 was $45.4 billion, according to official statistics. That, of course, was only the principal: debt servicing could scarcely keep pace with the country's meager growth rate between 1991 and 1997 of just 3.3 percent.[5]

Just before the Afghani volunteers began to arrive in the late 1980s, President Acquino had painstakingly negotiated a peace accord with the MNLF, rejected by the MILF. Governments were continuing their sporadic efforts toward compromise autonomy schemes for the Muslims when the first Afghans arrived on the scene, around the beginning of 1989. These were chiefly veterans of Professor Abdul Rasul Sayyaf, leader of the seventh, and officially the youngest, of the seven main groups of Afghan *moujahiddin* who fought the Soviets, and whose antecedents we shall review in Chapter 11. The Filipino Muslim leader of the Abu Sayyaf group transplanted from Afghanistan was Abduragak Abubakr Janjalani, a veteran of the fighting with the Russians. He and a group of "Afghani" colleagues, partly Filipino and partly Arab and other nationalities, proceeded to recruit young Filipino Islamic radicals in southern areas, many of them dropouts from high schools and universities in the southern Philippines. This small group of several hundred guerrillas, at first affiliated with MNLF but splitting from them and hoisting the flag of Abu Sayyaf, began to raid Christian plantations, abduct wealthy landowners and Catholic priests and seize their property. Such activity was also true of the larger MILF throughout the 1990s. In December 1998, Aburagak Janjalani was killed in a shoot-out with police in the village of Lamitan, on Basilan island.

A power struggle now ensued within the Philippines branch of Abu Sayyaf. The victor and new leader was the brother of the defunct founder. Their father was enough of an admirer of Libya's leader since 1969 to name the brother Qaddafi Janjalani. Colonel Qaddafi's Filipino namesake was, at first, a paramount leader of the group. He was ultimately responsible for the kidnapping and terrorist outrages claimed or acknowledged by Abu Sayyaf, especially in the islands of Basilan, Solo (sometimes called Sulu) and Tawi-Tawi in the southernmost part of the archipelago. All Western security sources consulted by this author agree that Abu Sayyaf has links to Osama bin Laden's al-Qaida and to Ramzi Ahmed Yousef, who was convicted of organizing the 1993 bombing of the World Trade Center in New York and has been associated with other acts described in Chapter 11.

Abu Sayyaf has consistently shunned the peace processes between the Manila governments and the MNLF, unequivocally demanding – like the larger MILF – an independent Muslim state in the southern Philippines. The group's specialties were not unlike those it exercised in postwar Afghanistan: bombings, assassinations, kidnappings and extortion from companies and business tycoons – those, that is, not willing to contribute voluntarily. In March 2000 the group branched out into seaborne piracy with the kidnapping, for ransom and political demands, including the freeing of such prisoners in the US as Ramzi Yousef, of a group of tourists vacationing on a Malaysian island, where the diving was first-rate, but security definitely not. The group began its terrorist career with a grenade attack in 1991, killing two foreign women. Next year, Abu Sayyaf militants threw a bomb at a dock in the southern city of Zamboanga. The motor-vessel *Doulous*, an international floating bookshop specializing in Bibles and Christian tracts and manned by Christian preachers, was moored there at the time. Several people were hurt.

Next, the group staged similar bombings against Zamboanga airport (not unlike the tactics taught by the CIA/Pakistani instructors and used against Soviet or Afghan Communist airfields in Afghanistan); and Roman Catholic churches, including, in 1993, a cathedral in Davao City, killing seven people. Targeting foreigners, as in the Malaysian kidnapping of foreign tourists to Solo island in the spring of 2000, was not a new project for the group. In 1993, its gunmen kidnapped Charles Walton, a language researcher at the American-based Summer Institute of Linguistics. Walton, then 61 years old, was freed 23 days later under circumstances never made entirely clear. In 1994, Abu Sayyaf kidnapped three Spanish nuns and a Spanish priest in separate raids. In 1998 their rehearsals for the outrages of 2000 included the abduction of two Hong Kong men, a Malaysian and a Taiwanese grandmother. But the pre-2000 outrage for which Abu Sayyaf is best remembered in the Philippines is a vicious assault on the Christian town of Ipil in Mindanao island. Gunmen destroyed the entire town center and massacred 53 civilians and federal soldiers.[6]

Philippine government suspicions or certainties about the Abu Sayyaf links to Osama bin Laden were reiterated in public on August 28, 1998 by Roberto Lastimoso, the director-general of the Philippine National Police. He told journalists in Manila that Muhammad Jamal al-Khalifa, married to bin Laden's sister, was evidently one of the main financiers of the group. Khalifa, said Lastimoso, channeled funds to the terrorists through "charitable endeavors", such as one in Basilan. These included water-well drilling projects and scholarships for Muslims in Mindanao. Filipino commentators recalled Abu Sayyaf's terrorist depradations in Mindanao, and that a caller claimed Abu Sayyaf responsibility for the 1994 Philippines Airlines bombing, the only successful one in a series of about a dozen attacks planned for the same day on Western airliners over the Pacific in which one passenger, a Japanese man, was killed. Lastimoso said that following the 1994 bombing of a commercial center in Zamboanga, a mainly Christian city, Khalifa and his associates seemed to disappear from the Philippines. A senior military official of the MILF, Al-Haj Murad, told journalists that one of Khalifa's wives was a Filipina Christian who had converted to Islam. Khalifa, said the Foreign Affairs Department in Manila, had indeed breached MILF defenses at Camp Bilal, Mindanao, and began clearing the area, after about 350 guerrillas holding it had fled. Nearby fighting had displaced more than 120,000 civilian villagers, said the

Philippine military. Major-General Diomedio Villanueva, commanding the military forces in the southern Philippines, said he had ordered troops to close all MILF camps in the region, including Camp Bilal. There were apparently none of the Abu Sayyaf. "The MILF has virtually set up a shadow government in the entire Lanao province and we cannot allow this to go on," said the general, claiming the MILF had been extorting money from civilians. About 250 MILF rebels and 213 government troops had been killed in clashes that began in the region in March, the military said.[7]

It was Philippines Defense Secretary Orlando Mercado who took it upon himself to publicize and deride the most extravagant demands of the Basilan kidnappers: the release of Ramzi Ahmed Yousef and Sheikh Omar Abdul Rahman, both serving life sentences in the United States for the February 1993 World Trade Center bombing and other extensive, though unaccomplished, attacks planned for New York City later that same year. The demands were "impossible" and "illogical," Mercado said. The American Embassy in Manila and the State Department in Washington added an official and absolute American refusal. Other Abu Sayyaf demands made in Basilan, also refused, were for the release of a man named Abu Haidal, apparently held in the United States, and who according to Philippine reports was the teacher of an unnamed leader of Abu Sayyaf. Further, the guerrillas demanded the release of two Abu Sayyaf militants held in Philippine jails, and the dismantling of a huge wooden cross erected on a mountain in Basilan in the 1970s.

Around April 25, just after Abu Sayyaf announced they had beheaded two of the male captives (later verified by the government) "as a gift to President Estrada because he had refused their demands," seaborne Abu Sayyaf gunmen – early dispatches called them "pirates" – descended on Sipadan, a small Malaysian island famed for its superb diving waters. From there, they kidnapped to Solo island 21 more hostages, all foreign tourists. The 21 included two Filipinos, three Germans, two French, two Finns, two South Africans and a Lebanese woman. Federal security forces approached the rebel camp and clashed with the Abu Sayyaf band. Nur Misuari, governor of the Muslim autonomous region of Mindanao who had unsuccessfully tried to negotiate several hostage releases, told a television interviewer that he understood one hostage was seriously hurt and another slightly injured by gunshots during the clash.

The gang's leader in Solo, calling himself Abu Escobar, told a local radio station that one hostage was shot dead and another had died of a heart attack. Colonel Ernesto de Guzman of the Philippine army announced that after the clash, the rebels had moved the hostages to another nearby hideout on the same island. An elderly German woman, Renate Wallert, 57, was reported seriously ill. Filipino Red Cross emissaries brought medicine. She was released. Both of the Abu Sayyaf kidnapping groups warned that they would kill more hostages unless government troops withdrew from siege positions near their camps. By mid-May the government said the Abu Sayyaf were demanding a ransom for the 21 tourists.

The government in Manila and foreign diplomats who had gathered there to monitor the situation appeared resigned to face long summer sieges.[8]

In May, a series of terrorist bombings causing casualties, including at shopping malls in Manila's upper-class district and bus stations, began to shake towns and cities in the islands. President Estrada returned a day early from a planned five-day trip to China to meet with security officials over the deteriorating situation, made momentarily worse by a destructive storm which hit Luzon island. Said Estrada: "terrorism, extortion, kidnappings for ransom, hostage-taking and other forms of violence" were ruining the economy. He called the Muslim separatists "those who wish to set up their own government and conduct terrorism [who] would never succeed." Estrada promised firm measures against them.

However, Estrada was arrested and the opposition declared that he should resign or be ousted. There was a summer of clashes between his opponents and his supporters. In July 2000 Estrada was formally charged before the highest court on charges of the capital offense of economic plunder, in addition to less serious charges linked with corruption. In November 2000 the Philippine Senate began impeachment proceedings against Estrada. Massive street demonstrations and pressure from the armed forces and most sectors of public opinion eventually forced him from office. Vice President Gloria Macapagal-Arroyo, daughter of former president Diosdado, and who had a PhD from Georgetown University, became president in January 2001. In April 2001 the Philippine Supreme Court ruled that Estrada had effectively resigned, ignoring his argument that he was merely on a leave of absence. The ruling also confirmed Mrs. Macapagal-Arroyo as president and deprived Estrada of his presidential immunity. This paved the way for his trial on corruption and bribery charges. His formal indictment on the plunder charges took place in July 2001.

As the summer of 2000 advanced, and still under Estrada's administration, Abu Sayyaf received at least $25 million in ransom money, paid by Colonel Qaddafi of Libya, who arranged for repatriation of the 21 former European captives to their homes with a stop in Tripoli and public displays of gratitude to Libya on the way. Geoffrey Schilling, an American from Oakland, California, was kidnapped earlier and released separately, after a long ordeal of jungle marches and tough captivity, but without any apparent payment of ransom.

Flush with their new cash from Libya and the arms, vehicles and supplies they were able to purchase with it, the bandits perpetrated new kidnappings and murderous raids throught the rest of 2000 and well into 2001. On June 11, 2001, they announced that they had beheaded Guillermo Sobrero, an American from Corona, California, kidnapped in May along with American Christian missionaries Martin and Gracia Burnham of Kansas and 17 Filipinos from Palawan island, 350 miles south of Manila. President Arroyo said she could not confirm the claim, but vowed to "decimate" Abu Sayyaf. She confirmed the edict she issued soon after taking office that no more ransom would be paid. Amid a new military campaign against the group, nine of the Filipino hostages escaped or were rescued, while two were found executed by the rebels. Four other hostages were taken from a hospital and church complex in Basilan island, and at least 15 more from the village of Lantawan on the same island.

US spokesmen at first cast doubt on the reported beheading of Sobrero, and FBI agents were sent to the Philippines to "advise" in the investigation of Abu Sayyaf, which kept renewing threats to kill the Burnham couple. The US government and the Vatican, solicitous of the welfare of the big Roman Catholic community in the Philippines, condemned the reported beheading and the continued violence. Sobrero's remains were not found, nor his death confirmed, until late summer of 2001. Meanwhile, in a grisly footnote to Sobrero's beheading, Abu Sayyaf tried to sell video footage to an unnamed US television network, to verify their boast of his beheading, President Arroyo's spokesman, Rigoberto Tiglao announced, and Reuter reported from Manila on June 14, 2001. Despite a new "peace accord" reached between Mrs. Arroyo's government and the Moro Islamic Liberation Front (MILF) at the end of June 2001, the warfare between the government and Abu Sayyaf, and Abu Sayyaf's depredations, were not affected.

After the terrorist attacks in New York and Washington on September 11, 2001, Abu Sayyaf became one of the list of 27 organizations and individuals, mostly affiliated with al-Qaida, whose assets were ordered frozen by President George W. Bush. In Manila, the Arroyo government followed the Bush order by affirming that it was investigating the financial dealings of at least two local charity groups with possible links to "Moro extremist groups." Philippines national security advisor Roilo Golez said his office was looking into the books of two or three private groups, one of which was apparently the International Islamic Relief Organization Inc. (IIRO), with possible links to the Abu Sayyaf. The IIRO had been formed in 1992 to channel funds to Muslim communities in Mindanao. The Philippine Congress passed a bill which would criminalize money laundering and ease stringent bank secrecy laws, to enable the Philippines Central Bank to crack down and freeze Abu Sayyaf-connected accounts, such as those of jailed Abu Sayyaf leader Hector Janjalani, from the group's founding family, the *Philadelphia Inquirer* reported from Manila on September 26, 2001.

In late 2001, as part of President Bush's post-September 11 "war on terrorism," and with the American Burnham missionary couple and a number of other hostages still held, US Defense Secretary Donald Rumsfeld announced the US military "advisors" had traveled to the Philippines. Some 30 US military personnel with counter-terrorism skills were on Basilan island to advise the Philippine army in the fight against Abu Sayyaf. American officials, reported the *New York Times* on October 30, 2001, "were likely to offer more than advice in coming days" and would probably provide weapons and training. A reporter for Agence-France Presse on October 28 reported he had seen Americans on Basilan island giving weapons training at a secluded Filipino Army Scout Rangers firing range. President Arroyo's spokespersons kept insisting, in statements reminiscent of those made by local and

American officials in the early days of American involvement in Vietnam in the 1960s, that the Americans would not get involved in combat.

The "advisors" had brought a pack of bloodhounds with them, so tracking Abu Sayyaf was evidently on the agenda. US officials confirmed that the al-Qaida network had made a serious effort to expand activities in East Asia, including Indonesia and Malaysia (where Abu Sayyaf had branched out and also become active), as well as the Philippines. President Arroyo told a World Economic Forum conference in Hong Kong on October 29 that the US military men were part of "a joint plan on how to deal with terrorism in the Philippines and the whole world."

The economic prospects in Mindanao were naturally affected most by the troubles. The large island accounts for 30 percent of the Philippines' total land area and 24 percent of its population, while its overall contribution to Philippines' GDP was estimated at a disproportionately lower 18 percent. Almost 60 percent of the country's rice and corn output came from the three provinces in Mindanao most involved in the conflict, which flamed into peak activity just at the start of the planting season. After at least 200,000 civilians had fled their homes to escape the violence, few remained home to plant, cultivate or harvest the crops. Philippines Senator Gregorio Honasan, a former military man who had served in past campaigns against the Muslim insurgents, said fighting had destroyed key infrastructure including roads and irrigation facilities essential to farming, and had also disrupted development projects. As for tourism, even worse damage – not unlike that which the Afghani-led Luxor massacre had caused in Egypt – was expected. Philippines tourism officials acknowledged ruefully that earlier targets of a 10 to 15 percent growth in arrivals in 2000 had become unattainable, after numerous countries in Europe and elsewhere had warned their nationals against travel to the Philippines.[9]

Once again, as in the United States, Canada, France, former Yugoslavia, Egypt, Algeria, the Russian Federation, the Sudan, Pakistan, Indian-ruled Kashmir, and Central Asian states, the Philippines found its own endemic social, economic and sectarian problems at the dawn of the twenty-first century aggravated by terrorism of two sorts. They had become inextricably mixed: grievance-based domestic violence, aggravated by imported zealotry and extremism, much of which had its origin in the holy warriors who had trained, fought, and then, in the new generation, trained again in Afghanistan. All this had been done originally in the name of fighting Russia and Communism. Now it was spreading around the world.

11 The Contagion Spreads: The Assault on America

The catastrophic attacks on New York's World Trade Center and the Pentagon in Washington, DC by suicidal airplane hijackers on September 11, 2001, were the horrendous climax of a series of assaults on America in the 1990s. These were planned, engineered and in some cases carried out by CIA-trained veterans of the 1979–89 Afghanistan war, or those schooled or influenced by them.

Few Americans seemed to comprehend what was happening around them in the decade of the Nineties, nor did most inquire about causes. Those directly involved noted the effects, but with the lack of causal understanding or historical thinking which often characterizes even senior members of the US governing and intelligence communities. Background relationships were not perceived or appreciated. Some thoughtful investigators, such as New York City's FBI director, Robert Fox, correctly identified the suspects after the February 1993 bombing of the World Trade Center – the unsuccessful, though lethal and damaging prelude to destruction of the twin towers in lower Manhattan's holocaust of September 2001. In 1993, Fox told newsmen in New York that "those guys" were trained by the CIA. This unpopular but true statement helped to get Fox transferred far away from his New York post a few weeks later.

Four months later, in June 1993, a new series of terrorist spectaculars, also in New York, and comparable with or even greater in scale than September 11, 2001 in the casualties they would have caused and the material mayhem they would have wreaked, was thwarted. What prevented them were the actions of an Egyptian "mole" or penetration agent working for the FBI, who had infiltrated the gang, a kind of prototype al-Qaida group operating in New York and New Jersey, and some very effective (and lucky) police work, which caught the conspirators red-handed. What made the identification and capture of the terrorists who had prepared and then provided logistical back-up for the September 11, 2001 attacks in New York and Washington more difficult was that none of the thousands of law-enforcement agents of all services, from local police to the FBI, had penetrated the terrorist network ahead of time.

Preparation for the attacks against the United States in 1993 and later, including their roots and their planning in South Asia, have to be viewed as part of a kind of giant prologue to the September 11, 2001 assault on America, which in turn triggered America's new war in South Asia during the fall and winter of 2001–02.

Similar, in some ways, to my own premonition in Washington in January 1980 of misfortunes and disasters which would result from the Christmas 1979 Soviet invasion of Afghanistan, was a brief but chilling glimpse of the future in New York in the spring of 1995.

I was speeding in a microbus taxi van from Manhattan across to Kennedy Airport on Long Island. Suddenly, Mahmoud, the bearded Pakistani driver, raised his voice. "By God, my friend," he said, "write in your newspapers, say on your television: we Muslims have suffered! I tell you, when Allah took our General Zia al-Haq from us, that was the start of the evil. My father grieved until he died." He was talking about the still publicly unsolved plane crash which killed Zia and senior US and Pakistani officials in August 1988 in Pakistan. After describing how he had emigrated to America and had managed to get a taxi license, so that his Pakistani girlfriend in New York wouldn't have to work before they married – women, he made it clear in Taliban-like terms, should not work – he added portentously: "The jihad died in Pakistan. Zia led us in a great jihad in Afghanistan. But the jihad will spread anyhow."

As we pulled up at the Kennedy Airport terminal, I asked him, "What about here? Is there jihad in America?" Mahmoud seemed to brake his van rather more suddenly than needed at the terminal building. "Yes," he snapped, "there is jihad in America. We are many Muslims. Here in New York, in New Jersey, everywhere. Jihad is our duty." As I collected my bags and paid him, Mahmoud handed me a folded pamphlet which I read in the check-in queue. "ISLAM ON TRIAL" it proclaimed, above a portrait of Sheikh Omar Abdel Rahman, sunglasses covering his blind eyes, his whiskers rampant. The sheikh would soon be tried for his role in allegedly instigating the February 1993 bombing of the World Trade Center; later convicted and jailed for life in a maximum-security Federal prison hospital facility in Missouri. The pamphlet Mahmoud gave me at Kennedy Airport quoted defense lawyers calling for his acquittal. He was guilty, contended attorney Ronald Kuby, of no more than "his interpretation of scripture – a profound dilemma for religion in an ostensibly free society."

Truly, I reflected during my flight back to the Middle East, "jihad in America" had already begun. For some members of the intelligence community, who chose not to discuss these matters publicly, it had begun in January 1993, a month before the World Trade Center bombing, with the case of Mir Aimal Kainsi. A veteran of the Afghanistan training and probably of combat, Kainsi ambushed, shot and killed two CIA employees and wounded several other people outside the main gate of CIA headquarters in Langley, Virginia. The FBI and other US services tracked him down, and with the help of the ISI – one of the occasions where Pakistani intelligence wholeheartedly cooperated with American law-enforcement – he was seized in Pakistan. He was flown to the US for trial on June 17, 1995, a few weeks after my encounter with Mahmoud.[1] This touched off reprisal killings of several Americans in Karachi a short time after his capture. He was sentenced to death in Virginia, the scene of his crime. Legal appeals delayed his execution, and he dropped out of the sight and certainly out of the mind, of the American public.

The spirit of jihad against America lived on. It flamed up spectacularly once again in the summer of 1998, in East Africa. On the morning of August 7, 1998, truck bombs devastated the area around the American embassies in Nairobi, Kenya and Dar es Salaam, Tanzania. The Nairobi bomb killed 247 people, including 12 Americans in a portion of the embassy which collapsed and wounded thousands. In the nearly simultaneous bombing in Dar es Salaam ten people died, and upwards of a hundred were wounded in the far less congested streets of the Tanzanian capital. The injured people lay, traumatized by shock, in pools of blood. Soon Nairobi's hospitals were crammed beyond capacity with emergency cases: men, women, children with severed limbs, blinded, mutilated. A total of over 5,000 people were injured in both cities.

The attacks, perceived almost immediately to bear the signature of Osama bin Laden and his al-Qaida organization formed years before in Afghanistan, should have been far less of a surprise to the US intelligence establishment than the twin towers and Pentagon disasters of September 11, 2001 (though, there had been vague advance warnings of those also).

A few insiders and some journalists had noted a warning broadcast only about 24 hours before the East African attacks. The warning was not signed by Osama bin Laden, al-Qaida, or even by the "International Islamic Front' of eight different Islamist organizations which had announced its creation for purposes of an anti-American jihad in May. Egypt's *Al-Gihad,* the terrorist organization responsible for President Sadat's murder in October 1981 and for much violence inside Egypt since, warned it was about to take reprisals against the United States – because, it said, the CIA had assisted the Albanians to arrest and extradite to Egypt several Egyptian Islamist militants, some of whom had been condemned to death in absentia. One week earlier, an exiled chief of *Al-Gihad*'s partner and sometime rival in terrorism, Egypt's *Gama' a al-Islamiya* or Islamic Group, which was behind the Luxor massacre of foreign tourists in November 1997, suddenly denied on his Internet web site that his organization was part of the "International Islamic Front," though his signature had been one of the eight announcing the Front's creation in February 1998. It sounded to expert Egyptian analysts of terrorism as though the Islamic Group leaders, or at least this one, knew of the horrific attacks being planned in East Africa and wanted to distance themselves from them.[2]

Washington, where President Clinton was under heavy fire because of his sexual scandal and the perjury accusations against him by independent prosecutor Kenneth Starr over his affair with former White House intern Monica Lewinsky, was galvanized by the attacks. Over 200 FBI agents and other intelligence teams and military units, including medical rescue teams, and even Israeli troops from Israel, were airborne for East Africa within hours.

The combined rescue and investigative efforts were, in retrospect, a kind of mini-rehearsal for the huge mobilization of humanitarian and law-enforcement resources in New York and Washington following the September 11, 2001 suicide attacks.

Soon, reports were coming in of threats to other US embassies, including those in Kampala, Uganda and Tirana, Albania. Later, these and a number of other US diplomatic missions throughout the world were temporarily evacuated, so seriously was the threat taken in Washington.

Within a few days, two suspects, a naturalized Kenyan of Palestinian birth named Muhammad Saddek Odeh and Muhammad Rashid al-'Owhali, a Yemeni, had been apprehended. Odeh was arrested in Pakistan after flying out of Nairobi and returned quickly to Nairobi after confessions to the Pakistanis. Owhali was seized in Kenya. Both were packed off in handcuffs in military aircraft to New York. There they were charged with murder, complicity in murder, use of munitions of massive power, and conspiracy.

Another accomplice from the Comores Islands, a former French colony in the Indian Ocean, named Abdallah Muhammad Fadhul, like the others (who admitted belonging to bin Laden's organization and some degree of guilt in the attacks) was a presumed member of al-Qaida.[3]

Within a very short time, it was clear to those who follow these events, that a total and deadly conflict was breaking out between the United States and its former ally and proxy (through Saudi Arabia) protégé, Osama bin Laden. From this time on, the progression to the climactic assaults of September 2001 became even clearer than it had been after the conspiracies and attacks of 1993, which now look like preludes to the main drama.

Just as they did in September 2001, the Washington policy-makers in August 1998 decided on swift retribution. President Clinton and his advisors resolved to strike back at two places regarded as bases or strongholds of Osama bin Laden, whom the suspect Muhammed Odeh had implicated as the originator of the embassy attacks. President Clinton summoned his National Security Advisor, Sandy Berger. He called back from Italy Secretary of State Madeleine Albright, who had been attending a gala wedding of the CNN network's Christiane Amanpour and former State Department spokesman James Rubin. Defense Secretary William Cohen, Joint Chiefs of Staff chairman General Hugh Shelton, and the latest of a long series of rapidly changing CIA directors, George Tenet, were called to join the crisis meetings.

Within hours, Clinton decided to hit Afghanistan, where bin Laden had his main operational bases, and the Sudan, believed to harbor a factory for chemical weapons components associated with bin Laden. It was decided not to risk any American personnel or aircraft – unlike the 2001–02 war against bin Laden and his Taliban hosts – but to use the weapon already used to hit Iraq's Saddam Hussein during the Gulf War and to punish him on several occasions after it: the remotely-guided Tomahawk cruise missile, which had done little damage to Saddam's cohorts, but had killed and wounded Iraqi civilians. About 20 Tomahawks would be fired, in this case, by US Navy ships in the Red Sea or the Indian Ocean, at several of bin Laden's camps, mostly near the village of Khost, not far from the Pakistan border. The camps had been planned and designed by the CIA and Pakistan's ISI, and constructed in the early 1980s with the human and engineering resources of Osama bin Laden and his associates. The second target was the Al Chifa pharmaceutical plant in Khartoum, Sudan. After all, reasoned Clinton and his aides, the Sudan, under Islamist Sheikh Hassan al-Turabi's influence, had cooperated closely with bin Laden during his stay there in the early 1990s. Western and Egyptian intellligence suspected him of complicity in many terrorist acts and conspiracies, including the attempted murder of President Mubarak in Addis Ababa, Ethiopia and the New York bombing conspiracies of 1993. The Al Chifa plant, reported the *New York Times* of August 25, was presumed to be cooperating with the Iraqi chemical weapons program and producing an important ingredient of VX nerve gas, ethyl methylphosphothionate.

In the cruise missile attack, codenamed "Infinite Reach," launched August 20, Taliban accounts said about 20 guerrilla fighters were killed in the camps, not including bin Laden himself, who was absent. Some Washington sources said that through its electronic monitoring of bin Laden's radiotelephone traffic and overhead satellite surveillance, the United States was aware of his absence. If it deliberately chose not to try to kill him, this was because a dead bin Laden would greatly enhance his already legendary charisma among violent Islamists everywhere. He would become a historic martyr whose death would stir his supporters to more frenzied acts of vengeance against the United States. This, of course, became a consideration which President George W. Bush's planners had to keep in mind, as they tried to hunt down bin Laden and his cronies during the winter war of 2001–02 in Afghanistan, and earlier than that, when, as reported in the *New York Times*, they financed a special Pakistani commando unit intended to track down bin Laden but which Pakistan's ISI never really intended to use, as ISI cultivated its comfortable relations with the Taliban.[4]

As for the Khartoum plant, which National Security Advisor Sandy Berger assured CNN audiences on August 23 was "indisputably" used to manufacture VX, a British engineer who had acted as Al Chifa's technical manager categorically rejected in a BBC interview any idea that the plant produced anything other than prescription medicines, vitamins and other pharmaceuticals badly needed in Sudan's impoverished society. A few days later, the Clinton administration through news leaks began to back off the story. They acknowledged that a dreadful error might have been made in the attack on Khartoum, although the US stoutly resisted Sudan's demand for an on-the-spot investigation by impartial United Nations investigators.[5] In July 2000, the plant's Saudi Arabian owner began a series of legal actions against the US to recover $50 million in damages.

The manhunt for the bin Laden bombers produced the arrest in Munich, Germany in late September of another suspect, Mahmoud Salim, 40, later extradited to the United States. An Egyptian-born US Army sergeant Muhammad Salem, who worked for bin Laden, also admitted guilty knowledge. Eventually, in September 2001, the four main conspirators were sentenced to life imprisonment, after long deliberations by a jury which had been unable to agree on inflicting the death penalty.

The earlier investigations of Mahmoud Salim, said by prosecution documents and court testimony to be a close associate of bin Laden, revealed an even more sinister aspect, a nuclear one. US investigators were still pursuing this aspect after new, publicized warnings in the fall of 2001, after the September 11 hijack attacks. They warned that bin Laden had sought, and perhaps found, nuclear material which might be used in some way as a weapon, even if only as radioactive waste in a "garbage bomb," or high-explosive device designed to scatter radioactive contamination.

By the time of his arrest at a car dealership outside Munich on a tip from Interpol, Salim was identified as a financial advisor and weapons procurer for bin Laden. As early as 1990, Salim, along with other al-Qaida members in Sudan, Afghanistan, Malaysia, the Philippines and elsewhere, began "financial transactions for the benefit of Al-Qaida and its affiliated groups." In 1992, the New York court documents said, the group had tried to obtain components for nuclear weapons, including enriched uranium, to attack US forces in Saudi Arabia, Yemen and Somalia. No concrete details about the supposed nuclear quest were released.[6]

A remarkably prescient preview of bin Laden's later escalating terrorist assault on America was provided for anyone who carefully read and digested Congressional testimony on September 3, 1998, by FBI director Louis J. Freeh. Neither Freeh nor anyone else foresaw that hijacked airliners, after years of careful planning which had probably already begun by 1998, would be turned into deadly missiles to destroy nerve centers of southern Manhattan in September 2001. However, the 1993 World Trade Center bombings, the aborted June 1993 plots to destroy Manhattan's main tunnels, bridges and other targets, followed by the US embassy bombings in East Africa in August 1998, had sufficiently awakened the FBI to begin comprehensive efforts to track the terrorists. Freeh's FBI agents had spread around the world and had (said its spokesmen and those of the CIA) buried its old rivalries with the CIA. As lead US anti-terrorist agency since 1995, the FBI was now actively working with the Agency's Counterterrorism Center and with a number of other intelligence and security agencies, military and civilian, in a new permanent consultative committee under security wraps in Washington.

In his testimony, Freeh cited the trend in anti-American terrorist attacks "toward large-scale incidents designed for maximum destruction, terror and impact." He recalled how the threat of what my Pakistani taxi driver in New York had called "jihad in America" had been brought home by the New York events of 1993. Next on Freeh's list came the attack with Sarin gas in the Tokyo subway system two years later, killing 12 commuters and, like the 1993 World Trade Center bombing, injuring well over a thousand people. Although there were no American victims in the Luxor attack in Egypt on foreign tourists in November 1997, Freeh confirmed that there were signs that the Luxor assault (like the kidnappings and murders perpetrated by the bin Laden-influenced Abu Sayyaf group in the Philippines) was meant to force the release of Sheikh Omar Abdel Rahman from his prison in Missouri. Freeh recalled that Sheikh Omar and his associates were convicted in 1995 for plotting (aside from the World Trade Center bombing) to murder President Mubarak while Mubarak visited New York in 1994. The same group was caught red-handed in a Queens, Long Island garage mixing fertilizer and fuel oil (one of the old, reliable CIA recipes in the Afghanistan training manuals, a recipe also used by Timothy McVeigh to blow up the federal building in Oklahoma City in 1997) for a lethal, do-it-yourself, home-grown bomb of great power. Their purpose, Freeh recalled, was to destroy if they could United Nations buildings, the Lincoln and Holland Tunnels and police and FBI headquarters, among other targets in New York. (Freeh might have added, but didn't, that they also discussed assassinating some leading pro-Israel congressmen.)

Freeh didn't mention the CIA–Afghanistan connection, a subject generally taboo since New York's regional FBI director, Robert Fox, mentioned the CIA training of several of the World Trade Center bombers on a 1993 television broadcast – and was transferred, "by coincidence," several weeks later. After rapidly reviewing how "Iran, Iraq, Sudan, Libya, Cuba and North Korea" were held to be guilty of state-sponsored terrorism, Freeh dealt with a second category: "autonomous, generally trans-national" organizations. These have their own personnel, financing and training facilities and are able to plan and mount operations around the world, including, Freeh said, in the United States. Hizbollah, he said, had been behind the 1983 truck bombings of the US Embassy and the US Marine barracks in Lebanon, as well as the bombing of the second US Embassy in East Beirut in 1984, and detention of US hostages in Lebanon.

Freeh's third category of terrorists were "locally affiliated," though global in scope, including those following Osama bin Laden. Prophetically, Freeh said such terrorists may pose the most urgent threat because "groups are often organized on an ad hoc, temporary basis, making them difficult for law enforcement to infiltrate or track. They can also exploit the mobility that technology and the lack of a rigorous base structure offers." This in effect analyzed, in advance, the transatlantic mobility shown by Muhammad Atta, the suicide pilot of the first hijacked airliner to hit the World Trade Center on September 11, 2001, and his colleagues, who had carefully pursued their studies and their networking in Europe, before moving to the United States to brush up on flying and navigating airlines in local US flying schools, and to prepare the complex logistics of their well-coordinated operation.

For years, Freeh recalled, the FBI had investigated leading "extra-territorial" cases. These included the June 25, 1996 bombing of the Khobar Towers American servicemen's housing complex in Saudi Arabia and finally the East African bombings of August 1998. The Khobar Towers truck bombing followed a smaller bomb attack several months earlier against joint US–Saudi military installations in Riyadh, killing three US civilians and two soldiers. The Khobar blast killed 19 American servicemen and wounded about 400 people. It forced the US to move the US Air Force personnel living there, and serving overflights of Iraq and other air operations from nearby Dhahran Air Base, to distant al-Kharj. This is a Saudi air base deep in the Nejd desert, far from inhabited towns. Freeh failed to mention in this speech the single factor which almost certainly led to his resignation in 2000: the total lack of cooperation received from the Saudi authorities, who refused to allow the FBI or CIA to interview suspects, and who had several of them beheaded before there was much opportunity for any thorough investigation. US justice and law-enforcement officials at various senior levels continuously expressed their frustration with the Saudi authorities. Some analysts concluded that the Saudis wished to cover the strongly suspected (though probably unproven) involvement of Iran's intelligence services with "Saudi" Hizbollah, members of the aggrieved Saudi Shi'ite Muslim minority in the kingdom's Eastern Province. Later, the United States, without consulting Saudi Arabia, indicted in absentia its own suspects in the Khobar affair.

Freeh referred to terrorist "renditions," by which he meant terrorists captured abroad and sent to the United States for trial (enemies of the US preferred to call them "kidnappings"), under a US presidential directive of the early Nineties setting out conditions for "rendition." He cited the case of Ramzi Ahmed Yousef, convicted mastermind of the World Trade Center bombing, whose real identity has always been in question and whom some US experts suspect of working for Iraqi intelligence, in liaison with bin Laden. Yousef was seized in a bin Laden-owned hostel, or safe house, in Pakistan by US and Pakistani ISI agents and extradited to New York on February 7, 1995, for later trial and conviction to life in prison. And, of course there had been the case of Mir Aimal Kainsi, the murderer of two CIA employees at the main gate of CIA headquarters in Langley, Virginia, in January 1993; also tracked by US and Pakistani agents and shipped to the US for trial.

The Clinton administration, finally recognizing the threat of the "Afghanis" for what it is, appointed another anti-terrorism "czar" in Washington. In early September of 1998, Secretary of State Madeleine Albright swore in a former ambassador to Britain and one-time Chairman of the Joint Chiefs of Staff, as chairman of two Accountability Review Boards, loaded with senior specialists in anti-terrorism, to investigate the East African embassy bombings. Admiral Crowe, as this author knew him at our first meeting, when Crowe commanded the US naval force in the Arab Gulf at Bahrain in 1968, is a rare combination of soldier, diplomat and intellectual. He is a man who has certainly gone beyond combating the post-Afghanistan terrorism phenomenon to take a long, hard look at its roots, especially the past judgement errors by US policy-makers which helped to bring it on.

Shortly after the August 20, 1998 cruise missile attacks on his camps and on Khartoum, Osama bin Laden threatened new retaliation against the United States. An Albanian gunman was shot at on August 23 by a security guard when trying to force his way into the US Embassy in Tirana. That embassy, and others elsewhere, had just been evacuated for security reasons. Bin Laden's hand, rightly or wrongly, was seen in this incident. It seems fairly certain, according to NATO intelligence sources, that bin Laden had visited Tirana at least once in disguise in 1994, as part of a "charitable" Saudi delegation, and had sought to recruit Muslim volunteers for al-Qaida in the Balkans, especially in Albania, Kosovo and Bosnia. In Bosnia, several hundred Afghan war veterans had fought as "volunteers" with the Bosnian Muslim regular army against the Serbs and Croats during the Balkan wars signaling

Yugoslavia's breakup in the early Nineties. The presumed presence of bin Laden operatives in Albania had caused more than one security alert for the American embassy and military mission in Tirana, and had caused postponement of several visits by senior Clinton administration officials to the Albanian capital.

Following the US cruise missile strike of August 1998, the Taliban authorities, faced with a massive military mobilization on Afghan borders by Iran, some of whose nationals, including diplomats, the Taliban kidnapped or killed during their summer 1998 conquest of northern Afghanistan, said they intended to restrain bin Laden. The senior Taliban leader, Mullah Muhammad Omar (who was to prove highly elusive when the US military and their Afghan allies of the Northern Alliance tried to pursue and trap him during the winter war of 2001–02), said in several interviews with local journalists that while bin Laden was still the militia's welcome guest, he had sent an envoy to that guest to remind him that it was Afghan territory which the Americans had attacked. The Taliban themselves reserved the right to respond. There could not be, Mullah Omar added, two parallel authorities in Afghanistan, and bin Laden was not there "to conduct political or military activities." Meanwhile, the government of Pakistan, through whose airspace the attacking missiles had struck, fired its civilian intelligence chief Manzoor Ahmed (not directly connected with the powerful military ISI). Prime Minister Nawaz Sharif's government had lost face by having to retract a false report that at least one of the American missiles had landed in Pakistan. The chief secretary of Pakistan's Northwest Frontier Province, Rustam Shah Momand, was removed over the same issue.[7]

The tangled and tortuous relationships between Pakistan, the Taliban and bin Laden's al-Qaida guerrillas, culminating in the American reprisal war in Afghanistan in 2001–02 following the airborne assaults on New York and Washington in September 2001, could be traced to an arbitrary starting point. In a sense, it had been identified by my Pakistani taxi driver in New York, when he bemoaned the mysterious death of General Zia al-Haq in August 1988. That occurrence upset Zia's many Islamist devotees. It began a slow-motion progression toward more internal troubles in Pakistan. The end of that trail was the multiple assault on America, beginning in early 1993 and continuing past the turn of the century. Along the way, Pakistan's ubiquitous and powerful ISI managed to use the American aid it had received for the Afghanistan jihad, aid which continued even after the jihad had ended and the Soviets had left, against Pakistan's main regional adversary, India.

To understand the phenomenon of bin Laden and his international network, one has to examine his relationships with the Pakistan of Zia al-Haq and with that of Zia's successors. These relationships were also linked to the place of the bin Laden family dynasty in Saudi Arabia, especially with Prince Turki bin Faisal. He was chief of Saudi intelligence during most of the Afghan war and the post-jihad period. It was almost certainly this close association with Osama bin Laden, his companies and his family, that led to Turki's firing and replacement by Crown Prince Abdallah, in the name of King Fahd, in September 2001, probably under heavy but hidden United States pressure. (At almost the same time, General Pervez Musharaf, Pakistan's military president, found it necessary to fire and replace General Mahmoud Ahmed, the ISI's chief and several other senior officers, all associated with the continued coddling of the Taliban, which the ISI had originally created in the early Nineties. General Musharaf had to make a 180-degree turn; stop supporting the Taliban and be seen, at least by the Americans, to be combating them instead, just as the Saudis did.)

Osama bin Laden was 23 years old as he finished his economics studies and courses in marketing at Jeddah University. (Later, he also received a degree in engineering at Riyadh University). Bin Laden began his friendship with Prince Turki when they discovered that they shared the same ideas about what they considered to be the decline and decadence of Islam and Islamic political dynamism. Osama also appreciated Prince Turki's honesty and antipathy to corruption, qualities not always found in the Arab world's royalty or secular rulers. Turki seems to have regarded Osama as a young man who burned with a pure, hard flame of devotion to religious principles. When the Soviets invaded Afghanistan in December 1979, Prince Turki sent bin Laden to Peshawar to scout out the possibilities of raising an Arab volunteer army.

In Pakistan, bin Laden quickly became acquainted with a tall, green-eyed and charismatic Palestinian, Abdallah Azzam, who had made a name for himself with fiery mosque sermons in Zarqa, Jordan, to Palestinians fleeing the Jordan army's crackdown on the PLO during and following Black September of 1970. Azzam later became one of the inspirers of the HAMAS movement. He rejected Yassir Arafat's mainstream PLO organization and the smaller Palestinian groups as too secular, in some cases too Marxist and not Islamic enough. He also felt that these movements were too dependent on the Soviet Great Satan, the usurper of Muslim Afghanistan. Azzam, in liaison with the generals running Pakistan's ISI, who were in turn under the direct command of President Zia al-Haq, outlined to bin Laden the need for weapons, transport and incomes for the families of the fighters. Bin Laden promised to be generous with financing.

Back in Riyadh, other members of the bin Laden construction firm and Prince Turki offered their blessings. They enabled Osama to begin fund-raising and organizational journeys throughout the Arab world. The bin Laden family further cemented their ties, begun in 1983, with the Saudi royal family and with Zia al-Haq. The group won the "contract of the century" in Saudi Arabia, worth $3 billion: the full restoration and where necessary, reconstruction of the holy places of Mecca and Medina. Delighted by his impeccable credentials, the CIA gave Osama free rein in Afghanistan, as did Pakistan's intelligence generals. They looked with a benign eye on a buildup of Sunni Muslim sectarian power in South Asia to counter the influence of Iranian Shi'ism of the Khomeiny variety. Bin Laden, according to the persistent legend which may well be true, proved himself a brave foot soldier by joining in the guerrilla fighting, in which he was wounded, against the Soviets near Jalalabad.

Always under the approving eye of Pakistan's ISI officers, he cultivated and guarded his good relations with the two main Afghan ethnic warlords, Gulbuddin Hekmatyar, a Pushtun and Ahmed Shah Massoud, a Tajik. Massoud later turned against both the Pushtun Taliban and bin Laden. He became the redoubtable commander of the Northern Alliance. He was finally murdered by Arab agents of the Taliban posing as television journalists in September 2001, striking the first of many heavy blows at the US attempt to use the Northern Alliance in its anti-Taliban campaign.

Even more crucial for his later alliance with the Taliban and his global enterprise in private terrorism, bin Laden used as a regional power base in Pakistan the Binoori mosque in Karachi's Newton district. The prayer leader there was a certain Mullah Muhammad Omar, then an unknown young cleric who had lost an eye in the war, and who by the late Nineties had risen to be the paramount leader of the Taliban, the most powerful man in Afghanistan. Later, bin Laden married Mullah Omar's daughter, cementing family ties, which are all-important in the Muslim world.

Operating from Karachi at first and later from his strongholds in Afghanistan, bin Laden's financial and construction empire set about building the base and training camps and landing strips in Afghanistan – under attack in the winter of 2001–02 by the United States, which had originally encouraged their building – for private jets of warlords of the anti-Soviet jihad, and for visiting Muslim and Arab dignitaries. Deeply buried bunkers and tunnels for command posts and telecommunications centers, the nightmare of the Pentagon planners trying to target them with huge penetration bombs in 2001, were carved out of the Afghan mountains. They were meant to make telecommunications of the moujahidin fighters proof against the radio traffic analysts and codebreakers of the Red Army, as well as to secure the munitions, weapons and fuel stores against attack by Soviet land and air forces.

Long before the war ended, bin Laden and his acolytes were preparing for the larger jihads to come against the impious Arab governments which, he felt, were beholden to the corrupt and satanic United States, with which, as an objective ally, he had been working to expel the Soviets. At the same time, Pakistan's growingly powerful ISI was already diverting some of the resources intended by the United States for the anti-Soviet war to the secular conflict with India over Kashmir, and the sectarian enmity of the ISI-supported militant Islamist groups against India's majority Hindu religion.

The bin Laden organizations prepared for the unholy wars to come by diversifying their financial investments. They bought into trucking, shipping and airline companies, especially among the oil states of the Arabian Peninsula and Gulf. The unexplained car bomb murder in 1989 of Abdallah Azzam, who had earlier recruited Muslim volunteers for the CIA's jihad in the United States, deeply shocked bin Laden. He moved close to his Algerian son-in-law, Bounoua Boudjema, who, as we saw earlier in this book, was a key leader of the Algerian armed Islamist rebels. French intelligence believes bin Laden helped to finance the Islamist bombings of the Paris metro and other targets in 1995. Bin Laden also hired mainly Algerian Afghan veterans as personal bodyguards.

Algerian-born Ahmed Ressam, another adherent of al-Qaida, was intended to be a key figure in bringing bin Laden's brand of jihad to the United States during the Christmas–New Year holidays of December 1999 and January 2000. In this period, Jordan intelligence, working with the US services, succeeded in thwarting major terrorist attacks planned against the Radisson Hotel in Amman and several tourist and pilgrimage sites in Jordan, frequented by American and Israeli visitors. Ressam, convicted in the summer of 2001 of planning to blow up Los Angeles International Airport, a project he confessed to, was seized by US Customs officers while trying to smuggle explosives in his car aboard a ferryboat from Vancouver, Canada, in December 1999. Anti-terrorist French judge Jean-Louis Brugiere, who had worked on most of the high-profile terrorism cases in France, traveled in January 2000 to the United States to join the investigation. Agence-France Presse reported on January 27, 2000 that French investigators linked Ressam to Fateh Kamel. A suspect held in France, Kamel had lived in Montreal and was "close" to Ressam, also based there. Kamel, with both Algerian and Canadian nationality, had been arrested by Jordan's vigilant intelligence operatives and extradited to France in April 1999. Kamel was a logistics specialist who had fought against the Russians in Afghanistan. A third Algerian, believed like Ressam and Kamel to have belonged to Algeria's radical Islamist *Groupe Islamique Armee* (GIA), affiliated with al-Qaida, shared an apartment with Ressam in Montreal. He was wanted in several countries for complicity in terrorism. Several other Algerians in the United States and Canada were suspected or proved to belong to the network supporting Ressam's intended mission.

Once the Soviets had departed Afghanistan in 1989, bin Laden also left the Afghan scene, without being drawn into the fratricidal struggles which began among the different Afghan political and ethnic clans. Back in Riyadh, Prince Turki apparently insisted that bin Laden maintain his training of mercenary volunteers centered on Peshawar. This would have been in line with the continuous and expanding training of Islamist militants by Pakistan's ISI for the struggle with India in Kashmir. However, while bin Laden seems to have wholeheartedly cooperated with the ISI in its Kashmir efforts, and may have also helped to finance them, bin Laden's purposes probably already differed from Turki's Saudi agenda.

In an interview with the Saudi-owned satellite TV channel MBC in November 2001, Prince Turki, after leaving his post as intelligence chief, described for the first time what he said was a failed attempt to get Mullah Omar, the Taliban's leader, to extradite bin Laden in 1998.

Turki became the first senior Saudi to say he was certain that bin Laden and al-Qaida were behind the attacks on the United States on September 11, 2001. He claimed that he had discussed bin Laden's handover to Saudi Arabia at a meeting in Kandahar, Afghanistan, in June 1998, two months before the embassy bombings in East Africa. Turki said he briefed Mullah Omar "on what bin Laden had done against the kingdom's interests and asked him to stop him and hand him over to us." At the time, bin Laden was already on a "wanted" list in his native Saudi Arabia for agitation against the royal family and the presence of US troops, whom he accused of "defiling" Islam's two holiest cities, Mecca and Medina. Omar agreed but then sidetracked the issue by advocating creation of a committee to study it. The embassy bombings in Nairobi and Dar es Salaam and the US counter-attack against Afghanistan and Khartoum followed this inconclusive meeting. When he returned to Afghanistan later in 1998, Mullah Omar, said Turki, had changed his mind. He flatly rejected the request to extradite bin Laden. Turki said he then told Omar, "You will regret it and the Afghan people will pay a high price for that."

Turki added that Mullah Omar and his former friend, bin Laden share the same ideology and that "the evil in them is the same."[7]

Bin Laden began to reorient the training of his troops in the al-Qaida organization. He moved away from more or less conventional anti-aircraft and anti-tank tactics used against the Soviets to urban guerrilla warfare, sabotage and terrorism – also skills imparted by the CIA, as we have seen, to the Pakistani and Afghan trainers of the moujahidin – aimed at destabilizing the societies and governments which were soon to become his targets, mainly but not exclusively in North Africa, Chechenya, the Philippines and the United States.

A change of command in Pakistan's ISI which followed the death of President Zia al-Haq in 1988 seems to have somewhat relaxed the ISI's direct hold on bin Laden's legions. Nevertheless, the ISI continued to rely on bin Laden's camp training system. This came to light with the American cruise missile attacks on the camps in the Khost area on August 20, 1998. The ISI turned to emphasizing support to the Kashmiri insurgents, and other operations aimed against the central power of India in New Delhi.

In the wake of the September 2001 attacks on the United States, the Bush administration, as it exerted great pressure and persuasion on Pakistan's General Musharaf to switch sides and support the US against the Taliban, rediscovered what journalists and intelligence operatives in the area had long known: not only had the ISI maintained a long relationship with bin Laden's people, it had used al-Qaida camps to train terrorists and underground fighters for battle with India in Kashmir and elsewhere. This reliance of the ISI on the bin Laden camps became evident in August 1998. The US cruise missile attacks on the camps near Khost killed or wounded several members of a Kashmiri group supported by Pakistan and believed to be training in the camps.

As Shamshad Ahmad, Pakistan's ambassador to the United Nations reminded two *New York Times* correspondents in October 2001, "After the Soviets were forced out of Afghanistan, you (the United States) left us in the lurch with all the problems stemming from the war: an influx of refugees, the drug and gun running, a Kalashnikov culture." The relative indifference of the Clinton administration to Pakistan's continued support for violent Kashmiri insurgent groups, as well as

Pakistan's nuclear weapons program and its human rights program was shown in a "ho hum" attitude of indifference to a secret memorandum written by Michael A. Sheehan, the State Department's counter-terrorism coordinator. It urged tougher efforts to cut financing to bin Laden and end the sanctuary and support offered to al-Qaida. Listing actions the US could take toward Pakistan, Afghanistan, Saudi Arabia, the United Arab Emirates and Yemen to persuade them to isolate al-Qaida, the memo called Pakistan the key. It urged that the administration make terrorism the main issue in relations with Islamabad.

As the *New York Times* put it, the Sheehan memo "landed with a resounding thud" and met general indifference. As the bin Laden threat grew – and, as became evident later – his planners began methodically preparing the next attacks on the US – and US pressure on Pakistan increased, the Pakistanis pretended to cooperate, but actually did very little. The CIA supplied and financed a special commando unit that Pakistan offered to create to capture bin Laden in Afghanistan as Ramzi Yousef and Mir Aimal Kainsi had been captured in the much easier environment of Pakistan. The idea went "nowhere," a former US official said, because "the ISI never intended to go after bin Laden. We got completely snookered."[8]

The United States almost "got snookered" again, following the September 2001 attacks in New York and Washington. At the end of September, according to the very authoritative intelligence column in the *Far Eastern Economic Review,* at least three Pakistani military intelligence officers, including a brigadier general and a colonel, crossed into Afghanistan. Although General Musharaf had already decreed that Pakistan would reverse its policies and support the United States instead of the Taliban, the officers' purpose was to help the Taliban prepare their defenses against the coming American onslaught and advise them on strategy. Moving without permission from Musharaf, the officers took with them several truckloads of ammunition, although the ISI and the army were under orders to stop military supplies to the Taliban.

When General Musharaf learned what had happened, ISI chief General Mahmoud Ahmed resigned, almost certainly at Musharaf's demand. His replacement, General Ehansul Haq, was ordered to overhaul the service and rid it of mid-level Islamist officers who had worked with the Taliban. On September 27, 2001, all ISI officers operating with the Taliban – and there were many – were ordered out of Afghanistan. On presidential orders there was a massive reshuffle in the senior army command on October 7, aimed at eliminating the hardline Islamist officers who had up to then devoted their careers to supporting the Taliban.[9] According an Indian research and intelligence report, the Kashmiri militant groups "could not have grown to their current [in the year 2000] size without the help of the ISI."

Among those causing India the most trouble are several which have been on and off the US State Department's list of terrorist groups: the Harkatul Mujahidin, the Lashkar-e-Taiba, the Hizbul Mujahidin, the Sipahe-Sahaba-Pakistan and the Lashkar-e-Jhangvi, which receive training from the ISI and enjoy support from

Islamist political parties in Pakistan.[10] Several of these groups were banned by General Musharaf, under apparent Indian and US pressure, in January 2002.

Cooperation between bin Laden and Iraq's dictator Saddam Hussein, the object of reporting and speculation about possible targeting of Iraq during the winter Afghanistan war of 2001–02, came to light only long after the allied "Operation Desert Storm" to expel Iraqi forces from Kuwait in 1991. When Saddam's forces invaded Kuwait in August 1990, Osama bin Laden expressed shock at Saudi King Fahd's decision, not only to invite the Americans to defend his kingdom but to agree to finance the Americans' defense efforts. He qualified this as "treason." Prince Turki, then still on excellent terms with bin Laden, reassured him that Americans would not be stationed near the Muslim holy places, and that they would leave Saudi Arabia once Saddam Hussein had been defeated. When in 1991 the US expeditionary force of over 400,000 departed but left several thousand permanently-stationed troops in the kingdom, bin Laden turned against the royal family, and began financing its Saudi opponents based in London. When King Fahd, at President Mubarak's request, deprived him of his Saudi nationality in 1994, bin Laden, as we saw earlier, moved to Khartoum. There he moved into a kind of business and commercial partnership with Sheikh Hassan al-Turabi and a Sudanese veteran of Afghanistan, Ghazi Salaheddine, Sudan's Minister of Information.

Until forced to leave the Sudan under American and Saudi pressure in 1996, bin Laden expanded his wealth and his global network of political, banking and terrorist contacts. He acquired a monopoly over Sudan's gum arabic, a colloidal substance used in resinous manufactures. The CIA seems to have definitively turned against its former partner bin Laden during this period, after the attacks on American personnel at Riyadh and Khobar.

Bin Laden flew back to Afghanistan in the summer of 1996, with baggage, wives and retainers. His friends, Gulbuddin Hekmatyar and Ahmed Shah Massoud, had been chased out of Kabul by the new Taliban rulers, probably with the blessings of the CIA. The fighters loyal to those two warlords were in many senses ideological forebears of the Taliban. But the followers of Mullah Muhammad Omar, whom bin Laden had befriended in the 1980s at the Binoori mosque in Karachi, had no use for them. On the contrary, they befriended bin Laden himself, perhaps believing, rightly or wrongly, that he still enjoyed the favors of some of their Saudi protectors and financiers. The Saudis were still betting heavily on the Taliban to eliminate all traces of Iranian influence, mainly in the form of the Shi'ite factions which the Saudis, as well as General Zia al-Haq and his successors in Islamabad, had always opposed.

In vain, the Saudis tried to persuade bin Laden not to support the royal family's opponents. One of these was Muhammad Massari, a dissident in London who sent thousands of faxes to sympathizers and others in the kingdom, spreading tales of corruption, oppression and police and prison abuse of political prisoners.

In February 1998, as preparations were already under way for the Nairobi and Dar es Salaam attacks, bin Laden met with at least four senior Islamist leaders. One was Ayman Zawahri, an Egyptian surgeon who left his lucrative practice in Cairo around 1995 to operate full-time as a founder and leader of Egypt's *Al-Gihad*. Since then, he has become bin Laden's most senior deputy. He frequently appeared in videos of bin Laden's communiqués and interviews, just prior to the September 11, 2001 attacks in the US. He is universally considered to have become the right arm, if not the logistical brains of bin Laden and the al-Qaida operations. Others at the February 1998 meeting included Abdel Salam Muhammed, chief of a radical Islamist group in Bangladesh; Fadi Errahmane Khalil, emir of the radical Pakistani Ansar movement; and the Egyptian Islamist exile Abu Yassir Ahmed Taha, representing Islamist groups in western North Africa. These men and some aides set up an "Islamic Struggle Front" dedicated to fighting "the Jews" (that is, Israel and all its friends and allies). They issued a fatwa declaring it to be legitimate to kill any American, civil or military.

Though few of the world's media noticed this, Washington did. The CIA, FBI and the Pentagon, even before bin Laden's outspoken and aggressive ABC News interview of June 1998 by John Miller, realized that bin Laden had in fact declared a worldwide jihad against all Americans. It was then that Prince Turki had to return to Saudi Arabia, empty-handed, after his futile mission to try to persuade Mullah Omar to hand over bin Laden.

Islamic extremism flourished in Pakistan after Zia al-Haq's mysterious death in August 1988 in the crash of his plane. That crash also killed General Akhtar Abdel Rahman Khan, former ISI chief and at the time of his death chairman of the Pakistani joint chiefs of staff and Zia's probable successor. Another victim, as we saw, was Arnold Raphel, US ambassador to Pakistan. His divorced wife, Mrs. Robin Raphel, later served as assistant US Secretary of State for South Asia. She was US ambassador to Tunisia when I discussed the crash with her in Tunis in March 1998. Arnold Raphel had been friends with President Zia for 12 years. Also lost were Brigadier General Herbert Wassom, the US defense attaché in Islamabad and eight Pakistani generals with their aides, as well as the aircrew. The presidential Pakistan Air Force C-130 suddenly dived and hit the ground shortly after takeoff a few miles north of Bahawalpur, Pakistan. The passengers had been watching a test demonstration of a US tank the Pentagon wanted to sell to Pakistan. The demonstration had been a failure.

A Pakistan board of inquiry eliminated normal accidents and mechanical failures, or an external attack by a missile. In a secret, unpublished finding, the board concluded that the pilot had been knocked out by a chemical agent, such as a quick-working nerve gas. Mrs. Raphel and other senior US sources dismiss this, and say that a later US Air Force inquiry pointed to a fault in the plane's hydraulic system.[11]

Some US media commentators mourned Zia's passing as that of one of America's best friends. However, Brigadier Mohammad Youssaf, the lately retired chief of the ISI's Afghanistan bureau, surmised that US policy-makers were actually not sorry to see Zia go. He felt that elements in the US administration were already trying to put the brakes on the Afghan Islamists and especially the Arab and other foreign volunteers helping them – not wanting it to be them, rather than the US-favored émigré Afghan "Transition Government" the CIA favored and which sat in exile in Peshawar, to enter Kabul and take power.

Youssaf's analysis was that as the holy war turned against the Communists, the jihad's patrons in Washington viewed the prospect of a total moujahidin victory and seizure of Kabul with alarm. They feared, he suggested, that an Islamist takeover in Kabul would see the jihad's paramount leaders, Gulbuddin Hekmatyar, Younis Khalis, Abdul Rasul Sayyaf and Hekmatyar's (and later the Taliban's) opponent, Burhaneddin Rabbani "establishing an Iranian-type religious dictatorship." In Youssaf's view, the American game was to curb the power of the Islamists, and to play on differences between the various actions and their commanders. General Akhtar, according to Youssaf, understood what was happening and opposed what he considered the CIA's maneuvering. Until Zia's sudden death, he supported the Pakistani intelligence chiefs' opposition to the CIA desire to issue arms and supplies directly to the fighters, without using the ISI as intermediary. The Americans partially achieved this in 1990, after the holy war had ended and the Russians were gone – but not until after major shifts on the Pakistani scene.[12]

Following the fatal plane crash, there was no power struggle. The handover to power of the new president, as provided in the constitution, was smooth. He was Ghulam Ishaq Khan, 73, who had been chairman of the Pakistani Senate. In May 1988, Zia had dismissed his prime minister, Muhammad Khan Juenjo and his cabinet for "incompetence, corruption and lack of attention to the Muslim faith." He formed a caretaker government in their place and he wanted the next election to be non-partisan. The Pakistani supreme court ruled differently on October 2, 1988. Parties were permitted to put up party candidates. Main contenders were the arch-conservative and Islamist party called the Islamic Democratic Alliance and the Pakistan People's Party (PPP). The latter was led by Miss Benazir Bhutto, the Radcliffe College- and Oxford University-educated daughter of Zufilcar Ali Bhutto, executed by Zia's regime. The PPP won the biggest block of seats. But the conservative Islamist establishment in the army and the ISI opposed Benazir. This was partly because she was less than enthusiastic about continuance of the jihad-related activities, led by Osama bin Laden and others, now that the Russians had left Afghanistan and the Soviet Union was beginning to collapse. President Ishaq Khan named Bhutto prime minister in December 1988. She won a vote of confidence in the national assembly.

At 35, Benazir Bhutto was the first woman leader in the modern history of any Muslim nation. Had she enjoyed the army's support, she might have had a chance to phase out the growing influence of the holy warriors who stayed on, and were now, as we saw, operating flourishing drugs and arms businesses to help finance their continuing operations, many of which – as in Kashmir and India's Punjab – had ISI support. Meanwhile Pakistan was being torn by the cult of arms and drugs resulting from the holy war – such as the inroads of heroin addiction in Pakistani society, friction among more than three million Afghan refugees, the mohajirs or Muslim refugees from India, and rising sectarian animosity inside Pakistan.

Benazir Bhutto was forced from power by a combination of the army and Nawaz Sharif, a power-broker who became prime minister. On April 15, 1999, a court in Rawalpindi convicted Bhutto and her businessman husband, Asif Ali Zardari, of corruption. Two judges ruled that they had taken kickbacks from a Swiss company which Bhutto had selected to monitor the collection of Pakistan's import duties. They sentenced them both to five years' prison and fined them $8.6 million. Mrs. Bhutto, in London at the time, said she would not return to Pakistan until the appeal had been heard.

After growing Islamist violence and sectarian fighting which served further to destroy an already crumbling economy, the army high command staged another coup on October 12, 1999. This time it was against the elected government of Nawaz Sharif, who had tried to dismiss General Pervez Musharaf, army commander-in-chief. Sharif tried to prevent Musharaf's plane from landing as it returned from a visit to Sri Lanka. General Musharaf sent troops to peacefully oust and arrest the Nawaz Sharif government. He declared martial law on October 15, suspending the constitution and dismissing parliament. In 2000 Sharif was tried and sentenced to life imprisonment for hijacking, attempted murder and other offenses. The government prosecutor, who had sought the death penalty, appealed; so did Sharif's defense lawyers, one of whom was murdered during the proceedings. Eventually, Sharif was allowed to depart for exile abroad.

By the summer of 2000, tension and fighting between India and Pakistan over Kashmir increased the danger of an Indo-Pakistan war, which US analysts feared might eventually be fought with nuclear weapons, which both countries had tested recently. An offensive, coordinated by the Pakistani army and the ISI, of Kashmiri militants ended in their withdrawal under pressure from US President Bill Clinton. Clinton visited South Asia in March 2000. He spent nearly five days in India, initiating a new "tilt toward India" and so reversing the policy of favoring Pakistan which Henry Kissinger had initiated during the 1971 Indo-Pakistan war. Indian commentators said this new wooing of India was giving way to the old US Pakistan-first policy in the fall of 2001, as a result of the renewed need of the US for Pakistan as a military base for its new war in Afghanistan.

During his trip in 2000, Clinton made only cursory stops in Bangladesh and Pakistan. On both stopovers, grave security threats curtailed his program. Washington's fears over the ISI's support for the militant Kashmiri groups and for the Taliban had become so great that the US Secret Service, which always sends agents in advance to countries initiating a US presidential visit, strongly opposed any visit at all by Clinton to Pakistan, out of concern for his safety. A least one of the Kashmiri groups had kidnapped and held Americans and others for ransom, and Islamists openly threatened and sometimes attacked Americans, especially in Karachi. President Clinton overruled the Secret Service and made the trip, but with extraordinary security precautions. The White House had an empty Air Force One, normally the presidential plane, flown to Pakistan. Clinton actually arrived in a small, unmarked plane. His motorcade into Islamabad halted under an overpass and Mr. Clinton changed cars. Clinton succeeded neither in inducing India and Pakistan to embrace nuclear disarmament, nor did General Musharaf hold out real hope of a Pakistani effort to induce the Taliban to surrender bin Laden, who was reported by some Western media, without any confirmation, to be suffering from a kidney or liver ailment, requiring treatment by an unnamed visiting Iraqi doctor – giving rise to more rumors about the Saddam Hussein connection.

It was in Pakistan that the real prelude to the climactic attacks in the United States in September 2001 occurred. For Ahmed Rashid, the seasoned and well-informed author of many articles and an outstanding book on the Taliban, the scene in 1995 demonstrated how events were linked in cities as widely separated as Karachi, Manila and New York. What happened in Islamabad on February 7, 1995, Rashid reported, "was a scene from a Hollywood thriller. Nine agents of the CIA and FBI teamed up with ISI officers. Acting on a tip from a South African Muslim informer named Mustaq Parker, who won a two million dollar reward and a new identity in the US as [a further] reward, the US–Pakistani team burst into a room in the Su Casa, a guesthouse in Islamabad owned by Osama bin Laden, their guns drawn and ready. Supine on the bed was the man then considered the world's most hunted terrorist, 27-year-old Ramzi Ahmed Yousef."[13] As we saw, he was wanted as the mastermind of the World Trade Center bombing of February 1993, and for his role in the plot to bomb strategic targets throughout New York City in June 1993.

Pakistan waived its ponderous extradition procedures, as Egypt had already done 18 months earlier for Mahmoud Abuhalima, an Egyptian veteran of the Afghan holy war wanted in the World Trade Center case. Some 36 hours after his seizure, Yousef was flown to New York, as Abuhalima had been flown from Egypt. President Bill Clinton publicly thanked Pakistan Prime Minister Benazir Bhutto. Many of the local Islamists condemned her as a stooge for Washington. Two days after Yousef was captured, a Pakistani court in Lahore sentenced two Christians, a boy of 14 and his uncle, to death for blasphemy against Islam – allegedly they had tossed scraps of paper with insults against the faith into a mosque. (Pakistani Christians often suffer the wrath of Islamists at Western actions. In late October 2001, over 20 Pakistani Roman Catholics paid with their lives when gunmen massacred them during mass in their church; an apparent reprisal for the US bombing of Afghanistan.) An appeals court acquitted the boy and his uncle. However, to save their lives from angry Islamist mobs demanding their murder, they were flown to asylum in Germany, a faraway country of which the two hapless Pakistanis knew little.

Worse was to come. Constant battles between Sunni and Shi'a Muslims in Karachi had already killed hundreds. Their feuding had been rendered lethal by huge stockpiles of weapons left over from the Afghanistan war. What was happening in Karachi was a smaller replica of Sunni–Shi'a strife in ruined Kabul. There, the

Shi'a minority was being outgunned and out-slaughtered by the Sunni majority forces of Burhaneddin Rabbani, the nominal Afghan president. Later, when the Taliban took control, they continued the job, nearly provoking war with Iran.

Benazir Bhutto's voice was one of those which, nearly unheeded in the United States, could have awakened Americans to the enormous terrorist threats facing the world from South Asia. Shortly before visiting the US in April 1995, she told Western newsmen and diplomats in Islamabad that Pakistan's very existence was threatened by the Afghan terrorist training camps and the spreading drug operations resulting from the 1979–89 war. Ramzi Ahmed Yousef, she disclosed, had intended to kill her. His own explosives wounded him while driving a booby-trapped car which was supposed to blow up her residence in Islamabad. Five weeks after Yousef's capture, a legion of 50 FBI agents flew to Pakistan and with local police, seized several more suspects. All were discovered through telephone taps and were linked to Ramzi Ahmed Yousef. Their nationalities read like a mini-catalogue of the foreign "Afghanis" still operating from the Peshawar area: an Iranian, a Sudanese, two Egyptians, two Pakistanis and a Syrian who operated the Islamic Relief Agency in Peshawar, financed by Kuwait.[14]

North of Peshawar, *New York Times* correspondent John F. Burns discovered, and was warned away from, the "university" of Dawal al-Jihad. It stood behind red clay walls and was shunned by taxi drivers and other locals. It was a school for terrorists. After talking with senior police officials, Burns described its reputation as a training place for terrorists who had operated in the Philippines, the Middle East, North Africa and New York City, in the 1993 plots. Its founder was Professor Abdul Rasul Sayyaf, an Afghani academic who claimed to be a graduate of Cairo's famed old al-Azhar Islamic university. A senior Pakistani military officer acknowledged that 20,000 volunteers were trained there by the ISI. Those who remained after the 1979–89 war stayed in the region, "looking for other wars to fight." Like leaders of the holy warriors, Ramzi Ahmed Yousef commuted back and forth across the frontier to Afghanistan between 1990 and his arrest in 1993.[15] Much of the finance for the Abu Sayyaf–ISI terrorist "university" most likely came first from Saudi government funds, and later, from Osama bin Laden. As we saw in the last chapter, Abu Sayyaf's own moujahidin movement had by 1990 moved a nucleus of its fighters to the Philippines and were operating there as terrorists and bandits under that name.

Another way station in the terrorists' long march from South Asia to New York in September 2001 was Jordan, under King Hussein until his death from cancer in February 1999, and then under his son, King Abdullah. The New Year's Eve plots, coinciding with the 1999–2000 millennium celebrations in Jordan and the Western US, had a long prelude in Jordan. Jordan's Islamists, who had a long history of benign attention, in the form of providing them, including Muslim Brotherhood members, with cabinet and other senior government posts, had long prospered in the strongly anti-socialist, anti-Communist and (towards the Islamists) benign atmosphere in Jordan. One of them, Abdallah Azzam, as we saw, had been a principal recruiter for the CIA's Afghanistan jihad. Another, Muhammad Salameh, the first Jordanian arrested and one of those convicted in the February 1993 World Trade Center bombing, had like Azzam bitterly opposed King Hussein's peace treaty signed with Israel in October 1994. The treaty was achieved only after weary years of constant effort; secret and less-secret contacts between Hussein and Israeli leaders, and the opposition of many of the Palestinians, comprising close to one-half of Jordan's five million people. In 1993, as part of the preliminaries for the settlement with Israel, Jordan security forces rounded up many and imprisoned a few Islamists: members or alumni of the strong and legal Muslim Brotherhood, and some members of the shadowy and far more radical Islamic Liberation Party. In the 1989 elections, just as some of the Jordanian and Palestinian Afghan war veterans began to return to Jordan, Islamists won in national elections fully 30 out of 80 parliamentary seats.

Meanwhile Muhammad Salameh had decided in 1987 to travel to the United States. As his family was poor and had no connections in the US, and Muhammad had only religious but no vocational or professional training, it was unlikely that he could get a visa through normal channels. His mother even ruled it out. Then one day he came home with a brand new Jordanian passport and a fresh US visa stamped into it. Jordanian officials said later that an "Afghan international network" – probably a predecessor of today's al-Qaida – procured US visas for young men with Islamist leanings. The mystery of how Muhammad Salameh got his visa was not cleared up in the New York trial records. Once he arrived in New York, he reported his passport lost. The US Embassy in Amman insisted they had never issued a visa to the future bomber and had no record of it.[16]

On May 24, 1993, a young Jordanian named Murad, an Afghan war veteran who had returned from Afghanistan only two months earlier, left by plane from Amman to report for new training and assignments in Afghanistan. He wouldn't meet an American journalist, so a senior Arab journalist in Amman, the author's friend, interviewed him. He disclosed that as of spring 1993, over three years after the Afghanistan war's end, young fighters were still being recruited in Jordan. Palestinians, Jordanians or others interested were steered to the Pakistani Embassy in Amman. If found acceptable, they were issued tickets to Islamabad. On arrival they called a number in Peshawar. Transport was sent to the airport to take them to a processing center. They were immediately given Afghan-type clothes and assigned to training camps. Murad's patron was Gulbuddin Hekmatyar. Each group, Murad said, had its own camps. Many were inside Afghanistan, and so beyond the reach of Pakistani, Egyptian and Algerian government agents sent to track them down. The least "pro-American," said Murad, were the Hekmatyar camps. The most pro-American were those of Burhaneddin Rabbani, the Tajik leader, and former acting president of Afghanistan. He opposed Hekmatyar and the Taliban, leading an armed struggle with the Northern Alliance against Hekmatyar in which much of Kabul and other Afghan cities had been destroyed since 1992.

Murad claimed proudly to have taken part in the tracking, trial and execution of a senior chief of KHAD, the former Afghan Communist secret police. In the Sudan, he said, there were many bases at secret locations. The "big man" financing them was Osama bin Laden. Overall political responsibility in the Sudan, Murad said, was in the hands of Sheikh Hassan al-Turabi. Murad confirmed that most Afghan veterans returning to Sudan, including himself, were routinely questioned by Jordanian intelligence. However, only members of a specific group, called *Jeish Muhammad* or Muhammad's Army (which was later placed on the US State Department's terrorist list), who tried to destabilize Jordan through acts of terrorism (mostly explosions in public places like cinemas and some government buildings) were held. Many of them were pardoned or amnestied.

Unlike Murad, Muhammad Salameh chose to go to the US and stay there. In New York he soon fell in with the circle of Islamist followers of the blind Egyptian Sheikh Omar Abdel Rahman, who had arrived in Brooklyn in July 1990. He had a US tourist visa, even though his name was on a list of terrorist suspects because of his record of militancy in Egypt. The US Embassy in Khartoum issued the visa. There, US diplomats claimed, a computer error in the English-language transliteration of the sheikh's name caused the error of issuing his visa. Later, it transpired that CIA officers, at Khartoum or elsewhere, had consciously assisted his entry. His initial hosts in New York were members of the Islamic Brotherhood, Inc., of 552–554 Atlantic Avenue, Brooklyn (Brooklyn's Arab quarter). The organization had successfully requested his entry as a guest preacher. Eventually the sheikh obtained a Green Card or Alien's Residence Permit. He used a multiple entry visa later stamped in his Egyptian passport to leave and enter the United States several times.[17]

Sheikh Omar began fund-raising and recruiting volunteers in the US for the anti-Soviet jihad. The mosques where he preached, first in Brooklyn, then in Jersey City, attracted first-generation Muslim immigrants. There were also Islamist recruits among Jordanians, Palestinians and others expelled from Kuwait and other Gulf emirates after the Gulf War, as a result of PLO leader Yassir Arafat's foolish embrace of Saddam Hussein during that war against Iraq. In March 1991, Mustafa Shalaby, a 39-year-old Egyptian immigrant and electrical contractor, was found murdered in his Brooklyn apartment. Police told New York investigative reporter Robert Friedman that he had been handling weapons supplies for Afghan guerrillas. He had also raised money for the legal defense of a man named El Sayyad Nossair, another Islamist who had been acquitted of murdering the radical Jewish Defense League chief, Rabbi Meier Kahane, but was jailed on weapons charges in the same case. Shalaby's killing was never solved. Sheikh Omar or someone working with him was suspected, because Shalaby had serious disagreements with the sheikh over money.

Directors of the Al Farouq Masjid mosque, in a storefront building on Atlantic Avenue, Brooklyn, expelled Sheikh Omar as preacher shortly after Kahane's murder. Sheikh Omar moved to the El Salaam mosque in Jersey City, New Jersey.

Its founder was Sultan Ibrahim al-Gawli, a wealthy, 55-year-old Egyptian businessman who had been convicted in 1986 by a Federal jury of conspiring to ship 150 pounds of C-4 plastic explosive to Israel for use by Palestinians in a planned Christmas bombing. Al-Gawli served 18 months in prison, then returned to Jersey City.[18]

The facts about the World Trade Center bombing in February 1993 and the second, aborted plot to destroy major targets in New York City in June of that year, were perhaps more widely reported and commented upon than any other terrorist case in the United States, until the final destruction of the Twin Towers by the suicide hijackers on September 11, 2001.[19]

Both the accomplished assault and the later, unaccomplished plans had the earmarks of the Afghan veterans' network, soon to be known as al-Qaida, all over them. The World Trade Center bombing in the Center's underground parking garage left a crater 200 feet wide and several storeys deep, a small pre-replica of the gaping abyss left in lower Manhattan by the September 2001 attack. The bomb was found to be of ammonium nitrate and fuel oil. This formula was taught in CIA manuals. Versions of these manuals were found in the possession of some of the conspirators, especially Ahmed Ajaj, a Palestinian who had first entered the US on September 9, 1991 and applied for political asylum from Israeli persecution, residing in Houston, Texas. In April 1992 he hastily left the country under an assumed name. In Peshawar and Afghanistan he came into contact with the bin Laden network and Ramzi Ahmed Yousef. He trained in weapons and explosives. Ajaj and Yousef flew together from Peshawar and arrived at New York's Kennedy Airport on September 1, 1992. Ajaj carried the bomb manuals and other incriminating materials which were found by US Customs. He escaped with only six months' imprisonment. Yousef, who claimed to be traveling alone, succeeded in entering the US and immediately began preparations with his co-conspirators for the February bombing. When he entered the US he claimed he had been beaten by Iraqi soldiers in Kuwait during the Gulf War, and asked for political asylum.[20]

Muhammad Salameh was arrested March 4, 1993. A day later, Egyptian immigrant Ibrahim Elghabrowny was arrested in Brooklyn for assaulting officers who searched his apartment. Chemical engineer Nidal Ayyad, who assembled the bomb, was arrested on March 10 at his Maplewood, New Jersey, apartment. The three suspects were indicted in Manhattan on March 17. A fourth Egyptian, an Afghan veteran named Mahmoud Abuhalima, was seized at his village in Egypt, turned over to US FBI agents on March 24, and flown to New York. Another suspect, Bilal Alkaisi, who had frequented an Afghan "refugee" facility, the Alkifah Refugee Center in Brooklyn (better known among the Arab community of Brooklyn as the "Jihad Office") was arrested in New Jersey on March 25. An explosives timer was later found in his apartment. Ramzi Ahmed Yousef, then still at large abroad, was indicted in absentia on March 31. He had boarded a plane out of New York for Pakistan on the day of the attack, after sharing an apartment with Salameh. Ahmed Ajaj was also taken into custody again at about the same time.

Long maneuvering followed between the US and Egypt over Sheikh Omar Abdel Rahman's status and whether Egypt would insist on his extradition (it didn't). Sheikh Omar was arrested and on August 25, he was indicted for conspiracy in the Trade Center attack, the June bomb conspiracy and the 1990 murder of Rabbi Meier Kahane. The charges said Sheikh Omar had instructed and advised other conspirators. El Sayyad Nossair was indicted on a charge of murder (Kahane's) to promote a larger and ongoing conspiracy. In all 15 men were named in the indictment. The main evidence used by the prosecution was 150 hours of taped, transcribed and translated conversations among the main conspirators, recorded by Imad Salem. He was an Egyptian working as a paid informer for the FBI. He claimed falsely to have been one of President Sadat's bodyguards, present at his murder in 1981. His bogus claims enabled the defense to cast doubt on his testimony, but in the end this made no difference to the outcome. The trial ended on March 4, 1994, in the US District Court in Manhattan. Salameh, Ajaj, Nidal Ayyad and Mahmoud Abuhalima were found guilty.

Ramzi Ahmed Yousef was then still at large, and so was an Iraqi, Ahmed Rahman Yasin, a former science student at Indiana University, so those two could not be tried. Yasin, still missing and wanted by the FBI in 2001, was almost certainly in Iraq. This and an Iraqi passport with another identity, that of an Abdel Bassit, often used by Yousef, raised questions by analysts who see the hand of Saddam Hussein in this attack and in others, including the climactic hijackings of September 2001. Bilal Alkaisi's case was separated from the others. He was supposed to be tried later, but dropped out of sight. Judge Kevin Duffy passed sentence on May 24, 1994. He called the defendants "cowards," an epithet that would also be applied to the successful suicide hijackers of 2001 by some commentators. The judge explained that 180 years of the sentences he passed were based on the cumulative life expectancy of the six people killed in the World Trade Center. The balance was for charges related to assault on a Federal officer. There was no possibility of parole.

In January 1995 another conspiracy trial opened in the Federal Court in New York, amid unprecedented security precautions against a possible terrorist attack. After a long and exhaustive choice of jurors from a pool of thousands, who were asked about their attitudes towards Arabs and Muslims, the trial proceeded. This time, one defendant was Clement Rodney Hampton-El, an Afro-American Muslim. He too had trained and served in a capacity, never clarified in public, in the Afghanistan war. His co-defendants rated him as a weapons expert.[21] The trial dragged through the summer of 1995. On October 1, 1995, Sheikh Omar and nine co-defendants were convicted of conspiracy to destroy American targets and also of planning the assassination of Egyptian President Mubarak during his New York visit earlier in the year. They were sentenced to long prison terms, against which their lawyers appealed, without success.

In January 1996 came a further trial for these and other offenses, including the 1990 murder of Rabbi Meier Kahane (the accused here was El Sayyad Nossair, earlier acquitted of the same offense). In one long marathon session on January 17, in a courthouse surrounded by armed police and barricades and searched by bomb-sniffing dogs, Sheikh Omar and nine co-defendants were tried together and sentenced, following individual pleas of each defendant's innocence. Once again, the main basis was Imad Salem's tape recordings. Sheikh Omar again got life in prison, this time for conspiring to murder President Mubarak. El Sayyad Nossair was sentenced to life without parole for the 1990 murder of Rabbi Kahane.[22] As in the 1995 trial, court records made public revealed none of the references to the Afghanistan jihad and the defendants' backgrounds, with the exception of a brief mention of the Afro-American defendant from Philadelphia, Rodney Hampton-El. The CIA, belatedly, was trying to cover its tracks.

The sentencing of Ramzi Ahmed Yousef on January 8, 1998 for his multiple assaults on American targets was, until then, the highest watermark of the blowback on America from the Afghanistan war. Yousef was condemned to 240 years in prison, plus life, for the February World Trade Center bombing. In earlier trials in Federal Court in New York in September and November 1996 Federal jurors convicted Yousef and Eyad Ismoil, a Palestinian, for murder and conspiracy. Ismoil had been in touch with Yousef and the other Trade Center plotters for months before the attack. Ismoil had driven the rented Ryder delivery van containing the 1,200 pound ammonium nitrate bomb into the Center's underground garage. Both Yousef and Ismoil had then immediately fled the US on airline flights. Ismoil was captured later in Jordan and flown to the US, in one of the many measures helpful to the United States taken by Jordan's ubiquitous intelligence service.

In retrospect, as this is written in late 2001, it is easy to read portents of the September 2001 attacks in the words of Yousef and his judges. Brian Parr, the FBI agent who had escorted a handcuffed Yousef on the flight to New York after his capture in Pakistan, had told the jury that Yousef hoped the explosion at the Trade Center would topple one of the two 110-foot towers into the other, killing tens of thousands of people, to let Americans know they were "at war," words similar to those in the communiqués and interviews of Yousef's presumed (though never proven) patron, Osama bin Laden. He is also said to have boasted to Parr that he had narrowly missed several opportunities to bomb all 12 airliners on a single day over the Pacific; to order a kamikaze-type suicide attack on CIA headquarters in Langley, Virginia (this was to actually happen on September 11, 2001, with the target the Pentagon instead of the CIA) – and to assassinate President Bill Clinton during an upcoming visit to the Philippines. Just before his sentencing, Yousef declared to the judge, "Yes, I am a terrorist and I am proud of it." America had invented terrorism, he added. He supported it "as long as it is used against the United States and Israel ... You are more than terrorists. You are butchers, liars and hypocrites."

Judge Duffy rose to the occasion with equally theatrical language. He recommended that Yousef remain in solitary confinement for his entire life; treatment, he added, historically reserved for those "who spread plague and pestilence throughout the world." Probably with the sensational murder trial of

the Afro-American football star and Hollywood celebrity O.J. Simpson in mind –
a number of those involved in the Simpson trial had cashed in with fat book,
television and cinema contracts – Judge Duffy acknowledged that "someone might
be perverse enough to buy your story." Accordingly, he fined Yousef $4.5 million
and ordered him to pay $250 million in restitution, so that any money from cinema,
television or book deals would go to the survivors of the six victims he had killed,
and to the thousand people the Center's bombing had wounded in New York.[23]

What was different about the terrible events of September 2001 was not the
objectives of the terrorists, which were essentially the same, on a far grander scale.
Quite different, on the other hand, were their backgrounds, motivations and indeed
their *modus operandi*.

From what is known at this writing in early winter of 2001–02, it was a different
breed of conspirators who hijacked the four United Airlines and American Airlines
planes on September 11, 2001. Three of the planes (one attempt was thwarted by
passengers and crew who fought the hijackers and brought about the fourth plane's
crash in open country in Pennsylvania, before it could head for its presumed target
of either the White House or the Capitol building in Washington) became guided
missiles. They toppled the Twin Towers, breached the Pentagon seriously and
killed about 3,000 people, leaving many thousands of others with serious or mortal
wounds, and with bereaved family members. The kamikaze pilots and those
supporting them were mostly quiet young men of "good families" displaying no
outward sign of religious zeal or fanaticism, unlike the Muhammad Salamehs
and Mahmoud Abuhalimas of modest backgrounds and often openly-declared
Islamist sentiments.

They were obviously supported by an al-Qaida network at least as sophisticated,
and probably more so, than that behind the suicide bombing of the US Navy
destroyer *Cole* in the big Yemeni port of Aden on October 12, 2000.

In a sense, the *Cole* attack in Yemen was another step up the ladder of escalation.
It proved that Osama bin Laden or his disciples or sympathizers could make good
bin Laden's threats against the US military in the Arabian Peninsula and Persian
Gulf – bin Laden's originally-declared target when he began operations in the early
1990s – and at the same time, carefully plan a coordinated operation in Asia, as one
of the preliminaries to the major assault on the United States in September 2001.

On October 12, 2000, the US Navy Arleigh Burke-class destroyer *Cole*,
commissioned in 1991 and worth, in 2001 funds, nearly one billion dollars, eased
slowly into the big harbor of Aden, at the southern tip of Yemen to refuel. Minutes
after it anchored, a small Zodiac-type boat with two men in it moved toward the
Cole, whose crew was preparing to relax on deck during what was scheduled to be
only a brief port call. Seconds before the small craft pulled alongside the destroyer,
one of the two men in it stood up and, according to witnesses aboard, seemed to
stand at attention. Then a horrendous explosion tore a house-sized hole in the
warship's side, killing 17 members of the ship's crew, wounding 39 others and, of
course, killing the suicide bombers and virtually pulverizing their remains. The

injured were first sent to Yemeni clinics ashore for treatment. They were subsequently evacuated by air, under arrangements quickly made by Mrs. Barbara Bodine, the US Ambassadress to Yemen and her staff, to the US air base at Ramstein, Germany and a French military hospital in the nearby republic and former French colony of Djibouti, on the northeast African coast.

Admiral Vern Clark, the Chief of US Naval Operations in Washington, DC, declared, with classic understatement, "this was clearly a terrorist act." No group or individual claimed responsibility. However, very soon, analysts like Vincent Cannistraro, the CIA's former anti-terrorist chief, were pointing the finger at Osama bin Laden and possible links between bin Laden's al-Qaida and Saddam Hussein's regime in Iraq. Within weeks, Yemeni investigators, offering limited help to a swarm of arriving FBI and US Navy security agents, found evidence linked to the blast, including the house ashore where the explosives had apparently been prepared, and had picked up a number of Arab suspects, many of whom were Afghan war veterans and most of whom were eventually released, but at least six of whom were eventually held for inconclusive trials. Richard Clarke, the Clinton administration's National Security Council advisor coordinating counter-terrorism efforts, said the huge explosion showed "a great deal of sophistication with explosives. There are some similarities that we see," he added, with the August 1998 US embassy bombings in East Africa. "There are similarities in the sophistication of the attack, the pre-planning of the attack. This is something that began long before the recent violence in the Middle East [meaning the Palestinian–Israel fighting which began with a new Palestinian *intifada,* the second since the 1990s, in September, just before the attack]. This took months to plan, and there are indications of safe houses, and planning, and moving of personnel in. That's a sophisticated attack."[24]

On October 30, 2000, a Norwegian heavy-lift ship, the *Blue Marlin,* picked up the stricken ship, whose crew of about 300, with reinforcements from the United States, had successfully battled to keep from foundering and sinking, from tugboats and carried it home to the US for the costly repairs, estimated at $150 million at least. "She left with some help from her friends, but she still left very proudly," Ambassador Bodine commented.

The investigation dragged slowly on through the year 2001. The US government in January announced a reward of up to $5 million for information leading to the arrest of those responsible. The US Navy conducted a Judge Advocate General investigation, aimed at determining "lessons learned" to help prevent future such attacks, and assess accountability of those involved. In February, Yemen President Ali Abdallah Saleh announced the arrest of two more Yemenis on their return from Afghanistan in connection with the bombing. In June, FBI and State Department investigators working in Aden moved their operation to the Yemeni capital, Sanaa, aboard a US C-130 which flew about 50 US investigators and their equipment from Aden to Sanaa Members of the US Marine Corps' Fleet Antiterrorism Security Team, sent to Aden to protect investigators, also moved to the Yemeni capital.

During the torrid summer months, the 100-degree plus Fahrenheit temperatures in Yemen and some intramural bickering in the US intelligence community apparently combined to slow the inquiries. Washington offered verbal carrots to Yemen when, on July 9, a special US Middle East envoy, William Burns, praised Yemen for helping the FBI probe the suicide bombing, offering some economic aid to Yemen in appreciation for its help. Soon, however, as the *New York Times* and other American media reported on August 21, despite the arrival of six fresh FBI investigators from the US to resume the investigation, it had virtually ground to a halt, mainly because Yemen had refused repeated US requests to widen the probe to include militant Islamist groups operating in the country. After the September 11 attacks in New York and Washington, the Bush administration, in presenting its case against Osama bin Laden to allied and friendly governments, said some of the same terrorists involved in the September 11 kamikaze assaults also had been linked to the East Africa embassy bombings and the attack on the *Cole*. On October 28, 2001, about two weeks after the start of the air war against the Taliban in Afghanistan, General Musharaf's Pakistani government arrested and turned over to American custody a Yemeni microbiology student wanted in connection with the bombing of the US destroyer.[25] Clearly, the most serious damage done by an enemy to an American warship since the Japanese Empire's surprise attack on the US Pacific Fleet at Pearl Harbor, December 7, 1941, would remain an open, unsolved case for many months or years, perhaps forever.

It was still too early, in the early winter of 2001–02, to tell whether this would also be true of the worst attack that ever occurred on United States soil, on September 11, 2001.

For many Americans, especially for the families and loved ones of the about 3,000 Americans dead or missing in the ruins of the collapsed World Trade Center Towers, the Pentagon, or in the scattered debris of the crash of the fourth hijacked plane in Pennsylvania, it was a nightmare from which there could be only the most gradual awakening, if indeed there could be one at all. Alastair Cooke, the venerable octogenarian BBC commentator who had been broadcasting his "Letter from America" on BBC radio's World Service since before World War II, described how he had switched on his TV set just before 9.00am on the morning of September 11, to see the horrifying image of the first hijacked airliner striking one of the twin towers, a few moments earlier.

Oh no, not another *Towering Inferno* film from Hollywood, he reflected. He quickly switched to another channel – where a well-known news commentator confirmed that it was really happening, and not a cinematographic event. Moments later, the second plane struck the other tower, eventually bringing both down, as the superheated steel skeletons of the buildings melted – a collapse which Ramzi Ahmed Yousef and his fellow-conspirators had dreamt of in 1993, but had been unable to achieve.

Within a few more minutes, the third airliner, turned missile, had, like the others, with all of their passengers and crews sharing the fiery death of the triumphant hijackers, slammed into a wing of the Pentagon, annihilating large sections of the US Defense Department and well over a hundred of its personnel. This author, frozen with dread as he watched the television pictures at home in Athens, Greece, after a few moments of wondering whether the first crash might not have been due to a monumental pilot or mechanical error, realized after the second strike that this was the worst enemy assault on the United States mainland since a British expeditionary force vengefully burned Washington, including the Capitol Building and the then residence of the US president, during the war of 1812.

President George W. Bush, informed as he visited a school in Florida, was hastily flown on Air Force One out of harm's way to two separate US Air Force bases in the southern and western US, before returning to Washington to take command, together with Vice-President Dick Cheney. In the meantime, US airspace was closed to all flights, as were all US airports, large and small. The nation was paralyzed for nearly 48 hours, wondering what next to expect. A massive salvage and rescue effort began almost at once in New York and Washington. Eventually it claimed the lives of nearly 400 New York firemen and policemen, many of whom had escaped from the twin towers after the impacts, only to race back into the buildings, scaling innumerable stairways to save lives and then lost their own as the 110-storey towers crashed to the ground in an apocalyptic cloud of dust and smoke.

As the toll of the dead and missing forever mounted into the thousands, the Americans and the rest of the Western world began to search for how to respond to what was swiftly being called, by a chorus of commentators, "the new terrorism," universally believed to be perpetrated by Osama bin Laden and his collaborators. President Bush spoke of the first war of the new century. He and his closest counselors, Secretary of State Colin Powell, National Security Advisor Condaleeza Rice, Secretary of Defense Donald Rumsfeld and all of the Pentagon's and CIA's senior staff began preparing for the inevitable riposte, which by October 7 became the start of a new air war. This time it was the bombing of Afghanistan, intended to destroy, if possible, the Taliban government and militias, and to root out Osama bin Laden and his followers, presumed to be hiding in the caves and underground bunkers which the CIA had helped them meticulously to prepare during the 1979–89 war against the Russians.

During the first days and weeks of heated emotion in the United States, the outpouring of dismayed grief mingled with patriotism – the sale of American flags, in all of their permutations from tee shirts to giant banners raised over homes and schools – gave rise to comparatively little real reflection. Where was the enemy, and how should he be struck? One commentator abroad summed up the questions: The terrorist peril – soon perceived by Americans to be augmented by an outbreak of apparent bio-warfare; mail-borne anthrax bacteria, which by November 2001 had sickened a score of Americans and killed several, raising fears of a new terrorist onslaught in the form of biological terrorism – needed a patient, daily response. Did it require a war?

The verdict of American opinion was yes, it did. The result of this verdict was the autumn and winter air and ground campaign launched against the Taliban, which was claiming civilian victims and once again, forcing the displacement of literally millions of Afghan refugees.

But much wider and more sweeping questions remained to trouble the anguished American psyche, and to stir the collective fears of Europeans, Asians, Africans and others around the world. Should the war be fought only against bin Laden's cohorts and their Taliban protectors? What about Pakistan's military and intelligence establishment, which had created the Taliban and at least, turned a blind eye to bin Laden's activities for so long? Or Iraq and its master, President Saddam Hussein, who almost daily mocked the United States, its leaders and its policies, and swore to even the score with Israel, as quickly as he could secure bases in neighboring Jordan or Syria to attack the Jewish state? What of other Muslim countries, even such allies as Saudi Arabia, which had also supported the Afghan war veterans, who now had to be hunted down and destroyed? Could such a war eventually boil over into a "crusade" – President Bush used the word, arousing the ferment of Muslims from Morocco to Indonesia with its atavistic overtones of the medieval Christian conquerors of Jerusalem, and soon had to retract it – against all of the world's billion Muslims?

Some of the reactions of American Christian fundamentalists, closely allied with America's extreme political Right, carried almost chiliastic overtones. "God," declared on television two influential "born again" Christian evangelists, Jerry Falwell and Pat Robertson, "has permitted the enemies of America to inflict on us what we probably deserved." Falwell added, enunciating all of the dark doctrines of the American Right: "It is the heathen, the abortionists, the feminists, the gays, the lesbians and the ACLU [American Civil Liberties Union, a liberal group lobbying for civil rights and freedom of expression] who, in trying to secularize America, supported this event." Falwell publicly apologized on September 18, after strong pressure from the White House.[26] However, across the United States, the insistent, and very understandable clamor, for retribution persisted and grew. This eased the tasks of President Bush's administration, as they mapped the possibilities and charted the Herculean diplomatic and military tasks facing them in building a "global coalition" for what CNN and other Western media baptized first the "strike against terrorism," and which came soon to be called simply the "new war."

The author, like hundreds if not thousands of other journalists the world over, instead of departing for Islamabad or northern Afghanistan with the armchair war correspondents or the frontline ones in Northern Alliance territory, joined the quest for information about the terrorists who had planned and perpetrated the September attacks. This quest took me to London, Paris, Hamburg, Munich, Rome and Milan. It further confirmed for me the thesis of this book; that the heightened violence and the new conflict were both, in effect, direct descendants of the policy decisions taken by the Soviet Union and the United States during the Cold War: by Moscow, to invade Afghanistan in 1979; by the United States and a set of allies, each with their own separate agendas and reasons, to counter that invasion with a proxy war, fought by the Afghans themselves, and the many thousands of volunteer Muslim mercenaries recruited around the world to come to their aid, but soon taken effectively in hand, more by Pakistan for its own ends than by the CIA which had conceived and planned the operation.

This war, however, had been triggered more by a new breed of quiet, discreet, well-educated and sometimes even affluent young men than by the often ill-educated youths, mainly alumni of the religious schools of Pakistan, the guerrilla training of the CIA-managed ISI training schools, or the ubiquitous camps of Osama bin Laden's network. Investigation showed traces of the plotters, before they traveled to the United States to join others already living there, in almost the entire European continent. However, there were two main centers: Germany and Italy.

Intelligence experts in Germany acknowledged that in continental Europe, al-Qaida had its strongest support network in Germany. Five Arab students, living and working together, mostly in Hamburg, for at least portions of nearly a decade, formed a hard-core terrorist planning cell. This was transplanted to the United States for advanced training in the flying techniques they needed to perform their September 2001 suicide missions. The leader was probably Muhammad Atta, 33, born in Cairo, Egypt, whose academic speciality was city planning, believed to be the pilot of the first aircraft which hit the north tower of the World Trade Center. Marwan al-Shehi, 23, a national of the United Arab Emirates, studied shipbuilding in Hamburg and was in the second aircraft, which struck the south tower of the Trade Center. Ziad Jarrah, 26, from Lebanon, studied aircraft engineering, and was apparently the hijacker-pilot of the aircraft that crashed in Pennsylvania. Said Bahaji, 26, with German nationality acquired from a German mother who had married a Moroccan man, was believed by German investigators in late 2001 to have been the possible main logistics planner of the group, flew to Pakistan on September 3 and was the object of an international arrest warrant. Finally, 29-year-old Ramzi Binalshibh, from Yemen, had registered in Hamburg for university courses, but disappeared in August 2001. He was also put on an international wanted list.

One of the key business contacts in Germany seems to have been Mamoun Darkazanli, owner of a Hamburg company listed by the US Treasury and the FBI as connected with the bin Laden network. Under questioning he denied involvement with terrorism, but apparently did not deny knowing bin Laden. One or more of the five-man Hamburg cell, German police and counter-intelligence officials said, spent some time in 2000 with a group of four men arrested on December 26 of that year for planning a terror attack in Strasbourg, France, and found with explosives and weapons. The German authorities and American FBI agents working with them discovered that the al-Qaida network in the 1980s, while the Afghan jihad was still raging, built up a loose organization composed of autonomous cells in Germany, Italy and elsewhere. Most of the members were Arabs. Fritz Behrens, interior minister of the German state of North Rhine-Westphalia, and another German official the author interviewed in Hamburg, estimated that there were 100 "sleepers," inactive bin Laden operatives waiting to be activated for attacks in Western Europe, living in Germany by September 2001.

The Munich branch of the German federal counter-intelligence service reported that "these 'Afghanistan warriors' have no connection with extremist organizations as far as organizational structures are concerned. Rather, they represent a loose network of small ... groups not under any common leadership but which keep contact with one another ... Al-Qaida operates [internationally] as a service point for Islamic terrorism. Regional groups act autonomously, but with support from Al-Qaida. Germany has been a safe haven [for them] in recent years." The German service's Stuttgart office said earlier that al-Qaida members use Germany as a transit base for activities elsewhere inside and outside Europe. Reinhard Wagner, German counter-intelligence official in Hamburg, said al-Qaida members "use amateur videos of wars, for instance in Chechnya, to recruit young men, mainly students." German investigators discovered what those in the US found out more belatedly: the terrorist networks, realizing that Western intelligence snoops regularly on normal telephone and radio communications, makes extensive use of personal couriers who, like Atta and his comrades in Hamburg, travel frequently in this capacity.

Students and university staff in Hamburg unanimously described the group as quiet, discreet, intelligent, clever and not disposed to display their political or extreme religious views in public – unlike many of the plotters in the earlier American terrorist conspiracies of the older group of Afghan war veterans. Muhammad Atta, during his eight-year stay at the Hamburg technical university, traveled a great deal between 1995 and 1997, saying he was visiting his family in Cairo, but probably traveling at least once to Afghanistan. (His father in Cairo, in European TV interviews, steadfastly denied that his well-bred, family-loving son, could have been remotely involved with terrorism; but could not explain his disappearance after September 11.) However, other students who knew Atta in Hamburg said he returned from his trips abroad more inclined to say his prayers regularly at the mosque, near the university, and wearing a beard.

Atta's colleague Said Bahaji, whose German mother indignantly refused to believe in her son's involvement in the conspiracy and who insisted on believing his story that his September 3 trip to Pakistan was for an "internship" there, was seen, it seems, more often at the mosque than the others. His Turkish-German wife or girlfriend of many years followed Muslim dress codes, but told investigators, when she finally informed them that Bahaji was up to no good (she was later granted permanent asylum and a new identity), that she had suspected nothing bad for years. Neither had his fellow students on campus, where he wore Western clothes, like the other cell members, and never talked politics or religion.[27]

The Italian dimension of the pre-September 2001 bin Laden network in Europe was disclosed by a series of investigations in Milan and Rome, by the ABC News

Rome office and by reporters working for Italian radio stations. In January 2001, an Italian police wiretap in Milan intercepted a call between two suspected bin Laden operatives. "They've arrested our brothers ... half of the group. They found the arms warehouse," one caller said. The intercept led to the arrest, three months later, of Essid Sami ben Khemais, a 33-year-old Tunisian and five others in Italy. At this writing, Milan prosecuting judge Stefano Dambruoso was completing a case against those arrested and against a Tunisian-born Belgian national and an Iraqi living in Germany. Italian authorities said they had evidence of links between al-Qaida adherents in Italy, Britain, Germany, Belgium, Switzerland, Spain and France. Dozens of suspects were detained in those countries. Wiretapped conversations by members of the group – who did not use the communications precautions observed by bin Laden operatives elsewhere – discussed bombing and incendiary techniques used successfully in Chechenya. Ben Khemais, who used the *nom de guerre* "Saber" before his extradition from Germany to Italy, in another conversation mentioned a "drug" which when concealed in tomato cans could be used to "knock out" people at the scene of a bomb explosion.

One of the suspects, Tareq Maaroufi, the naturalized Belgian of Tunisian descent, was convicted in Belgium in the 1990s for involvement in the Algerian GIA terrorist group. US intelligence officials believe he was involved in a planned attack on the US Embassy in Rome, leading to temporary evacuation of the mission on January 5, 2001. Italian authorities closely monitored Milan's Islamic Cultural Institute, whose former director was Anwar Shaaban, an Egyptian investigated by Milan prosecutors before being killed in 1995 as one of the Afghan war veterans in the Bosnian Muslim army. An Italian report called the Institute "a substantial crossroads" for Egyptian terrorists. None of this group of suspects seemed to have any links to the September 2001 attacks in the United States. Many, however, were believed to be plotting grandiose terror attacks, supposed to coincide roughly with the 1999–2000 millennium celebrations in France (Strasbourg and the US Embassy in Paris), Italy (the Rome Embassy in January 2001) and Belgium. Significantly, these European suspects were far less prudent or discreet than the Hamburg cell members had been.[28]

This narrative, incomplete as it is, has to close somewhere, and for now, it will be here. The United States, in its "war against terror," seemed to be drawn deeper into a hi-tech but low-intensity new war in Asia which in many ways resembled a giant police operation; a manhunt for Osama bin Laden and senior al-Qaida and Taliban chiefs. Since 1979, when the Brezhnev Kremlin and the Carter administration in Washington made their fateful decisions, resulting in the invasion of Afghanistan and the means of resistance to that invasion, the world has been, and still is, suffering the consequences. From Peshawar, Islamabad and Kabul to Cairo, Khartoum, Algiers, Moscow, Central Asia, East Africa, the Philippines, and finally, New York in September 2001, the trail of the Afghan war veterans has been long and bloodstained. Arguably, the Soviet Union of Leonid Brezhnev and his politburo cronies, had, by invading Afghanistan in December 1979, doomed itself. Historians may decide that this was not the original sin, but rather the final sin, and the terminal error, of a dying Soviet Union – the predecessor of a revived Russia, aspiring to some form of capitalism and democracy. Now, at the start of the twenty-first century, it is at least temporarily the ally of the United States in a common battle against radical Islamists, whom the United States had made its earlier allies against the Communist adversary. What the Soviet invasion of 1979 did do was give America an opening for a crusade, conducted by Afghans and foreign Muslim mercenaries, who then turned on their benefactors and employers. In the new century, the world will continue to experience this blowback, which reached a crescendo in the events in New York, Washington and South Asia in the winter of 2001–02.

Perhaps future governments, whether in the United States, the United Kingdom, Russia or less powerful and influential nations, will take to heart this important lesson of late twentieth-century history: When you decide to go to war against your current main enemy, take a good, long look at the people behind you whom you choose as your friends, allies or mercenary fighters. Look well to see whether these allies already have unsheathed their daggers – and are pointing them at your back.

Epilogue:
The War against Terror

The lessons of the second Afghanistan war of our time, triggered by the worst terrorist attack in remembered history, have proved numerous and bitter for all concerned. These lessons – military, political, historical and above all human – or most of them, were similar to those of the 1979–89 war and *après guerre*: the dangers of using fractious mercenaries as proxies; the hostility, indifference or uncertain support of many of the less-favored classes among the world's over one billion Muslims; the failures of Western intelligence to understand the Islamist terrorist movements, or accurately to predict their actions.

Balanced against this was the obvious relief, joy and euphoria of Afghan people, especially women and their children, at being freed from the cruel and unnatural social constraints and repressive laws applied by the Taliban, as the allies successively liberated larger and larger regions from the Taliban yoke in the early winter of 2001–02. People literally danced for joy; returned to their own music for entertainment; turned on their television and radio sets; dusted off works of art which had portrayed living beings. Men shaved their beards and got haircuts; many women discarded their all-covering *burqahs* and returned to teaching, nursing and other jobs forbidden to them by the Taliban since the early 1990s

At the start of the fall and winter military campaign against Afghanistan's Taliban rulers, in October 2001, President George W. Bush and his senior advisors hoped, and told the American and world public, that it could destroy Osama bin Laden, his al-Qaida terrorist center and the Taliban regime that protected them largely through a series of air strikes applied with state-of-the-art high technology, and with an almost total lack of American casualties. This strategy had been applied in the Gulf war against Iraq in 1991 and the Kosovo war against Serbia in 1999. It was revived, with the addition of commando raids and the support of anti-Taliban opposition groups in Afghanistan. In Washington and apparently in London, though with lesser enthusiasm in other capitals participating in the coalition, such as Islamabad, Riyadh, Paris, Berlin or Rome, it was expected that thousands of fighters would defect from Taliban ranks.

This was not the case at the start of the war in October, but it did happen later. In November, thousands of new tribal volunteers from Pakistan tried to flock across the border to swell Taliban ranks. But after the fall of Mazar-i-Sharif and Kabul itself, as well as Herat and Jalalabad, to the proxy forces of the Afghan Northern Alliance, (renamed the National Union), the allied noose tightened around other Taliban strongholds such as Kandahar, and Kunduz, the last Taliban bastion in the north, as the Taliban retreated and these strongholds too fell, leaving US Special

Forces and Marines, with their Afghan allies, to probe al-Qaida's presumed hideouts in the mountainous Tora Bora caves and caverns, near the Pakistani frontier.

Everywhere, a thunderous bombing campaign by many US and a few British warplanes softened the enemy resistance. And slowly, the steel of the allies tightened around the presumed hideouts of Osama bin Laden and his al-Qaida movement, as thousands of Taliban fighters deserted, changed sides, or simply shaved their beards, hid their weapons, and merged with the local populations. Those who remained in towns like Kunduz and tried to fight to the end were the foreign mercenaries of the Taliban and bin Laden: Pakistanis, Arabs, Indonesians, Uighurs and other Muslims who had flocked to the banner of jihad from all parts of the world.

What was lacking, following the first allied military successes of November, was a widely-based coalition government, composed of minority Tajik, Uzbek or Hazara components, as well as the majority Pushtun element which had formed the tribal backbone of the Taliban. Efforts under the aegis of the United Nations, led by the highly able Algerian diplomat Lakhdar Brahimi, sought to fashion such a government, with many political cooks stirring the Afghan broth, from the 87-year-old, exiled former king, Zahir Shah and his entourage, to the Pushtun warlords who became regional governors and village headmen, as the Taliban retreated. By December an interim government had been agreed upon at a conference in Bonn, Germany, attended by representatives of all the main Afghan ethnic and tribal factions. It began to function in Kabul, protected in part by a peacekeeping force sponsored by the UN and led by a contingent of several hundred British troops.

The tunnels, caves and the homes of ordinary Afghan citizens, often hardly distinguishable from the fighters, often proved to be as tough to single out, penetrate or destroy as the Russian invaders had found them to be in the 1979–89 war. Warned by allied and some of its own intelligence experts, the US Defense Department planners agreed to accept aid, including troop contingents it had initially shunned from such NATO allies as France, Germany and Italy. Even Japan, stretching its constitutional constraints against involving its Self-Defense Forces, committed since its defeat in World War II in 1945 not to undertake military actions abroad, sent a small force of warships and planeloads of humanitarian aid.

Arab and Muslim public opinion had opposed the bombing campaign from the start, especially when it became apparent that no bombing pause was intended during the month-long Ramadan Muslim holy month of fasting, which ended just before Christmas 2001. However, the street demonstrations and other public opposition eased as the allied hi-tech military campaign succeeded. European public opinion, though gratified by the November successes against the Taliban and al-Qaida, had been at first appalled at the vast movement of millions of often starving and freezing refugees displaced by the war, and the daily pummeling of an impoverished country, already devastated by over twenty years of war and four years of punishing drought. The US administration, relieved at the outpouring of international humanitarian aid, also accepted the European offers of military aid, partly to show that the global anti-terrorist coalition demanded by President Bush was not just a myth.

It was disclosed that not only US Special Military Forces were operating on the ground in Afghanistan, but also that the CIA's own paramilitary units had entered the fray, carrying out reconnaissance, behind-the-lines spying and other covert operations. The CIA suffered its first battle casualty in the new war when a CIA officer was killed in a revolt of al-Qaida war prisoners captured during the fighting at Mazar-i-Sharif.

However, the CIA's pre-war prescience about what was to come on the terrorist front had left much to be desired. For some reason unknown at this writing, for example, little or no heed was paid in Washington to an ominous warning passed on by King Abdullah's royal Jordanian intelligence service. Sometime during the late summer, United States officials, and separately, German intelligence contacts in Amman, were advised that the assiduous Jordanian service had heard that there would shortly be a "major attack" on American soil involving airplanes, though hijacking was not mentioned. The Jordanian service, which as we saw in this book, had been relentlessly tracking other Islamist terrorists and the specifically al-Qaida conspiracies for years, had even learned the Arabic code name used by the conspirators for the operations: *Al Urous al-Kabir*, or "The Grand Wedding." Which US service received this alert, and how it was passed up the chain of command in Washington (if it was), is unknown to the author at this writing. Chancellor Gerhard Schroeder's German government in Berlin did not take it seriously.

Not that red flags of danger had not been displayed inside the United States: In March 2001, a US government commission, chaired by two former senators, Gary Hart, a Colorado Democrat and Warren Rudman, the New Hampshire Republican, published a 146-page book titled *Road Map for National Security: Imperative for Change*. It called for the creation of the cabinet-level post of Homeland Security – which was done by President Bush after September 11 – and warned: "The combination of unconventional weapons proliferation with the persistence of international terrorism will end the relative invulnerability of the United States homeland to catastrophic attack." The report also correctly prophesied: "A direct attack against American citizens on American soil is likely over the next quarter century. The risk is not only death and destruction but also a demoralization that could undermine US global leadership. In the face of this threat, our nation has no coherent or integrated governmental structure."

Outside the United States, a bewildering array of at least 12 different and often competing intelligence agencies reported on every conceivable aspect of military, political, economic, social and even cultural trends. The ubiquitous National Security Agency (NSA) in Fort Meade, Maryland, cooperating with the similar but much smaller corresponding agencies of Britain, Canada, Australia and New Zealand, trawled through the world's electronic communications. But the conspirators preparing the September 2001 attacks had apparently managed to evade detection even by this multi-billion-dollar network of electronic snoopers.

In November 2001, a US presidential commission recommended that the NSA, the National Reconnaissance Office (NRO) which runs satellite intelligence systems and the National Imagery and Mapping Agency, which handles visual mapping systems from the air and outer space, be put under the directorship of the CIA. When implemented, after the expected battles over turf and jurisdiction between agencies, this would become the "largest overhaul of the US intelligence community in decades and is intended to help consolidate programs and reduce rivalries" within the gigantic US intelligence community, as *Washington Post* intelligence expert Walter Pincus reported on November 8, 2001.

Hindsight, of course, is always easier than foresight, and this is as true for the present writer as for everyone else. However, since much of this book has been an attempt to catalog historical errors of US policy, I am closing it with some reflections of a very distinguished, retired US intelligence officer and businessman who has spent his career, as have I as a journalist, largely in the Middle East. I happen to share these ideas, so I set them forth here. I realize that I will be called "unpatriotic", or worse, by some fellow Americans for doing so, but here goes.

The US bombing campaign initiated on October 7, 2001, with some British participation, was an understandable and, in military terms, successful act of angry frustration with what happened in New York and Washington a month earlier. The military successes against the Taliban left the political problem. Could all the king's horses, and all the king's men, piece together the shattered political entity which had once been a kind of country?

The Bush administration should have capitalized on the initial and unprecedented wave of international outrage and sympathy for the American victims. First, it should have called on all governments even remotely concerned for a huge law-enforcement effort, to track down and capture the criminals. The United Nations, whose secretary-general, Kofi Annan, was branded a "criminal" in one of Osama bin Laden's televised outbursts, should have been asked to head this worldwide effort, which was rightly perceived by President Bush, Mr. Annan and many others, as an "existential threat to civilized international society," in the words of the veteran observer whose thoughts I share. The basic agreement of Russia, which offered use of bases near Afghanistan in the former Soviet Muslim republics bordering Afghanistan , and 1979–89 holy war ally China, which offered at least moral support, provided a huge opportunity for such a UN-sponsored world campaign. Both Russia, in rebellious Muslim Chechenya, and China, in the fractious Muslim Uighur tribes of China's Far West, in Xinjiang, had their own fierce agenda in opposing bin Laden and the Taliban, whom they both accused of aiding their adversaries.

There was still time, in the winter of 2001–02, to get the UN Security Council, dominated by the triumvirate US–Russia–China, and with the usual support of the other NATO allies, to develop an international protocol or code defining and regulating violent and criminal political action, perhaps avoiding the use of the word "terrorism" which always raises the familiar "one man's terrorist is another man's freedom fighter" cliché.

With the authority of the United Nations behind it, the US, in the absence of the bombing campaign in Afghanistan, could woo and perhaps enlist some real support of smaller nations like Iran, Syria and Libya, whom we have so often accused of "harboring" terrorists. Assuming that bin Laden did not find asylum in some fringe or outlaw state, such as Somalia, there seems to me a reasonable chance that he might be so brought to justice and deferred before an international tribunal, rather than the American criminal courts which have tried other terrorists involved in the 1990s assaults on Americans at home and abroad. By the end of 2001, the United States was detaining hundreds of Afghan war prisoners at the big American base at Guantanamo Bay, Cuba. There was serious talk of organizing US military courts to try suspected terrorists. Whether the Guantanamo detainees, whom the US called "illegal combatants," should be granted the rights of regular prisoners of war under the Geneva Conventions, as urged by many governments and human rights groups, became a subject of serious controversy by February 2002.

An imaginative and sweeping gesture would be a new American initiative to launch a worldwide new development effort, a kind of "Marshall Plan" on a world scale, avoiding the now pejorative noun, "globalization." It would aim at leveling some of the terrible economic, environmental and health problems which have created such growing poverty and misery, which, after all, are root causes of terrorism. Along with this should be real pressure on some friends and allies of the United States, not the least of them Saudi Arabia, to solve their human rights problems, which exist around the world, and found only their most extreme form in the abuses of the Afghan Taliban.

Last, but perhaps most important for those of us who have dealt most of our lives with the Middle East – and truly, I believe, for the rest of the world – would be a concerted effort by US administrations, present and future, finally to solve the Palestine–Israel problem in a manner that is just and equitable for both sides. Like Stalin's Soviet Union, the United States was present and approving at Israel's creation in 1948. The Arab world (and not only the Palestinians themselves) collectively regarded this as a violation of President Franklin D. Roosevelt's 1944 promise to King Abdelazziz ibn Saud not to change the status of British-mandated Palestine without consulting the Arabs first. No matter: Israel, the needed and eternal haven for the survivors of the Nazi holocaust and their descendants, of course, is here to stay. But as the only existing and important national state which has insisted on maintaining for two generations now the military occupation of another people's territory, it is out of line with most of the the world community, and finds unwavering support only from the United States.

In October 2001, Yassir Arafat and his advisors indignantly rejected the demagogic claim by Osama bin Laden that he, too, was fighting with them for a liberated Palestine. Bin Laden realized that the Palestinian cause is by far the most popular cause among the world's billion or more Muslims and Arabs, and so tried to raise his own banner and image alongside that of the Palestinians, as a champion of Jerusalem's "liberation." Arafat and his Palestinian Authority angrily rejected this, denouncing al-Qaida's violence and refusing its support.

The ageing leadership of the Palestinians around Yassir Arafat, or the Israelis around Ariel Sharon or another Israeli prime minister, may not be up to the task of reaching what this author advocated in his book, *Green March, Black September*, back in 1972: a compromise on a settlement and creation, in fact, of an Arab Palestinian state. Such a solution has already existed, in the dreams and aspirations of Palestinian people, Muslim and Christian, and in that of many thoughtful Jews for years. It is up to the United States to lead. It must forcefully mediate, and if necessary, impose, such a solution, which alone can assure the future security of Israel's people, the Palestinian Arabs, and of people in the entire region.

Yes, I agree with the reader who will tell me that this is a tremendously over-ambitious agenda. But I believe that it's not "mission impossible." And I think that if it is seriously attempted, the second Afghanistan war in a generation, costing like others before it thousands of lives and billions of dollars, may succeed in restoring a measure of the hope and stability that earlier wars, both holy and unholy, failed to bring to the Afghan people.

Notes

1: CARTER AND BREZHNEV IN THE VALLEY OF DECISION

1. Quoted from Hon. George N. Curzon, *Russia in Central Asia*, in Peter Yopp (ed.), *The Traveler's Dictionary of Quotation* (London and New York: Routledge, 1988), p. 1.
2. Trevor Mostyn and Albert Hourani (eds.), *The Cambridge Encyclopedia of the Middle East and North Africa* (Cambridge and New York: Cambridge University Press, 1988), pp. 294–6.
3. Vassily Safronchuk, "Afghanistan in the Taraki Period," *International Affairs*, Moscow January 1991, pp. 86–7.
4. Safronchuk, *International Affairs*, January 1991, pp. 90–2.
5. Diego Cordovez and Selig S. Harrison, *Out of Afghanistan, the Inside Story of the Soviet Withdrawal* (New York: Oxford University Press, 1995), p. 14.
6. Andrei Gromyko's unsent letter to the Politburo is quoted in full in his son Anatoly Gromyko's book, *Vi Labyreentach Kremlya (In the Labyrinth of the Kremlin*, Moscow: Avtok, 1997) pp. 387–8. Translated for my use by Natalie Kovalenko.
7. "Resolution of the CC of the CPSU" and "The CPSU on the events in Afghanistan, December 27–28, 1997, Top Secret." Original Soviet document and translation. See Appendix for full texts.
8. Preceding quotes from Oslo conference in private transcripts furnished to the author by participants. Cogan material from Charles C. Cogan, "Partners in Time, the CIA and Afghanistan," in *World Policy Journal*, World Policy Institute of the New School for Social Research, New York, Summer 1993, vol. X, no. 2, pp. 373–4. Mr. Cogan was chief of the Near East and South Asia division of the CIA's Directorate of Operations (DOD), the Agency's clandestine service.
9. Cogan, "Partners in Time, the CIA and Afghanistan," *World Policy Journal*, vol. X, no. 2, p. 74.
10. Interview with Brzezinski by Vincent Javert in *Le Nouvel Observateur*, Paris, January 15–21, 1998, p. 76.
11. Quoted in "Asie Centrale: la guerre des pipelines," *Le Nouvel Observateur*, January 15–21, 1998, p. 75.
12. Archie Roosevelt, *For Lust of Knowing, Memoirs of an Intelligence Officer* (London: Weidenfeld & Nicholson, 1988), p. 332.
13. Ibid., pp. 432–3.
14. Jimmy Carter, *Keeping Faith, Memoirs of a President* (New York: Bantam Books, 1982), p. 143.
15. Stansfield Turner, *Secrecy and Democracy, the CIA in Transition* (London: Sidgewick & Jackson, 1986), pp. 84–5.
16. Haykal's original account of the Safari Club is found in Mohammad Haykal, *Iran, the Untold Story* (New York: Pantheon Books, 1982), pp. 112–115.
17. Mohammad Haykal, *Iran the Untold Story*, pp. 113–116 and Roger Faligot and Pascal Krop, *La Piscine, the French Secret Service Since 1944* (Oxford: Blackwell), pp. 254–8.
18. Alexandre de Marenches with Christine Ockrent, *Dans le Secret des Princes: Perceptions et Actions* (Paris: Editions Stock, 1986), pp. 211–14.

2:   ANWAR AL-SADAT

1. Zbigniew Brzezinski, *Power and Principle, Memoirs of the National Security Adviser 1977–1981* (London: Weidenfeld & Nicholson, 1983), *passim*. See also Jimmy Carter, *Keeping Faith*; pp. 264–5; 471–3; 573 and 590.
2. Abdel Azim Ramadan, "Fundamentalist Influence in Egypt: the Strategies of the Muslim Brotherhood and the Takfir Groups," in Martin E. Marty and Scott Appleby (eds.), *Fundamentalisms and the State* (Chicago and London: The University of Chicago Press, 1993), pp. 152–4.
3. Private interviews in Jerusalem, January 1997.
4. *October* magazine, Cairo, December 1979, p. 1.
5. David Hirst and Irene Beeson, *Sadat* (London: Faber & Faber, 1981), pp. 342–5 and personal communications in Cairo, 1982.
6. Much of the foregoing material can be found in Mohammed Haseinine Haykal's books *Autumn of Fury* (London: Corgi Books, 1983), pp. 223–6 and *Illusions of Triumph* (London: HarperCollins, 1992), pp. 45, 67 and 87. The ideas and information were amplified in two long conversations with Haykal, one recorded on camera for ABC News; in Cairo and Mansuriyeh, Egypt, March and April 1993, and in interviews with several Cairo attorneys and a judge.
7. Ramadan, *Fundamentalisms and the State*, pp. 171–2.
8. Mary Anne Weaver, "The Trial of the Sheikh," *New Yorker*, March 6, 1993, pp.71–81, *passim*, quotations from pp. 77–80; personal interviews in Cairo, 1993.
9. NBC News Transcript, *Today Show*, September 23, 1981.
10. Mary Anne Weaver, pp. 76–81 and interviews with Haykal, op. cit.
11. Author's personal investigations for ABC News in Cairo, April and May 1993.

3:   ZIA AL-HAQ

1. Rudyard Kipling, letter from Lord Dufferin to Lord Landsdowne, 1888, quoted in Yopp (ed.) *The Traveler's Dictionary of Quotation*, p. 684.
2. Ayesha Jalal, *Democracy and Authoritarianism in South Asia* (Cambridge and New York: Cambridge University Press, 1995), p. 27.
3. Mumtaz Ahmed, "Islamic Fundamentalism in South Asia," in Martin E. Marty and Scott Appleby (eds.), *Fundamentalisms Observed* (Chicago: University of Chicago Press, 1994) vol. 1, pp. 462–3.
4. Ibid., pp. 470–1.
5. William L. Langer (ed.), *New Illustrated Encyclopedia of World History* (New York: Abrams Inc., 1972), vol. 2, p. 1213.
6. Ayesha Jalal, *Democracy and Authoritarianism in South Asia*, p. 38.
7. Langer, *Encyclopedia of World History*, vol. 2, p. 1213.
8. See Seymour M. Hersh, "On the Nuclear Edge," *New Yorker*, March 29, 1993, p. 56.
9. Author's interviews with Ardeshir Zahedi, the Shah's former foreign minister and ambassador to the US, and at Zahedi's residence in Switzerland March 1995.
10. Ayesha Jalal, *Democracy and Authoritarianism in South Asia*, pp. 86–105.
11. Mohammad Youssaf and Mark Adkin, *The Bear Trap, Afghanistan's Untold Story* (London: Leo Cooper, 1992), p. 23.
12. Conversation with Charles Cogan, Washington, DC, June 1996; same with a senior US diplomat in North Africa, March 1998.
13. Private interviews, Washington DC, March 1981.
14. James Adams, *Trading in Death, the Modern Arms Race* (London: Pan Books, 1990), p. 67.

15. Wilhelm Dietl, *Brueckenkopf Afghanistan, Machtpolitik im Mittleren Osten* (Munich: Kinder Verlag, 1984), p. 276 and author's personal interviews with Dietl in 1992 and 1993.
16. State Department Bureau of Intelligence and Research (BIS) report (Secret), "Pakistan's Short-Term Prospects," August 24, 1979, in *Documents from the US Espionage Den*, vol. 46–2, p. 54.
17. James Risen, "Column One, in Defense of CIA's Derring-Do," *Los Angeles Times*, January 4, 1996, Part A, p. 1.
18. Mohammad Youssaf and Mark Adkin, *The Bear Trap*, pp. 40–1 and a series of private communications in 1992–93.
19. Private research by a Muslim colleague in Kabul, winter 1985–86.

4: DENG XIAOPING

1. Transcript of Harold Brown's news conference in Beijing, released by the Pentagon, January 9, 1980.
2. Audiotape of ABC News "Issues and Answers" program, January 13, 1980.
3. For background on the intelligence sites in Iran, see John K. Cooley, *Payback, America's Long War in the Middle East* (Mclean, Va. & London: Brassey's 1981), pp. 12–17. For background on Chinese intelligence, see Roger Faligot and Remi Kauffer, *Les Maitres Espions, Histoire Mondiale du Renseignement, Tome 2, De la guerre froid a nos jours* (Paris: Robert Laffont,1994), pp. 116–17; also Jeffrey T. Richolson and Desmond Ball, *The Ties That Bind, Intelligence Cooperation Between the UK–USA Countries, Canada, Australia and New Zealand*, second edition (Boston: Unwin Hyman, 1990), pp. 171–2.
4. Roger Faligot and Remi Kauffer, *The Chinese Secret Service* (Paris and London: Robert Laffont and Headline Book Publishing Co., 1989), English version, pp. 389–90.
5. Henry Kissinger, *Years of Upheaval* (London: Weidenfeld & Nicholson and Michael Joseph, 1982), p. 61.
6. Faligot and Kauffer, *The Chinese Secret Service*, pp. 439–40.
7. Faligot and Kauffer, *Les Maitres Espions, Tome 2*, pp. 116–17, Jeffrey T. Richolson and Desmond Ball, *The Ties That Bind*, pp. 171–2.
8. Faligot and Kauffer, *Les Maitres Espions*, p. 177.
9. Erich Schmidt-Eenboom, *Schnueffler ohne Nase, Der BND – die unheimlichen mMacht im Staat* (Dusseldorf: Econ Verlag, 1993), p. 245.
10. Private interview in Munich, Germany, 1993.
11. *Boston Globe*, January 17, 1980, p. 3.
12. *White Book on Foreign Intervention in Afghanistan* (Kabul: Afghan Foreign Ministry, undated), p. 20.
13. Private communication from an American military source, 1993.
14. Mohammad Youssaf and Mark Adkin, *The Bear Trap*, pp. 83–5.
15. Ibid., p. 120.
16. Ibid., p. 121.
17. Interview in Cairo, 1993, with a senior journalist who visited the warriors in Pakistan and Afghanistan repeatedly in the 1980s.
18. Ibrahim Ma Zhaio-chin, "Islam in China: the Internal Dimension" (London: Institute of Muslim Minority Affairs), vol. 7, no. 2, July 1986, pp. 373 and 379.
19. Gerald Segal, *China Changes Shape*, p. 29.
20. Lillian Craig Harris, *China Considers the Middle East* (London and New York: I.B. Tauris & Co., Ltd., 1993), pp. xv–xvi and pp. 53–6.
21. Ibid., p. 58ff.
22. Ibid., p. 143.

5:   RECRUITERS, TRAINERS, TRAINEES AND ASSORTED SPOOKS

1. John M. Collins, *Green Berets, Seals and Spetznaz, US and Soviet Special Military Operations* (Washington, DC: Pergamon-Brasseys, 1987), pp. 2–3.
2. Major R. B. Andersen, "Special Forces Forge Training Spec Ops Warriors of the '90s,' in *Soldier of Fortune* magazine, November 1989, p. 46.
3. John M. Collins, *Green Berets*, pp. 4–5.
4. Ibid., p. 6.
5. Mumtaz Ahmed, "Islamic Fundamentalism in South Asia," in Marty and Appleby (eds.), *Fundamentalisms Observed*, p. 510.
6. For a full discussion, see Mumtaz Ahmed, *Fundamentalisms Observed*, pp. 511–23 *passim*.
7. ABC News transcript, July 10, 1993.
8. Ronald Kessler, *Inside the CIA* (New York: Pocket Books, 1992), p. 128.
9. Ibid., p. 5.
10. Richard Marcinko with John Weisman, *Rogue Warrior* (New York: Pocket Books, 1992), p. 54.
11. Ibid., p. 291.
12. Personal communication, 1992 and Ronald Kessler, *Inside the CIA*, p. 53.
13. Stephen Dorril, *The Silent Conspiracy, Inside the Intelligence Services in the 1980s* (London: Mandarin Books, William Heinemann Ltd., 1994), pp. 382–91.
14. Ibid., pp. 392–3.
15. Stephen Dorril, *The Silent Conspiracy*, pp. 266–9.
16. Jim Graves, "Interview with General Rahmatollah Safi," *Soldier of Fortune* magazine, February 1988, p. 15.
17. James Adams, *Secret Armies, the Explosive Inside Story of the World's Most Elite Warriors* (New York: Bantam Books, 1989), pp. 154–5.
18. Richard Deacon, *British Secret Service* (London: Grafton Books, Collins, 1991), pp. 465–6.
19. Mike Williams, "Omega Jihad," *Soldier of Fortune*, September 1988, pp. 40–4.
20. Roger Faligot and Pascal Kropp, *La Piscine*, pp. 273–5. See also John K. Cooley, *Libyan Sandstorm, the Complete Story of Qaddafi's Revolution* (New York: New Republic Books of Holt, Rinehart & Winston, 1981), pp. 117–24.
21. Roger Faligot and Remy Kauffer, *Les Maitres Espions*, pp. 261–3.
22. Author's interview in Tunis, April 1998, with Ahmed Mestiri, former Tunisian Foreign Minister and UN negotiator in Afghanistan, who met Massoud several times.
23. Ronald Payne, *Mossad, Israel's Most Secret Service* (London: Corgi Books, 1990), p. 188.
24. Ahmed Taheri, *Holy Terror, The Inside Story of Islamic Terrorism* (London: Sphere Books, Hutchinson Ltd., 1987), pp. 95–100.
25. Olivier Roy, *Islam and Resistance in Afghanistan*, pp. 50–1 and 230–6.
26. Samuel Segev, *The Iranian Triangle, the Untold Story of Israel's Role in the Iran-Contra Affair* (New York: The Free Press, 1987), p. 275.

6:   DONORS, BANKERS AND PROFITEERS

1. Edward Girardet, "Russia's War in Afghanistan," in *Central Asian Survey*, vol. 2, no. 4, July 1983, p. 48.
2. Interviews with Arab journalists in Cairo and Amman, 1993 and 1994.
3. John Jameson, "SOF Afghanistan, the Master of Kabul," in *Soldier of Fortune* magazine, May 1989, p. 46.

4. *Strategic Studies* journal, Islamabad, Summer 1982, p. 34 and p. 46, note 48.
5. Bob Woodward, *Veil, the Secret Wars of the CIA 1981–1987* (London: Headline Books, 1987), pp. 79 and 297.
6. Tim Weiner, "The Pentagon's Secret Stash," *Mother Jones* magazine, March–April 1982, pp. 22–8.
7. For more details on ISA and Duncan, see James Adams, Secret Armies, pp. 207–11 and John K. Cooley, *Payback*, pp. 115–16.
8. Michael Barone and Grant Ujifusa, *The Almanac of American Politics 1990* (Washington, DC: The National Journal, 1990), pp. 158–9.
9. Ibid., p. 734.
10. Ibid., p. 263.
11. Bob Woodward, *Veil*, pp. 315–16.
12. As reported by all major Western newspapers and agencies, quoted by Stephen Dorril, in *The Silent Conspiracy*, p. 297.
13. *The Encyclopedia Britannica Yearbook*, 1993, p. 117.
14. *Middle East Economic Survey*, Nicosia, vol. V, no. 5, December 8, 1976, p. 2.
15. Private communications from several US diplomats active in the Mideast in the 1960s and 1970s; and Peter Truell and Larry Gurwin, BCCI, *the Inside Story of the World's Most Corrupt Financial Empire* (London: Bloomsbury, 1992), pp. 120–1.
16. *The Economist*, London, August 19, 1995, p. 91.
17. Private communications in London, 1990–91 and Stephen Dorril, *The Silent Conspiracy*, pp. 292–3.
18. *Guardian*, London, May 19, 1984, p. 1 and July 12, 1984, p. 1; *The Times*, London, March 29, 1984, p. 3 and July 5, 1984, p. 1; ABC News broadcasts by the author from London on same dates.
19. Beaty and Gwynne, *The Outlaw Bank*, pp. 118–119; author's personal investigative files.
20. Private communication, Washington, DC, March 1993.
21. Peter Truell and Larry Gerwin, BCCI, *the Inside Story of the World's Most Corrupt Financial Empire* (London: Bloomsbury, 1992), p. 143.
22. Beaty and Gwynne, *The Outlaw Bank*, p. 315.
23. Ibid., pp. 316–18.
24. "Talking with Terror's Banker, an Exclusive Interview with Osama bin Laden," ABC News transcript, May 28, 1998, *passim*.
25. Michael Field, *A Hundred Million Dollars A Day* (New York: Praeger Publishers Inc., 1976), pp. 186–7.
26. Robert Lacey, *The Kingdom* (London: Fontana/Collins, 1981), p. 507.
27. US State Department, "Issues Factsheet on bin Laden," and private communications in Cairo, summer 1994.
28. *Rose al Youssef* magazine, Cairo, summarized in *The Egyptian Gazette*, October 10, 1993, p. 1.
29. "Issues Factsheet on bin Laden," pp. 2–3, and private communications in Cairo, summer 1994.
30. *New York Times*, April 8, 1994, pp. 1 and 3.
31. "Issues Factsheet on bin Laden," p. 2.
32. Private communications in London, July 1996.
33. Private communications in Paris, September 1996.

7: POPPY FIELDS, KILLING FIELDS AND DRUGLORDS

1. A scholarly book, also a fascinating read, on the original sect of the assassins is Bernard Lewis, *The Assassins* (London: Weidenfeld & Nicholson, 1967), or in paperback, (London: Al-Saqi Books, 1985).

2. Alfred J. McCoy, *The Politics of Heroin*, pp. 87–8.
3. Ibid., p. 106.
4. Roger Faligot and Pascal Krop, *La Piscine*, pp. 244–51.
5. Roger Faligot & Pascal Krop, *La Piscine*, pp. 261–2; S.C. Gwynne, *The Outlaw Bank*, pp. 303–6 and interview with de Marenches in *Time* magazine, June 13, 1994.
6. Brian Fremantle, *The Fix, Inside the World Drug Trade* (New York: Tim Doherty Associates, 1986), pp. 180–1; Andrew Cockburn, *The Threat, Inside the Soviet Military Machine* (London: Hutchinson, 1983), p. 40.
7. Olivier Roy, *Islam and Resistance in Afghanistan*, p. 42.
8. Lt. Col. Yury Shvedov and team (names do not appear in book), *Voina V' Afghanistanyeh* (War in Afghanistan), (Moscow: Ministry of Defense, Institute of Military History, 1991), pp. 131–2. Translations by Natalie Kovalenko.
9. Ibid., pp. 136–8.
10. Ibid., pp. 139–40.
11. Alfred J. McCoy, *The Politics of Heroin*, pp. 438–9.
12. Alfred J. McCoy and Alan A. Black, "US Narcotics Policy: An Anatomy of Failure," in *War on Drugs* (McCoy and Black, eds.), (Boulder, Colorado: Westview Press, 1992), p. 9.
13. Robert Parry, "Contra-Cocaine Evidence of Premeditation," in *The Consortium* (investigative newsletter), June 1, 1998, pp. 3–4.
14. Brian Fremantle, *The Fix*, p. 32.
15. Scott B. MacDonald, "Afghanistan's Drug Trade," in *Society* (journal), July–August 1992, p. 61.
16. UNDCP, Afghanistan Drug Control and Rehabilitation Program, "General Facts on Opium Poppy Cultivation in Afghanistan," undated illustrated brochure, p. 4 and Stephane Allix, *La Petite Cuillere de Scheherazade, sur la Route de l'Heroine* (Paris: Editions Ramsay, 1998), preface by Larry Collins, pp. 11–14.
17. BBC World Service (radio) news, 1700 gmt, August 31, 1998.
18. Stephane Allix, *La Petite Cuillere*, pp. 99–108.
19. Jean Ziegler, *Les Seigneurs du Crime* (Paris: Editions du Seuil, 1997), pp. 45–66.
20. Ibid., p. 65.
21. Ibid., pp. 63–5.
22. Stephane Allix, *La Petite Cuillere*, p. 106.
23. AFP, Islamabad, March 12, 1995.
24. *The Economist*, October 5, 1996, pp. 21–2.
25. Barnett R. Rubin, "Women and Pipelines: Afghanistan's proxy wars," *International Affairs*, 73,2 (1997), pp. 283–6.
26. Personal communication, March 1997, in Nicosia, Cyprus. Emphasis is the author's.
27. Barnett R. Rubin, "Women and Pipelines," p. 286.
28. "Taliban gain control of 1,100 billion cubic meters of natural-gas reserves in Shibergan," *Dharb-I-M'umnin*, Taliban publication in Afghanistan, Internet, undated.
29. Jobin Goodarzi, "Washington and the Taliban, Strange Bedfellows," *Middle East International*, October 25, 1996.
30. Stephane Allix, *La Petite Cuillere*, p. 32.
31. AFP and Associated Press dispatches, August 11–15, 1998.
32. Stephane Allix, *La Petite Cuillere*, pp. 48–52.
33. Ibid., pp. 55–61.
34. Ibid., pp. 62–3.
35. Xinhua (New China) news agency, Tehran, March 3, 1998.
36. Stephane Allix, *La Petite Cuillere*, pp. 113–18.

37. Lucian Kim, "Taliban Jars Central Asia," *The Christian Science Monitor*, August 14, 1998.
38. "Uzbekistan," report of the Observatoire Geopolitique des Drogues (OGD), annual report 1995–96, Paris, internet, undated, pp. 2–3.
39. Ibid., p. 46.
40. *World Almanac and Book of Facts 1997* (Mahwah, NJ: World Almanac Books, 1998), p. 788.
41. Stephane Allix, *La Petite Cuillere*, p. 181–5.
42. Ibid., p. 185.
43. Ibid., pp. 218–21.

8: RUSSIA: BITTER AFTERTASTE AND RELUCTANT RETURN

1. Conversation with Vladimir Ilyin, Moscow, February 12, 1994.
2. Personal interviews in Moscow, February 1994.
3. Hedrick Smith, *The New Russians* (London: Hutchinson, 1992), pp. 469–70.
4. Alexander Solzhenitsyn wrote *Rebuilding Russia* in July 1990. It was first published in the USSR in September 1990 under the title "How to Revitalize Russia" in the mass-circulation daily *Komsomolskaya Pravda*. These quotes are from *Rebuilding Russia*, translated and annotated by Alexis Flimmof (New York: Farrar, Strauss & Giroux, 1991), pp. 3–4.
5. Hedrick Smith, *The New Russia*, pp. 469–70.
6. Gary Lee and Rick Atkinson, "Apostasy in the Soviet Ranks: Even a Political Officer Says Lenin Made Mistakes," *International Herald Tribune*, November 23, 1990, p. 1.
7. James Risen, *New York Times News Service*, "Russia's New Role in Afghan Conflict," in the *International Herald Tribune*, July 27, 1998, p. 3.
8. See Philip Bowring, "Central Asia at Risk in Afghanistan," *International Herald Tribune*, February 2, 1994, p. 6. The meeting with the Uzbek diplomat took place on the occasion of a lecture by the author at the Middle East Institute, Washington, DC, November 18, 1994.
9. See John K. Cooley, *International Herald Tribune*, op-ed page, August 17, 1998.
10. Arkady Vaksberg, *The Soviet Mafia*, translated by John and Elizabeth Roberts (London: Weidenfeld & Nicholson, 1991), pp. 247–50.
11. Observatoire Geopolitique de Drogues (OGD), 1995–96 report, internet, pp. 1–5.
12. AFP dispatch, Peshawar, Pakistan, March 7, 1994.
13. See John K. Cooley, *Payback*, p. 123.
14. Charles J. Hanely (AP correspondent), "Deadly quest for shoulder-fired lightning," in the *Cyprus Weekly*, Nicosia, November 26–December 2, 1993; also Michael Fleet, "Mafiosi Feud Hits Suburbia," in the *Sunday Telegraph Magazine*, May 1, 1994, p. 1. Statistics on Chechenya from Wolfgang Michal, "Der Kaukasische Teufelskreise," in *Geo* magazine, Hamburg, February 1994, inserted and unpaged map and graphics supplement.
15. Robin Wright and John M. Broder, "US Bidding to Regain Stingers Sent to Afghans," *Los Angeles Times*, July 23, 1993, pp. A1 and A4.
16. Astrid von Borcke, "Unforeseen Consequences of a Soviet Intervention, the Movement of the 'Afghans' in Militant Islamism," annotated monograph in English (Cologne: Bundesinstitut fuer Ostwissenschaftliche und internationale Studien, June 1996).
17. Anthony Hyman, "Muslim Minorities in Central Asia," in *Dialogue*, newsletter published by the Public Affairs Committee for Shi'a Muslims, London, May 1994, p. 2.
18. Astrid von Borcke, "Unforeseen Consequences," pp. 6–7.

19. Dennis A. Pluchinsky, "Terrorism in the Former Soviet Union: a Primer, a Puzzle, a Prognosis, in *Studies in Conflict and Terrorism*, a journal (Taylor, 1998), internet version, pp. 134–7.
20. Astrid von Borcke, "Unforeseen Consequences," p. 7.

9: THE CONTAGION SPREADS: EGYPT AND THE MAGHREB

1. *Amnesty International Report 1998* (London; Amnesty International, 1998), pp. 158–9; "New US Envoy: Iran was involved in Luxor massacres," *Jerusalem Post*, "Gehorsam gegen Allah," *Der Spiegel* magazine, 48/1997, internet version, pp. 1–3; "Horror on the Nile," ABC's Nightline program, December 3, 1997, ABC News transcript.
2. Personal interviews with travelers from Egypt, Nicosia, Cyprus, November 1997.
3. Joseph Kechechian and Jeanne Nazimek, "Challenges to the Military in Egypt," in *Middle East Policy* (journal), vol. 5, 1997, pp. 125–33, *passim*.
4. *Amnesty International Report 1998*, p. 158.
5. "Challenges to the Military in Egypt," p. 126.
6. Ibid., p.127–40.
7. Mary Anne Weaver, "Letter from Cairo: Revolution by Stealth," *New Yorker*, January 8, 1998, pp. 38–48.
8. Some details drawn from Slimane Zeghidawi's chronological history of Algeria in the illustrated French magazine *Geo*, March 1998, pp. 94–5.
9. Martin Marty and Scott Appleby (eds.) *Fundamentalisms and the State*, p. 637, also personal communications from Francis Ghilles in London, 1992.
10. John-Thor Dahlburg, "Algerian Veterans, the Nucleus for Mayhem," *Los Angeles Times*, August 5,1996, p. A11.
11. AFP, Algiers, December 14, 1997.
12. Personal communication, French informant Paris, April 1994.
13. Dahlburg, "Algerian Veterans," *Los Angeles Times*, August 5, 1996, p. A11.
14. AFP, Algiers, December 14, 1997.
15. Dominique Lagarde, "Les Contrats US en Algerie," *L'Express*, November 20, 1997.
16. Reuter, Washington DC, January 5, 1998.
17. Astrid von Borcke, "Unforeseen Consequences of a Soviet Intervention," pp.18–19.
18. AFP, Bonn, October 10, 1997.
19. Xinhua News Agency, Kuwait, October 10, 1997.
20. Louis Martinez, "Algerie, le business de la violence," *Le Nouvel Observateur*, January 15, 1998, p. 73.
21. Arnold Hoettinger, *Islamischer Fundamentalismus* (Zurich, Verlag Neue Zuercher Zeitung, 1993), pp. 85–6 and author's interviews in Tunis, March 1998.
22. Francois Sudan, "Algerie-Maroc, un cadeau qui ne coute rien," *Jeune Afrique*, Paris, September 7–13, 1998, p. 5.
23. Arnold Hoettinger, *Islamischer Fundamentalismus*, pp. 92–3.

10: MORE CONTAGION: THE PHILIPPINES

1. Dr. Maria von Barrata (ed.), *Der Fischer Weltalmanach* (Fischer Taschenbuch Verlag, Frankfurt am Main, 1999), p. 619. Much of the foregoing statistics and history are from the same volume, pp. 619–21 and from standard American and British reference works such as the *Columbia Encyclopedia*; the *World Almanac* and the *Information Please* almanacs for the years 1999 and 2000.

2. Ronald E. Dolin (ed.), *Philippines: A Country Study* (Federal Research Division, Library of Congress, June 1991), page 2 of the section entitled "Muslim Filipinos," internet version. I have closely followed sections of this study, as well as using the article on the Republic of the Philippines on pp. 2133–5 in the *Columbia Encyclopedia*, Fifth Edition (New York: Columbia University Press/Houghton Mifflin, 1993).
3. Von Barrata, *Fischer Weltalmanach* , pp. 622–3.
4. John Pilger, *Hidden Agendas* (London & Sidney: Vintage Books, 1998), pp. 3 and 208.
5. Von Barrata, *Fischer Weltalmanach*, p. 622.
6. "Al-Harakat Islamia," two-page study by the International Center for Counter-Terrorism (ICT), Nataniya, Israel, April 2000, *passim*, internet version.
7. AFP dispatch, Zamboanga, April 14, 2000.
8. Kyodo World News Service (Japan), May 3, 2000; AFP dispatch, Manila, May 12, 2000.
9. Cecil Morella, "Philippines' economic prospects threatened by terrorism, rebellion," AFP Manila, May 21, 2000.

11: THE CONTAGION SPREADS: THE ASSAULT ON AMERICA

1. "Counter-Terrorism Policy: Louis J. Freeh," testimony before the Senate Judiciary Committee, September 3, 1998, in *Congressional Testimony*, Federal Documents Clearing House, internet edition, pp. 4–5.
2. AFP, Cairo, quoting Diaa Rashwar of the Al-Ahram Center for Strategic Studies.
3. Most of the world's media reported these developments, August 7 to 12, 1998.
4. James Risen and Judith Miller, "Pakistani Intelligence Had Links to Al Qaeda, US Officials Say," *New York Times*, October 29, 2001.
5. Private communications to author in Washington, DC, September 10–12, 1998.
6. Private communications to author in Washington, DC, September 10–12, 1998.
7. Associated Press dispatch, Cairo, November 3, 2001.
8. James Risen and Judith Miller, "Pakistani Intelligence ...," *New York Times*, October 29, 2001.
9. *Far Eastern Economic Review,* October 18, 2001.
10. "Pakistan's Jehadi Apparatus: Goals and Methods," by Sumita Kumar, Research Officer, IDSA-India, undated but posted online sometime in late 2000.
11. Personal communications in Tunis in March 1998 and Washington, DC in 1999.
12. James Risen and Judith Miller, "Pakistani Intelligence ...," *New York Times*, October 29, 2001.
13. Quoted in Roger Faligot and Remi Kauffer, *Les Maitres Espions,* p. 231.
14. Reuter, Islamabad, March 17, 1995.
15. John F. Burns, *New York Times,* March 13, 1995.
16. *Jordan Times,* Amman, July 9, 1994.
17. Conversation with US Ambassador Robert Pelletreau in Cairo, July 1993, and a file of about 30 documents released to Karen Burnes of ABC News under the Freedom of Information Act by the US State Department (letter of January 31, 1994).
18. Robert I. Friedman, *The Village Voice*, March 20, 1993 and all major newspapers of the dates indicated.
19. Official accounts are well summarized in "Foreign Terrorists in America," Congressional Testimony before the Senate Judiciary Committee's subcommittee on Technology, Terrorism and Information, February 24, 1998, *passim*.
20. All major newspapers and ABC News reports, January 9–10 and March 1–15, 1995.
21. *New York Times*, October 2, 1985.

22. Melissa Block, reporter, on Morning Edition, National Public Radio, Washington, DC, January 18, 1996.
23. *New York Times,* September 6, 1996.
24. CNN.com, October 23, 2000.
25. Combined media reports, summarized online by intellnet.org, November 5, 2001.
26. "Etats-Unis, exces du puissance," by Steven C. Clemons, vice-president of the New America Foundation, Washington, DC, in *Le Monde Diplomatique,* Paris, October 2001, p. 1.
27. Personal interviews by the author in Hamburg, September 2001, and two articles by Hugh Williamson in the *Financial Times,* September 27, 2001.
28. ABC News memoranda, personal interviews in Milan, Italy in October 2001 and an ICIJ Investigative Report, by Leo Sisti and Maud Beelman, October 3, 2001 (online).

Appendix I : Press Release from United States Attorney, Southern District of New York, November 4, 1998

PRESS RELEASE

MARY JO WHITE, the United States Attorney for the Southern District of New York, and LEWIS D. SCHILIRO, Assistant Director in Charge of the New York FBI Office, announced that USAMA BIN LADEN and MUHAMMAD ATEF, a/k/a "Abu Hafs," were indicted today in Manhattan federal court for the August 7, 1998, bombings of the United States embassies in Nairobi, Kenya, and Dar es Salaam, Tanzania, and for conspiring to kill American nationals outside of the United States.

The United States Department of State also announced today rewards of up to $5 million each for information leading to the arrest or conviction of BIN LADEN and ATEF.

The first count of the Indictment charges that BIN LADEN and ATEF, along with co-defendants WADIH EL HAGE, FAZUL ABDULLAH MOHAMMED, MOHAMMED SADEEK ODEH, and MOHAMMED RASHED DAOUD AL-'OWHALI, acted together with other members of "al Qaeda," a worldwide terrorist organization led by BIN LADEN, in a conspiracy to murder United States nationals. The objectives of this international terrorist conspiracy allegedly included: killing members of the American military stationed in Saudi Arabia and Somalia; killing United States nationals employed at the United States Embassies in Nairobi, Kenya, and Dar es Salaam, Tanzania; and concealing the activities of the co-conspirators by, among other things, establishing front companies, providing false identity and travel documents, engaging in coded correspondence and providing false information to the authorities in various countries.

BIN LADEN's organization al Qaeda allegedly functioned both on its own and through some of the terrorist organizations that operated under its umbrella, including the Al Jihad group based in Egypt, the Islamic Group (also known as the "el Gamaa Islamia" or simply "Gamaa't"), led at one time by Sheik Omar Abdel Rahman, and a number of jihad groups in other countries, including the Sudan, Egypt, Saudi Arabia, Yemen and Somalia. Al Qaeda also allegedly maintained cells and personnel in a number of countries to facilitate its activities, including in Kenya, Tanzania, the United Kingdom and the United States.

According to the Indictment, BIN LADEN and al Qaeda forged alliances with the National Islamic Front in the Sudan and with representatives of the government of Iran, and its associated terrorist group Hezballah, with the goal of working together against their perceived common enemies in the West, particularly the United States.

In order to further this international conspiracy to murder United States nationals, BIN LADEN and other co-conspirators are alleged to have committed the following acts: (1) providing training camps for use by al Qaeda and its affiliates; (2) recruiting United States citizens including the defendant EL HAGE to help facilitate the goals of al Qaeda; (3) purchasing weapons and explosives; and (4) establishing headquarters and businesses in the Sudan.

The Indictment also alleges that *fatwahs* were issued by BIN LADEN and a committee of al Qaeda members urging other members and associates of al Qaeda to kill Americans.

According to the Indictment, several of these *fatwahs* called for attacks on American troops stationed in Saudi Arabia and Somalia. The Indictment also alleges that American troops were indeed attacked and killed by persons who received training from al Qaeda members or those trained by al Qaeda. The Indictment specifically charges that the August 7, 1998, bombings of the United States embassies in Kenya and Tanzania as actions taken in furtherance of this conspiracy to kill American nationals.

BIN LADEN and ATEF, along with ABDULLAH MOHAMMED, ODEH and AL-'OWHALI, are charged with bombing the two embassies and causing the deaths of more than 200 persons and injuring more than 4,500 others. Those five defendants are also charged with murdering all of the civilians killed in the embassy bombings. The Indictment names all of the victims of the bombings and each victim is charged as a separate count of murder for a total of 224 counts of murder against BIN LADEN, ATEF, ABDULLAH MOHAMMED, ODEH, and AL-'OWHALI.

Ms. WHITE and Mr. SCHILIRO said the investigation of this case is being conducted by the Joint Terrorist Task Force composed of the FBI, the New York City Police Department, the United States Department of State, the United States Secret Service, the United States Immigration and Naturalization Service, the Federal Aviation Administration, the United States Marshals Service, the Bureau of Alcohol, Tobacco, and Firearms, the New York State Police and the Port Authority of New York and New Jersey.

Ms. WHITE and Mr. SCHILIRO praised the Governments of Kenya, Tanzania and the Comoros Islands for their cooperation in this investigation and praised all the investigative efforts and cooperation of the agencies involved in the case. They also said that the investigation is continuing.

United States Attorney General Janet Reno stated: "This is an important step forward in our fight against terrorism. It sends a message that no terrorist can flout our laws and murder innocent civilians."

Ms. WHITE stated: "Usama Bin Laden and his military commander Muhammad Atef are charged with the most heinous acts of violence ever committed against American diplomatic posts. These acts caused the deaths of hundreds of citizens of Kenya, Tanzania and the United States. All those responsible for these brutal and cowardly acts, from the leaders and organizers to all of those who had any role in these crimes in East Africa, will be brought to justice."

Mr. SCHILIRO stated: "This investigation has been given the highest priority. Our investigative strategy is clear: We will identify, locate and prosecute all those responsible right up the line, from those who constructed and delivered the bombs to those who paid for them and ordered it done. This has been an investigation which has involved the largest deployment of FBI agents abroad, including members of the Joint Terrorist Task Force. Working closely with the law enforcement authorities in Kenya and Tanzania, our investigators have made significant progress, yet much remains to be done."

BIN LADEN and ATEF, both of whom are fugitives, face a maximum sentence of life imprisonment without the possibility of parole, or death.

Assistant United States Attorneys PATRICK J. FITZGERALD, KENNETH M. KARAS and MICHAEL J. GARCIA are in charge of the prosecution.

The charges contained in the Indictment are merely accusations, and the defendants are presumed innocent unless and until proven guilty.

98–240

[This text, and the full indictment texts are available on the New York Field Office web site at http://www.fbi.gov/fo/nyfo/prladen.htm]

Appendix II: The Resolution of the CPSU Central Committee

(THE FOLLOWING IS HANDWRITTEN)

Chairman - comrade L.I. Brezhnev
Present: Suslov M.A., Grishin V.V., Kirilenko A.P., Pelshe A.I., Ustinov D.F., Chernenko K.U., Andropov U.V., Gromyko A.A., Tikhonov N.A., Ponomarev B.N.

Resolution of the CC of the CPSU

On the situation in "A"

1. To approve the considerations and measures described by comrades Andropov U.V., Ustinov D.F., Gromyko A.A.

To allow them to introduce minor non-principal corrections in the realization of these measures.

The questions, to be solved by the CC, must be submitted to the Politbureau in due time.

To assign comrades Andropov U.V., Ustinov D.F., Gromyko A.A. with the realization of all these measures.

2. To assign comrades Andropov U.V., Ustinov D.F., Gromyko A.A. to inform the Politbureau of the CC on course of the practical realization of the planned measures.

General Secretary of the CC   L. Brezhnev

(Signatures of) "For" Andropov, "For" Ustinov, "For" Gromyko, ?, Suslov, Grishin, Kirilenko, Chernenko, Tikhonov, ?Brezhnev? 25/XII ? 26/XII "For" Shyerbitsky 26/XII

P176/175 of 12/XII

See page 246, overleaf

Председательствовал тов. Л.И. Брежнев

Присутствовали: Суслов М.А., Пельше А.Я., Кириленко А.П., Романов Г.В.,
Черненко К.У., Андропов Ю.В., Гришин В.В., Громыко А.А., Тихонов Н.А.,
Горбачёв Ф., Устинов Д.Ф., Пономарёв Б.Н.

Постановление ЦК КПСС

К положению в „А"

[здесь наложено множество рукописных подписей и пометок, включая:]

За — ... Андропова Ю.В.,
за — ... Громыко А.А.

Разрешить ... осуществить
этих мероприятий ... вносить
коррективы тактического
характера.

Вопросы, требующие решения
ЦК, своевременно вносить
в Политбюро

Осуществление всех этих меропр-
ятий возложить на т.т. Андропов
Ю.В., Устинова Д.Ф., Громыко А.А.

2. Поручить т.т. Андропову Ю.В.,
Устинову Д.Ф., Громыко А.А.
информировать Политбюро ЦК
о ходе выполнения намеченных
мероприятий.

[подпись] Л. Брежнев

[пометка: 26.12.79]

+ + +

The CPSU Central Committee

On the events in Afghanistan
December 27–28, 1979

After the coup d'etat and murdering of the General Secretary of the NDPA Central
Committee, Chairman of the Revolutionary Council of Afghanistan N.M. Taraky,
committed by Amin this September, the situation in Afghanistan has drastically
aggravated, becoming loaded with crisis.

Kh. Amin imposed a regime of personal dictatorship in the country, in fact lowering
the NDPA Central Committee and the Revolutionary Council to the position of purely
formal bodies. Persons with family relations to Kh. Amin or dedicated to him were
appointed to the leading positions both in the party and in the state. Many members of the
NDPA Central Committee, the Revolutionary Council and the Afghan government were
expelled from the party and arrested. In general the repressions and physical elimination
were aimed against active participants of the April revolution, people manifesting their
sympathy to the Soviet Union, those who defended Lenin's standards of party life. Kh.
Amin deceived the party and the people by his declarations that the Soviet Union
allegedly approved of Taraky's removal from the party and from the government.

On the direct orders of Kh. Amin, in Afghanistan, there began to circulate notoriously
invented gossips, discrediting the Soviet Union and besmirching the work of Soviet
personnel in Afghanistan, who were limited in contacts with Afghan representatives.

At the same time there were attempts to establish contacts with the Americans within
the framework of the "more balanced foreign policy course" approved by Kh. Amin. Kh.
Amin was practicing confidential contacts with charge d'affaires of the USA in Kabul.
The DRA government began to create favorable conditions for the work of the American
cultural center, on the order of Kh. Amin the DRA special services stopped their work
against the US embassy.

Kh. Amin tried to strengthen his position by reaching a compromise with the leaders of
the internal counterrevolution. Through his entrusted persons he got in contact with the
leaders of the right-wing Muslim opposition.

The political repressions were becoming massive. Since the September events alone,
in Afghanistan there were eliminated without court and trial more than 600 NDPA
members, military men and other people, suspected in anti-Amin mood. In fact,
disbanding of the party was the perspective of the nearest future.

All that combined with the objective difficulties and the specific conditions in
Afghanistan put the development of the revolutionary process into extremely difficult
conditions, stepped up the activities of the counterrevolutionary forces, which practically
established their control in many provinces of the country. Using foreign support, which
was intensified when Amin was in office, they were trying to achieve a principal change
of the military and political situation in the country, to liquidate the revolutionary
achievements.

The dictator's methods of the country management, repressions, massive executions,
violations of the laws brought massive discontent in the country. In the capital, there

began to appear numerous leaflets exposing the antisocial nature of the present regime, urging the people to unite in the fight against the "Amin's clique." The discontent spread to the Army too. A major part of the officers expressed their indignation with the dominance of incompetent proteges of Kh. Amin. In fact, a broad anti-Amin front was formed in the country.

Demonstrating the worries about the fate of the revolution and independence of the country, closely following the strengthening of the anti-Amin moods in Afghanistan, being in emigration, Karmal Babrak and Asadulla Sarvary started to unite all the anti-Amin groups both inside and outside the country for the sake of saving the Motherland and the revolution. It was taken into consideration that the "Parcham" group, being underground under the leadership of the underground Central Committee had carried out a significant work on joining all the healthy forces including Taraky's supporters from the "Khalk" group.

Former discrepancies were removed, the split in the NDPA was eliminated. The "Khalkovists" (represented by Sarvary) and the "Parchamists" (represented by Babrak) announced the final merge of the party. Babrak was elected the leader of the new party center, Sarvary was elected his deputy.

In the extremely difficult conditions, which were threatening the achievements of the April revolution and the security interests of our country, there emerged a necessity of rendering additional military assistance to Afghanistan, especially since the former DRA government had turned to us with such a request. In accordance with the provisions of the Soviet–Afghan treaty of 1978, the decision was made to send the necessary contingent of the Soviet Army to Afghanistan.

On the upraise of the patriotic moods of rather broad masses of the Afghanistan population because of the deployment of the Soviet troops, made in strict observation of the provisions of the Soviet–Afghan treaty of 1978, the forces in opposition to Kh. Amin organized an armed rebellion which ended up in overthrowing the regime of Kh. Amin. That rebellion was widely supported by the working people, intellectuals, a major part of the Afghan Army, state structures, which greeted the creation of a new leadership of the DRA and the NDPA.

The new government and the Revolutionary Council composed of the representatives of the former groups of "Parcham" and "Khalk", representatives of the military and non-party members were formed on a wide and representative basis.

In their program memorandums the new authorities declared their struggle to achieve a complete victory of the national-democratic, anti-feudal, anti-imperialist revolution, protection of the national independence and the sovereignty of Afghanistan. In the sphere of the foreign policy they declared the course on all-round strengthening of the friendship and cooperation with the USSR. Having taken into account the mistakes made by the former regime, the new leadership in its practical work intends to pay serious attention to the extensive democratizing of the social life, ensuring observation of the laws, widening of the social basis and strengthening of the local authorities, pursuing a flexible policy towards the religion, tribes and ethnic minorities.

One of the first steps which attracted the attention of the Afghan public was the release of a large group of political prisoners, including prominent political and military leaders of the country. Many of them (Kadyr, Keshtmand, Rafy and others) were enthusiastic and actively joined the work in the new Revolutionary Council and the government.

Broad masses of the population listened to the announcement on the overthrowing of Kh. Amin with unconcealed joy and expressed their readiness to support the declared program of the government. The commanding officers of all the major units of Afghan Army have declared their support to the new leadership of the party and the DRA government. The attitude toward Soviet servicemen and experts remains generally good-natured. The situation in the country becomes normal.

It is noted in the political circles of Kabul that Babrak's government, will obviously have to overcome significant difficulties in the spheres of home policy and economy, inherited from the former regime, but they express their hope that the NDPA will manage to solve these problems with the help of the USSR. Babrak is characterized as one of the best theoretically prepared leaders of the NDPA, with a sober and objective estimation of the situation in Afghanistan, he was always noted for his sincere sympathy to the Soviet Union, enjoyed excellent reputation in the party and in the country. In this relation confidence is expressed that the new DRA leadership will manage to find efficient ways to achieve a complete stabilization of the situation in the country.

(Signed by) U. Andropov, A. Gromyko, D. Ustinov, B. Ponomarev

31 December 1979

No 2519–A

(handwritten):
To the archive
?.I.80

Index

Note on Arabic names: The prefix 'al-' in personal names has been retained but ignored, so that al-Sadat is listed under S. 'bin' is treated as a primary element and appears under B. Names with multiple elements are listed under the one most commonly used (e.g. Abdel Rahman rather than Rahman)